race to the
South Pole

ROALD AMUNDSEN

WHITE STAR PUBLISHERS

GRAPHIC DESIGN

PATRIZIA BALOCCO LOVISETTI

© 2007 White Star s.p.a.
Via Candido Sassone, 22/24
13100 Vercelli, Italy
www.whitestar.it

ISBN: 978-88-544-0217-1

Printed in Italy by Grafica Veneta s.p.a.

Excerpts from Roald Amundsen, *The South Pole, an account of Norwegian
Antartic expedition in the* Fram, *1910-1912,* translated from the Norwegian by
A.G. Chater, London, John Murray, 1912.

CONTENTS

THE FIRST ACCOUNT

On February 10, 1911, we started for the South to establish depots, and continued our journey until April 11. We formed three depots and stored in them 3 tons of provisions, including 22 hundredweight of seal meat. As there were no landmarks, we had to indicate the position of our depots by flags, which were posted at a distance of about four miles to the east and west. The first barrier afforded the best going, and was specially adapted for dog-sledging. Thus, on February 15 we did 62 miles with sledges. Each sledge weighed 660 pounds, and we had six dogs for each. The upper barrier ("barrier surface") was smooth and even. There were a few crevasses here and there, but we only found them dangerous at one or two points. The barrier went in long, regular undulations. The weather was very favorable, with calm or light winds. The lowest temperature at this station was -49° F, which was taken on March 4.

When we returned to winter quarters on February 5 from the first trip, we found that the *Fram* had already left us. With joy and pride we heard from those who had stayed behind that our gallant captain had succeeded in sailing her farther south than any former ship. So the good old *Fram* has shown the flag of Norway both farthest north and farthest south. The most southerly latitude reached by the *Fram* was 78° 41'.

Before the winter set in we had 60 tons of seal meat in our winter quarters; this was enough for ourselves and our 110 dogs. We had built eight kennels and a number of connecting tents and snow huts. When we had provided for the dogs, we thought of ourselves. Our little hut was almost entirely covered with snow. Not till the middle of April did we decide to adopt artificial light in the hut. This we did with the help of a Lux lamp of 200 candle-power, which gave an excellent light and kept the indoor temperature at about 68° F throughout the winter. The ventilation was very satisfactory, and we got sufficient fresh air. The hut was directly connected with the house in which we had our workshop, larder, storeroom, and cellar, besides a single bathroom and observatory. Thus we had everything indoors and easily got at, in case the weather should be so cold and stormy that we could not venture out.

The sun left us on April 22, and we did not see it again for four months. We spent the winter in altering our whole equipment, which our depot journeys had shown to be too heavy and clumsy for the smooth barrier surface. At the same time we carried out all the scientific work for which there was opportunity. We made a number of surprising meteorological observations. There was very little snow, in spite of there being open water in the neighbourhood. We had expected to observe higher temperatures in the course of the winter, but the thermometer remained very low. During five months temperatures were observed varying between -58° and -74° F. We had the lowest (-74° F) on August 13; the weather was calm. On August 1 we had -72° F with a wind of 13 miles an hour. The mean temperature for the year was -15° F. We expected blizzard after blizzard, but had only two moderate

8

storms. We made many excellent observations of the *aurora australis* in all parts of the heavens. Our bill of health was the best possible throughout the whole winter. When the sun returned on August 24 it shone upon men who were healthy in mind and body, and ready to begin the task that lay before them.

We had brought the sledges the day before to the starting-point of the southern journey. At the beginning of September the temperature rose, and it was decided to commence the journey. On September 8 a party of eight men set out, with seven sledges and 90 dogs, provisioned for 90 days. The surface was excellent, and the temperature not so bad as it might have been. But on the following day we saw that we had started too early. The temperature then fell, and remained for some days between -58°F and -75°F. Personally we did not suffer at all, as we had good fur clothing, but with the dogs it was another matter. They grew lanker and lanker every day, and we soon saw that they would not be able to stand it in the long run. At our depot in latitude 80° we agreed to turn back and await the arrival of spring. After having stored our provisions, we returned to the hut. Excepting the loss of a few dogs and one or two frostbitten heels, all was well. It was not till the middle of October that the spring began in earnest. Seals and birds were sighted. The temperature remained steady, between -5° and -22°F.

Meanwhile we had abandoned the original plan, by which all were to go to the south. Five men were to do this, while three others made a trip to the east, to visit King Edward VII Land. This trip did not form part of our program, but as the English did not reach this land last summer, as had been their intention, we agreed that it would be best to undertake this journey in addition.

On October 20 the southern party left. It consisted of five men with four sledges and 52 dogs, and had provisions for four months. Everything was in excellent order, and we had made up our minds to take it easy during the first part of the journey, so that we and the dogs might not be too fatigued, and we therefore decided to make a little halt on the 22nd at the depot that lay in latitude 80°. However, we missed the mark owing to thick fog, but after two or three miles' march we found the place again.

When we had rested here and given the dogs as much seal meat as they were able to eat, we started again on the 26th. The temperature remained steady, between -5° and -22° F. At first we had made up our minds not to drive more than twelve to eighteen miles a day; but this proved to be too little, thanks to our strong and willing animals. At lat. 80° we began to erect snow beacons, about the height of a man, to show us the way home. On the 31st we reached the depot in lat. 81°. We halted for a day and fed the dogs on pemmican. On November 5 we reached the depot in 82°, where for the last time the dogs got as much to eat as they could manage.

On the 8th we started southward again, and now made a daily march of about thirty miles. In order to relieve the heavily laden sledges, we formed a depot at every parallel we reached. The journey from lat. 82° to 83° was a pure pleasure trip, on account of the surface and the temperature, which were as favourable as one could wish. Everything went swimmingly until the 9th, when we sighted South Victoria Land and the continuation of the mountain chain, which Shackleton gives on his map, running southeast from Beardmore Glacier. On the same day we reached lat. 83°, and established here Depot No. 4.

On the 11th we made the interesting discovery that the Ross Barrier ended in an elevation on the south-east, formed between a chain of mountains running south-eastward from South Victoria Land and another chain on the opposite side, which runs south-westward in continuation of King Edward VII. Land. On the 13th we reached lat. 84°, where we established a depot. On the 16th we got to 85°, where again we formed a depot. From our winter quarters at Framheim we had marched due south the whole time.

On November 17, in lat. 85°, we came to a spot where the land barrier intersected our route, though for the time being this did not cause us any difficulty. The barrier here rises in the form of a wave to a height of about 300 feet, and its limit is shown by a few large fissures. Here we established our main depot. We took supplies for sixty days on the sledges and left behind enough provisions for thirty days.

The land under which we now lay, and which we were to attack, looked perfectly impossible, with peaks along the barrier which rose to heights of from 2,000 to 10,000 feet. Farther south we saw more peaks, of 15,000 feet or higher. Next day we began to climb. The first part of the work was easy, as the ground rose gradually with smooth snow-slopes below the mountain-side. Our dogs working well, it did not take us long to get over these slopes.

At the next point we met with some small, very steep glaciers, and here we had to harness twenty dogs to each sledge and take the four sledges in two journeys. Some places were so steep that it was difficult to use our ski. Several times we were compelled by deep crevasses to turn back. On the first day we climbed 2,000 feet. The next day we crossed small glaciers, and camped at a height of 4,635 feet. On the third day we were obliged to descend the great Axel Heiberg Glacier, which separates the mountains of the coast from those farther south.

On the following day the longest part of our climbing began. Many detours had to be made to avoid broad fissures and open crevasses. Most of them were filled up, as in all probability the glacier had long ago ceased to move; but we had to be very careful, nevertheless, as we could never know the depth of snow that covered them. Our camp that night was in very picturesque surroundings, at a height of about 5,000 feet.

The glacier was here imprisoned between two mountains of 15,000 feet, which we named after Fridtjof Nansen and Don Pedro Christophersen.

At the bottom of the glacier we saw Ole Engelstad's great snow-cone rising in the air to 19,000 feet. The glacier was much broken up in this narrow defile; enormous crevasses seemed as if they would stop our going farther, but fortunately it was not so bad as it looked.

Our dogs, which during the last few days had covered a distance of nearly 440 miles, put in a very good piece of work that day, as they did twenty-two miles on ground rising to 5,770 feet. It was an almost incredible record. It only took us four days from the barrier to reach the immense inland plateau. We camped at a height of 7,600 feet. Here we had to kill twenty-four of our brave dogs, keeping eighteen – six for each of our three sledges. We halted here for four days on account of bad weather. On November 25 we were tired of waiting, and started again. On the 26th we were overtaken by a raging blizzard. In the thick, driving snow we could see absolutely nothing; but we felt that, contrary to what we had expected – namely, a further ascent – we were going rapidly downhill. The hypsometer that day showed a descent of 600 feet. We continued our march next day in a strong wind and thick, driving snow. Our faces were badly frozen. There was no danger, but we simply could see nothing. Next day, according to our reckoning, we reached lat. 86°. The hypsometer showed a fall of 800 feet. The following day passed in the same way. The weather cleared up about noon, and there appeared to our astonished eyes a mighty mountain range to the east of us, and not far away. But the vision only lasted a moment, and then disappeared again in the driving snow. On the 29th the weather became calmer and the sun shone – a pleasant surprise. Our course lay over a great glacier, which ran in a southerly direction. On its eastern side was a chain of mountains running to the southeast. We had no view of its western part, as this was lost in a thick fog. At the foot of the Devil's Glacier we established a depot in lat. 86° 21', calculated for six days. The hypsometer showed 8,000 feet above sea level. On November 30 we began to ascend the glacier. The lower part was much broken up and dangerous, and the thin bridges of snow over the crevasses often broke under us. From our camp that evening we had a splendid view of the mountains to the east. Mount Helmer Hansen was the most remarkable of them all; it was 12,000 feet high, and covered by a glacier so rugged that in all probability it would have been impossible to find foothold on it. Here were also Mounts Oskar Wisting, Sverre Hassel, and Olav Bjaaland, grandly lighted up by the rays of the sun. In the distance, and only visible from time to time through the driving mists, we saw Mount Thorvald Nilsen, with peaks rising to 15,000 feet. We could only see those parts of them that lay nearest to us. It took us three days to get over the Devil's Glacier, as the weather was unusually misty.

On December 1 we left the glacier in high spirits. It was cut up by innumerable crevasses and holes. We were now at a height of

9,370 feet. In the mist and driving snow it looked as if we had a frozen lake before us; but it proved to be a sloping plateau of ice, full of small blocks of ice. Our walk across this frozen lake was not pleasant. The ground under our feet was evidently hollow, and it sounded as if we were walking on empty barrels. First a man fell through, then a couple of dogs; but they got up again all right. We could not, of course, use our ski on this smooth-polished ice, but we got on fairly well with the sledges. We called this place the Devil's Ballroom. This part of our march was the most unpleasant of the whole trip. On December 2 we reached our greatest elevation. According to the hypsometer and our aneroid barometer we were at a height of 11,075 feet – this was in lat. 87° 51'. On December 8 the bad weather came to an end, the sun shone on us once more, and we were able to take our observations again. It proved that the observations and our reckoning of the distance covered gave exactly the same result – namely, 88° 16' S. lat. Before us lay an absolutely flat plateau, only broken by small crevices. In the afternoon we passed 88° 23', Shackleton's farthest south. We pitched our camp in 88° 25', and established our last depot – No. 10. From 88° 25' the plateau began to descend evenly and very slowly. We reached 88° 29' on December 9. On December 10, 88° 56'; December 11, 89° 15'; December 12, 89° 30'; December 13, 89° 45'.

Up to this moment the observations and our reckoning had shown a surprising agreement. We reckoned that we should be at the Pole on December 14. On the afternoon of that day we had brilliant weather – a light wind from the south-east with a temperature of -10° F. The sledges were going very well. The day passed without any occurrence worth mentioning, and at three o' clock in the afternoon we halted, as according to our reckoning we had reached our goal.

We all assembled about the Norwegian flag – a handsome silken flag – which we took and planted all together, and gave the immense plateau on which the Pole is situated the name of "King Haakon VII.'s Plateau."

It was a vast plain of the same character in every direction, mile after mile. During the afternoon we traversed the neighbourhood of the camp, and on the following day, as the weather was fine, we were occupied from six in the morning till seven in the evening in taking observations, which gave us 89° 55' as the result. In order to take observations as near the Pole as possible, we went on, as near true south as we could, for the remaining 9 kilometres. On December 16 we pitched our camp in brilliant sunshine, with the best conditions for taking observations. Four of us took observations every hour of the day – twenty-four in all. The results of these will be submitted to the examination of experts.

We have thus taken observations as near to the Pole as was humanly possible with the instruments at our disposal. We had a sextant and artificial horizon calculated for a radius of 8 kilometres.

On December 17 we were ready to go. We raised on the spot a little circular tent, and planted above it the Norwegian flag and the *Fram*'s pennant. The Norwegian camp at the South Pole was given the name of "Polheim." The distance from our winter quarters to the Pole was about 870 English miles, so that we had covered on an average 15 1/2 miles a day.

We began the return journey on December 17. The weather was unusually favourable, and this made our return considerably easier than the march to the Pole. We arrived at "Framheim," our winter quarters, in January, 1912, with two sledges and eleven dogs, all well. On the homeward journey we covered an average of 22 1/2 miles a day. The lowest temperature we observed on this trip was -24° F., and the highest +23° F.

The principal result – besides the attainment of the Pole – is the determination of the extent and character of the Ross Barrier. Next to this, the discovery of a connection between South Victoria Land and, probably, King Edward VII. Land through their continuation in huge mountain-ranges, which run to the south-east and were seen as far south as lat. 88° 8', but which in all probability are continued right across the Antarctic Continent. We gave the name of "Queen Maud's Mountains" to the whole range of these newly discovered mountains, about 530 miles in length.

The expedition to King Edward VII. Land, under Lieutenant Prestrud, has achieved excellent results. Scott's discovery was confirmed, and the examination of the Bay of Whales and the Ice Barrier, which the party carried out, is of great interest. Good geological collections have been obtained from King Edward VII. Land and South Victoria Land.

The *Fram* arrived at the Bay of Whales on January 9, having been delayed in the "Roaring Forties " by easterly winds.

On January 16 the Japanese expedition arrived at the Bay of Whales, and landed on the Barrier near our winter quarters.

We left the Bay of Whales on January 30. We had a long voyage on account of contrary wind.

We are all in the best of health.

Roald Amundsen

Hobart,
March 8, 1912

INTRODUCTION

When the explorer comes home victorious, everyone goes out to cheer him. We are all proud of his achievement – proud on behalf of the nation and of humanity. We think it is a new feather in our cap, and one we have come by cheaply.

How many of those who join in the cheering were there when the expedition was fitting out, when it was short of bare necessities, when support and assistance were most urgently wanted? Was there then any race to be first? At such a time the leader has usually found himself almost alone; too often he has had to confess that his greatest difficulties were those he had to overcome at home before he could set sail. So it was with Columbus, and so it has been with many since his time.

So it was, too, with Roald Amundsen – not only the first time, when he sailed in the *Gjöa* with the double object of discovering the Magnetic North Pole and of making the North-West Passage, but this time again, when in 1910 he left the fjord on his great expedition in the *Fram*, to drift right across the North Polar Sea. What anxieties that man has gone through, which might have been spared him if there had been more appreciation on the part of those who had it in their power to make things easier! And Amundsen had then shown what stuff he was made of: both the great objects of the *Gjöa's* expedition were achieved. He has always reached the goal he has aimed at, this man who sailed his little yacht over the whole Arctic Ocean, round the north of America, on the course that had been sought in vain for four hundred years. If he staked his life and abilities, would it not have been natural if we had been proud of having such a man to support?

But was it so? For a long time he struggled to complete his equipment. Money was still lacking, and little interest was shown in him and his work, outside the few who have always helped so far as was in their power. He himself gave everything he possessed in the world. But this time, as last, he nevertheless had to put to sea loaded with anxieties and debts, and, as before, he sailed out quietly on a summer night.

Autumn was drawing on. One day there came a letter from him. In order to raise the money he could not get at home for his North Polar expedition he was going to the South Pole first. People stood still – did not know what to say. This was an unheard-of thing, to make for the North Pole by way of the South Pole! To make such an immense and entirely new addition to his plans without asking leave! Some thought it grand; more thought it doubtful; but there were many who cried out that it was inadmissible, disloyal – nay, there were some who wanted to have him stopped. But nothing of this reached him. He had steered his course as he himself had set it, without looking back.

Then by degrees it was forgotten, and everyone went on with his own affairs. The mists were upon us day after day, week after week – the mists that are kind to little men and swallow up all that is great and towers above them.

Suddenly a bright spring day cuts through the bank of fog. There is a new message. People stop again and look up. High above them shines a deed, a man. A wave of joy runs through the souls of men; their eyes are bright as the flags that wave about them.

Why? On account of the great geographical discoveries, the important scientific results? Oh no; that will come later, for the few specialists. This is something all can understand. A victory of human mind and human strength over the dominion and powers of Nature; a deed that lifts us above the grey monotony of daily life; a view over shining plains, with lofty mountains against the cold blue sky, and lands covered by ice-sheets of inconceivable extent; a vision of long-vanished glacial times; the triumph of the living over the stiffened realm of death. There is a ring of steeled, purposeful human will – through icy frosts, snowstorms, and death.

For the victory is not due to the great inventions of the present day and the many new appliances of every kind. The means used are of immense antiquity, the same as were known to the nomad thousands of years ago, when he pushed forward across the snow-covered plains of Siberia and Northern Europe. But everything, great and small, was thoroughly thought out, and the plan was splendidly executed. It is the man that matters, here as everywhere.

Like everything great, it all looks so plain and simple. Of course, that is just as it had to be, we think. Apart from the discoveries and experiences of earlier explorers – which, of course, were a necessary condition of success – both the plan and its execution are the ripe fruit of Norwegian life and experience in ancient and modern times. The Norwegians' daily winter life in snow and frost, our peasants' constant use of ski and ski-sledge in forest and mountain, our sailors' yearly whaling and sealing life in the Polar Sea, our explorers' journeys in the Arctic regions – it was all this, with the dog as a draught animal borrowed from the primitive races, that formed the foundation of the plan and rendered its execution possible – when the man appeared.

Therefore, when the man is there, it carries him through all difficulties as if they did not exist; every one of them has been foreseen and encountered in advance. Let no one come and prate about luck and chance. Amundsen's luck is that of the strong man who looks ahead. How like him and the whole expedition is his telegram home – as simple and straightforward as if it concerned a holiday tour in the mountains. It speaks of what is achieved, not of their hardships. Every word a manly one. That is the mark of the right man, quiet and strong.

It is still too early to measure the extent of the new discoveries, but the cablegram has already dispersed the mists so far that the outlines are beginning to shape themselves. That fairyland of ice, so different from all other lands, is gradually rising out of the clouds.

In this wonderful world of ice Amundsen has found his own way. From first to last he and his companions have traversed entirely unknown regions on their ski, and there are not many expeditions in history that have brought under the foot of man so long a range of country hitherto unseen by human eye. People thought it a matter of course that he would make for Beardmore Glacier, which Shackleton had discovered, and by that route come out on to the high snow plateau near the Pole, since there he would be sure of getting forward. We who knew Amundsen thought it would be more like him to avoid a place for the very reason that it had been trodden by others. Happily we were right. Not at any point does his route touch that of the Englishmen – except by the Pole itself.

This is a great gain to research. When in a year's time we have Captain Scott back safe and sound with all his discoveries and observations on the other route, Amundsen's results will greatly increase in value, since the conditions will then be illuminated from two sides. The simultaneous advance towards the Pole from two separate points was precisely the most fortunate thing that could happen for science. The region investigated becomes so much greater, the discoveries so many more, and the importance of the observations is more than doubled, often multiplied many times. Take, for instance, the meteorological conditions: a single series of observations from one spot no doubt has its value, but if we get a simultaneous series from another spot in the same region, the value of both becomes very much greater, because we then have an opportunity of understanding the movements of the atmosphere. And so with other investigations. Scott's expedition will certainly bring back rich and important results in many departments, but the value of his observations will also be enhanced when placed side by side with Amundsen's.

An important addition to Amundsen's expedition to the Pole is the sledge journey of Lieutenant Prestrud and his two companions eastward to the unknown King Edward VII. Land, which Scott discovered in 1902. It looks rather as if this land was connected with the masses of land and immense mountain-chains that Amundsen found near the Pole. We see new problems looming up.

But it was not only these journeys over ice-sheets and mountain-ranges that were carried out in masterly fashion. Our gratitude is also due to Captain Nilsen and his men. They brought the *Fram* backwards and forwards, twice each way, through those ice-filled southern waters that many experts even held to be so dangerous that the *Fram* would not be able to come through them, and on both trips this was done with the speed and punctuality of a ship on her regular route. The *Fram*'s builder, the excellent Colin Archer, has reason to be proud of the way in which his "child" has performed her latest task – this vessel that has been farthest north and farthest south on our globe. But Captain Nilsen and the crew of the *Fram* have done more than this; they have carried out a work of research which in scientific value may be compared with what their comrades have accomplished in the unknown world of ice, although most people will not be able to recognize this. While Amundsen and his companions were passing the winter in the South, Captain Nilsen, in the *Fram*, investigated the ocean between South America and Africa. At no fewer than sixty stations they took a number of temperatures, samples of water, and specimens of the plankton in this little-known region, to a depth of 2,000 fathoms and more. They thus made the first two sections that have ever been taken of the South Atlantic, and added new regions of the unknown ocean depths to human knowledge. The *Fram*'s sections are the longest and most complete that are known in any part of the ocean.

Would it be unreasonable if those who have endured and achieved so much had now come home to rest? But Amundsen points onward. So much for that; now for the real object. Next year his course will be through Behring Strait into the ice and frost and darkness of the North, to drift right across the North Polar Sea – five years, at least. It seems almost superhuman; but he is the man for that, too. *Fram* is his ship, "forward" is his motto, and he will come through. He will carry out his main expedition, the one that is now before him, as surely and steadily as that he has just come from.

But while we are waiting, let us rejoice over what has already been achieved. Let us follow the narrow sledge-tracks that the little black dots of dogs and men have drawn across the endless white surface down there in the South – like a railroad of exploration into the heart of the unknown. The wind in its everlasting flight sweeps over these tracks in the desert of snow. Soon all will be blotted out.

But the rails of science are laid; our knowledge is richer than before.

And the light of the achievement shines for all time.

Fridtjof Nansen.

Lysaker,
May 3, 1912.

CHAPTER 1

THE HISTORY OF THE SOUTH POLE

"Life is a ball in the hands of chance."

Brisbane, Queensland, April 13, 1912.

Here I am, sitting in the shade of palms, surrounded by the most wonderful vegetation, enjoying the most magnificent fruits, and writing – the history of the South Pole. What an infinite distance seems to separate that region from these surroundings! And yet it is only four months since my gallant comrades and I reached the coveted spot.

I write the history of the South Pole! If anyone had hinted a word of anything of the sort four or five years ago, I should have looked upon him as incurably mad. And yet the madman would have been right. One circumstance has followed on the heels of another, and everything has turned out so entirely different from what I had imagined.

On December 14, 1911, five men stood at the southern end of our earth's axis, planted the Norwegian flag there, and named the region after the man for whom they would all gladly have offered their lives – King Haakon VII. Thus the veil was torn aside for all time, and one of the greatest of our earth's secrets had ceased to exist.

Since I was one of the five who, on that December afternoon, took part in this unveiling, it has fallen to my lot to write – the history of the South Pole.

Antarctic exploration is very ancient. Even before our conception of the earth's form had taken definite shape, voyages to the South began. It is true that not many of the explorers of those distant times reached what we now understand by the Antarctic regions, but still the intention and the possibility were there, and justify the name of Antarctic exploration. The motive force of these undertakings was – as has so often been the case – the hope of gain. Rulers greedy of power saw in their mind's eye an increase of their possessions. Men thirsting for gold dreamed of an unsuspected wealth of the alluring metal. Enthusiastic missionaries rejoiced at the thought of a multitude of lost sheep. The scientifically trained world waited modestly in the background. But they have all had their share: politics, trade, religion, and science.

The history of Antarctic discovery may be divided at the outset into two categories. In the first of these I would include the numerous voyagers who, without any definite idea of the form or conditions of the southern hemisphere, set their course toward the South, to make what landfall they could. These need only be mentioned briefly before passing to the second group, that of Antarctic travellers in the proper sense of the term, who, with a knowledge of the form of the earth, set out across the ocean, aiming to strike the Antarctic monster – in the heart, if fortune favoured them.

We must always remember with gratitude and admiration the first sailors who steered their vessels through storms and mists, and increased our knowledge of the lands of ice in the

26

South. People of the present day, who are so well supplied with information about the most distant parts of the earth, and have all our modern means of communication at their command, find it difficult to understand the intrepid courage that is implied by the voyages of these men.

They shaped their course toward the dark unknown, constantly exposed to being engulfed and destroyed by the vague, mysterious dangers that lay in wait for them somewhere in that dim vastness.

The beginnings were small, but by degrees much was won. One stretch of country after another was discovered and subjected to the power of man. Knowledge of the appearance of our globe became ever greater and took more definite shape. Our gratitude to these first discoverers should be profound. And yet even to-day we hear people ask in surprise: What is the use of these voyages of exploration? What good do they do us? Little brains, I always answer to myself, have only room for thoughts of bread and butter.

The first name on the roll of discovery is that of Prince Henry of Portugal, surnamed the Navigator, who is ever to be remembered as the earliest promoter of geographical research. To his efforts was due the first crossing of the Equator, about 1470. With Bartholomew Diaz another great step in advance was made. Sailing from Lisbon in 1487, he reached Algoa Bay, and without doubt passed the fortieth parallel on his southward voyage. Vasco da Gama's voyage of 1497 is too well known to need description. After him came men like Cabral and Vespucci, who increased our knowledge, and de Gonneville, who added to the romance of exploration.

We then meet with the greatest of the older explorers, Ferdinand Magellan, a Portuguese by birth, though sailing in the service of Spain. Setting out in 1519, he discovered the connection between the Atlantic and Pacific Oceans in the strait that bears his name. No one before him had penetrated so far South – to about lat. 52° S. One of his ships, the *Victoria*, accomplished the first circumnavigation of the world, and thus established in the popular mind the fact that the earth was really round. From that time the idea of the Antarctic regions assumed definite shape. There must be something in the South: whether land or water the future was to determine.

In 1578 we come to the renowned English seaman, Sir Francis Drake. Though he was accounted a buccaneer, we owe him honour for the geographical discoveries he made. He rounded Cape Horn and proved that Tierra del Fuego was a great group of islands and not part of an Antarctic continent, as many had thought.

The Dutchman, Dirk Gerritsz, who took part in a plundering expedition to India in 1599 by way of the Straits of Magellan, is said to have been blown out of his course after passing the straits, and to have found himself in lat. 64° S. under high land covered with snow. This has been assumed to be the South Shetland Islands, but the account of the voyage is open to doubt.

In the seventeenth century we have the discoveries of Tasman, and towards its close English adventurers reported having reached high latitudes in the South Atlantic. The English Astronomer Royal, Halley, undertook a scientific voyage to the South in 1699 for the purpose of making magnetic observations, and met with ice in 52° S., from which latitude he returned to the north. The Frenchman, Bouvet (1738), was the first to follow the southern ice-pack for any considerable distance, and to bring reports of the immense, flat-topped Antarctic icebergs.

In 1756 the Spanish trading-ship *Leon* came home and reported high, snow-covered land in lat. 55° S. to the east of Cape Horn. The probability is that this was what we now know by the name of South Georgia. The Frenchman, Marion-Dufresne, discovered, in 1772, the Marion and Crozet Islands. In the same year Joseph de Kerguélen-Trémarec – another Frenchman – reached Kerguelen Land.

This concludes the series of expeditions that I have thought it proper to class in the first group. "Antarctica," the sixth continent itself, still lay unseen and untrodden. But human courage and intelligence were now actively stirred to lift the veil and reveal the many secrets that were concealed within the Antarctic Circle.

Captain James Cook – one of the boldest and most capable seamen the world has known – opens the series of Antarctic expeditions properly so-called. The British Admiralty sent him out with orders to discover the great southern continent, or prove that it did not exist. The expedition, consisting of two ships, the *Resolution* and the *Adventure*, left Plymouth on July 13, 1772. After a short stay at Madeira it reached Cape Town on October 30. Here Cook received news of the discovery of Kerguelen and of the Marion and Crozet Islands. In the course of his voyage to the south Cook passed 300 miles to the south of the land reported by Bouvet, and thereby established the fact that the land in question – if it existed – was not continuous with the great southern continent.

On January 17, 1773, the Antarctic Circle was crossed for the first time – a memorable day in the annals of Antarctic exploration. Shortly afterwards a solid pack was encountered, and Cook was forced to return to the north. A course was laid for the newly discovered islands – Kerguelen, Marion, and the Crozets – and it was proved that they had nothing to do with the great southern land. In the course of his further voyages in Antarctic waters Cook completed the most southerly circumnavigation of the globe, and showed that there was no connection between any of the lands or islands that had been discovered and the great mysterious "Antarctica." His highest latitude (January 30, 1774) was 71° 10' S.

Cook's voyages had important commercial results, as his reports of the enormous number of seals round South Georgia brought many sealers, both English and American, to those waters, and these sealers, in turn, increased the field of geographical discovery.

In 1819 the discovery of the South Shetlands by the Englishman, Captain William Smith, is to be recorded. And this discovery led to that of the Palmer Archipelago to the south of them. The next scientific expedition to the Antarctic regions was that despatched by the Emperor Alexander I. of Russia, under the command of Captain Thaddeus von Bellingshausen. It was composed of two ships, and sailed from Cronstadt on July 15, 1819. To this expedition belongs the honour of having discovered the first land to the south of the Antarctic Circle – Peter I. Island and Alexander I. Land.

The next star in the Antarctic firmament is the British sea-man, James Weddell. He made two voyages in a sealer of 160 tons, the *Jane* of Leith, in 1819 and 1822, being accompanied on the second occasion by the cutter *Beaufoy*. In February, 1823, Weddell had the satisfaction of beating Cook's record by reaching a latitude of 74° 15' S. in the sea now known as Wed-dell Sea, which in that year was clear of ice.

The English firm of shipowners, Enderby Brothers, plays a not unimportant part in Antarctic exploration. The Enderbys had carried on sealing in southern waters since 1785. They were greatly interested, not only in the commercial, but also in the scientific results of these voyages, and chose their captains accordingly. In 1830 the firm sent out John Biscoe on a sealing voyage in the Antarctic Ocean with the brig *Tula* and the cutter *Lively*. The result of this voyage was the sighting of Enderby Land in lat. 66° 25' S., long. 49° 18' E. In the following year Adelaide, Biscoe, and Pitt Islands, on the west coast of Graham Land were charted, and Graham Land itself was seen for the first time. Kemp, another of Enderby's skippers, reported land in lat. 66° S., and about long. 60° E.

In 1839 yet another skipper of the same firm, John Balleny, in the schooner *Eliza Scott*, discovered the Balleny Islands.

We then come to the celebrated French sailor, Admiral Jules Sébastien Dumont d'Urville. He left Toulon in September, 1837, with a scientifically equipped expedition, in the ships *Astrolabe* and *Zélée*. The intention was to follow in Weddell's track, and endeavour to carry the French flag still nearer to the Pole. Ear-ly in 1838 Louis Philippe Land and Joinville Island were dis-covered and named. Two years later we again find d'Urville's

31

vessels in Antarctic waters, with the object of investigating the magnetic conditions in the vicinity of the South Magnetic Pole. Land was discovered in lat. 66° 30' S. and long. 138° 21' E. With the exception of a few bare islets, the whole of this land was completely covered with snow. It was given the name of Adélie Land, and a part of the ice-barrier lying to the west of it was called Côte Clarie, on the supposition that it must envelop a line of coast.

The American naval officer, Lieutenant Charles Wilkes, sailed in August, 1838, with a fleet of six vessels. The expedition was sent out by Congress, and carried twelve scientific observers. In February, 1839, the whole of this imposing Antarctic fleet was collected in Orange Harbour in the south of Tierra del Fuego, where the work was divided among the various vessels. As to the results of this expedition it is difficult to express an opinion. Certain it is that Wilkes Land has subsequently been sailed over in many places by several expeditions. Of what may have been the cause of this inaccurate cartography it is impossible to form any opinion. It appears, however, from the account of the whole voyage, that the undertaking was seriously conducted.

Then the bright star appears – the man whose name will ever be remembered as one of the most intrepid polar explorers and one of the most capable seamen the world has produced – Admiral Sir James Clark Ross.

The results of his expedition are well known. Ross himself commanded the *Erebus* and Commander Francis Crozier the *Terror*. The former vessel, of 370 tons, had been originally built for throwing bombs; her construction was therefore extraordinarily solid. The *Terror*, 340 tons, had been previously employed in Arctic waters, and on this account had been already strengthened. In provisioning the ships, every possible precaution was taken against scurvy, with the dangers of which Ross was familiar from his experience in Arctic waters.

The vessels sailed from England in September, 1839, calling at many of the Atlantic Islands, and arrived in Christmas Harbour, Kerguelen Land, in the following May. Here they stayed two months, making magnetic observations, and then proceeded to Hobart.

Sir John Franklin, the eminent polar explorer, was at that time Governor of Tasmania, and Ross could not have wished for a better one. Interested as Franklin naturally was in the expedition, he afforded it all the help he possibly could. During his stay in Tasmania Ross received information of what had been accomplished by Wilkes and Dumont d'Urville in the very region which the Admiralty had sent him to explore. The effect of this news was that Ross changed his plans, and decided to proceed along the 170th meridian E., and if possible to reach the Magnetic Pole from the eastward. Here was another fortuitous circumstance in the long chain of events. If Ross had not received this intelligence, it is quite possible that the epoch-making geographical discoveries associated with his name would have been delayed for many years.

On November 12, 1840, Sir John Franklin went on board the *Erebus* to accompany his friend Ross out of port. Strange are the ways of life! There stood Franklin on the deck of the ship which a few years later was to be his deathbed. Little did he suspect, as he sailed out of Hobart through Storm Bay – the bay that is now wreathed by the flourishing orchards of Tasmania – that he would meet his death in a high northern latitude on board the same vessel, in storms and frost. But so it was.

After calling at the Auckland Islands and at Campbell Island, Ross again steered for the South, and the Antarctic Circle was crossed on New Year's Day, 1841. The ships were now faced by the ice-pack, but to Ross this was not the dangerous enemy it had appeared to earlier explorers with their more weakly constructed vessels. Ross plunged boldly into the pack with his fortified ships, and, taking advantage of the narrow leads, he came out four days later, after many severe buffets, into the open sea to the South. Ross had reached the sea now named after him, and the boldest voyage known in Antarctic exploration was accomplished.

Few people of the present day are capable of rightly appreciating this heroic deed; this brilliant proof of human courage and energy. With two ponderous craft – regular "tubs" according to our ideas – these men sailed right into the heart of the pack, which all previous polar explorers had regarded as certain death. It is not merely difficult to grasp this; it is simply impossible – to us, who with a motion of the hand can set the screw going, and wriggle out of the first difficulty we encounter. These men were heroes – heroes in the highest sense of the word.

It was in lat. 69° 15' S. and long. 176° 15' E. that Ross found the open sea. On the following day the horizon was perfectly clear of ice. What joy that man must have felt when he saw that he had a clear way to the South! The course was set for the Magnetic Pole, and the hope of soon reaching it burned in the hearts of all. Then – just as they had accustomed themselves to the idea of open sea, perhaps to the Magnetic Pole itself – the crow's-nest reported "High land right ahead." This was the mountainous coast of South Victoria Land.

What a fairyland this must have seemed to the first voyagers who approached it! Mighty mountain-ranges with summits from 7,000 to 10,000 feet high, some covered with snow and some quite bare – lofty and rugged, precipitous and wild.

It became apparent that the Magnetic Pole was some 500 miles distant – far inland, behind the snow-covered ridges. On the morning of January 12 they came close under a little island, and Ross with a few companions rowed ashore and took possession of the country. They could not reach the mainland itself on account of the thick belt of ice that lay along the coast.

The expedition continued to work its way southward, making fresh discoveries. On January 28 the two lofty summits, Mount Erebus and Mount Terror, were sighted for the first time. The former was seen to be an active volcano, from which smoke and flames shot up into the sky. It must have been a wonderfully fine sight, this flaming fire in the midst of the white, frozen landscape. Captain Scott has since given the island, on which the mountains lie, the name of Ross Island, after the intrepid navigator.

Naturally there were great expectations on board. If they had penetrated so far south, there might be no limit to their further progress. But, as had happened so many times before, their hopes were disappointed. From Ross Island, as far to the eastward as the eye could see, there extended a lofty, impenetrable wall of ice. To sail through it was as impossible as sailing through the cliffs of Dover, Ross says in his description. All they could do was to try to get round it. And then began the first examination of that part of the great Antarctic Barrier which has since been named the Ross Barrier.

The wall of ice was followed to the eastward for a distance of 250 miles. Its upper surface was seen to be perfectly flat. The most easterly point reached was long. 167° W., and the highest latitude 78° 4' S. No opening having been found, the ships returned to the west, in order to try once more whether there was any possibility of reaching the Magnetic Pole. But this attempt soon had to be abandoned on account of the lateness of the season, and in April, 1841, Ross returned to Hobart.

His second voyage was full of dangers and thrilling incidents, but added little to the tale of his discoveries. On February 22, 1842, the ships came in sight of the Barrier, and, following it to the east, found that it turned north-eastward. Here Ross recorded an "appearance of land" in the very region in which Captain Scott, sixty years later, discovered King Edward VII. Land.

On December 17, 1842, Ross set out on his third and last Antarctic voyage. His object this time was to reach a high latitude along the coast of Louis Philippe Land, if possible, or alternatively by following Weddell's track. Both attempts were frustrated by the ice conditions.

On sighting Joinville Land, the officers of the *Terror* thought they could see smoke from active volcanoes, but Ross and his men did not confirm this. About fifty years later active volcanoes were actually discovered by the Norwegian, Captain C. A. Larsen, in the *Jason*. A few minor geographical discoveries were made, but none of any great importance.

This concluded Ross's attempts to reach the South Pole. A magnificent work had been achieved, and the honour of having opened up the way by which, at last, the Pole was reached must be ascribed to Ross.

The *Pagoda*, commanded by Lieutenant Moore, was the next vessel to make for the South. Her chief object was to make magnetic observations in high latitudes south of the Indian Ocean. The first ice was met with in lat. 53° 30' S., on January 25,1845. On February 5 the Antarctic Circle was crossed in long. 30° 45' E. The most southerly latitude attained on this voyage was 67° 50', in long. 39°41' E. This was the last expedition to visit the Antarctic regions in a ship propelled by sails alone.

The next great event in the history of the southern seas is the *Challenger* expedition. This was an entirely scientific expedition, splendidly equipped and conducted. The achievements of this expedition are, however, so well known over the whole civilized world that I do not think it necessary to dwell upon them. Less known, but no less efficient in their work, were the whalers round the South Shetlands and in the regions to the south of them. The days of sailing-ships were now past, and vessels with auxiliary steam appear on the scene.

Before passing on to these, I must briefly mention a man who throughout his life insisted on the necessity and utility of Antarctic expeditions – Professor Georg von Neumayer. Never has Antarctic research had a warmer, nobler, and more high-minded champion. So long as "Antarctica" endures, the name of Neumayer will always be connected with it.

The steam whaler *Grönland* left Hamburg on July 22, 1872, in command of Captain Eduard Dallmann, bound for the South Shetlands. Many interesting geographical discoveries were made on this voyage. Amongst other whalers may be mentioned the *Balæna*, the *Diana*, the *Active*, and the *Polar Star* of Dundee.

In 1892 the whole of this fleet stood to the South to hunt for whales in the vicinity of the South Shetlands. They each brought home with them some fresh piece of information. On board the *Balæna* was Dr. William S. Bruce. This is the first time we meet with him on his way to the South, but it was not to be the last.

Simultaneously with the Scottish whaling fleet, the Norwegian whaling captain, C. A. Larsen, appears in the regions to the south of the South Shetlands. It is not too much to say of Captain Larsen that of all those who have visited the Antarctic regions in search of whales, he has unquestionably brought home the best and most abundant scientific results. To him we owe the discovery of large stretches of the east coast of Graham Land, King Oscar II. Land, Foyn's Land, etc. He brought us news of two active volcanoes, and many groups of islands. But perhaps the greatest interest attaches to the fossils he brought home from Seymour Island – the first to be obtained from the Antarctic regions.

In November, 1894, Captain Evensen in the *Hertha* succeeded in approaching nearer to Alexander I. Land than either Bellingshausen or Biscoe. But the search for whales claimed his attention, and he considered it his duty to devote himself to that before anything else. A grand opportunity was lost: there can be no doubt that, if Captain Evensen had been free, he would here have had a chance of achieving even better work than he did – bold, capable, and enterprising as he is.

The next whaling expedition to make its mark in the South

Polar regions is that of the *Antarctic*, under Captain Leonard Kristensen. Kristensen was an extraordinarily capable man, and achieved the remarkable record of being the first to set foot on the sixth continent, the great southern land – "Antarctica." This was at Cape Adare, Victoria Land, in January, 1895.

An epoch-making phase of Antarctic research is now ushered in by the Belgian expedition in the *Belgica*, under the leadership of Commander Adrien de Gerlache. Hardly anyone has had a harder fight to set his enterprise on foot than Gerlache. He was successful, however, and on August 16, 1897, the *Belgica* left Antwerp.

The scientific staff had been chosen with great care, and Gerlache had been able to secure the services of exceedingly able men. His second in command, Lieutenant G. Lecointe, a Belgian, possessed every qualification for his difficult position. It must be remembered that the *Belgica's* company was as cosmopolitan as it could be – Belgians, Frenchmen, Americans, Norwegians, Swedes, Rumanians, Poles, etc. – and it was the business of the second in command to keep all these men together and get the best possible work out of them. And Lecointe acquitted himself admirably; amiable and firm, he secured the respect of all.

As a navigator and astronomer he was unsurpassable, and when he afterwards took over the magnetic work he rendered great services in this department also. Lecointe will always be remembered as one of the main supports of this expedition. Lieutenant Emile Danco, another Belgian, was the physicist of the expedition. Unfortunately this gifted young man died at an early stage of the voyage – a sad loss to the expedition. The magnetic observations were then taken over by Lecointe.

The biologist was the Rumanian, Emile Racovitza. The immense mass of material Racovitza brought home speaks better than I can for his ability. Besides a keen interest in his work, he possessed qualities which made him the most agreeable and interesting of companions. Henryk Arçtowski and Antoine Dobrowolski were both Poles. Their share of the work was the sky and the sea; they carried out oceanographical and meteorological observations.

Henry Arçtowski was also the geologist of the expedition – an all-round man. It was a strenuous task he had, that of constantly watching wind and weather. Conscientious as he was, he never let slip an opportunity of adding to the scientific results of the voyage.

Frederick A. Cook, of Brooklyn, was surgeon to the expedition – beloved and respected by all. As a medical man, his calm and convincing presence had an excellent effect. As things turned out, the greatest responsibility fell upon Cook, but he mastered the situation in a wonderful way. Through his practical qualities he finally became indispensable. It cannot be denied that the Belgian Antarctic expedition owes a great debt to Cook.

The object of the expedition was to penetrate to the South Magnetic Pole, but this had to be abandoned at an early stage for want of time. A somewhat long stay in the interesting channels of Tierra del Fuego delayed their departure till January 13, 1898. On that date the *Belgica* left Staten Island and stood to the South.

An interesting series of soundings was made between Cape Horn and the South Shetlands. As these waters had not previously been investigated, these soundings were, of course, of great importance. The principal work of the expedition, from a geographical point of view, was carried out on the north coast of Graham Land. A large channel running to the south-west was discovered, dividing a part of Palmer Land from the mainland – Danco's Land. The strait was afterwards named by the Belgian authorities "Gerlache Strait." Three weeks were spent in charting it and making scientific observations. An excellent collection of material was made.

This work was completed by February 12, and the *Belgica* left Gerlache Strait southward along the coast of Graham Land, at a date when all previous expeditions had been in a hurry to turn their faces homeward. On the 15th the Antarctic Circle was crossed on a south-westerly course. Next day they sighted Alexander Land, but could not approach nearer to it than twenty miles on account of impenetrable pack-ice. On February 28 they had reached lat. 70° 20' S. and long. 85° W. Then a breeze from the north sprang up and opened large channels in the ice, leading southward. They turned to the south, and plunged at haphazard into the Antarctic floes.

On March 3 they reached lat. 70° 30' S., where all further progress was hopeless. An attempt to get out again was in vain – they were caught in the trap. They then had to make the best of it. Many have been disposed to blame Gerlache for having gone into the ice, badly equipped as he was, at a time of year when he ought rather to have been making his way out, and they may be right. But let us look at the question from the other side as well.

After years of effort he had at last succeeded in getting the expedition away. Gerlache knew for a certainty that unless he returned with results that would please the public, he might just as well never return at all. Then the thickly packed ice opened, and long channels appeared, leading as far southward as the eye could reach. Who could tell? Perhaps they led to the Pole itself. There was little to lose, much to gain; he decided to risk it. Of course, it was not right, but we can easily understand it. The *Belgica* now had thirteen long months before her. Preparations were commenced at once for the winter. As many seals and penguins as could be found were shot, and placed in store. The scientific staff was constantly active, and brilliant oceanographical, meteorological, and magnetic work was accomplished.

On May 17 the sun disappeared, not to be seen again for seventy days. The first Antarctic night had begun. What would it bring? The *Belgica* was not fitted for wintering in the ice. For one thing, personal equipment was insufficient. They had to do the best they could by making clothes out of blankets, and the most extraordinary devices were contrived in the course of the winter. Necessity is the mother of invention.

On June 5 Danco died of heart-failure. On the same day they had a narrow escape of being squeezed in the ice. Fortunately the enormous block of ice passed under the vessel and lifted her up without doing her any damage. Otherwise, the first part of the winter passed off well. Afterwards sickness appeared, and threatened the most serious danger to the expedition – scurvy and insanity. One of them by itself would have been bad enough. Scurvy especially increased, and did such havoc that finally there was not a single man who escaped being attacked by this fearful disease.

Cook's behaviour at this time won the respect and devotion of all. It is not too much to say that Cook was the most popular man of the expedition, and he deserved it. From morning to night he was occupied with his many patients, and when the sun returned it happened not infrequently that, after a strenuous day's work, the doctor sacrificed his night's sleep to go hunting seals and penguins, in order to provide the fresh meat that was so greatly needed by all.

On July 22 the sun returned. It was not a pleasant sight that it shone upon. The Antarctic winter had set its mark upon all, and green, wasted faces stared at the returning light. Time went on, and the summer arrived. They waited day by day to see a change in the ice. But no; the ice they had entered so light-heartedly was not to be so easy to get out of again. New Year's Day came and went without any change in the ice.

The situation now began to be seriously threatening. Another winter in the ice would mean death and destruction on a large scale. Disease and insufficient nourishment would soon make an end of most of the ship's company. Again Cook came to the aid of the expedition. In conjunction with Racovitza he had thought out a very ingenious way of sawing a channel, and thus reaching the nearest lead. The proposal was submitted to the leader of the expedition and accepted by him; both the plan and the method of carrying it out were well considered. After three weeks' hard work, day and night, they at last reached the lead.

Cook was incontestably the leading spirit in this work, and gained such honour among the members of the expedition that I think it just to mention it. Upright, honourable, capable, and conscientious in the extreme – such is the memory we retain of Frederick A. Cook from those days. Little did his comrades suspect that a few years later he would be regarded as one of the greatest humbugs the world has ever seen. This is a psychological enigma well worth studying to those who care to do so.

But the Belgica was not yet clear of the ice. After having worked her way out into the lead and a little way on, she was stopped by absolutely close pack, within sight of the open sea. For a whole month the expedition lay here, reaping the same experiences as Ross on his second voyage with the Erebus and Terror. The immense seas raised the heavy ice high in the air, and flung it against the sides of the vessel. That month was a hell upon earth. Strangely enough, the *Belgica* escaped undamaged, and steamed into Punta Arenas in the Straits of Magellan on March 28, 1899. Modern scientific Antarctic exploration had now been initiated, and de Gerlache had won his place for all time in the first rank of Antarctic explorers.

While the *Belgica* was trying her hardest to get out of the ice, another vessel was making equally strenuous efforts to get in. This was the Southern Cross, the ship of the English expedition, under the leadership of Carstens Borchgrevink. This expedition's field of work lay on the opposite side of the Pole, in Ross's footsteps. On February 11, 1899, the Southern Cross entered Ross Sea in lat. 70° S. and long. 174° E., nearly sixty years after Ross had left it.

A party was landed at Cape Adare, where it wintered. The ship wintered in New Zealand. In January, 1900, the land party was taken off, and an examination of the Barrier was carried out with the vessel. This expedition succeeded for the first time in ascending the Barrier, which from Ross's day had been looked upon as inaccessible. The Barrier formed a little bight at the spot where the landing was made, and the ice sloped gradually down to the sea.

We must acknowledge that by ascending the Barrier, Borchgrevink opened a way to the south, and threw aside the greatest obstacle to the expeditions that followed. The Southern Cross returned to civilization in March, 1900.

The *Valdivia's* expedition, under Professor Chun, of Leipzig, must be mentioned, though in our day it can hardly be regarded as an Antarctic expedition. On this voyage the position of Bouvet Island was established once for all as lat. 54° 26' S., long. 3° 24' E. The ice was followed from long. 8° E. to 58° E., as closely as the vessel could venture to approach. Abundance of oceanographical material was brought home.

Antarctic exploration now shoots rapidly ahead, and the twentieth century opens with the splendidly equipped British and German expeditions in the *Discovery* and the *Gauss*, both national undertakings. Captain Robert F. Scott was given command of the *Discovery's* expedition, and it could not have been placed in better hands. The second in command was Lieutenant Armitage, who had taken part in the Jackson-Harmsworth North Polar expedition. The other officers were Royds, Barne, and Shackleton. Lieutenant Skelton was chief engineer and photographer to the expedition. Two surgeons were on board – Dr. Koettlitz, a former member of the Jackson-Harmsworth expedition, and Dr. Wilson. The latter was also the artist of the expedition. Bernacchi was the physicist, Hodgson the biologist, and Ferrar the geologist.

On August 6, 1901, the expedition left Cowes, and arrived at Simon's Bay on October 3. On the 14th it sailed again for New Zealand. The official plan was to determine as accurately as possible the nature and extent of the South Polar lands that might be found, and to make a magnetic survey. It was left to the leader of the expedition to decide whether it should winter in the ice.

It was arranged beforehand that a relief ship should visit and communicate with the expedition in the following year. The first ice was met with in the neighbourhood of the Antarctic Circle on January 1, 1902, and a few days later the open Ross Sea was reached. After several landings had been made at Cape Adare and other points, the *Discovery* made a very interesting examination of the Barrier to the eastward. At this part of the voyage King Edward VII. Land was discovered, but the thick ice-floes prevented the expedition from landing. On the way back the ship entered the same bight that Borchgrevink had visited in 1900, and a balloon ascent was made on the Barrier. The bay was called Balloon Inlet.

From here the ship returned to McMurdo Bay, so named by Ross. Here the *Discovery* wintered, in a far higher latitude than any previous expedition. In the course of the autumn it was discovered that the land on which the expedition had its winter quarters was an island, separated from the mainland by McMurdo Sound. It was given the name of Ross Island.

Sledge journeys began with the spring. Depots were laid down, and the final march to the South was begun on November 2, 1902, by Scott, Shackleton, and Wilson. They had nineteen dogs to begin with. On November 27 they passed the 80th parallel. Owing to the nature of the ground their progress was not rapid; the highest latitude was reached on December 30 – 82° 17' S. New land was discovered – a continuation of South Victoria Land. One summit after another rose higher and higher to the south. The return journey was a difficult one. The dogs succumbed one after another, and the men themselves had to draw the sledges. It went well enough so long as all were in health; but suddenly Shackleton was incapacitated by scurvy, and there were only two left to pull the sledges. On February 3 they reached the ship again, after an absence of ninety-three days. Meanwhile Armitage and Skelton had reached, for the first time in history, the high Antarctic inland plateau at an altitude of 9,000 feet above the sea.

The relief ship *Morning* had left Lyttelton on December 9. On her way south Scott Island was discovered, and on January 25 the Discovery's masts were seen. But McMurdo Sound lay ice-bound all that year, and the *Morning* returned home on March 3.

The expedition passed a second winter in the ice, and in the following spring Captain Scott led a sledge journey to the west on the ice plateau. In January, 1904, the Morning returned, accompanied by the *Terra Nova*, formerly a Newfoundland sealing vessel. They brought orders from home that the *Discovery* was to be abandoned if she could not be got out. Preparations were made for carrying out the order, but finally, after explosives had been used, a sudden break-up of the ice set the vessel free.

All the coal that could be spared was put on board the *Discovery* from the relief ships, and Scott carried his researches further. If at that time he had had more coal, it is probable that this active explorer would have accomplished even greater things than he did. Wilkes's "Ringgold's Knoll" and "Eld's Peak" were wiped off the map, and nothing was seen of "Cape Hudson," though the *Discovery* passed well within sight of its supposed position. On March 14 Scott anchored in Ross Harbour, Auckland Islands. With rich results, the expedition returned home in September, 1904.

Meanwhile the German expedition under Professor Erich von Drygalski had been doing excellent work in another quarter. The plan of the expedition was to explore the Antarctic regions to the south of Kerguelen Land, after having first built a station on that island and landed a scientific staff, who were to work there, while the main expedition proceeded into the ice. Its ship, the *Gauss*, had been built at Kiel with the *Fram* as a model.

The *Gauss's* navigator was Captain Hans Ruser, a skilful seaman of the Hamburg-American line. Drygalski had chosen his scientific staff with knowledge and care, and it is certain that he could not have obtained better assistants. The expedition left Kiel on August 11, 1901, bound for Cape Town. An extraordinarily complete oceanographical, meteorological, and magnetic survey was made during this part of the voyage.

After visiting the Crozet Islands, the *Gauss* anchored in Royal Sound, Kerguelen Land, on December 31. The expedition stayed here a month, and then steered for the south to explore the regions between Kemp Land and Knox Land. They had already encountered a number of bergs in lat. 60° S. On February 14 they made a sounding of 1,730 fathoms near the supposed position of Wilkes's Termination Land. Progress was very slow hereabout on account of the thick floes.

Suddenly, on February 19, they had a sounding of 132 fathoms, and on the morning of February 21 land was sighted, entirely covered with ice and snow. A violent storm took the *Gauss* by surprise, collected a mass of icebergs around her, and filled up the intervening space with floes, so that there could be no question of making any way. They had to swallow the bitter pill, and prepare to spend the winter where they were. Observatories were built of ice, and sledge journeys were undertaken as soon as the surface permitted. They reached land in three and a half days, and there discovered a bare mountain, about 1,000 feet high, fifty miles from the ship. The land was named Kaiser Wilhelm II. Land, and the mountain the Gaussberg.

They occupied the winter in observations of every possible kind. The weather was extremely stormy and severe, but their winter harbour, under the lee of great stranded bergs, proved to be a good one. They were never once exposed to unpleasant surprises. On February 8, 1903, the *Gauss* was able to begin to move again. From the time she reached the open sea until her arrival at Cape Town on June 9, scientific observations were continued. High land had been seen to the eastward on the bearing of Wilkes's Termination Land, and an amount of scientific work had been accomplished of which the German nation may well be proud. Few Antarctic expeditions have had such a thoroughly scientific equipment as that of the *Gauss*, both as regards appliances and personnel.

The Swedish Antarctic expedition under Dr. Otto Nordenskjöld left Gothenburg on October 16, 1901, in the *Antarctic*, commanded by Captain C. A. Larsen, already mentioned. The scientific staff was composed of nine specialists. After calling at the Falkland Islands and Staten Island, a course was made for the South Shetlands, which came in sight on January 10, 1902. After exploring the coast of Louis Philippe Land, the ship visited Weddell Sea in the hope of getting southward along King Oscar II. Land, but the ice conditions were difficult, and it was impossible to reach the coast. Nordenskjöld and five men were then landed on Snow Hill Island, with materials for an observatory and winter quarters and the necessary provisions. The ship continued her course northward to the open sea.

The first winter on Snow Hill Island was unusually stormy and cold, but during the spring several interesting sledge journeys were made. When summer arrived the *Antarctic* did not appear, and the land party were obliged to prepare for a second winter. In the following spring, October, 1903, Nordenskjöld made a sledge journey to explore the neighbourhood of Mount Haddington, and a closer examination showed that the mountain lay on an island. In attempting to work round this island, he one day stumbled upon three figures, doubtfully human, which might at first sight have been taken for some of our African brethren straying thus far to the south. It took Nordenskjöld a long time to recognize in these beings Dr. Gunnar Andersson, Lieutenant Duse, and their companion during the winter, a Norwegian sailor named Grunden.

The way it came about was this. The *Antarctic* had made repeated attempts to reach the winter station, but the state of the ice was bad, and they had to give up the idea of getting through. Andersson, Duse and Grunden were then landed in the vicinity, to bring news to the winter quarters as soon as the ice permitted them to arrive there. They had been obliged to build themselves a stone hut, in which they had passed the winter. This experience is one of the most interesting one can read of in the history of the Polar regions. Badly equipped as they were, they had to have recourse, like Robinson Crusoe, to their inventive faculties. The most extraordinary contrivances were devised in the course of the winter, and when spring came the three men stepped out of their hole, well and hearty, ready to tackle their work.

This was such a remarkable feat that everyone who has some knowledge of Polar conditions must yield them his admiration. But there is more to tell. On November 8, when both parties were united at Snow Hill, they were unexpectedly joined by Captain Irizar, of the Argentine gunboat *Uruguay*, and one of his officers. Some anxiety had been felt owing to the absence of news of the Antarctic, and the Argentine Government had sent the *Uruguay* to the South to search for the expedition. But what in the world had become of Captain Larsen and the *Antarctic*? This was the question the others asked themselves.

The same night – it sounds almost incredible – there was a knock at the door of the hut, and in walked Captain Larsen with five of his men. They brought the sad intelligence that the good ship *Antarctic* was no more. The crew had saved themselves on the nearest island, while the vessel sank, severely damaged by ice. They, too, had had to build themselves a stone hut and get through the winter as best they could. They certainly did not have an easy time, and I can imagine that the responsibility weighed heavily on him who had to bear it. One man died; the others came through it well. Much of the excellent material collected by the expedition was lost by the sinking of the *Antarctic*, but a good deal was brought home. Both from a scientific and from a popular point of view this expedition may be considered one of the most interesting the South Polar regions have to show.

We then come to the Scotsman, Dr. William S. Bruce, in the *Scotia*. We have met with Bruce before: first in the *Balæna* in 1892, and afterwards with Mr. Andrew Coats in Spitzbergen. The latter voyage was a fortunate one for Bruce, as it provided him with the means of fitting out his expedition in the *Scotia* to Antarctic waters.

The vessel left the Clyde on November 2,1902, under the command of Captain Thomas Robertson, of Dundee. Bruce had secured the assistance of Mossman, Rudmose Brown and Dr. Pirie for the scientific work. In the following February the Antarctic Circle was crossed, and on the 22nd of that month the ship was brought to a standstill in lat. 70° 25' S. The winter was spent at Laurie Island, one of the South Orkneys. Returning to the south, the *Scotia* reached, in March, 1904, lat. 74° 1' S., long. 22° W., where the sea rapidly shoaled to 159 fathoms. Further progress was impossible owing to ice. Hilly country was sighted beyond the barrier, and named "Coats Land," after Bruce's chief supporters.

In the foremost rank of the Antarctic explorers of our time stands the French savant and yachtsman, Dr. Jean Charcot. In the course of his two expeditions of 1903–1905 and 1908–1910 he succeeded in opening up a large extent of the unknown continent. We owe to him a closer acquaintance with Alexander I. Land, and the discovery of Loubet, Fallières and Charcot Lands is also his work. His expeditions were splendidly equipped, and the scientific results were extraordinarily rich. The point that compels our special admiration in Charcot's voyages is that he chose one of the most difficult fields of the Antarctic zone to work in. The ice conditions here are extremely unfavourable, and navigation in the highest degree risky. A coast full of submerged reefs and a sea strewn with icebergs was what the Frenchmen had to contend with. The exploration of such regions demands capable men and stout vessels.

Sir Ernest Shackleton! – the name has a brisk sound. At its mere mention we see before us a man of indomitable will and boundless courage. He has shown us what the will and energy of a single man can perform. He gained his first experience of Antarctic exploration as a member of the British expedition in the *Discovery*, under Captain Scott. It was a good school. Scott, Wilson, and Shackleton, formed the southern party, with the highest latitude as their goal. They reached 82° 17' S. – a great record at that time. Being attacked by scurvy, Shackleton had to go home at the first opportunity.

Shortly after his return Shackleton began to make active preparations. Few people had any faith in Shackleton. Wasn't it he who was sent home from the *Discovery* after the first year? What does he want to go out for again? He has shown well enough that he can't stand the work! Shackleton had a hard struggle to find the necessary funds. He left England unheeded and loaded with debts in August, 1907, on board the *Nimrod*, bound for the South Pole. With surprising frankness he declared his intention of trying to reach the Pole itself. So far as I know, he was the first who ventured to say straight out that the Pole was his object. This hearty frankness was the first thing that struck me, and made me look more closely at the man. Later on I followed his steps with the greatest interest. The expedition, unnoticed when it left England, was soon forgotten. At most, people connected the name of Shackleton with the rank of "Lieutenant R.N.R." And the months went by ....

Then suddenly came a piece of news that made a great stir. It was in the latter half of March, 1909. The telegraphic instruments were busy all over the world; letter by letter, word by word, they ticked out the message, until it could be clearly read that one of the most wonderful achievements of Polar exploration had been accomplished. Everyone was spellbound. Was it possible? Could it be true? Shackleton, Lieutenant R.N.R., had fought his way to lat. 88° 23' S. Seldom has a man enjoyed a greater triumph; seldom has a man deserved it better. As the details of Sir Ernest Shackleton's expedition will be fresh in the minds of English readers, it is unnecessary to recapitulate them here. A few points may, however, be noted, for comparison with the *Fram's* expedition.

The plan was to leave New Zealand at the beginning of 1908 and go into winter quarters on the Antarctic continent with the necessary provisions and equipment, while the vessel returned to New Zealand and came back to take off the land party in the following year. The land party that wintered in the South was divided into three. One party was to go eastward to King Edward VII. Land and explore it, the second was to go westward to the South Magnetic Pole, and the third southward toward the Geographical Pole.

In the plan submitted to the Royal Geographical Society Shackleton says: "I do not intend to sacrifice the scientific utility of the expedition to a mere record-breaking journey, but say frankly, all the same, that one of my great efforts will be to reach the Southern Geographical Pole." It was further intended that the *Nimrod* should explore Wilkes Land.

As draught animals Shackleton had both ponies and dogs, but chiefly ponies. The dogs were regarded more as a reserve. Shackleton's experience was that the Ice Barrier was best suited for ponies. They also took a motor-car, besides the usual equipment of sledges, ski, tents, etc.

Leaving Lyttelton on January 1, 1908, the *Nimrod* reached the ice-pack on the 15th, and arrived in the open Ross Sea in lat. 70° 43' S., long. 178° 58' E. The Ross Barrier was sighted on January 23. The original intention was to follow this, and try to land the shore party in Barrier Inlet, which was practically the beginning of King Edward VII. Land; but it was found that Barrier Inlet had disappeared, owing to miles of the Barrier having calved away. In its place was a long, wide bay, which Shackleton named the Bay of Whales. This discovery determined him not to attempt to winter on the Barrier, but on solid land. At this part of the voyage the course of the *Nimrod* coincided very nearly with that of the *Fram* on her second outward trip.

After an unsuccessful attempt to reach King Edward VII. Land, Shackleton turned to the west and took up his winter quarters on Ross Island in McMurdo Sound. The southern party, composed of Shackleton, Adams, Marshall, and Wild, started on October 29, 1908, with four sledges, four ponies, and provisions for ninety-one days. On November 26 Scott's farthest south, 82° 17' S. was passed. By the time lat. 84° was reached all the ponies were dead, and the men had to draw the sledges themselves. They were then faced by the long and difficult ascent of Beardmore Glacier, and it was not until seventeen days later that they came out on the high plateau surrounding the Pole. At last, on January 9, 1909, they were compelled to return by shortness of provisions, having planted Queen Alexandra's flag in lat. 88° 23' S., long. 162° E.

Everyone who reads Shackleton's diary must feel a boundless admiration for these four heroes. History can scarcely show a clearer proof of what men can accomplish when they exert their full strength of will and body. These men have raised a monument, not only to themselves and their achievement, but also to the honour of their native land and the whole of civilized humanity. Shackleton's exploit is the most brilliant incident in the history of Antarctic exploration. The distance covered, out and back, was 1,530 geographical miles. The time occupied was 127 days – 73 days out and 54 days back. The average daily march was about 12 miles.

Meanwhile the other party, composed of Professor David, Mawson, and Mackay, had set off to determine the position of the South Magnetic Pole. They had neither ponies nor dogs, and had therefore to depend solely on their own powers. It seems almost incredible, but these men succeeded in working their way on foot over sea-ice and land-ice, cracks and crevasses, hard snow and loose snow, to the Magnetic Pole, and making observations there. What was better still, they all came back safe and sound. The total distance covered was 1,260 geographical miles. It must have been a proud day for the two parties of the expedition when they met again on the deck of the Nimrod, and could tell each other of their experiences. More than any of their predecessors, these men had succeeded in raising the veil that lay over "Antarctica."

But a little corner remained.

CHAPTER 2

PLAN AND PREPARATIONS

"The deity of success is a woman, and she insists on being won, not courted. You've got to seize her and bear her off, instead of standing under her window with a mandolin."

Kex Beach

"The North Pole is reached."

In a flash the news spread over the world. The goal of which so many had dreamed, for which so many had laboured and suffered and sacrificed their lives, was attained. It was in September, 1909, that the news reached us. At the same instant I saw quite clearly that the original plan of the *Fram's* third voyage – the exploration of the North Polar basin – hung in the balance. If the expedition was to be saved, it was necessary to act quickly and without hesitation. Just as rapidly as the message had travelled over the cables I decided on my change of front – to turn to the right-about, and face to the South.

It was true that I had announced in my plan that the *Fram's* third voyage would be in every way a scientific expedition, and would have nothing to do with record-breaking; it was also true that many of the contributors who had so warmly supported me had done so with the original plan before them; but in view of

57

the altered circumstances, and the small prospect I now had of obtaining funds for my original plan, I considered it neither mean nor unfair to my supporters to strike a blow that would at once put the whole enterprise on its feet, retrieve the heavy expenses that the expedition had already incurred, and save the contributions from being wasted.

It was therefore with a clear conscience that I decided to postpone my original plan for a year or two, in order to try in the meantime to raise the funds that were still lacking. The North Pole, the last problem but one of popular interest in Polar exploration, was solved. If I was now to succeed in arousing interest in my undertaking, there was nothing left for me but to try to solve the last great problem – the South Pole.

I know that I have been reproached for not having at once made the extended plan public, so that not only my supporters, but the explorers who were preparing to visit the same regions might have knowledge of it. I was well aware that these reproaches would come, and had therefore carefully weighed this side of the matter. As regards the former – the contributors to my expedition – my mind was soon at rest. They were all men of position, and above discussing the application of the sums they had dedicated to the enterprise. I knew that I enjoyed such confidence among these people that they would all judge the circumstances aright, and know that when the time came their contributions would be used for the purpose for which they were given. And I have already received countless proofs that I was not mistaken.

Nor did I feel any great scruples with regard to the other Antarctic expeditions that were being planned at the time. I knew

I should be able to inform Captain Scott of the extension of my plans before he left civilization, and therefore a few months sooner or later could be of no great importance. Scott's plan and equipment were so widely different from my own that I regarded the telegram that I sent him later, with the information that we were bound for the Antarctic regions, rather as a mark of courtesy than as a communication which might cause him to alter his programme in the slightest degree. The British expedition was designed entirely for scientific research. The Pole was only a side-issue, whereas in my extended plan it was the main object. On this little détour science would have to look after itself; but of course I knew very well that we could not reach the Pole by the route I had determined to take without enriching in a considerable degree several branches of science.

Our preparations were entirely different, and I doubt whether Captain Scott, with his great knowledge of Antarctic exploration, would have departed in any point from the experience he had gained and altered his equipment in accordance with that which I found it best to employ. For I came far short of Scott both in experience and means. As regards Lieutenant Shirase in the Kainan Maru, I understood it to be his plan to devote his whole attention to King Edward VII. Land.

After thus thoroughly considering these questions, I came to the conclusions I have stated, and my plan was irrevocably fixed. If at that juncture I had made my intention public, it would only have given occasion for a lot of newspaper discussion, and possibly have ended in the project being stifled at its birth. Everything had to be got ready quietly and calmly. My brother, upon whose absolute silence I could blindly rely, was the only person I let into the secret of my change of plan, and he did me many important services during the time when we alone shared the knowledge. Then Lieutenant Thorvald Nilsen – at that time first officer of the *Fram*, now her commander – returned home, and I considered it my duty to inform him immediately of my resolve. The way in which he received it made me feel safe in my choice of him. I saw that in him I had found not only a capable and trustworthy man, but a good comrade as well; and this was a point of the highest importance. If the relations between the chief and the second in command are good, much unpleasantness and many unnecessary worries can be avoided. Besides which, a good understanding in this quarter gives an example to the whole ship. It was a great relief to me when Captain Nilsen came home in January, 1910, and was able to help – which he did with a good will, a capability, and a reliability that I have no words to commend.

The following was the plan of the *Fram's* southern voyage: Departure from Norway at latest before the middle of August. Madeira was to be the first and only place of call. From there a course was to be made on the best route for a sailing-ship – for the *Fram* cannot be regarded as anything else – southward through the Atlantic, and then to the east, passing to the south of the Cape of Good Hope and Australia, and finally pushing through the pack and into Ross Sea about New Year, 1911.

As a base of operations I had chosen the most southerly point we could reach with the vessel – the Bay of Whales in the great Antarctic Barrier. We hoped to arrive here about January 15. After having landed the selected shore party – about ten men – with materials for a house, equipment, and provisions for two years, the *Fram* was to go out again and up to Buenos Aires, in order to carry out from there an oceanographical voyage across the Atlantic to the coast of Africa and back. In October she was to return to the Bay of Whales and take off the shore party. So much, but no more, could be settled beforehand. The further progress of the expedition could only be determined later, when the work in the South was finished.

My knowledge of the Ross Barrier was due to descriptions alone; but I had so carefully studied all the literature that treats of these regions, that, on first encountering this mighty mass of ice, I felt as if I had known it for many years.

After thorough consideration, I fixed upon the Bay of Whales as a winter station, for several reasons. In the first place, because we could there go farther south in the ship than at any other point – a whole degree farther south than Scott could hope to get in McMurdo Sound, where he was to have his station. And this would be of very great importance in the subsequent sledge journey toward the Pole. Another great advantage was that we came right on to our field of work, and could see from our hut door the conditions and surface we should have to deal with. Besides this, I was justified in supposing that the surface southward from this part of the Barrier would be considerably better, and offer fewer difficulties than the piled-up ice along the land. In addition, animal life in the Bay of Whales was, according to the descriptions, extraordinarily rich, and offered all the fresh meat we required in the form of seals, penguins, etc.

Besides these purely technical and material advantages which the Barrier seemed to possess as a winter station, it offered a specially favourable site for an investigation of the meteorological conditions, since here one would be unobstructed by land on all sides. It would be possible to study the character of the Barrier by daily observations on the very spot better than anywhere else. Such interesting phenomena as the movement, feeding, and calving of this immense mass of ice could, of course, be studied very fully at this spot.

Last, but not least, there was the enormous advantage that it was comparatively easy to reach in the vessel. No expedition had yet been prevented from coming in here.

I knew that this plan of wintering on the Barrier itself would be exposed to severe criticism as recklessness, foolhardiness, and so forth, for it was generally assumed that the Barrier was afloat here, as in other places. Indeed, it was thought to be so even by those who had themselves seen it. Shackleton's description of the conditions at the time of his visit did not seem very promising. Mile after mile had broken away, and he thanked God he had not made his camp there. Although I have a very great regard for Shackleton, his work and his experience, I believe that in this case his conclusion was too hasty – fortunately, I must add. For if, when Shackleton passed the Bay of Whales on January, 24, 1908, and saw the ice of the bay in process of breaking up and drifting out, he had waited a few hours, or at the most a couple of days, the problem of the South Pole would probably have been solved long before December, 1911. With his keen sight and sound judgment, it would not have taken him long to determine that the inner part of the bay does not consist of floating barrier, but that the Barrier there rests upon a good, solid foundation, probably in the form of small islands, skerries, or shoals, and from this point he and his able companions would have disposed of the South Polar question once for all. But circumstances willed it otherwise, and the veil was only lifted, not torn away.

I had devoted special study to this peculiar formation in the Barrier, and had arrived at the conclusion that the inlet that exists to-day in the Ross Barrier under the name of the Bay of Whales is nothing else than the self-same bight that was observed by Sir James Clark Ross – no doubt with great changes of outline, but still the same. For seventy years, then, this formation – with the exception of the pieces that had broken away – had persisted in the same place. I therefore concluded that it could be no accidental formation. What, once, in the dawn of time, arrested the mighty stream of ice at this spot and formed a lasting bay in its edge, which with few exceptions runs in an almost straight line, was not merely a passing whim of the fearful force that came crashing on, but something even stronger than that – something that was firmer than the hard ice – namely, the solid land. Here in this spot, then, the Barrier piled itself up and formed the bay we now call the Bay of Whales. The observations we made during our stay there confirm the correctness of this theory. I therefore had no misgivings in placing our station on this part of the Barrier.

The plan of the shore party was, as soon as the hut was built and provisions landed, to carry supplies into the field, and lay down depots as far to the south as possible. I hoped to get such a quantity of provisions brought down to lat. 80° S., that we should be able to regard this latitude as the real starting-place of the actual sledge journey to the Pole. We shall see later that this hope was more than fulfilled, and a labour many times greater than this was performed. By the time this depot work was accomplished winter would be before us, and with the knowledge we had of the conditions in the Antarctic regions, every precaution would have to be taken to meet the coldest and probably the most stormy weather that any Polar expedition had hitherto encountered. My object was, when winter had once set in, and everything in the station was in good working order, to concentrate all our forces upon the one object – that of reaching the Pole.

I intended to try to get people with me who were specially fitted for outdoor work in the cold. Even more necessary was it to find men who were experienced dog-drivers; I saw what a decisive bearing this would have on the result. There are advantages and disadvantages in having experienced people with one on an expedition like this. The advantages are obvious. If a variety of experiences are brought together and used with common sense, of course a great deal can be achieved. The experience of one man will often come in opportunely where that of another falls short. The experiences of several will supplement each other, and form something like a perfect whole; this is what I hoped to obtain. But there is no rose without a thorn; if it has its advantages, it also has its drawbacks. The drawback to which one is liable in this case is that someone or other may think he possesses so much experience that every opinion but his own is worthless. It is, of course, regrettable when experience takes this turn, but with patience and common sense it can be broken of it. In any case, the advantages are so great and predominant that I had determined to have experienced men to the greatest extent possible. It was my plan to devote the entire winter to working at our outfit, and to get it as near to perfection as possible. Another thing to which we should have to give some time was the killing of a sufficient number of seals to provide fresh meat both for ourselves and our dogs for the whole time. Scurvy, the worst enemy of Polar expeditions, must be kept off at all costs, and to achieve this it was my intention to use fresh meat every day. It proved easy to carry out this rule, since everyone, without exception, preferred seal meat to tinned foods. And when spring came I hoped that my companions and I would be ready, fit and well, with an outfit complete in every way.

The plan was to leave the station as early in the spring as possible. If we had set out to capture this record, we must at any cost get there first. Everything must be staked upon this. From the very moment when I had formed the plan, I had made up my mind that our course from the Bay of Whales must be set due south, and follow the same meridian, if possible, right up to the Pole. The effect of this would be that we should traverse an entirely new region, and gain other results besides beating the record.

I was greatly astonished to hear, on my return from the South, that some people had actually believed we had set our course from the Bay of Whales for Beardmore Glacier – Shackleton's route – and followed it to the south. Let me hasten to assure them that this idea never for a single instant crossed my mind when I made the plan. Scott had announced that he was going to take Shackleton's route, and that decided the matter. During our long stay at Framheim not one of us ever hinted at the possibility of such a course. Without discussion Scott's route was declared out of bounds.

No; due south was our way, and the country would have to be difficult indeed to stop our getting on to the plateau. Our plan was to go south, and not to leave the meridian unless we were forced to do so by insuperable difficulties. I foresaw, of course, that there would be some who would attack me and accuse me of "shabby rivalry," etc., and they would perhaps have had some shadow of justification if we had really thought of taking Captain Scott's route. But it never occurred to us for a moment. Our starting-point lay 350 geographical miles from Scott's winter quarters in McMurdo Sound, so there could be no question of encroaching upon his sphere of action. Moreover, Professor Nansen, in his direct and convincing way, has put an end once for all to this twaddle, so that I need not dwell upon it any longer.

I worked out the plan, as here given, at my home on Bundefjord, near Christiania, in September, 1909, and as it was laid, so was it carried out to the last detail. That my estimate of the time it would take was not so very far out is proved by the final sentence of the plan: "Thus we shall be back from the Polar journey on January 25." It was on January 25, 1912, that we came into Framheim after our successful journey to the Pole.

This was not the only time our calculations proved correct; Captain Nilsen showed himself to be a veritable magician in this way. While I contented myself with reckoning dates, he did not hesitate to go into hours. He calculated that we should reach the Barrier on January 15, 1911; this is a distance of 16,000 geographical miles from Norway. We were at the Barrier on January 14, one day before the time. There was not much wrong with that estimate. In accordance with the Storthing's resolution of

February 9, 1909, the *Fram* was lent for the use of the expedition, and a sum of 75,000 kroner (4,132 pounds sterling) was voted for repairs and necessary alterations.

The provisions were chosen with the greatest care, and packed with every precaution. All groceries were soldered in tin boxes, and then enclosed in strong wooden cases. The packing of tinned provisions is of enormous importance to a Polar expedition; it is impossible to give too much attention to this part of the supplies. Any carelessness, any perfunctory packing on the part of the factory, will as a rule lead to scurvy. It is an interesting fact that on the four Norwegian Polar expeditions – the three voyages of the *Fram* and the *Gjöa's* voyage – not a single case of scurvy occurred. This is good evidence of the care with which these expeditions were provisioned. In this matter we owe a deep debt of gratitude above all to Professor Sophus Torup, who has always been the supervising authority in the matter of provisioning, this time as well as on the former occasions.

Great praise is also due to the factories that supplied our tinned goods. By their excellent and conscientious work they deserved well of the expedition. In this case a part of the supplies was entrusted to a Stavanger factory, which, in addition to the goods supplied to order, with great generosity placed at the disposal of the expedition provisions to the value of 2,000 kroner (£110). The other half of the tinned foods required was ordered from a firm at Moss. The manager of this firm undertook at the same time to prepare the necessary pemmican for men and dogs, and executed this commission in a way that I cannot sufficiently praise. Thanks to this excellent preparation, the health both of men and dogs on the journey to the Pole was always remarkably good. The pemmican we took was essentially different from that which former expeditions had used. Previously the pemmican had contained nothing but the desired mixture of dried meat and lard; ours had, besides these, vegetables and oatmeal, an addition which greatly improves its flavour, and, as far as we could judge, makes it easier to digest.

This kind of pemmican was first produced for the use of the Norwegian Army; it was intended to take the place of the "emergency ration." The experiment was not concluded at the time the expedition left, but it may be hoped that the result has proved satisfactory. A more stimulating, nourishing, and appetizing food, it would be impossible to find.

But besides the pemmican for ourselves, that for our dogs was equally important, for they are just as liable to be attacked by scurvy as we men. The same care had therefore to be devoted to the preparation of their food. We obtained from Moss two kinds of pemmican, one made with fish and the other with meat. Both kinds contained, besides the dried fish (or meat) and lard, a certain proportion of dried milk and middlings. Both kinds were equally excellent, and the dogs were always in splendid condition. The pemmican was divided into rations of 1 pound 1.5 ounces, and could be served out to the dogs as it was. But before we should be able to use this pemmican we had a five months' voyage before us, and for this part of the expedition I had to look for a reliable supply of dried fish. This I found through the agent of the expedition at Tromsö, Mr. Fritz Zappfe. Two well-known firms also placed large quantities of the best dried fish at my disposal. With all this excellent fish and some barrels of lard we succeeded in bringing our dogs through in the best of condition.

One of the most important of our preparations was to find good dogs. As I have said, I had to act with decision and promptitude if I was to succeed in getting everything in order. The day after my decision was made, therefore, I was on my way to Copenhagen, where the Inspectors for Greenland, Messrs. Daugaard-Jensen and Bentzen, were to be found at that moment. The director of the Royal Greenland Trading Company, Mr. Rydberg, showed, as before, the most friendly interest in my undertaking, and gave the inspectors a free hand. I then negotiated with these gentlemen, and they undertook to provide 100 of the finest Greenland dogs and to deliver them in Norway in July, 1910. The dog question was thus as good as solved, since the choice was placed in the most expert hands. I was personally acquainted with Inspector Daugaard-Jensen from former dealings with him, and knew that whatever he undertook would be performed with the greatest conscientiousness. The administration of the Royal Greenland Trading Company gave permission for the dogs to be conveyed free of charge on board the Hans Egede and delivered at Christiansand.

Before I proceed to our further equipment, I must say a few more words about the dogs. The greatest difference between Scott's and my equipment lay undoubtedly in our choice of draught animals. We had heard that Scott, relying on his own experience, and that of Shackleton, had come to the conclusion that Manchurian ponies were superior to dogs on the Barrier. Among those who were acquainted with the Eskimo dog, I do not suppose I was the only one who was startled on first hearing this. Afterwards, as I read the different narratives and was able to form an accurate opinion of the conditions of surface and going, my astonishment became even greater. Although I had never seen this part of the Antarctic regions, I was not long in forming an opinion diametrically opposed to that of Shackleton and Scott, for the conditions both of going and surface were precisely what one would desire for sledging with Eskimo dogs, to judge from the descriptions of these explorers. If Peary could make a record trip on the Arctic ice with dogs, one ought, surely, with equally good tackle, to be able to beat Peary's record on the splendidly even surface of the Barrier. There must be some misunderstanding or other at the bottom of the Englishmen's estimate of the Eskimo dog's utility in the Polar regions. Can it be that the dog has not understood his master? Or is it the master who has not understood his dog? The right footing must be established from the outset; the dog must understand that he has to obey in everything, and the master must know how to make himself respected. If obedience is once established, I am convinced that the dog will be superior to all other draught animals over these long distances.

Another very important reason for using the dog is that this small creature can much more easily cross the numerous slight snow-bridges that are not to be avoided on the Barrier and on the glaciers. If a dog falls into a crevasse there is no great harm done; a tug at his harness and he is out again; but it is another matter with a pony. This comparatively large and heavy animal of course falls through far more easily, and if this happens, it is a long and stiff job to get the beast hauled up again – unless, indeed, the traces have broken and the pony lies at the bottom of a crevasse 1,000 feet deep.

And then there is the obvious advantage that dog can be fed on dog. One can reduce one's pack little by little, slaughtering the feebler ones and feeding the chosen with them. In this way they get fresh meat. Our dogs lived on dog's flesh and pemmican the whole way, and this enabled them to do splendid work.

And if we ourselves wanted a piece of fresh meat we could cut off a delicate little fillet; it tasted to us as good as the best beef. The dogs do not object at all; as long as they get their share they do not mind what part of their comrade's carcass it comes from. All that was left after one of these canine meals was the teeth of the victim – and if it had been a really hard day, these also disappeared.

If we take a step farther, from the Barrier to the plateau, it would seem that every doubt of the dog's superiority must disappear. Not only can one get the dogs up over the huge glaciers that lead to the plateau, but one can make full use of them the whole way. Ponies, on the other hand, have to be left at the foot of the glacier, while the men themselves have the doubtful pleasure of acting as ponies. As I understand Shackleton's account, there can be no question of hauling the ponies over the steep and crevassed glaciers. It must be rather hard to have to abandon one's motive power voluntarily when only a quarter of the distance has been covered. I for my part prefer to use it all the way.

From the very beginning I saw that the first part of our expedition, from Norway to the Barrier, would be the most dangerous section. If we could only reach the Barrier with our dogs safe and well, the future would be bright enough. Fortunately all my comrades took the same view of the matter, and with their cooperation we succeeded not only in bringing the dogs safely to our field of operations, but in landing them in far better condition than when we received them. Their number was also considerably increased on the way, which seems to be another proof of a flourishing state of things. To protect them against damp and heat we laid a loose deck of planed boards about 3 inches above the fixed deck, an arrangement by which all the rain and spray ran underneath the dogs. In this way we kept them out of the water, which must always be running from side to side on the deck of a deep-laden vessel on her way to the Antarctic Ocean. Going through the tropics this loose deck did double service. It always afforded a somewhat cool surface, as there was a fresh current of air between the two decks. The main deck, which was black with tar, would have been unbearably hot for the animals; the false deck was high, and kept fairly white during the whole voyage. We carried awnings in addition, chiefly on account of the dogs. These awnings could be stretched over the whole vessel and give the dogs constant protection from the burning sun.

I still cannot help smiling when I think of the compassionate voices that were raised here and there – and even made their way into print – about the "cruelty to animals" on board the *Fram*. Presumably these cries came from tender-hearted individuals who themselves kept watch-dogs tied up.

Besides our four-footed companions, we took with us a two-footed one, not so much on account of the serious work in the Polar regions as for pleasant entertainment on the way. This was our canary "Fridtjof." It was one of the many presents made to the expedition, and not the least welcome of them. It began to sing as soon as it came on board, and has now kept it going on two circumnavigations through the most inhospitable waters of the earth. It probably holds the record as a Polar traveller among its kind.

Later on we had a considerable collection of various families: pigs, fowls, sheep, cats, and – rats. Yes, unfortunately, we knew what it was to have rats on board, the most repulsive of all creatures, and the worst vermin I know of. But we have declared war against them, and off they shall go before the *Fram* starts on her next voyage. We got them in Buenos Aires, and the best thing will be to bury them in their native land.

On account of the rather straitened circumstances the expedition had to contend with, I had to look twice at every shilling before I spent it. Articles of clothing are an important factor in a Polar expedition, and I consider it necessary that the expedition should provide each of its members with the actual "Polar clothing." If one left this part of the equipment to each individual, I am afraid things would look badly before the journey was done. I must admit that there was some temptation to do this. It would have been very much cheaper if I had simply given each man a list of what clothes he was required to provide for himself. But by so doing I should have missed the opportunity of personally supervising the quality of the clothing to the extent I desired.

It was not an outfit that cut a dash by its appearance, but it was warm and strong. From the commissariat stores at Horten I obtained many excellent articles. I owe Captain Pedersen, the present chief of the Commissariat Department, my heartiest thanks for the courtesy he always showed me when I came to get things out of him. Through him I had about 200 blankets served out to me. Now, the reader must not imagine a bed and bedding, such as he may see exhibited in the windows of furniture shops, with thick, white blankets, so delicate that in spite of their thickness they look as if they might float away of their own accord, so light and fine do they appear. It was not blankets like these that Captain Pedersen gave us; we should not have known what to do with them if he had. The blankets the commissariat gave us were of an entirely different sort. As to their colour – well, I can only call it indeterminable – and they did not give one the impression that they would float away either, if one let go of them. No, they would keep on the ground right enough; they were felted and pressed together into a thick, hard mass. From the dawn of time they had served our brave warriors at sea, and it is by no means impossible that some of them had gruesome stories to tell of the days of Tordenskjold. The first thing I did, on obtaining possession of these treasures, was to get them into the dyeing-vat. They were unrecognizable when I got them back – in ultramarine blue, or whatever it was called. The metamorphosis was complete: their warlike past was wiped out.

My intention was to have these two hundred blankets made into Polar clothing, and I took counsel with myself how I might get this done. To disclose the origin of the stuff would be an unfortunate policy. No tailor in the world would make clothes out of old blankets, I was pretty sure of that. I had to hit upon some stratagem. I heard of a man who was a capable worker at his trade, and asked him to come and see me. My office looked exactly like a woollen warehouse, with blankets everywhere. The tailor arrived. "Was that the stuff?" "Yes, that was it. Just imported from abroad. A great bargain. A lot of samples dirt cheap." I had put on my most innocent and unconcerned expression. I saw the tailor glance at me sideways; I suppose he thought the samples were rather large. "A closely woven stuff," said he, holding it up to the light. "I could almost swear it was 'felted.'" We went carefully through every single sample, and took the number. It was a long and tedious business, and I was glad when I saw that at last we were nearing the end. Over in a corner there lay a few more; we had reached the one hundred and ninety-third, so there could not be many in the pile. I was occupied with something else, and the tailor went through the remainder by himself. I was just congratulating myself on the apparently fortunate result of the morning's work when I was startled by an exclamation from the man in the corner. It sounded like the bellow of a mad bull. Alas! there stood the tailor enveloped in ultramarine, and swinging over his head a blanket, the couleur changeante of which left no doubt as to the origin of the "directly imported" goods. With a look of thunder the man quitted me, and I sank in black despair. I never saw him again. The fact was that in my hurry I had forgotten the sample blanket that Captain Pedersen had sent me. That was the cause of the catastrophe.

Well, I finally succeeded in getting the work executed, and it is certain that no expedition has ever had warmer and stronger clothing than this. It was in great favour on board.

I also thought it best to provide good oilskins, and especially good sea-boots for every man. The sea-boots were therefore made to measure, and of the very best material. I had them made by the firm I have always regarded as the best in that branch. How, then, shall I describe our grief when, on the day we were to wear our beautiful sea-boots, we discovered that most of them were useless? Some of the men could dance a hornpipe in theirs without taking the boots off the deck. Others, by exerting all their strength, could not squeeze their foot through the narrow way and reach paradise. The leg was so narrow that even the most delicate little foot could not get through it, and to make up for this the foot of the boot was so huge that it could comfortably accommodate twice as much as its owner could show. Very few were able to wear their boots. We tried changing, but that was no use; the boots were not made for any creatures of this planet. But sailors are sailors wherever they may be; it is not easy to beat them. Most of them knew the proverb that one pair of boots that fit is better than ten pairs that you can't put on, and had brought their own with them. And so we got out of that difficulty.

We took three sets of linen underclothing for every man, to wear in the warm regions. This part of the equipment was left to each individual; most men possess a few old shirts, and not much more is wanted through the tropics. For the cold regions there were two sets of extra thick woollen underclothing, two thick hand-knitted woollen jerseys, six pairs of knitted stockings, Iceland and other lighter jackets, socks and stockings from the penitentiary.

Besides these we had a quantity of clothing from the army depots. I owe many thanks to General Keilhau for the kind way in which he fell in with all my wishes. From this quarter we obtained outer clothing for both cold and warm climates, under-clothes, boots, shoes, wind-clothing, and cloths of different kinds.

As the last item of our personal equipment I may mention that each man had a suit of sealskin from Greenland. Then there were such things as darning-wool, sewing-yarn, needles of all possible sizes, buttons, scissors, tapes – broad and narrow, black and white, blue and red. I may safely assert that nothing was forgotten; we were well and amply equipped in every way.

Another side of our preparations which claimed some attention was the fitting up of the quarters we were to inhabit, the saloons and cabins. What an immense difference it makes if one lives in comfortable surroundings. For my part, I can do twice the amount of work when I see tidiness and comfort around me. The saloons on the *Fram* were very handsomely and taste-fully fitted. Here we owe, in the first place, our respectful thanks to King Haakon and Queen Maud for the photographs they presented to us; they were the most precious of our gifts. The ladies of Horten gave us a number of pretty things for decorating the cabins, and they will no doubt be glad to hear of the admiration they aroused wherever we went. "Is this really a Polar ship?" people asked; "we expected to see nothing but wooden benches and bare walls." And they began to talk about "boudoirs" and things of that sort. Besides splendid embroideries, our walls were decorated with the most wonderful photographs; it would have rejoiced the giver of these to hear all the words of praise that have been bestowed upon them.

The sleeping quarters I left to individual taste: every man could take a bit of his home in his own little compartment. The bedclothes came from the naval factory at Horten; they were first-class work, like everything else that came from there. We owe our best thanks to the giver of the soft blankets that have so often been our joy and put warmth into us after a bitter day; they came from a woollen mill at Trondhjem.

I must also mention our paper-supply, which was in all respects as fine and elegant as it could possibly be: the most exquisite notepaper, stamped with a picture of the *Fram* and the name of the expedition, in large and small size, broad and narrow, old style and new style – every kind of notepaper, in fact. Of pens and penholders, pencils, black and coloured, india-rubber, Indian ink, drawing-pins and other kinds of pins, ink and ink-powder, white chalk and red chalk, gum arabic and other gums, date-holders and almanacs, ship's logs and private diaries, notebooks and sledging diaries, and many other things of the same sort, we have such a stock that we shall be able to circumnavigate the earth several times more before running short. This gift does honour to the firm which sent it; every time I have sent a letter or written in my diary, I have had a grateful thought for the givers.

From one of the largest houses in Christiania we had a complete set of kitchen utensils and breakfast and dinner services, all of the best kind. The cups, plates, knives, forks, spoons, jugs, glasses, etc., were all marked with the ship's name.

We carried an extraordinarily copious library; presents of books were showered upon us in great quantities. I suppose the *Fram's* library at the present moment contains at least 3,000 volumes. For our entertainment we also had a good many different games. One of these became our favourite pastime in leisure evenings down in the South. Packs of cards we had by the dozen, and many of them have already been well used. A gramophone with a large supply of records was, I think, our best friend. Of musical instruments we had a piano, a violin, a flute, mandolins, not forgetting a mouth-organ and an accordion. All the publishers had been kind enough to send us music, so that we could cultivate this art as much as we wished.

Christmas presents streamed in from all sides; I suppose we had about five hundred on board. Christmas-trees and decorations for them, with many other things to amuse us at Christmas, were sent with us by friends and acquaintances. People have indeed been kind to us, and I can assure the givers that all their presents have been, and are still, much appreciated.

We were well supplied with wines and spirits, thanks to one of the largest firms of wine-merchants in Christiania. An occasional glass of wine or a tot of spirits were things that we all, without exception, were very glad of. The question of alcohol on Polar expeditions has often been discussed. Personally, I regard alcohol, used in moderation, as a medicine in the Polar regions – I mean, of course, so long as one is in winter quarters. It is another matter on sledge journeys: there we all know from experience that alcohol must be banished – not because a drink of spirits can do any harm, but on account of the weight and space. On sledging journeys one has, of course, to save weight as much as possible, and to take only what is strictly necessary; and I do not include alcohol under the head of strictly necessary things. Nor was it only in winter quarters that we had use for alcohol, but also on the long, monotonous voyage through raw, cold, and stormy regions. A tot of spirits is often a very good thing when one goes below after a bitter watch on deck and is just turning in. A total abstainer will no doubt turn up his nose and ask whether a cup of good warm coffee would not do as well. For my part, I think the quantity of coffee people pour into themselves at such times is far more harmful than a little Lysholmer snaps. And think of the important part a glass of wine or toddy plays in social gatherings on such a voyage. Two men who have fallen out a little in the course of the week are reconciled at once by the scent of rum; the past is forgotten, and they start afresh in friendly co-operation. Take alcohol away from these little festivities, and you will soon see the difference. It is a sad thing, someone will say, that men absolutely must have alcohol to put them in a good humour – and I am quite ready to agree. But seeing that our nature is what it is, we must try to make the best of it. It seems as though we civilized human beings must have stimulating drinks, and that being so, we have to follow our own convictions. I am for a glass of toddy. Let who will eat plum-cake and swill hot coffee – heartburn and other troubles are often the result of this kind of refreshment. A little toddy doesn't hurt anybody.

The consumption of alcohol on the *Fram*'s third voyage was as follows: One dram and fifteen drops at dinner on Wednesdays and Sundays, and a glass of toddy on Saturday evenings. On holidays there was an additional allowance. We were all well supplied with tobacco and cigars from various firms at home and abroad. We had enough cigars to allow us one each on Saturday evenings and after dinner on Sundays.

Two Christiania manufacturers sent us their finest bonbons and drops, and a foreign firm gave us "Gala Peter," so that it was no rare thing to see the Polar explorers helping themselves to a sweetmeat or a piece of chocolate. An establishment at Drammen gave us as much fruit syrup as we could drink, and if the giver only knew how many times we blessed the excellent product he supplied, I am sure he would be pleased. On the homeward march from the Pole we looked forward every day to getting nearer to our supply of syrup.

From three different firms in Christiania we received all our requirements in the way of cheese, biscuits, tea, sugar, and coffee. The packing of the last-named was so efficient that, although the coffee was roasted, it is still as fresh and aromatic as the day it left the warehouse. Another firm sent us soap enough for five years, and one uses a good deal of that commodity even on a Polar voyage. A man in Christiania had seen to the care of our skin, hair, and teeth, and it is not his fault if we have not delicate skins, abundant growth of hair, and teeth like pearls, for the outfit was certainly complete enough.

An important item of the equipment is the medical department, and here my advisers were Dr. Jacob Roll and Dr. Holth; therefore nothing was wanting. A chemist in Christiania supplied all the necessary medicines as a contribution, carefully chosen, and beautifully arranged. Unfortunately no doctor accompanied the expedition, so that I was obliged to take all the responsibility myself.

Lieutenant Gjertsen, who had a pronounced aptitude both for drawing teeth and amputating legs, went through a "lightning course" at the hospital and the dental hospital. He clearly showed that much may be learnt in a short time by giving one's mind to it. With surprising rapidity and apparent confidence Lieutenant Gjertsen disposed of the most complicated cases – whether invariably to the patient's advantage is another question, which I shall leave undecided. He drew teeth with a dexterity that strongly reminded one of the conjurer's art; one moment he showed an empty pair of forceps, the next there was a big molar in their grip. The yells one heard while the operation was in progress seemed to indicate that it was not entirely painless.

A match factory gave us all the safety matches we wanted. They were packed so securely that we could quite well have towed the cases after us in the sea all the way, and found the matches perfectly dry on arrival. We had a quantity of ammunition and explosives. As the whole of the lower hold was full of petroleum, the *Fram* had a rather dangerous cargo on board. We therefore took all possible precautions against fire; extinguishing apparatus was fitted in every cabin and wherever practicable, and pumps with hose were always in readiness on deck. The necessary ice-tools, such as saws from 2 to 6 metres long, ice-drills, etc., were not forgotten.

We had a number of scientific instruments with us. Professors Nansen and Helland-Hansen had devoted many an hour to our oceanographical equipment, which was therefore a model of what such an equipment should be. Lieutenants Prestrud and Gjertsen had both gone through the necessary course in oceanography under Helland-Hansen at the Bergen biological station. I myself had spent a summer there, and taken part in one of the oceanographical courses. Professor Helland-Hansen was a brilliant teacher; I am afraid I cannot assert that I was an equally brilliant pupil.

Professor Mohn had given us a complete meteorological out-fit. Among the instruments belonging to the *Fram* I may mention a pendulum apparatus, an excellent astronomical theodolite, and a sextant. Lieutenant Prestrud studied the use of the pendulum apparatus under Professor Schiotz and the use of the astronomical theodolite under Professor Geelmuyden. We had in addition several sextants and artificial horizons, both glass and mercury. We had binoculars of all sizes, from the largest to the smallest.

So far I have been dealing with our general outfit, and shall now pass to the special equipment of the shore party. The hut we took out was built on my property on Bundefjord, so that I was able to watch the work as it progressed. It was built by the brothers Hans and Jörgen Stubberud, and was throughout a splendid piece of work, which did honour to both the brothers. The materials proved excellent in every way. The hut was 26 feet long by 13 feet wide; its height from the floor to the ridge of the roof was about 12 feet. It was built as an ordinary Norwegian house, with pointed gable, and had two rooms. One of these was 19 1/2 feet long, and was to serve as our dormitory, dining-room, and sitting-room; the other room was 6 1/2 feet long, and was to be Lindström's kitchen. From the kitchen a double trap-door led to the loft, where we intended to keep a quantity of provisions and outfit. The walls consisted of 3-inch planks, with air space between; panels outside and inside, with air space between them and the plank walling. For insulation we used cellulose pulp. The floor and the ceiling between the rooms and the loft were double, while the upper roof was single. The doors were extraordinarily thick and strong, and fitted into oblique grooves, so that they closed very tightly. There were two windows – a triple one in the end wall of the main room, and a double one in the kitchen. For the covering of the roof we took out roofing-paper, and for the floor linoleum. In the main room there were two air-pipes, one to admit fresh air, the other for the exhaust. There were bunks for ten men in two stages, six on one wall and four on the other. The furniture of the room consisted of a table, a stool for each man, and a Lux lamp.

One half of the kitchen was occupied by the range, the other by shelves and cooking utensils. The hut was tarred several times, and every part was carefully marked, so that it could easily be set up. To fasten it to the ground and prevent the Antarctic storms from blowing it away I had strong eyebolts screwed into each end of the roof-ridge and the four corners of the roof; we carried six strong eyebolts, a metre long, to be rammed into the barrier; between these bolts and those on the hut, steel wires were to be stretched, which could be drawn quite tight. We also had two spare cables, which could be stretched over the roof if the gales were too severe. The two ventilating pipes and the chimney were secured outside with strong stays.

As will be seen, every precaution was taken to make the hut warm and comfortable, and to hold it down on the ground. We also took on board a quantity of loose timber, boards and planks.

Besides the hut we took with us fifteen tents for sixteen men each. Ten of these were old, but good; they were served out to us from the naval stores; the other five were new, and we bought them from the army depots. It was our intention to use the tents as temporary houses; they were easily and quickly set up, and were strong and warm. On the voyage to the South Rönne sewed new floors of good, strong canvas to the five new tents.

All cases of provisions that were intended for winter quarters were marked and stowed separately in the hold in such a way that they could be put out on to the ice at once.

We had ten sledges made by a firm of sporting outfitters in Christiania. They were built like the old Nansen sledges, but rather broader, and were 12 feet long. The runners were of the best American hickory, shod with steel. The other parts were of good, tough Norwegian ash. To each sledge belonged a pair of spare runners, which could easily be fitted underneath by means of clamps, and as easily removed when not required. The steel shoeing of the runners was well coated with red lead, and the spare runners with tar. These sledges were extremely strongly built, and could stand all kinds of work on every sort of surface. At that time I did not know the conditions on the Barrier as I afterwards came to know them. Of course, these sledges were very heavy.

We took twenty pairs of skis, all of the finest hickory; they were 8 feet long, and proportionately narrow. I chose them of this length with a view to being able to cross the numerous cracks in the glaciers; the greater the surface over which the weight could be distributed, the better prospect we should have of slipping over the snow-bridges. We had forty ski-poles, with ebonite points. The ski-bindings were a combination of the Huitfeldt and the Höyer Ellefsen bindings. We also had quantities of loose straps.

We had six three-man tents, all made in the navy workshops. The workmanship could not have been better; they were the strongest and most practical tents that have ever been used. They were made of the closest canvas, with the floor in one piece. One man was sufficient to set up the tent in the stiffest breeze; I have come to the conclusion that the fewer poles a tent has, the easier it is to set up, which seems quite natural. These tents have only one pole. How often one reads in narratives of Polar travel that it took such and such a time – often hours – to set up the tent, and then, when at last it was up, one lay expecting it to be blown down at any moment. There was no question of this with our tents. They were up in a twinkling, and stood against all kinds of wind; we could lie securely in our sleeping-bags, and let it blow.

The arrangement of the door was on the usual sack principle, which is now recognized as the only serviceable one for the Polar regions. The sack patent is quite simple, like all patents that are any good. You cut an opening in the tent of the size you wish; then you take a sack, which you leave open at both ends, and sew one end fast round the opening of the tent. The funnel formed by the open sack is then the entrance. When you have come in, you gather up the open end of the funnel or sack, and tie it together. Not a particle of snow can get into a tent with the floor sewed on and an entrance of this kind, even in the worst storm.

The cases for sledging provisions were made of fairly thin, tough ash, which came from the estate of Palsgaard in Jutland, and the material did all it promised. These cases were 1 foot square and 15 1/2 inches high. They had only a little round opening on the top, closed with an aluminium lid, which fitted exactly like the lid of a milk-can. Large lids weaken the cases, and I had therefore chosen this form. We did not have to throw off the lashing of the case to get the lid off, and this is a very great advantage; we could always get at it. A case with a large lid, covered by the lashing, gives constant trouble; the whole lashing has to be undone for every little thing one wants out of the case. This is not always convenient; if one is tired and slack, it may sometimes happen that one will put off till to-morrow what ought to be done to-day, especially when it is bitterly cold. The handier one's sledging outfit, the sooner one gets into the tent and to rest, and that is no small consideration on a long journey.

Our outfit of clothing was abundant and more complete, I suppose, than that of any former Polar expedition. We may divide it into two classes, the outfit for specially low temperatures and that for more moderate temperatures. It must be remembered that no one had yet wintered on the Barrier, so we had to be prepared for anything. In order to be able to grapple with any degree of cold, we were supplied with the richest assortment of reindeer-skin clothing; we had it specially thick, medium, and quite light. It took a long time to get these skin clothes prepared. First the reindeer-skins had to be bought in a raw state, and this was done for me by Mr. Zappfe at Tromsö, Karasjok, and Kaatokeino. Let me take the opportunity of thanking this man for the many and great services he has rendered me, not only during my preparations for the third voyage of the *Fram*, but in the fitting out of the *Gjöa* expedition as well. With his help I have succeeded in obtaining things that I should otherwise never have been able to get. He shrank from no amount of work, but went on till he had found what I wanted. This time he procured nearly two hundred and fifty good reindeer-skins, dressed by the Lapps, and sent them to Christiania. Here I had great trouble in finding a man who could sew skins, but at last I found one. We then went to work to make clothes after the pattern of the Netchelli Eskimo, and the sewing went on early and late – thick anoraks and thin ones, heavy breeches and light, winter stockings and summer stockings. We also had a dozen thin sleeping-bags, which I thought of using inside the big thick ones if the cold should be too severe. Everything was finished, but not until the last moment. The outer sleeping-bags were made by Mr. Brandt, furrier, of Bergen, and they were so excellent, both in material and making-up, that no one in the world could have done better; it was a model piece of work. To save this outer sleeping-bag, we had it provided with a cover of the lightest canvas, which was a good deal longer than the bag itself. It was easy to tie the end of the cover together like the mouth of the sack, and this kept the snow out of the bag during the day's march. In this way we always kept ourselves free from the annoyance of drifting snow. We attached great importance to having the bags made of the very best sort of skin, and took care that the thin skin of the belly was removed. I have seen sleeping-bags of the finest reindeer-skin spoilt in a comparatively short time if they contained a few patches of this thin skin, as of course the cold penetrates more easily through the thin skin, and gives rise to dampness in the form of rime on meeting the warmth of the body. These thin patches remain damp whenever one is in the bag, and in a short time they lose their hair. The damp spreads, like decay in wood, and continually attacks the surrounding skin, with the result that one fine day you find yourself with a hairless sleeping-bag. One cannot be too careful in the choice of skins. For the sake of economy, the makers of reindeer-skin sleeping-bags are in the habit of sewing them in such a way that the direction of the hair is towards the opening of the bag. Of course this suits the shape of the skins best, but it does not suit the man who is going to use the bag. For it is no easy matter to crawl into a sleeping-bag which is only just wide enough to allow one to get in, and if the way of the hair is against one it is doubly difficult. I had them all made as one-man bags, with lacing round the neck; this did not, of course, meet with the approval of all, as will be seen later. The upper part of this thick sleeping-bag was made of thinner reindeer-skin, so that we might be able to tie it closely round the neck; the thick skin will not draw so well and fit so closely as the thin.

Our clothing in moderate temperatures consisted of thick woollen underclothing and Burberry windproof overalls. This underclothing was specially designed for the purpose; I had myself watched the preparation of the material, and knew that it contained nothing but pure wool. We had overalls of two different materials: Burberry "gabardine" and the ordinary green kind that is used in Norway in the winter. For sledge journeys, where one has to save weight, and to work in loose, easy garments, I must unhesitatingly recommend Burberry. It is extraordinarily light and strong, and keeps the wind completely out. For hard work I prefer the green kind. It keeps out the wind equally well, but is heavier and more bulky, and less comfortable to wear on a long march. Our Burberry wind-clothes were made in the form of anorak (blouse) and trousers, both very roomy. The others consisted of trousers and jacket with hood.

Our mits were for the most part such as one can buy in any shop; we wanted nothing else in and around winter quarters. Outside the mits we wore an outer covering of windproof material, so as not to wear them out too quickly. These mits are not very strong, though they are good and warm. Besides these, we had ten pairs of ordinary kid mits, which were bought at a glove-shop in Christiania, and were practically impossible to wear out. I wore mine from Framheim to the Pole and back again, and afterwards on the voyage to Tasmania. The lining, of course, was torn in places, but the seams of the mits were just as perfect as the day I bought them. Taking into consideration the fact that I went on skis the whole way and used two poles, it will be understood that the mits were strongly made. We also had a number of woollen gloves, which, curiously enough, the others greatly prized. For myself, I was never able to wear such things; they simply freeze the fingers off me.

But most important of all is the covering of the feet, for the feet are the most exposed members and the most difficult to protect. One can look after the hands; if they grow cold it is easy to beat them into warmth again. Not so with the feet; they are covered up in the morning, and this is a sufficiently troublesome piece of work to make one disinclined to undo it again until one is turning in. They cannot be seen in the course of the day, and one has to depend entirely on feeling; but feeling in this case often plays curious tricks. How often has it happened that men have had their feet frozen off without knowing it! For if they had known it, they could not possibly have let it go so far. The fact is that in this case sensation is a somewhat doubtful guide, for the feet lose all sensation. It is true that there is a transitional stage, when one feels the cold smarting in one's toes, and tries to get rid of it by stamping the feet. As a rule this is successful; the warmth returns, or the circulation is restored; but it occasionally happens that sensation is lost at the very moment when these precautions are taken. And then one must be an old hand to know what has happened. Many men conclude that, as they no longer feel the unpleasant smarting sensation, all is well; and at the evening inspection a frozen foot of tallow-like appearance presents itself. An event of this kind may ruin the most elaborately prepared enterprise, and it is therefore advisable in the matter of feet to carry one's caution to lengths which may seem ridiculous.

Now, it is a fact that if one can wear soft foot-gear exclusively the risk of frost-bite is far less than if one is compelled to wear stiff boots; in soft foot-gear, of course, the foot can move far more easily and keep warm. But we were to take skis and to get full use out of them, so that in any case we had to have a stiff sole for the sake of the bindings. It is of no use to have a good binding unless you can use it in the right way. In my opinion, on a long journey such as that we had before us, the skis must be perfectly steady. I do not know anything that tires me more than a bad fastening – that is, one that allows the foot to shift in the binding. I want the skis to be a part of oneself, so that one always has full command of them. I have tried many patents, for I have always been afraid of a stiff fastening in cold temperatures; but all these patents, without exception, are worthless in the long-run. I decided this time to try a combination of stiff and soft foot-gear, so that we could use the splendid Huitfeldt-Höyer Ellefsen bindings; but this was no easy matter. Of our whole outfit nothing caused me more worry or gave us all more work in the course of the expedition than the stiff outer covering which we had to have; but we solved the problem at last. I applied to one of the leading makers of ski-boots in Christiania, and explained the difficulty to him; fortunately I had found a man who was evidently interested in the question. We agreed that he should make a sample pair after the pattern of ski-boots. The sole was to be thick and stiff – for we had to be prepared to use crampons – but the uppers as soft as possible. In order to avoid leather, which usually becomes stiff and easily cracked in the cold, he was to use a combination of leather and thin canvas for the uppers – leather nearest the sole, and canvas above it.

The measurements were taken from my foot, which is not exactly a child's foot, with two pairs of reindeer-skin stockings on, and ten pairs were made. I well remember seeing these boots in civilized Christiania. They were exhibited in the boot-maker's windows – I used to go a long way round to avoid coming face to face with these monsters in public. We are all a trifle vain, and dislike having our own shortcomings shown up in electric light. If I had ever cherished any illusions on the subject of "a dainty little foot," I am sure the last trace of such vanity died out on the day I passed the shoemaker's window and beheld my own boots. I never went that way again until I was certain that the exhibition was closed. One thing is certain, that the boots were a fine piece of workmanship. We shall hear later on of the alterations they had to undergo before we at last made them as large as we wanted, for the giant boots turned out much too small!

Among other equipment I must mention our excellent Primus cooking apparatus. This all came complete from a firm in Stockholm. For cooking on sledge journeys the Primus stove ranks above all others; it gives a great deal of heat, uses little oil, and requires no attention – advantages which are important enough anywhere, but especially when sledging. There is never any trouble with this apparatus; it has come as near perfection as possible. We took five Nansen cookers with us. This cooker utilizes the heat more completely than any other; but I have one objection to make to it – it takes up space. We used it on our depot journeys, but were unfortunately obliged to give it up on the main southern journey. We were so many in a tent, and space was so limited, that I dared not risk using it. If one has room enough, it is ideal in my opinion.

We had with us ten pairs of snow-shoes and one hundred sets of dog-harness of the Alaska Eskimo pattern. The Alaska Eskimo drive their dogs in tandem; the whole pull is thus straight ahead in the direction the sledge is going, and this is undoubtedly the best way of utilizing the power. I had made up my mind to adopt the same system in sledging on the Barrier. Another great advantage it had was that the dogs would pass singly across fissures, so that the danger of falling through was considerably reduced. The exertion of pulling is also less trying with Alaska harness than with the Greenland kind, as the Alaska harness has a shallow, padded collar, which is slipped over the animal's head and makes the weight of the pull come on his shoulders, whereas the Greenland harness presses on his chest. Raw places, which occur rather frequently with the Greenland harness, are almost entirely avoided with the other. All the sets of harness were made in the navy workshops, and after their long and hard use they are as good as ever. There could be no better recommendation than this.

Of instruments and apparatus for the sledge journeys we carried two sextants, three artificial horizons, of which two were glass horizons with dark glasses, and one a mercury horizon, and four spirit compasses, made in Christiania. They were excellent little compasses, but unfortunately useless in cold weather – that is to say, when the temperature went below -40° F.; at this point the liquid froze. I had drawn the maker's attention to this beforehand and asked him to use as pure a spirit as possible. What his object was I still do not know, but the spirit he employed was highly dilute.

The best proof of this was that the liquid in our compasses froze before the spirits in a flask. We were naturally inconvenienced by this. Besides these we had an ordinary little pocket-compass, two pairs of binoculars, one by Zeiss and the other by Goertz, and snow-goggles from Dr. Schanz. We had various kinds of glasses for these, so that we could change when we were tired of one colour. During the whole stay on the Barrier I myself wore a pair of ordinary spectacles with yellow glasses of quite a light tint. These are prepared by a chemical process in such a way that they nullify the harmful colours in the sun's rays. How excellent these glasses are appears clearly enough from the fact that I never had the slightest touch of snow-blindness on the southern journey, although the spectacles were perfectly open and allowed the light to enter freely everywhere. It will perhaps be suggested that I am less susceptible to this ailment than others, but I know from personal experience that such is not the case. I have previously had several severe attacks of snow-blindness.

We had two photographic cameras, an air thermometer, two aneroids with altitude scale to 15,000 feet, and two hypsometers. The hypsometer is only an instrument for determining the boiling-point, which gives one the height above the sea. The method is both simple and reliable.

The medical stores for sledging were given by a London firm, and the way in which the things were packed speaks for the whole outfit. There is not a speck of rust on needles, scissors, knives, or anything else, although they have been exposed to much damp. Our own medical outfit, which was bought in Christiania, and according to the vendor's statement unusually well packed, became in a short time so damaged that the whole of it is now entirely spoilt.

The sledging provisions must be mentioned briefly. I have already spoken of the pemmican. I have never considered it necessary to take a whole grocer's shop with me when sledging; the food should be simple and nourishing, and that is enough – a rich and varied menu is for people who have no work to do. Besides the pemmican, we had biscuits, milk-powder, and chocolate. The biscuits were a present from a well-known Norwegian factory, and did all honour to their origin. They were specially baked for us, and were made of oatmeal with the addition of dried milk and a little sugar; they were extremely nourishing and pleasant to the taste. Thanks to efficient packing, they kept fresh and crisp all the time. These biscuits formed a great part of our daily diet, and undoubtedly contributed in no small degree to the successful result. Milk-powder is a comparatively new commodity with us, but it deserves to be better known. It came from the district of Jæderen. Neither heat nor cold, dryness nor wet, could hurt it; we had large quantities of it lying out in small, thin linen bags in every possible state of the weather: the powder was as good the last day as the first. We also took dried milk from a firm in Wisconsin; this milk had an addition of malt and sugar, and was, in my opinion, excellent; it also kept good the whole time. The chocolate came from a world-renowned firm, and was beyond all praise. The whole supply was a very acceptable gift.

We are bringing all the purveyors of our sledging provisions samples of their goods that have made the journey to the South Pole and back, in gratitude for the kind assistance they afforded us.

CHAPTER 3

ON THE WAY TO THE SOUTH

The month of May, 1910, ran its course, beautiful as only a spring month in Norway can be – a lovely dream of verdure and flowers. But unfortunately we had little time to admire all the splendour that surrounded us; our watchword was "Away" – away from beautiful sights, as quickly as possible.

From the beginning of the month the *Fram* lay moored to her buoy outside the old walls of Akershus. Fresh and trim she came from the yard at Horten; you could see the shine on her new paint a long way off. Involuntarily one thought of holidays and yachting tours at the sight of her; but the thought was soon banished. The first day after her arrival, the vessel's deck assumed the most everyday appearance that could be desired: the loading had begun.

A long procession of cases of provisions made its way unceasingly from the basement of the Historical Museum down into the roomy hold of the *Fram,* where Lieutenant Nilsen and the three Nordlanders were ready to receive them. This process was not an altogether simple one; on the contrary, it was a very serious affair. It was not enough to know that all the cases were duly on board; the problem was to know exactly where each particular case was placed, and, at the same time, to stow them all in such a way that they could easily be got at in future. This was a difficult piece of work, and it was not rendered any more easy by the attention that had to be paid to the numerous hatches leading down into the lower hold, where the big petroleum tanks stood. All these hatches had to be left accessible, otherwise we should have been cut off from pumping the oil into the engine-room.

However, Nilsen and his assistants accomplished their task with brilliant success. Among the hundreds of cases there was not one that was misplaced; not one that was stowed so that it could not instantly be brought into the light of day.

While the provisioning was going on, the rest of the equipment was also being taken on board. Each member of the expedition was busily engaged in looking after the needs of his own department in the best way possible. Nor was this a question of trifles: one may cudgel one's brains endlessly in advance, but some new requirement will constantly be cropping up – until one puts a full stop to it by casting off and sailing. This event was becoming imminent with the arrival of June.

The day before leaving Christiania we had the honour and pleasure of receiving a visit from the King and Queen of Norway on board the *Fram*. Having been informed beforehand of their Majesties' coming, we endeavoured as far as possible to bring some order into the chaos that reigned on board. I do not know that we were particularly successful, but I am sure that every one of the *Fram*'s crew will always remember with respectful gratitude King Haakon's cordial words of farewell.

On the same occasion the expedition received from their Majesties the gift of a beautiful silver jug, which afterwards formed the most handsome ornament of our table on every festive occasion.

On June 3, early in the forenoon, the *Fram* left Christiania, bound at first for my home on Bundefjord. The object of her call there was to take on board the house for the winter station, which stood ready built in the garden. Our excellent carpenter Jörgen Stubberud had superintended the construction of this strong building. It was now rapidly taken to pieces, and every single plank and beam was carefully numbered. We had quite an imposing pile of materials to get aboard, where even before there was not much room to spare. The bulk of it was stowed forward, and the remainder in the hold.

The more experienced among the members of the expedition were evidently absorbed in profound conjectures as to the meaning of this "observation house," as the newspapers had christened it. It may willingly be admitted that they had good reason for their speculations. By an observation house is usually meant a comparatively simple construction, sufficient to provide the necessary shelter from wind and weather. Our house, on the other hand, was a model of solidity, with three double walls, double roof and floor. Its arrangements included ten inviting bunks, a kitchener, and a table; the latter, moreover, had a brand-new American-cloth cover. "I can understand that they want to keep themselves warm when they're making observations," said Helmer Hanssen; "but what they want with a cloth on the table I can't make out."

On the afternoon of June 6 it was announced that everything was ready, and in the evening we all assembled at a simple farewell supper in the garden. I took the opportunity of wishing good luck to every man in turn, and finally we united in a "God preserve the King and Fatherland!" Then we broke up. The last man to get into the boat was the second in command; he arrived armed with a horseshoe. In his opinion it is quite incredible what luck an old horseshoe will bring. Possibly he is right. Anyhow, the horseshoe was firmly nailed to the mast in the *Fram*'s saloon, and there it still hangs.

When on board, we promptly set to work to get up the anchor. The Bolinder motor hummed, and the heavy cable rattled in through the hawse-hole. Precisely at midnight the anchor let go of the bottom, and just as the Seventh of June, rolled in over us, the *Fram* stood out of Christiania Fjord for the third time. Twice already had a band of stout-hearted men brought this ship back with honour after years of service. Would it be vouchsafed to us to uphold this honourable tradition? Such were, no doubt, the thoughts with which most of us were occupied as our vessel glided over the motionless fjord in the light summer night. The start was made under the sign of the Seventh of June, and this was taken as a promising omen; but among our bright and confident hopes there crept a shadow of melancholy. The hillsides, the woods, the fjord – all were so bewitchingly fair and so dear to us. They called to us with their allurement, but the Diesel motor knew no pity. Its tuff-tuff went on brutally through the stillness. A little boat, in which were some of my nearest relations, dropped gradually astern. There was a glimpse of white handkerchiefs in the twilight, and then – farewell!

The next morning we were moored in the inner harbour at Horten. An apparently innocent lighter came alongside at once, but the lighter's cargo was not quite so innocent as its appearance. It consisted of no less than half a ton of gun-cotton and rifle ammunition, a somewhat unpleasant, but none the less necessary, item of our equipment. Besides taking on board the ammunition, we availed ourselves of the opportunity of completing our water-supply. When this was done, we lost no time in getting away. As we passed the warships lying in the harbour they manned ship, and the bands played the National Anthem. Outside Vealös we had the pleasure of waving a last farewell to a man to whom the expedition will always owe a debt of gratitude, Captain Christian Blom, Superintendent of the dockyard, who had supervised the extensive repairs to the *Fram* with unrelaxing interest and obligingness. He slipped past us in his sailing-boat; I do not remember if he got a cheer. If he did not, it was a mistake.

Now we were on our way to the South, as the heading of this chapter announces, though not yet in earnest. We had an additional task before us: the oceanographical cruise in the Atlantic. This necessitated a considerable détour on the way. The scientific results of this cruise will be dealt with by specialists in due course; if it is briefly referred to here, this is chiefly for the sake of continuity. After consultation with Professor Nansen, the plan was to begin investigations in the region to the south of Ireland, and thence to work our way westward as far as time and circumstances permitted. The work was to be resumed on the homeward voyage in the direction of the North of Scotland. For various reasons this programme afterwards had to be considerably reduced.

For the first few days after leaving Norway we were favoured with the most splendid summer weather. The North Sea was as calm as a millpond; the *Fram* had little more motion than when she was lying in Bundefjord. This was all the better for us, as we could hardly be said to be absolutely ready for sea when we passed Færder, and came into the capricious Skagerak. Hard pressed as we had been for time, it had not been possible to lash and stow the last of our cargo as securely as was desirable; a stiff breeze at the mouth of the fjord would therefore have been rather inconvenient. As it was, everything was arranged admirably, but to do this we had to work night and day. I have been told that on former occasions sea-sickness made fearful ravages on board the *Fram* but from this trial we also had an easy escape. Nearly all the members of the expedition were used to the sea, and the few who, perhaps, were not so entirely proof against it had a whole week of fine weather to get into training. So far as I know, not a single case occurred of this unpleasant and justly dreaded complaint.

After passing the Dogger Bank we had a very welcome north-east breeze; with the help of the sails we could now increase the not very reckless speed that the motor was capable of accomplishing. Before we sailed, the most contradictory accounts were current of the *Fram's* sailing qualities. There were some who asserted that the ship could not be got through the water at all, while with equal force the contrary view was maintained – that she was a notable fast sailer. As might be supposed, the truth as usual lay about half-way between these two extremes. The ship was no racer, nor was she an absolute log. We ran before the north-east wind towards the English Channel at a speed of about seven knots, and with that we were satisfied for the time being. The important question for us was whether we should keep the favourable wind till we were well through the Straits of Dover, and, preferably, a good way down Channel. Our engine power was far too limited to make it of any use trying to go against the wind, and we should have been obliged in that case to have recourse to the sailing-ship's method – beating. Tacking in the English Channel – the busiest part of the world's seas – is in itself no very pleasant work; for us it would be so much the worse, as it would greatly encroach on the time that could be devoted to oceanographical investigations. But the east wind held with praiseworthy steadiness. In the course of a few days we were through the Channel, and about a week after leaving Norway we were able to take the first oceanographical station at the point arranged according to the plan. Hitherto everything had gone as smoothly as we could wish, but now, for a change, difficulties began to appear, first in the form of unfavourable weather When the north-wester begins to blow in the North Atlantic, it is generally a good while before it drops again, and this time it did not belie its reputation. Far from getting to the westward, we were threatened for a time with being driven on to the Irish coast. It was not quite so bad as that, but we soon found ourselves obliged to shorten the route originally laid down very considerably. A contributing cause of this determination was the fact that the motor was out of order. Whether it was the fault of the oil or a defect in the engine itself our engineer was not clear. It was therefore necessary to make for home in good time, in case of extensive repairs being required. In spite of these difficulties, we had a quite respectable collection of samples of water and temperatures at different depths before we set our course for Norway at the beginning of July, with Bergen as our destination.

During the passage from the Pentland Firth we had a violent gale from the north, which gave us an opportunity of experiencing how the *Fram* behaved in bad weather. The trial was by no means an easy one. It was blowing a gale, with a cross sea; we kept going practically under full sail, and had the satisfaction of seeing our ship make over nine knots. In the rather severe rolling the collar of the mast in the fore-cabin was loosened a little; this let the water in, and there was a slight flooding of Lieutenant Nilsen's cabin and mine. The others, whose berths were to port, were on the weather side, and kept dry. We came out of it all with the loss of a few boxes of cigars, which were wet through. They were not entirely lost for all that; Rönne took charge of them, and regaled himself with salt and mouldy cigars for six months afterwards. Going eight or nine knots an hour, we did not make much of the distance between Scotland and Norway. On the afternoon of Saturday, July 9, the wind dropped, and at the same time the lookout reported land in sight. This was Siggen on Bömmelö. In the course of the night we came under the coast, and on Sunday morning, July 10, we ran into Sælbjömsfjord. We had no detailed chart of this inlet, but after making a great noise with our powerful air-siren, we at last roused the inmates of the pilot-station, and a pilot came aboard. He showed visible signs of surprise when he found out, by reading the name on the ship's side, that it was the *Fram* he had before him. "Lord, I thought you were a Russian!" he exclaimed. This supposition was presumably intended to serve as a sort of excuse for his small hurry in coming on board.

It was a lovely trip through the fjords to Bergen, as warm and pleasant in here as it had been bitter and cold outside. We had a dead calm all day, and with the four knots an hour, which was all the motor could manage, it was late in the evening when we anchored off the naval dockyard in Solheimsvik. Our stay in Bergen happened at the time of the exhibition, and the committee paid the expedition the compliment of giving all its members free passes.

Business of one kind and another compelled me to go to Christiania, leaving the *Fram* in charge of Lieutenant Nilsen. They had their hands more than full on board. Diesel's firm in Stockholm sent their experienced fitter, Aspelund, who at once set to work to overhaul the motor thoroughly. The work that had to be done was executed gratis by the Laxevaag engineering works. After going into the matter thoroughly, it was decided to change the solar oil we had on board for refined petroleum. Through the courtesy of the West of Norway Petroleum Company, we got this done on very favourable terms at the company's storage dock in Skaalevik. This was troublesome work, but it paid in the future.

The samples of water from our trip were taken to the biological station, where Kutschin at once went to work with the filtering (determination of the proportion of chlorine).

Our German shipmate, the oceanographer Schroer, left us at Bergen. On July 23 the *Fram* left Bergen, and arrived on the following day at Christiansand, where I met her. Here we again had a series of busy days. In one of the Custom-house warehouses were piled a quantity of things that had to go on board: no less than 400 bundles of dried fish, all our ski and sledging outfit, a waggon-load of timber, etc. At Fredriksholm, out on Flekkerö, we had found room for perhaps the most important of all – the passengers, the ninety-seven Eskimo dogs, which had arrived from Greenland in the middle of July on the steamer Hans Egede. The ship had had a rather long and rough passage, and the dogs were not in very good condition on their arrival, but they had not been many days on the island under the supervision of Hassel and Lindström before they were again in full vigour. A plentiful supply of fresh meat worked wonders. The usually peaceful island, with the remains of the old fortress, resounded day by day, and sometimes at night, with the most glorious concerts of howling. These musical performances attracted a number of inquisitive visitors, who were anxious to submit the members of the chorus to a closer examination, and therefore, at certain times, the public were admitted to see the animals. It soon turned out that the majority of the dogs, far from being ferocious or shy, were, on the contrary, very appreciative of these visits. They sometimes came in for an extra tit-bit in the form of a sandwich or something of the sort. Besides which, it was a little diversion in their life of captivity, so uncongenial to an Arctic dog; for every one of them was securely chained up. This was necessary, especially to prevent fighting among themselves. It happened not infrequently that one or more of them got loose, but the two guardians were always ready to capture the runaways. One enterprising rascal started to swim over the sound to the nearest land – the object of his expedition was undoubtedly certain unsuspecting sheep that were grazing by the shore – but his swim was interrupted in time.

After the *Fram*'s arrival Wisting took over the position of dog-keeper in Hassel's place. He and Lindström stayed close to the island where the dogs were. Wisting had a way of his own with his four-footed subjects, and was soon on a confidential footing with them. He also showed himself to be possessed of considerable veterinary skill – an exceedingly useful qualification in this case, where there was often some injury or other to be attended to. As I have already mentioned, up to this time no member of the expedition, except Lieutenant Nilsen, knew anything of the extension of plan that had been made. Therefore, amongst the things that came on board, and amongst the preparations that were made during our stay at Christiansand, there must have been a great deal that appeared very strange to those who, for the present, were only looking forward to a voyage round Cape Horn to San Francisco. What was the object of taking all these dogs on board and transporting them all that long way? And if it came to that, would any of them survive the voyage round the formidable promontory? Besides, were there not dogs enough, and good dogs too, in Alaska? Why was the whole after-deck full of coal? What was the use of all these planks and boards? Would it not have been much more convenient to take all that kind of goods on board in 'Frisco? These and many similar questions began to pass from man to man; indeed, their very faces began to resemble notes of interrogation. Not that anyone asked me – far from it; it was the second in command who had to bear the brunt and answer as well as he could – an extremely thankless and unpleasant task for a man who already had his hands more than full.

In order to relieve his difficult situation, I resolved, shortly before leaving Christiansand, to inform Lieutenants Prestrud and Gjertsen of the true state of affairs. After having signed an undertaking of secrecy, they received full information of the intended dash to the South Pole, and an explanation of the reasons for keeping the whole thing secret. When asked whether they wished to take part in the new plan, they both answered at once in the affirmative, and that settled it.

There were now three men on board – all the officers – who were acquainted with the situation, and were thus in a position to parry troublesome questions and remove possible anxieties on the part of the uninitiated.

Two of the members of the expedition joined during the stay at Christiansand – Hassel and Lindström – and one change was made: the engineer Eliassen was discharged. It was no easy matter to find a man who possessed the qualifications for taking over the post of engineer to the *Fram*. Few, or perhaps no one, in Norway could be expected to have much knowledge of motors of the size of ours. The only thing to be done was to go to the place where the engine was built – to Sweden. Diesel's firm in Stockholm helped us out of the difficulty; they sent us the man, and it afterwards turned out that he was the right man. Knut Sundbeck was his name. A chapter might be written on the good work that man did, and the quiet, unostentatious way in which he did it. From the very beginning he had assisted in the construction of the *Fram*'s motor, so that he knew his engine thoroughly. He treated it as his darling; therefore there was never anything the matter with it. It may truly be said that he did honour to his firm and the nation to which he belongs.

Meanwhile we were hard at work, getting ready to sail. We

decided to leave before the middle of August – the sooner the better. The *Fram* had been in dry dock, where the hull was thoroughly coated with composition. Heavily laden as the ship was, the false keel was a good deal injured by the severe pressure on the blocks, but with the help of a diver the damage was quickly made good.

The many hundred bundles of dried fish were squeezed into the main hold, full as it was. All sledging and ski outfit was carefully stowed away, so as to be protected as far as possible from damp. These things had to be kept dry, otherwise they, would become warped and useless. Bjaaland had charge of this outfit, and he knew how it should be treated.

As is right and proper, when all the goods had been shipped, it was the turn of the passengers. The *Fram* was anchored off Fredriksholm, and the necessary preparations were immediately made for receiving our four-footed friends. Under the expert direction of Bjaaland and Stubberud, as many as possible of the crew were set to work with axe and saw, and in the course of a few hours the *Fram* had got a new deck. This consisted of loose pieces of decking, which could easily be raised and removed for flushing and cleaning. This false deck rested on three-inch planks nailed to the ship's deck; between the latter and the loose deck there was therefore a considerable space, the object of which was a double one – namely, to let the water, which would unavoidably be shipped on such a voyage, run off rapidly, and to allow air to circulate, and thus keep the space below the animals as cool as possible. The arrangement afterwards proved very successful.

The bulwarks on the fore-part of the *Fram*'s deck consisted of an iron railing covered with wire-netting. In order to provide both shade and shelter from the wind, a lining of boards was now put up along the inside of the railing, and chains were fastened in all possible and impossible places to tie the dogs up to. There could be no question of letting them go loose – to begin with, at any rate; possibly, we might hope to be able to set them free later on, when they knew their masters better and were more familiar with their surroundings generally.

Late in the afternoon of August 9 we were ready to receive our new shipmates, and they were conveyed across from the island in a big lighter, twenty at a time. Wisting and Lindström superintended the work of transport, and maintained order capitally. They had succeeded in gaining the dogs' confidence, and at the same time their complete respect – just what was wanted, in fact. At the *Fram*'s gangway the dogs came in for an active and determined reception, and before they had recovered from their surprise and fright, they were securely fastened on deck and given to understand with all politeness that the best thing they could do for the time being was to accept the situation with calmness. The whole proceeding went so rapidly that in the course of a couple of hours we had all the ninety-seven dogs on board and had found room for them; but it must be added that the *Fram*'s deck was utilized to the utmost. We had thought we should be able to keep the bridge free, but this could not be done if we were to take them all with us. The last boat-load, fourteen in number, had to be accommodated there. All that was left was a little free space for the man at the wheel. As for the officer of the watch, it looked as if he would be badly off for elbow-room; there was reason to fear that he would be compelled to kill time by standing stock-still in one spot through the whole watch; but just then there was no time for small troubles of this sort. No sooner was the last dog on board than we set about putting all visitors ashore, and then the motor began working the windlass under the forecastle. "The anchor's up!" Full speed ahead, and the voyage towards our goal, 16,000 miles away, was begun. Quietly and unobserved we went out of the fjord at dusk; a few of our friends accompanied us out.

After the pilot had left us outside Flekkerö, it was not long before the darkness of the August evening hid the outlines of the country from our view; but Oxö and Ryvingen flashed their farewells to us all through the night.

We had been lucky with wind and weather at the commencement of our Atlantic cruise in the early summer; this time we were, if possible, even more favoured. It was perfectly calm when we sailed, and the North Sea lay perfectly calm for several days after. What we had to do now was to become familiar with and used to, all these dogs, and this was enormously facilitated by the fact that for the first week we experienced nothing but fine weather.

Before we sailed there was no lack of all kinds of prophecies of the evil that would befall us with our dogs. We heard a number of these predictions; presumably a great many more were whispered about, but did not reach our ears. The unfortunate beasts were to fare terribly badly. The heat of the tropics would make short work of the greater part of them. If any were left, they would have but a miserable respite before being washed overboard or drowned in the seas that would come on deck in the west wind belt. To keep them alive with a few bits of dried fish was an impossibility, etc.

As everyone knows, all these predictions were very far from being fulfilled; the exact opposite happened. Since then I expect most of us who made the trip have been asked the question – Was not that voyage to the South an excessively wearisome and tedious business? Didn't you get sick of all those dogs? How on earth did you manage to keep them alive?

It goes without saying that a five months' voyage in such waters as we were navigating must necessarily present a good deal of monotony; how much will depend on what resources one has for providing occupation. In this respect we had in these very dogs just what was wanted. No doubt it was work that very often called for the exercise of patience; nevertheless, like any other work, it furnished diversion and amusement, and so much the more since we here had to deal with living creatures that had sense enough fully to appreciate and reciprocate in their own way any advance that was made to them.

From the very first I tried in every way to insist upon the paramount importance to our whole enterprise of getting our draught animals successfully conveyed to our destination. If we had any watchword at this time it was: "Dogs first, and dogs all the time." The result speaks best for the way in which this watchword was followed. The following was the arrangement we made: The dogs, who at first were always tied up on the same spot, were divided into parties of ten; to each party one or two keepers were assigned, with full responsibility for their animals and their treatment. For my own share I took the fourteen that lived on the bridge. Feeding the animals was a manoeuvre that required the presence of all hands on deck; it therefore took place when the watch was changed. The Arctic dog's greatest enjoyment in life is putting away his food; it may be safely asserted that the way to his heart lies through his dish of meat. We acted on this principle, and the result did not disappoint us. After the lapse of a few days the different squads were the best of friends with their respective keepers.

As may be supposed, it was not altogether to the taste of the dogs to stand chained up all the time; their temperament is far too lively for that. We would gladly have allowed them the pleasure of running about and thus getting healthy exercise, but for the present we dared not run the risk of letting the whole pack loose. A little more education was required first. It was easy enough to win their affection; to provide them with a good education was of course a more difficult matter. It was quite touching to see their joy and gratitude when one gave up a little time to their entertainment. One's first meeting with them in the morning was specially cordial. Their feelings were then apt to find vent in a chorus of joyful howls; this was called forth by the very sight of their masters, but they asked more than that. They were not satisfied until we had gone round, patting and talking to every one. If by chance one was so careless as to miss a dog, he at once showed the most unmistakable signs of disappointment.

There can hardly be an animal that is capable of expressing its feelings to the same extent as the dog. Joy, sorrow, gratitude, scruples of conscience, are all reflected as plainly as could be desired in his behaviour, and above all in his eyes. We human beings are apt to cherish the conviction that we have a monopoly of what is called a living soul; the eyes, it is said, are the mirror of this soul. That is all right enough; but now take a look at a dog's eyes, study them attentively. How often do we see something "human" in their expression, the same variations that we meet with in human eyes. This, at all events, is something that strikingly resembles "soul." We will leave the question open for those who are interested in its solution, and will here only mention another point, which seems to show that a dog is something more than a mere machine of flesh and blood – his pronounced individuality. There were about a hundred dogs on board the *Fram*. Gradually, as we got to know each one of them by daily intercourse, they each revealed some characteristic trait, some peculiarity. Hardly two of them were alike, either in disposition or in appearance. To an observant eye there was here ample opportunity for the most amusing exercise. If now and then one grew a little tired of one's fellow-men – which, I must admit, seldom happened – there was, as a rule, diversion to be found in the society of the animals. I say, as a rule; there were, of course, exceptions. It was not an unmixed pleasure having the whole deck full of dogs for all those months; our patience was severely tested many a time. But in spite of all the trouble and inconvenience to which the transport of the dogs necessarily gave rise, I am certainly right in saying that these months of sea voyage would have seemed far more monotonous and tedious if we had been without our passengers.

During the first four or five days we had now been making our way towards the Straits of Dover, and the hope began to dawn within us that this time, as last, we should slip through without any great difficulty. There had been five days of absolute calm; why should it not last out the week? But it did not. As we passed the lightship at the western end of the Goodwins the fine weather left us, and in its place came the south-west wind with rain, fog, and foul weather in its train. In the course of half an hour it became so thick that it was impossible to see more than two or three ship's lengths ahead; but if we could see nothing, we heard all the more. The ceaseless shrieks of many steam-whistles and sirens told us only too plainly what a crowd of vessels we were in. It was not exactly a pleasant situation; our excellent ship had many good points, but they did not prevent her being extraordinarily slow and awkward in turning. This is an element of great danger in these waters. It must be remembered that a possible accident – whether our own fault or not – would to us be absolutely fatal. We had so little time to spare that the resulting delay might ruin the whole enterprise. An ordinary trading vessel can take the risk; by careful manoeuvring a skipper can almost always keep out of the way. Collisions are, as a rule, the result of rashness or carelessness on one side or the other. The rash one has to pay; the careful one may perhaps make money out of it. Carefulness on our part was a matter of course; it would have been a poor consolation to us if another ship had had to pay for her carelessness. We could not take that risk; therefore, little as we liked doing so, we put into the Downs and anchored there.

Right opposite to us we had the town of Deal, then in the height of its season. The only amusement we had was to observe all these apparently unconcerned people, who passed their time in bathing, or walking about the white, inviting sands. They had no need to worry themselves much about what quarter the wind blew from. Our only wish was that it would veer, or in any case drop. Our communication with the land was limited to sending ashore telegrams and letters for home.

By the next morning our patience was already quite exhausted, but not so with the south-wester. It kept going as steadily as ever, but it was clear weather, and therefore we decided at once to make an attempt to get to the west. There was nothing to be done but to have recourse to the ancient method of beating. We cleared one point, and then another, but more than that we could not manage for the time being. We took one bearing after another; no, there was no visible progress. Off Dungeness we had to anchor again, and once more console ourselves with the much-vaunted balm of patience. This time we escaped with passing the night there. The wind now thought fit to veer sufficiently to let us get out at daybreak, but it was still a contrary wind, and we had to beat almost all the way down the English Channel. A whole week was spent in doing these three hundred miles; that was rather hard, considering the distance we had to go.

I fancy most of us gave a good sigh of relief when at last we were clear of the Scilly Isles. The everlasting south-west wind was still blowing, but that did not matter so much now. The main thing was that we found ourselves in open sea with the whole Atlantic before us. Perhaps one must have sailed in the *Fram* to be able fully to understand what a blessing it was to feel ourselves altogether clear of the surrounding land and the many sailing-ships in the Channel – to say nothing of constantly working the ship with a deck swarming with dogs. On our first voyage through the Channel in June we had caught two or three carrier pigeons, which had come to rest in the rigging utterly tired out. On the approach of darkness we were able to get hold of them without difficulty. Their numbers and marks were noted, and after they had been taken care of for a couple of days and had recovered their strength, we let them go. They circled once or twice round the mast-heads, and then made for the English coast.

I think this episode led to our taking a few carrier pigeons with us when we left Christiansand; Lieutenant Nilsen, as a former owner of pigeons, was to take charge of them. Then a nice house was made for them, and the pigeons lived happily in their new abode on the top of the whale-boat amidships. Now, in some way or other the second in command found out that the circulation of air in the pigeon-house was faulty; to remedy this defect, he one day set the door a little ajar. Air certainly got into the house, but the pigeons came out. A joker, on discovering that the birds had flown, wrote up "To Let" in big letters on the wall of the pigeon-house. The second in command was not in a very gentle frame of mind that day. As far as I know, this escape took place in the Channel. The pigeons found their way home to Norway.

The Bay of Biscay has a bad name among seamen, and it fully deserves it; that tempestuous corner of the sea conceals for ever in its depths so many a stout ship and her crew. We for our part, however, had good hopes of escaping unharmed, considering the time of year, and our hopes were fulfilled. We had better luck than we dared to anticipate. Our stubborn opponent, the south-west wind, got tired at last of trying to stop our progress; it was no use. We went slowly, it was true, but still we got along. Of the meteorological lessons of our youth, we especially recalled at that moment the frequent northerly winds off the coast of Portugal, and as a pleasant surprise we already had them far up in the Bay. This was an agreeable change after all our close-hauled tacking in the Channel. The north wind held almost as bravely as the south-west had done before, and at what was to our ideas quite a respectable rate, we went southward day after day towards the fine-weather zone, where we could be sure of a fair wind, and where a sailor's life is, as a rule, a pleasant one.

For that matter, as far as seamanship was concerned, our work had gone on smoothly enough, even during these first difficult weeks. There were always willing and practised hands enough for what was wanted, even though the work to be done was frequently of a not very pleasant kind. Take washing decks, for instance. Every seaman will have something to say about what this is like on board ships that carry live animals, especially when these are carried on deck, in the way of all work that has to be done. I have always held the opinion that a Polar ship ought not, any more than any other vessel, to be a wholesale establishment for dirt and filth, however many dogs there may be on board. On the contrary, I should say that on voyages of this kind it is more than ever vitally necessary to keep one's surroundings as clean and sweet as possible. The important thing is to get rid of anything that may have a demoralizing and depressing effect. The influence of uncleanliness in this way is so well known that it is needless to preach about it here.

My views were shared by everyone on board the *Fram*, and everything was done to act in accordance with them, in spite of what may be considered great difficulties. Twice a day the whole deck was thoroughly washed down, besides all the extra turns at odd times with bucket and scrubber. At least once a week the whole of the loose deck was taken up, and each separate part of it thoroughly washed, until it was as clean as when it was laid down at Christiansand. This was a labour that required great patience and perseverance on the part of those who had to perform it, but I never saw any shortcomings. "Let's just see and get it clean," they said.

At night, when it was not always easy to see what one was doing, it might often happen that one heard some more or less heated exclamations from those who had to handle coils of rope in working the ship. I need not hint more explicitly at the cause of them, if it is remembered that there were dogs lying about everywhere, who had eaten and drunk well in the course of the day. But after a time the oaths gave way to jokes. There is nothing in the world that custom does not help us to get over.

It is the universal practice on board ship to divide the day and night into watches of four hours; the two watches into which the crew is divided relieve each other every four hours. But on vessels that sail to the Arctic Ocean, it is customary to have watches of six hours. We adopted the latter plan, which, on its being put to the vote, proved to have a compact majority in its favour. By this arrangement of watches we only had to turn out twice in the course of twenty-four hours, and the watch below had had a proper sleep whenever it turned out. If one has to eat, smoke, and perhaps chat a little during four hours' watch below, it does not leave much time for sleeping;

and if there should be a call for all hands on deck, it means no sleep at all.

To cope with the work of the engine-room, we had from the beginning the two engineers, Sundbeck and Nödtvedt; they took watch and watch, four hours each. When the motor was in use for a long time continuously, this was a rather severe duty, and on the whole it was just as well to have a man in reserve. I therefore decided to have a third man trained as reserve engineer. Kristensen applied for this post, and it may be said in his praise that he accomplished the change remarkably well. Thorough deck-hand as he was, there might have been reason to fear that he would repent of the transfer; but no, he quickly became life and soul an engineer. This did not prevent our seeing him on deck again many a time during the passage through the west wind belt, when there was need of a good man during a gale.

The motor, which during the Atlantic cruise had been a constant source of uneasiness and anxiety, regained our entire confidence under Sundbeck's capable command; it hummed so that it was a pleasure to hear it. To judge from the sound of the engine-room, one would have thought the *Fram* was moving through the water with the speed of a torpedo-boat. If this was not the case, the engine was not to blame; possibly, the screw had a share of it. The latter ought probably to have been somewhat larger, though experts are not agreed about this; in any case, there was something radically wrong with our propeller. Whenever there was a little seaway, it was apt to work loose in the brasses. This disadvantage is of very common occurrence in vessels which have to be fitted with lifting propellers on account of the ice, and we did not escape it. The only remedy was to lift the whole propeller-frame and renew the brasses – an extremely difficult work when it had to be done in the open sea and on as lively a ship as the *Fram*.

Day by day we had the satisfaction of seeing how the dogs found themselves more and more at home on board. Perhaps, even among ourselves, there were one or two who had felt some doubt at first of what the solution of the dog question would be, but in any case all such doubts were soon swept away. Even at an early stage of the voyage we had every reason to hope that we should land our animals safe and sound. What we had to see to in the first place was to let them have as much and as good food as circumstances permitted. As already mentioned, we had provided ourselves with dried fish for their consumption. Eskimo dogs do not suffer very greatly from daintiness, but an exclusive diet of dried fish would seem rather monotonous in the long-run, even to their appetites, and a certain addition of fatty substances was necessary, otherwise we should have some trouble with them. We had on board several great barrels of tallow or fat, but our store was not so large that we did not have to economize. In order to make the supply of fat last, and at the same time to induce our boarders to take as much dried fish as possible, we invented a mixture which was called by a sailor's term – dænge. This must not be confused with "thrashing," which was also served out liberally from time to time, but the dænge was more in demand. It consisted of a mixture of chopped-up fish, tallow, and maize-meal, all boiled together into a sort of porridge. This dish was served three times a week, and the dogs were simply mad for it. They very soon learned to keep count of the days when this mess was to be expected, and as soon as they heard the rattling of the tin dishes in which the separate portions were carried round, they set up such a noise that it was impossible to hear oneself speak. Both the preparation and the serving out of this extra ration were at times rather troublesome, but it was well worth it. It is quite certain that our complement of dogs would have made a poor show on arrival at the Bay of Whales if we had shrunk from the trouble.

The dried fish was not nearly so popular as the dænge, but to make up for that there was plenty of it. Not that the dogs themselves ever thought they could have enough; indeed, they were always stealing from their neighbours, perhaps more for the sake of the sport than for anything else. In any case, as a sport it was extremely popular, and it took many a good hiding to get the rascals to understand that it could not be allowed. I am afraid, though, that they kept up their thieving even after they knew very well that it was wrong; the habit was too old to be corrected. Another habit, and a very bad one, that these Eskimo dogs have fallen into in the course of ages, and of which we tried to break them, at all events during the sea voyage, is their tendency to hold howling concerts. What the real meaning of these performances may be, whether they are a pastime, or an expression of gratification or the reverse, we could never decide to our satisfaction. They began suddenly and without warning. The whole pack might be lying perfectly still and quiet, when a single individual, who for that occasion had taken upon himself the part of leader of the chorus, would set up a long, blood-curdling yowl. If they were left to themselves, it was not long before the whole pack joined in, and this infernal din was kept going at full steam for two or three minutes. The only amusing thing about the entertainment was its conclusion. They all stopped short at the same instant, just as a well-trained chorus obeys the baton of its conductor. Those of us, however, who happened to be in our bunks, found nothing at all amusing in these concerts, either in the finale or anything else, for they were calculated to tear the soundest sleeper from his slumbers. But if one only took care to stop the leader in his efforts the whole affair was nipped in the bud, and we usually succeeded in doing this. If there were some who at first were anxious about their night's rest, these fears were soon dispersed.

On leaving Norway we had ninety-seven dogs in all, and of these no less than ten were bitches. This fact justified us in expecting an increase of the canine population on our voyage to the South, and our expectations were very soon fulfilled. The first "happy event " occurred when we had been no more than three weeks at sea. An incident of this kind may seem in itself of no great importance; to us, living under conditions in which one day was almost exactly like another, it was more than enough to be an object of the greatest interest. Therefore, when the report went round that "Camilla" had got four shapely youngsters, there was general rejoicing. Two of the pups, who happened to be of the male sex, were allowed to live; the females were sent out of this world long before their eyes were opened to its joys and sorrows. It might be thought that, seeing we had nearly a hundred grown-up dogs on board, there would be little opportunity for looking after puppies; that this was done, nevertheless, with all the care that could be wished, is due in the first instance to the touching affection of the second in command for the little ones. From the very first moment he was their avowed protector. Gradually, as the numbers increased, there was a difficulty in finding room on the already well-occupied deck. "I'll take them in my bunk," said the second in command. It did not come to that, but if it had been necessary he would certainly have done so. The example was catching. Later on, when the little chaps were weaned, and had begun to take other nourishment, one might see regularly, after every meal, one after another of the crew coming on deck with some carefully scraped-up bits of food on his plate; the little hungry mouths were to have what was left over.

Something more than patience and punctual performance of duty is displayed in such things as those of which I have been speaking; it is love of, and a living interest in, one's work. From what I saw and heard every day, I was certain that these necessary incentives were present; although, as far as most of the men were concerned, our object was still the protracted one of drifting for years in the Arctic ice. The extension of the plan – the far more imminent battle with the ice-floes of the South – was still undreamt of by the majority of the ship's company. I considered it necessary to keep it to myself for a little while yet – until our departure from the port we were now making for: Funchal, Madeira. It may possibly appear to many people that I was running a pretty big risk in thus putting off till the last moment the duty of informing my comrades of the very considerable détour we were to make. Suppose some, or perhaps all, of them had objected! It must be admitted that it was a big risk, but there were so many risks that had to be taken at that time.

However, as I got to know each man during these first few weeks of our long voyage, I soon arrived at the conviction that there was nobody on board the *Fram* who would try to put difficulties in the way. On the contrary, I had more and more reason to hope that they would all receive the news with joy when they heard it; for then their whole prospect would be so different. Everything had gone with surprising ease up to this time; in future it would go even better.

It was not without a certain longing that I looked forward to our arrival at Madeira: it would be grand to be able to speak out! No doubt the others who knew of the plan were equally eager. Secrets are neither amusing nor easy to carry about – least of all on board a ship, where one has to live at such close quarters as we had. We were chatting together every day, of course, and the uninitiated could not be deterred from leading the conversation round to the ugly difficulties that would embitter our lives and hinder our progress when rounding the Horn. It was likely enough that we should manage to bring the dogs safely through the tropics once, but whether we should succeed in doing so twice was more doubtful; and so on to infinity. It is easier to imagine than to describe how awkward all this was, and how cunningly one had to choose one's words to avoid saying too much. Among inexperienced men there would have been no great difficulty, but it must be remembered that on the *Fram* pretty nearly every second man had spent years of his life in Polar voyages: a single slight hint to them would have been enough to expose the whole plan. That neither those on board nor anyone else discovered it prematurely can only be explained by its being so obvious.

Our ship was a good deal too dependent on wind and weather to enable us to make any accurate estimate of the time our voyage would occupy, especially as regards those latitudes in which the winds are variable. The estimate for the whole voyage was based on an average speed of four knots, and at this very modest rate, as it may seem, we ought to arrive at the Ice Barrier about the middle of January, 1911. As will be seen later, this was realized with remarkable exactness. For reaching Madeira we had allowed a month as a reasonable time. We did a good deal better than this, as we were able to leave Funchal a month to the day after our departure from Christiansand. We were always ready to forgive the estimate when it was at fault in this way.

The delay to which we had been subjected in the English Channel was fortunately made up along the coast of Spain and to the south of it. The north wind held until we were in the north-east trade, and then we were all right. On September 5 our observations at noon told us that we might expect to see the lights that evening, and at 10 p.m. the light of San Lorenzo on the little island of Fora, near Madeira, was reported from the rigging.

CHAPTER 4

FROM MADEIRA TO THE BARRIER

On the following morning we anchored in Funchal Roads. My brother was to arrive at Funchal, by arrangement, early enough to be sure of preceding us there. It was, however, a good while before we saw anything of him, and we were already flattering ourselves that we had arrived first when he was suddenly observed in a boat coming under our stern. We were able to tell him that all was well on board, and he brought us a big packet of letters and newspapers that gave us news of home. A little officious gentleman, who said he was a doctor, and as such had come in an official capacity to inquire as to the state of our health, was in an amazing hurry to leave the ship again when, at the top of the gangway, he found himself confronted with a score of dogs' jaws, which at the moment were opened wide on account of the heat. The learned man's interest in our health had suddenly vanished; his thoughts flew to the safety of his own life and limbs.

As Funchal was the last place where we could communicate with the outside world, arrangements were made for completing our supplies in every possible way, and in particular we had to take on board all the fresh water we could. The consumption of this commodity would be very large, and the possibility of running short had to be avoided at any price. For the time being we could do no more than fill all our tanks and every imaginable receptacle with the precious fluid, and this was done. We took about 1,000 gallons in the long-boat that was carried just above the main hatch. This was rather a risky experiment, which might have had awkward consequences in the event of the vessel rolling; but we consoled ourselves with the hope of fine weather and a smooth sea during the next few weeks. During the stay at Funchal the dogs had two good meals of fresh meat as a very welcome variety in their diet; a fair-sized carcass of a horse disappeared with impressive rapidity at each of these banquets. For our own use we naturally took a plentiful supply of vegetables and fruits, which were here to be had in abundance; it was the last opportunity we should have of regaling ourselves with such luxuries.

Our stay at Funchal was somewhat longer than was intended at first, as the engineers found it necessary to take up the propeller and examine the brasses. This work would occupy two days, and while the three mechanics were toiling in the heat, the rest of the ship's company took the opportunity of becoming acquainted with the town and its surroundings; the crew had a day's leave, half at a time. An excursion was arranged to one of the numerous hotels that are situated on the heights about the town. The ascent is easily made by means of a funicular railway, and in the course of the half-hour it takes to reach the top one is able to get an idea of the luxuriant fertility of the island. At the hotels one finds a good cuisine, and, of course, still better wine. It is scarcely necessary to add that we did full justice to both.

Roald Amundsen

I *Here Roald Amundsen (1872-1928) is atypically dressed: he is not wearing the heavy jacket he used on his expeditions.*

II *The prow of the* Fram, *the ship Nansen gave Amundsen for his expedition to the South Pole.*
(All the photographs are from Roald Amundsen, *La conquista del Polo Sud*, Treves, Milan, 1913)

III *From left to right: The crew of the* Fram: *Rönne, Lindström, Hansen, Kristensen, Stubberud, Beck, Olsen, Johansen and Nödtvedt.*
(From Roald Amundsen, *La conquista del Polo Sud*, Treves, Milan, 1913)

IV top *The members of the expedition spend an evening in the warmth of Framheim, mending clothes with a needle and thread.*

IV bottom and V top *Several factors gave Amundsen an edge over Scott in the race to the South Pole: the use of very little – but highly reliable – gear, particularly skis and sled dogs, proved to be decisive.*

V center *Soundings are taken to measure the thickness of the ice pack.*

V bottom *A seal approaches Framheim as expedition members look on.*
(All the photographs are from Roald Amundsen, *La conquista del Polo Sud*, Treves, Milan, 1913)

VI top *Sverre Hassel uses a sextant and an artificial horizon to take measurements near the South Pole.* (From Roald Amundsen, *La conquista del Polo Sud*, Treves, Milan, 1913)

VI bottom *To register his success, Amundsen set up this tent at the South Pole on December 14, 1911, on which he hoisted the Norwegian flag.* (© Norsk Folkemuseum)

VII *The map shows the routes of the great explorers of the past who tried to reach the South Pole.* (From Roald Amundsen, *La conquista del Polo Sud*, Treves, Milan, 1913)

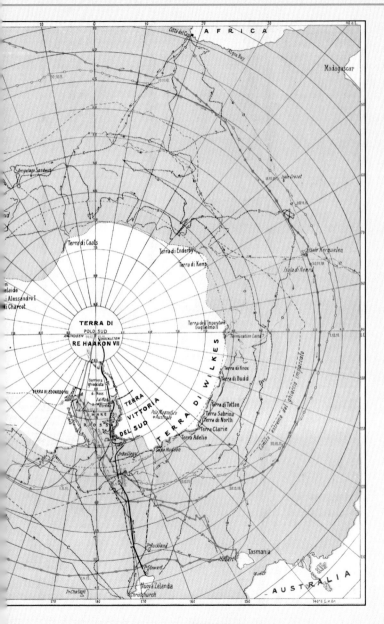

VII

VIII *Amundsen in his "polar" gear: a suit lined entirely with fur.* (From Roald Amundsen, *La conquista del Polo Sud*, Treves, Milan, 1913)

For the descent a more primitive means of transport was employed: we came down on sledges. It may be startling to hear of sledging in Madeira, but I must explain that the sledges had wooden runners, and that the road was paved with a black stone that was very smooth. We went at a creditable pace down the steep inclines, each sledge being drawn or pushed by three or four swarthy natives, who seemed to be possessed of first-rate legs and lungs.

It may be mentioned as a curiosity that the newspapers of Funchal did not hesitate to connect our expedition with the South Pole. The native journalists had no idea of the value of the startling piece of news they were circulating. It was a canard invented on the supposition that when a Polar ship steers to the south, she must, of course, be making for the South Pole. In this case the canard happened to be true. Fortunately for us, it did not fly beyond the shores of Madeira.

By the afternoon of September 9 we could begin to make our preparations for departure. The engineers had replaced the propeller and tested it; all supplies were on board, and the chronometers had been checked. All that remained was to get rid of the importunate bumboat – men who swarmed round the vessel in their little craft, each looking like a small floating shop. These obtrusive fellows were quickly sent off down the gangway: besides ourselves only my brother was left on board. Now that we were thus completely isolated from the outer world, the long-expected moment had arrived when I could proceed to inform all my comrades of my decision, now a year old, to make for the South. I believe all who were on board will long remember that sultry afternoon in Funchal Roads. All hands were called on deck: what they thought of I do not know, but it was hardly Antarctica and the South Pole. Lieutenant Nilsen carried a big rolled-up chart; I could see that this chart was the object of many interrogative glances.

Not many words were needed before everyone could see where the wind lay, and what course we should steer hencefor-ward. The second in command unrolled his big chart of the southern hemisphere, and I briefly explained the extended plan, as well as my reasons for keeping it secret until this time. Now and again I had to glance at their faces. At first, as might be expected, they showed the most unmistakable signs of sur-prise; but this expression swiftly changed, and before I had fin-ished they were all bright with smiles. I was now sure of the an-swer I should get when I finally asked each man whether he was willing to go on, and as the names were called, every single man had his "Yes" ready. Although, as I have said, I had expected it to turn out as it did, it is difficult to express the joy I felt at see-ing how promptly my comrades placed themselves at my ser-vice on this momentous occasion. It appeared, however, that I was not the only one who was pleased. There was so much life and good spirits on board that evening that one would have thought the work was successfully accomplished instead of be-ing hardly begun.

For the present, however, there was not much time to spare for discussing the news. We had first to see about getting away; afterwards there would be many months before us. Two hours' grace was allowed, in which every man could write to his peo-ple at home about what had just passed. The letters were prob-ably not very long ones; at all events, they were soon finished.

The mail was handed over to my brother to take to Christiania, from whence the letters were sent to their respective destinations; but this did not take place until after the alteration of our plans had been published in the Press.

It had been easy enough to tell my comrades the news, and they could not have given it a better reception; it was another question what people at home would say when the intelligence reached their ears. We afterwards heard that both favourable and unfavourable opinions were expressed. For the moment we could not trouble ourselves very greatly with that side of the matter; my brother had undertaken to announce the way we had taken, and I cannot say that I envied him the task. After we had all given him a final hearty shake of the hand he left us, and thereby our communication with the busy world was broken off. We were left to our own resources. No one can say that the situation oppressed us greatly. Our long voyage was entered upon as though it were a dance; there was not a trace of the more or less melancholy feeling that usually accompanies any parting. The men joked and laughed, while witticisms, both good and bad, were bandied about on the subject of our original situation. The anchor came up more quickly than usual, and after the motor had helped us to escape from the oppressive heat of the harbour, we had the satisfaction of seeing every sail filled with the fresh and cooling north-east trade.

The dogs, who must have found the stay at Funchal rather too warm for their taste, expressed their delight at the welcome breeze by getting up a concert. We felt we could not grudge them the pleasure this time.

It was pure enjoyment to come on deck the morning after

leaving Madeira; there was an added note of friendliness in every man's "Good-morning," and a smile twinkled in the corner of every eye. The entirely new turn things had taken, and the sudden change to fresh fields for thought and imagination, acted as a beneficent stimulus to those who, the day before, had contemplated a trip round the Horn. I think what chiefly amused them was their failure to smell a rat before. "How could I have been such an ass as not to think of it long ago?" said Beck, as he sent a nearly new quid into the sea. "Of course, it was as plain as a pikestaff. Here we are with all these dogs, this fine 'observation house,' with its big kitchen-range and shiny cloth on the table, and everything else. Any fool might have seen what it meant." I consoled him with the remark that it is always easy to be wise after the event, and that I thought it very lucky no one had discovered our destination prematurely.

Those of us who had been obliged hitherto to keep to themselves what they knew, and to resort to all kinds of stratagems to avoid making any disclosure, were certainly no less pleased at being rid of the secret; now they could talk freely to their heart's content. If we had previously had to resort to mystification, there was now nothing to prevent our laying our cards on the table. So many a conversation had come to a standstill because those who had a number of questions to ask did not dare to put them, and those who could have told held their tongues. Hereafter it would be a very long time before we were at a loss for subjects of conversation; a theme had suddenly presented itself, so varied and comprehensive that it was difficult at first to know where to begin. There were many men on board the *Fram* with a wealth of experience gained during years spent within the Arctic Circle, but to almost all of us the great Antarctic continent was a terra incognita. I myself was the only man on board who had seen Antarctica; perhaps one or two of my companions had in former days passed in the vicinity of an Antarctic iceberg on a voyage round Cape Horn, but that was all.

What had previously been accomplished in the way of exploration in the South, and the narratives of the men who had endeavoured to extend our knowledge of that inhospitable continent, were also things that very few of the ship's company had had time or opportunity to study, nor had they perhaps had any reason to do so. Now there was every possible reason. I considered it an imperative necessity that every man should acquaint himself as far as possible with the work of previous expeditions; this was the only way of becoming in some measure familiar with the conditions in which we should have to work. For this reason the *Fram* carried a whole library of Antarctic literature, containing everything that has been written by the long succession of explorers in these regions, from James Cook and James Clark Ross to Captain Scott and Sir Ernest Shackleton. And, indeed, good use was made of this library. The works of the two last-named explorers were in chief request; they were read from cover to cover by all who could do so, and, well written and excellently illustrated as these narratives are, they were highly instructive. But if ample time was thus devoted to the theoretical study of our problem, the practical preparations were not neglected. As soon as we were in the trade-winds, where the virtually constant direction and force of the wind permitted a reduction of the watch on deck, the various specialists went to work to put our extensive wintering outfit in the best possible order. It is true that every precaution had been taken beforehand to have every part of the equipment as good and as well adapted to its purpose as possible, but the whole of it, nevertheless, required a thorough overhauling. With so complicated an outfit as ours was, one is never really at the end of one's work; it will always be found that some improvement or other can be made. It will appear later that we had our hands more than full of the preparations for the sledge journey, not only during the long sea voyage, but also during the still longer Antarctic winter.

Our sailmaker, Rönne, was transformed into a – well, let us call it tailor. Rönne's pride was a sewing-machine, which he had obtained from the yard at Horten after considerable use of his persuasive tongue. His greatest sorrow on the voyage was that, on arriving at the Barrier, he would be obliged to hand over his treasure to the shore party. He could not understand what we wanted with a sewing-machine at Framheim. The first thing he did when the *Fram* reached Buenos Aires was to explain to the local representative of the Singer Sewing Machine Company how absolutely necessary it was to have his loss made good. His gift of persuasion helped him again, and he got a new machine.

For that matter, it was not surprising that Rönne was fond of his machine. He could use it for all sorts of things – sailmaker's, shoemaker's, saddler's, and tailor's work was all turned out with equal celerity. He established his workshop in the chart-house, and there the machine hummed incessantly through the tropics, the west wind belt, and the ice-floes too; for, quick as our sailmaker was with his fingers, the orders poured in even more quickly. Rönne was one of those men whose ambition it is to get as much work as possible done in the shortest possible time, and with increasing astonishment he saw that here he would never be finished; he might go at it as hard as he liked – there was always something more. To reckon up all that he delivered from his workshop during these months would take us too long; it is enough to say that all the work was remarkably well done, and executed with admirable rapidity. Perhaps one of the things he personally prided himself most on having made was the little three-man tent which was afterwards left at the South Pole. It was a little masterpiece of a tent, made of thin silk, which, when folded together, would easily have gone into a fair-sized pocket, and weighed hardly a kilogram.

At this time we could not count with certainty on the possibility of all those who made the southern journey reaching latitude 90°. On the contrary, we had to be prepared for the probability of some of the party being obliged to turn back. It was intended that we should use the tent in question, in case it might be decided to let two or three men make the final dash, and therefore it was made as small and light as possible. Fortunately we had no need to use it, as every man reached the goal; and we then found that the best way of disposing of Rönne's work of art was to let it stay there as a mark.

Our sailmaker had no dogs of his own to look after; he had no time for that. On the other hand, he often assisted me in attending to my fourteen friends up on the bridge; but he seemed to have some difficulty in getting on terms of familiarity with the dogs and all that belonged to them. It did not quite agree with his idea of life on board ship to have a deck swarming with dogs. He regarded this abnormal state of things with a sort of scornful compassion. "So you carry dogs, too, aboard this ship," he would say, every time he came on deck and found himself face to face with the "brutes." The poor brutes, I am sure, made no attempt to attack Rönne's person more than anyone else's, but he seemed for a long time to have great doubts about it. I don't think he felt perfectly safe until the dogs had been muzzled.

A part of our equipment to which we gave special care was, of course, the skis; in all probability they would be our chief weapon in the coming fight. However much we might have to learn from Scott's and Shackleton's narratives, it was difficult for us to understand their statements that the use of skis on the Barrier was not a success. From the descriptions that were given of the nature of the surface and the general conditions, we were forced to the opposite conclusion, that skis were the only means to employ. Nothing was spared to provide a good skiing outfit, and we had an experienced man in charge of it – Olav Bjaaland. It is sufficient to mention his name. When, on leaving Norway, it was a question of finding a good place for our twenty pairs of skis, we found we should have to share our own quarters with them; they were all disposed under the ceiling of the fore-cabin. At any rate, we had no better place to put them. Bjaaland, who during the last month or two had tried his hand at the unaccustomed work of a seaman, went back to his old trade of ski-maker and carpenter when we came into the trade-winds. Both ski and bindings were delivered ready for use by Hagen and Co., of Christiania; it remained to adapt them, and fit the backstraps to each man's boots, so that all might be ready for use on arrival at the Barrier. A full skiing outfit had been provided for every man, so that those who were to be left on board might also have a run now and then during their stay at the ice edge.

For each of our ten sledges, Bjaaland made during the voyage a pair of loose runners, which it was intended to use in the same way as the Eskimo use theirs. These primitive people have – or, at all events, had – no material that was suited for shoeing sledge-runners. They get over the difficulty by covering the runners with a coating of ice. No doubt it requires a great deal of practice and patience to put on this kind of shoeing properly, but when it is once on there can be no question that this device throws all others into the shade. As I say, we had intended to try this on the Barrier; we found, however, that the pulling power of our teams was so good as to allow us to retain our steel-shod runners with an easy conscience.

For the first fourteen days after leaving Madeira the northeast trade was fresh enough to enable us to keep up our average rate, or a little more, with the help of the sails alone. The engine was therefore allowed a rest, and the engineers had an opportunity of cleaning and polishing it; this they did early and late, till it seemed as if they could never get it bright enough. Nödtvedt now had a chance of devoting himself to the occupation which is his delight in this world – that of the blacksmith; and, indeed, there was opportunity enough for his use of the hammer and anvil. If Rönne had plenty of sewing, Nödtvedt had no less forging – sledge-fittings, knives, pickaxes, bars and bolts, patent hooks by the hundred for dogs, chains, and so on to infinity. The clang and sparks of the anvil were going all day long till we were well into the Indian Ocean. And in the westerly belt the blacksmith's lot was not an enviable one; it is not always easy to hit the nail on the head when one's feet rest on so unstable a foundation as the *Fram*'s deck, nor is it altogether pleasant when the forge is filled with water several times a day.

While we were fitting out for the voyage, the cry was constantly raised in certain quarters at home that the old *Fram*'s hull was in a shocking state. It was said to be in bad repair, to leak like a sieve – in fact, to be altogether rotten. It throws a curious light on these reports when we look at the voyages that the *Fram* has accomplished in the last two years. For twenty months out of twenty-four she has kept going in open sea, and that, too, in waters which make very serious demands on a vessel's strength. She is just as good as when she sailed, and could easily do it all over again without any repairs. We who were on board all knew perfectly well before we sailed how groundless and foolish these cries about her "rottenness" were; we knew, too, that there is scarcely a wooden ship afloat on which it is not necessary to use the pumps now and then. When the engine was stopped, we found it was sufficient to take a ten minutes' turn at the hand-pump every morning; that was all the "leaking" amounted to. Oh no! there was nothing wrong with the *Fram*'s hull. On the other hand, there might be a word or two to say about the rigging; if this was not all it should have been, the fault lay entirely with the plaguy considerations of our budget. On the foremast we had two squaresails; there ought to have been four. On the jib-boom there were two staysails; there was room enough for three, but the money would not run to it. In the Trades we tried to make up for the deficiency by rigging a studding-sail alongside the foresail and a sky-sail above the topsail. I will not assert that these improvised sails contributed to improve the vessel's appearance, but they got her along, and that is a great deal more important. We made very fair progress southward during these September days, and before the month was half over we had come a good way into the tropical belt. No particularly tropical heat was felt, at any rate by us men; and as a rule the heat is not severely felt on board ship in open sea so long as the vessel is moving. On a sailing-ship, lying becalmed with the sun in the zenith, it might be warmer than one would wish; but in case of calms we had the engine to help us, so that there was always a little breeze – that is, on deck. Down below it was worse; sometimes "hoggishly mild," as Beck used to put it. Our otherwise comfortable cabins had one fault; there were no portholes in the ship's side, and therefore we could not get a draught; but most of us managed without shifting our quarters. Of the two saloons, the fore-saloon was decidedly preferable in warm weather; in a cold climate probably the reverse would be the case. We were able to secure a thorough draught of air forward through the alleyway leading to the forecastle; it was difficult to get a good circulation aft, where they also had the warm proximity of the engine. The engineers, of course, had the hottest place, but the ever-inventive Sundbeck devised a means of improving the ventilation of the engine-room, so that even there they were not so badly off under the circumstances.

One often hears it asked, Which is to be preferred, severe heat or severe cold? It is not easy to give a definite answer; neither of the two is pleasant, and it must remain a matter of taste which is least so. On board ship no doubt most people will vote for heat, as, even if the days are rather distressing, one has the glorious nights to make up for them. A bitterly cold day is poorly compensated for by an even colder night.

One decided advantage of a warm climate for men who have to be frequently in and out of their clothes and their bunks is the simplicity of costume which it allows. When you wear hardly anything it takes a very short time to dress.

If we had been able to take the opinion of our dogs on their existence in the tropics, they would probably have answered as one dog: "Thanks, let us get back to rather cooler surroundings." Their coats were not exactly calculated for a temperature of 90° in the shade, and the worst of it was that they could not change them. It is, by the way, a misunderstanding to suppose that these animals absolutely must have hard frost to be comfortable; on the contrary, they prefer to be nice and warm. Here in the tropics of course they had rather too much of a good thing, but they did not suffer from the heat. By stretching awnings over the whole ship we contrived that they should all be constantly in the shade, and so long as they were not directly exposed to the sun's rays, there was no fear of anything going wrong. How well they came through it appears best from the fact that not one of them was on the sick-list on account of the heat. During the whole voyage only two deaths occurred from sickness – one was the case of a bitch that died after giving birth to eight pups – which might just as easily have caused her death under other conditions. What was the cause of death in the other case we were unable to find out; at any rate, it was not an infectious disease. One of our greatest fears was the possibility of an epidemic among the dogs, but thanks to the care with which they had been picked, there was never a sign of anything of the sort.

In the neighbourhood of the Equator, between the north-east and the south-east trades, lies what is called the "belt of calms." The position and extent of this belt vary somewhat with the season. If you are extremely lucky, it may happen that one trade-wind will practically take you over into the other; but, as a rule, this region will cause quite a serious delay to sailing-ships; either there are frequent calms, or shifting and unsteady winds. We arrived there at an unfavourable time of the year and lost the north-east trade as early as ten degrees north of the line. If we had had the calms we looked for, we could have got across with the help of the engine in a reasonably short time, but we saw very little sign of calms. As a rule, there was an ob-stinate south wind blowing, and it would not have taken very much of it to make the last few degrees of north latitude stiffer than we cared for.

The delay was annoying enough, but we had another disap-pointment of a more serious kind, for, curiously enough, we never had a proper shower of rain. Generally in these latitudes one encounters extremely heavy downpours, which make it possible to collect water by the barrelful in a very short space of time. We had hoped in this way to increase our store of fresh water, which was not so large but that extreme economy had to be practised if we were to avoid running short. However, this hope failed us, practically speaking. We managed to catch a lit-tle water, but it was altogether insufficient, and the husbanding of our supply had to be enforced in future with authority. The dogs required their daily ration, and they got it – measured out to a hair's-breadth. Our own consumption was limited to what was strictly necessary; soups were banished from the bill of fare, they used too much of the precious fluid; washing in fresh water was forbidden. It must not be supposed from this that we had no opportunity of washing. We had a plentiful supply of soap, which lathered just as well in salt water as in fresh, and was thus capable of keeping ourselves and our clothes as clean as before. If for a time we had felt a certain anxiety about our water-supply, these fears were banished comparatively quickly, as the reserve we had taken in the long-boat on deck lasted an incredibly long time, almost twice as long as we had dared to hope, and this saved the situation, or very nearly so. If the worst came to the worst, we should be obliged to call at one of the numerous groups of islands that would lie in our route later on.

For over six weeks the dogs had now been chained up in the places assigned to them when they came on board. In the course of that time most of them had become so tame and tractable that we thought we might soon let them loose. This would be a welcome change for them, and, what was more important, it would give them an opportunity for exercise. To tell the truth, we also expected some amusement from it; there would certainly be a proper shindy when all this pack got loose. But before we gave them their liberty we were obliged to disarm them, otherwise the inevitable free fight would be liable to result in one or more of them being left on the battle-field, and we could not afford that. Every one of them was provided with a strong muzzle; then we let them loose and waited to see what would happen. At first nothing at all happened; it looked as if they had abandoned once for all the thought of ever moving from the spot they had occupied so long At last a solitary individual had the bright idea of attempting a walk along the deck.

But he should not have done so; it was dangerous to move about here. The unaccustomed sight of a loose dog at once aroused his nearest neighbours. A dozen of them flung themselves upon the unfortunate animal who had been the first to leave his place, rejoicing in the thought of planting their teeth in his sinful body. But to their disappointment the enjoyment was not so great as they expected. The confounded strap round their jaws made it impossible to get hold of the skin; the utmost they could do was to pull a few tufts of hair out of the object of their violent onslaught. This affair of outposts gave the signal for a general engagement all along the line. What an unholy row there was for the next couple of hours! The hair flew, but skins remained intact. The muzzles saved a good many lives that afternoon.

These fights are the chief amusement of the Eskimo dogs; they follow the sport with genuine passion. There would be no great objection to it if they had not the peculiar habit of always combining to set upon a single dog, who is chosen as their victim for the occasion; they all make for this one, and if they are left to themselves they will not stop until they have made an end of the poor beast. In this way a valuable dog may be destroyed in a moment.

We therefore naturally made every effort from the first to quench their love of fighting, and the dogs very soon began to understand that we were not particularly fond of their combats; but we had here to deal with a natural characteristic, which it was impossible to eradicate; in any case, one could never be sure that nature would not reassert itself over discipline. When the dogs had once been let loose, they remained free to run about wherever they liked for the remainder of the voyage; only at meal-times were they tied up. It was quite extraordinary how they managed to hide themselves in every hole and comer; on some mornings there was hardly a dog to be seen when daylight came. Of course they visited every place where they ought not to have gone. Several of them repeatedly took the opportunity of tumbling into the forehold, when the hatches were open; but a fall of 25 feet did not seem to trouble them in the least. One even found his way into the engine-room, difficult as it might seem to gain access to it, and curled himself up between the piston-rods. Fortunately for the visitor, the engine was not started while he was there.

When the first furious battles had been fought out, a calm soon settled upon the dogs' spirits. It was easy to notice a feeling of shame and disappointment in the champions when they found that all their efforts led to nothing. The sport had lost its principal charm as soon as they saw what a poor chance there was of tasting blood.

From what has here been said, and perhaps from other accounts of the nature of Arctic dogs, it may appear as though the mutual relations of these animals consisted exclusively of fighting. This, however, is far from being the case. On the contrary, they very often form friendships, which are sometimes so strong that one dog simply cannot live without the other. Before we let the dogs loose we had remarked that there were a few who, for some reason or other, did not seem as happy as they should have been: they were more shy and restless than the others. No particular notice was taken of this, and no one tried to find out the cause of it. The day we let them loose we discovered what had been the matter with the ones that had moped: they had some old friend who had chanced to be placed in some other part of the deck, and this separation had been the cause of their low spirits. It was really touching to see the joy they showed on meeting again; they became quite different animals. Of course in these cases a change of places was arranged between the different groups, so that those who had associated from their own inclination would in future be members of the same team.

We had expected to reach the Equator by October 1, but the unfavourable conditions of wind that we met with to the north of it caused us to be a little behind our reckoning, though not much. On the afternoon of October 4 the *Fram* crossed the line. Thus an important stage of the voyage was concluded: the feeling that we had now reached southern latitudes was enough to put us all in holiday humour, and we felt we must get up a modest entertainment. According to ancient custom, crossing the line should be celebrated by a visit from Father Neptune himself, whose part is taken for the occasion by someone chosen from among the ship's company. If in the course of his inspection this august personage comes upon anyone who is unable to prove that he has already crossed the famous circle, he is handed over at once to the attendants, to be "shaved and baptized." This process, which is not always carried out with exaggerated gentleness, causes much amusement, and forms a welcome variety in the monotonous life of a long sea voyage, and probably many on board the *Fram* looked forward with eagerness to Neptune's visit, but he did not come. There simply was no room for him on our already well-occupied deck.

We contented ourselves with a special dinner, followed by coffee, liqueurs, and cigars. Coffee was served on the fore-deck, where by moving a number of the dogs we had contrived to get a few square yards of space. There was no lack of entertainment. A violin and mandolin orchestra, composed of Prestrud, Sundbeck, and Beck, contributed several pieces, and our excellent gramophone was heard for the first time. Just as it started the waltz from "The Count of Luxembourg," there appeared in the companion-way a real ballet-girl, masked, and in very short skirts. This unexpected apparition from a better world was greeted with warm applause, which was no less vigorous when the fair one had given proof of her skill in the art of dancing. Behind the mask could be detected Gjertsen's face, but both costume and dance were in the highest degree feminine. Rönne was not satisfied until he had the "lady" on his knees – hurrah for illusion!

The gramophone now changed to a swinging American cake-walk, and at the same moment there opportunely appeared on the scene a nigger in a tail-coat, a silk hat, and – a pair of wooden shoes. Black as he was, we saw at once that it was the second in command who had thus disguised himself. The mere sight of him was enough to set us all shrieking with laughter, but he made his great success when he began to dance. He was intensely amusing.

It did us a great deal of good to have a little amusement just then, for this part of the voyage was a trial of patience more than anything else. Possibly we were rather hard to please, but the south-east trade, which we were expecting to meet every day, was, in our opinion, far too late in coming, and when at length it arrived, it did not behave at all as becomes a wind that has the reputation of being the steadiest in the world. Besides being far too light, according to our requirements, it permitted itself such irregularities as swinging between the points of south and east, but was mostly in the neighbourhood of the former. For us, who had to lie all the time close-hauled to the westward, this had the effect of increasing our western longitude a great deal faster than our latitude. We were rapidly approaching the north-eastern point of South America – Cape San Roque. Fortunately we escaped any closer contact with this headland, which shoots so far out into the Atlantic. The wind at last shifted aft, but it was so light that the motor had to be constantly in use. Slowly but surely we now went southward, and the temperature again began to approach the limits that are fitting according to a Northerner's ideas. The tiresome, rather low awning could be removed, and it was a relief to be rid of it, as one could then walk upright everywhere.

On October 16, according to the observations at noon, we were in the vicinity of the island of South Trinidad, one of the lonely oases in the watery desert of the South Atlantic. It was our intention to go close under the island, and possibly to attempt a landing; but unfortunately the motor had to be stopped for cleaning, and this prevented our approaching it by daylight. We caught a glimpse of the land at dusk, which was, at all events, enough to check our chronometers.

South of the 20th degree of latitude the south-east trade was nearly done with, and we were really not sorry to be rid of it; it remained light and scant to the last, and sailing on a wind is not a strong point with the *Fram*. In the part of the ocean where we now were there was a hope of getting a good wind, and it was wanted if we were to come out right: we had now covered 6,000 miles, but there were still 10,000 before us, and the days went by with astonishing rapidity. The end of October brought the change we wanted; with a fresh northerly breeze she went gallantly southward, and before the end of the month we were down in lat. 40°. Here we had reached the waters where we were almost certain to have all the wind we wished, and from the right quarter. From now our course was eastward along what is known as the southern west wind belt. This belt extends between the 40th and 50th parallels all round the earth, and is distinguished by the constant occurrence of westerly winds, which as a rule blow with great violence. We had put our trust in these west winds; if they failed us we should be in a mess. But no sooner had we reached their domain than they were upon us with full force; it was no gentle treatment that we received, but the effect was excellent – we raced to the eastward. An intended call at Gough Island had to be abandoned; the sea was running too high for us to venture to approach the narrow little harbour. The month of October had put us a good deal behindhand, but now we were making up the distance we had lost. We had reckoned on being south of the Cape of Good Hope within two months after leaving Madeira, and this turned out correct. The day we passed the meridian of the Cape we had the first regular gale; the seas ran threateningly high, but now for the first time our splendid little ship showed what she was worth. A single one of these gigantic waves would have cleared our decks in an instant if it had come on board, but the *Fram* did not permit any such impertinence. When they came up behind the vessel, and we might expect at any moment to see them break over the low after-deck, she just raised herself with an elegant movement, and the wave had to be content with slipping underneath. An albatross could not have managed the situation better. It is said that the *Fram* was built for the ice, and that cannot, of course, be denied; but at the same time it is certain that when Colin Archer created his famous masterpiece of an ice boat, she was just as much a masterpiece of a sea boat – a vessel it would be difficult to match for seaworthiness. To be able to avoid the seas as the *Fram* did, she had to roll, and this we had every opportunity of finding out. The whole long passage through the westerly belt was one continual rolling; but in course of time one got used even to that discomfort. It was awkward enough, but less disagreeable than shipping water. Perhaps it was worse for those who had to work in the galley: it is no laughing matter to be cook, when for weeks together you cannot put down so much as a coffee-cup without its immediately turning a somersault. It requires both patience and strong will to carry it through, but the two – Lindström and Olsen – who looked after our food under these difficult conditions, had the gift of taking it all from the humorous point of view, and that was well.

As regards the dogs, it mattered little to them whether a gale was blowing, so long as the rain kept off. They hate rain; wet in any form is the worst one can offer an Arctic dog. If the deck was wet, they would not lie down, but would remain standing motionless for hours, trying to take a nap in that uncomfortable position. Of course, they did not get much sleep in that way, but to make up for it they could sleep all day and all night when the weather was fine. South of the Cape we lost two dogs; they went overboard one dark night when the ship was rolling tremendously. We had a coal-bunker on the port side of the after-deck, reaching up to the height of the bulwarks; probably these fellows had been practising boarding drill, and lost their balance. We took precautions that the same thing should not happen again.

Fortunately for our animals, the weather in the westerly belt was subject to very frequent changes. No doubt they had many a sleepless night, with rain, sleet, and hail; but on the other hand they never had to wait very long for a cheerful glimpse of the sun. The wind is for the most part of cyclonic character, shifting suddenly from one quarter to another, and these shifts always involve a change of weather. When the barometer begins to fall, it is a sure warning of an approaching north-westerly wind, which is always accompanied by precipitation, and increases in force until the fall of the barometer ceases. When this occurs, there follows either a short pause, or else the wind suddenly shifts to the south-west, and blows from that quarter with increasing violence, while the barometer rises rapidly. The change of wind is almost always followed by a clearing of the weather.

A circumstance which contributes an element of risk to navigation in the latitudes where we found ourselves is the possibility of colliding with an iceberg in darkness or thick weather; for it sometimes happens that these sinister monsters in the course of their wanderings find their way well up into the "forties." The probability of a collision is of course in itself not very great, and it can be reduced to a minimum by taking proper precautions. At night an attentive and practised look-out man will always be able to see the blink of the ice at a fairly long distance. From the time when we had to reckon with any likelihood of meeting icebergs, the temperature of the water was also taken every two hours during the night.

As Kerguelen Island lay almost directly in the course we intended to follow, it was decided for several reasons that we should call there, and pay a visit to the Norwegian whaling-station. Latterly many of the dogs had begun to grow thin, and it seemed probable that this was owing to their not having enough fatty substances in their food; on Kerguelen Island there would presumably be an opportunity of getting all the fat we wanted. As to water, we had, it was true, just enough to last us with economy, but it would do no harm to fill up the tanks. I was also hoping that there would be a chance of engaging three or four extra hands, for the *Fram* would be rather short-handed with only ten men to sail her out of the ice and round the Horn to Buenos Aires after the rest of us had been landed on the Barrier. Another reason for the contemplated visit was that it would be an agreeable diversion. We now only had to get there as quickly as possible, and the west wind helped us splendidly; one stiff breeze succeeded another, without our having any excessive weather. Our daily distance at this time amounted as a rule to about one hundred and fifty miles; in one twenty-four hours we made one hundred and seventy-four miles. This was our best day's work of the whole voyage, and it is no bad performance for a vessel like the *Fram,* with her limited sail area and her heavily-laden hull.

On the afternoon of November 28 we sighted land. It was on-ly a barren rocky knoll, and according to our determination of the position it would be the island called Bligh's Cap, which lies a few miles north of Kerguelen Island; but as the weather was not very clear, and we were unacquainted with the channels, we preferred to lie-to for the night before approaching any nearer. Early next morning the weather cleared, and we got accurate bearings. A course was laid for Royal Sound, where we supposed the whaling-station to be situated. We were going well in the fresh morning breeze, and were just about to round the last headland, when all at once a gale sprang up again, the bare and uninviting coast was hidden in heavy rain, and we had the choice of waiting for an indefinite time or continuing our voyage. Without much hesitation we chose the latter alternative. It might be tempting enough to come in contact with other men, especially as they were fellow-countrymen, but it was even more tempting to have done with the remaining 4,000 miles that lay between us and the Barrier as quickly as possible. It turned out that we had chosen rightly. December brought us a fair wind, even fresher than that of November, and by the middle of the month we had already covered half the distance between Kerguelen Island and our goal. We fortified the dogs from time to time with a liberal allowance of butter, which had a marvellous effect. There was nothing wrong with ourselves; we were all in the best of health, and our spirits rose as we drew nearer our goal.

That the state of our health was so remarkably good during the whole voyage must be ascribed in a material degree to the excellence of our provisions. During the trip from home to Madeira we had lived sumptuously on some little pigs that we took with us, but after these luxuries we had to take to tinned meat for good. The change was not felt much, as we had excellent and palatable things with us. There was a separate service for the two cabins, but the food was precisely the same in each. Breakfast was at eight, consisting of American hot cakes, with marmalade or jam, cheese, fresh bread, and coffee or cocoa. Dinner as a rule was composed of one dish of meat and sweets. As has already been said, we could not afford to have soup regularly on account of the water it required, and it was only served on Sundays. The second course usually consisted of Californian fruit. It was our aim all through to employ fruit, vegetables, and jam, to the greatest possible extent; there is undoubtedly no better means of avoiding sickness. At dinner we always drank syrup and water; every Wednesday and Saturday we were treated to a glass of spirits. I knew from my own experience how delicious a cup of coffee tastes when one turns out to go on watch at night. However sleepy and grumpy one may be, a gulp of hot coffee quickly makes a better man of one; therefore coffee for the night watch was a permanent institution on board the *Fram*.

By about Christmas we had reached nearly the 150th meridian in lat. 56° S. This left not much more than 900 miles before we might expect to meet with the pack-ice. Our glorious west wind, which had driven us forward for weeks, and freed us from all anxiety about arriving too late, was now a thing of the past. For a change we again had to contend for some days with calms and contrary wind. The day before Christmas Eve brought rain and a gale from the south-west, which was not very cheerful. If we were to keep Christmas with any festivity, fine weather was wanted, otherwise the everlasting rolling would spoil all our attempts. No doubt we should all have got over it if it had fallen to our lot to experience a Christmas Eve with storm, shortened sail, and other delights; worse things had happened before. On the other hand, there was not one of us who would not be the better for a little comfort and relaxation; our life had been monotonous and commonplace enough for a long time. But, as I said, the day before Christmas Eve was not at all promising. The only sign of the approaching holiday was the fact that Lindström, in spite of the rolling, was busy baking Christmas cakes. We suggested that he might just as well give us each our share at once, as it is well known that the cakes are best when they come straight out of the oven, but Lindström would not hear of it. His cakes vanished for the time being under lock and key, and we had to be content with the smell of them.

Christmas Eve arrived with finer weather and a smoother sea than we had seen for weeks. The ship was perfectly steady, and there was nothing to prevent our making every preparation for the festivity. As the day wore on Christmas was in full swing. The fore-cabin was washed and cleaned up till the Ripolin paint and the brass shone with equal brilliance; Rönne decorated the workroom with signal flags, and the good old "Happy Christmas" greeted us in a transparency over the door of the saloon. Inside Nilsen was busily engaged, showing great talents as a decorator. The gramophone was rigged up in my cabin on a board hung from the ceiling. A proposed concert of piano, violin, and mandolin had to be abandoned, as the piano was altogether out of tune.

The various members of our little community appeared one after another, dressed and tidied up so that many of them were scarcely recognizable. The stubbly chins were all smooth, and that makes a great difference. At five o'clock the engine was stopped, and all hands assembled in the fore-cabin, leaving only the man at the wheel on deck. Our cosy cabins had a fairy-like appearance in the subdued light of the many-coloured lamps, and we were all in the Christmas humour at once. The decorations did honour to him who had carried them out and to those who had given us the greater part of them – Mrs. Schroer, and the proprietor of the Oyster Cellar at Christiania, Mr. Ditlev-Hansen.

Then we took our seats round the table, which groaned beneath Lindström's masterpieces in the culinary art. I slipped behind the curtain of my cabin for an instant, and set the gramophone going. Herold sang us "Glade Jul."

The song did not fail of its effect; it was difficult to see in the subdued light, but I fancy that among the band of hardy men that sat round the table there was scarcely one who had not a tear in the corner of his eye. The thoughts of all took the same direction, I am certain – they flew homeward to the old country in the North, and we could wish nothing better than that those we had left behind should be as well off as ourselves. The melancholy feeling soon gave way to gaiety and laughter; in the course of the dinner the first mate fired off a topical song written by himself, which had an immense success. In each verse the little weaknesses of someone present were exhibited in more or less strong relief, and in between there were marginal remarks in prose. Both in text and performance the author fully attained the object of his work – that of thoroughly exercising our risible muscles.

In the after-cabin a well-furnished coffee-table was set out, on which there was a large assortment of Lindström's Christmas baking, with a mighty kransekake from Hansen's towering in the midst. While we were doing all possible honour to these luxuries, Lindström was busily engaged forward, and when we went back after our coffee we found there a beautiful Christmas-tree in all its glory. The tree was an artificial one, but so perfectly imitated that it might have come straight from the forest. This was also a present from Mrs. Schroer.

Then came the distribution of Christmas presents. Among the many kind friends who had thought of us I must mention the Ladies' Committees in Horten and Fredrikstad, and the telephone employees of Christiania. They all have a claim to our warmest gratitude for the share they had in making our Christmas what it was – a bright memory of the long voyage.

By ten o'clock in the evening the candles of the Christmas-tree were burnt out, and the festivity was at an end. It had been successful from first to last, and we all had something to live on in our thoughts when our everyday duties again claimed us.

In that part of the voyage which we now had before us – the region between the Australian continent and the Antarctic belt of pack-ice – we were prepared for all sorts of trials in the way of unfavourable weather conditions. We had read and heard so much of what others had had to face in these waters that we involuntarily connected them with all the horrors that may befall a sailor. Not that we had a moment's fear for the ship; we knew her well enough to be sure that it would take some very extraordinary weather to do her any harm. If we were afraid of anything, it was of delay.

But we were spared either delay or any other trouble; by noon on Christmas Day we had just what was wanted to keep our spirits at festival pitch; a fresh north-westerly wind, just strong enough to push us along handsomely toward our destination. It afterwards hauled a little more to the west, and lasted the greater part of Christmas week, until on December 30 we were in long. 170° E. and lat. 60° S. With that we had at last come far enough to the east, and could now begin to steer a southerly course; hardly had we put the helm over before the wind changed to a stiff northerly breeze Nothing could possibly be better; in this way it would not take us long to dispose of the remaining degrees of latitude. Our faithful companions of the westerly belt – the albatrosses – had now disappeared, and we could soon begin to look out for the first representatives of the winged inhabitants of Antarctica.

After a careful consideration of the experiences of our predecessors, it was decided to lay our course so that we should cross the 65th parallel in long. 175° E. What we had to do was to get as quickly as possible through the belt of pack-ice that blocked the way to Ross Sea to the south of it, which is always open in summer. Some ships had been detained as much as six weeks in this belt of ice; others had gone through in a few hours. We unhesitatingly preferred to follow the latter example, and therefore took the course that the luckier ones had indicated.

Of course, the width of the ice-belt may be subject to somewhat fortuitous changes, but it seems, nevertheless, that as a rule the region between the 175th and the 180th degrees of longitude offers the best chance of getting through rapidly; in any case, one ought not to enter the ice farther to the west. At noon on New Year's Eve we were in lat. 62° 15' S. We had reached the end of the old year, and really it had gone incredibly quickly. Like all its predecessors, the year had brought its share of success and failure; but the main thing was that at its close we found ourselves pretty nearly where we ought to be to make good our calculations – and all safe and well. Conscious of this, we said good-bye to 1910 in all friendliness over a good glass of toddy in the evening, and wished each other all possible luck in 1911.

At three in the morning of New Year's Day the officer of the watch called me with news that the first iceberg was in sight. I had to go up and see it. Yes, there it lay, far to windward, shining like a castle in the rays of the morning sun. It was a big, flat-topped berg of the typical Antarctic form. It will perhaps seem paradoxical when I say that we all greeted this first sight of the ice with satisfaction and joy; an iceberg is usually the last thing to gladden sailors' hearts, but we were not looking at the risk just then. The meeting with the imposing colossus had another significance that had a stronger claim on our interest – the pack-ice could not be far off. We were all longing as one man to be in it; it would be a grand variation in the monotonous life we had led for so long, and which we were beginning to be a little tired of. Merely to be able to run a few yards on an ice-floe appeared to us an event of importance, and we rejoiced no less at the prospect of giving our dogs a good meal of seal's flesh, while we ourselves would have no objection to a little change of diet.

The number of icebergs increased during the afternoon and

night, and with such neighbours it suited us very well to have daylight all through the twenty-four hours, as we now had. The weather could not have been better – fine and clear, with a light but still favourable wind. At 8 p.m. on January 2 the Antarctic Circle was crossed, and an hour or two later the crow's-nest was able to report the ice-belt ahead. For the time being it did not look like obstructing us to any great extent; the floes were collected in long lines, with broad channels of open water between them. We steered right in. Our position was then long. 176° E. and lat. 66° 30' S. The ice immediately stopped all swell, the vessel's deck again became a stable platform, and after two months' incessant exercise of our sea-legs we could once more move about freely. That was a treat in itself.

At nine in the morning of the next day we had our first opportunity of seal-hunting; a big Weddell seal was observed on a floe right ahead. It took our approach with the utmost calmness, not thinking it worth while to budge an inch until a couple of rifle-bullets had convinced it of the seriousness of the situation. It then made an attempt to reach the water, but it was too late. Two men were already on the floe, and the valuable spoil was secured. In the course of a quarter of an hour the beast lay on our deck, flayed and cut up by practised hands; this gave us at one stroke at least four hundredweight of dog food, as well as a good many rations for men. We made the same coup three times more in the course of the day, and thus had over a ton of fresh meat and blubber.

It need scarcely be said that there was a great feast on board that day. The dogs did their utmost to avail themselves of the opportunity; they simply ate till their legs would no longer carry them, and we could grant them this gratification with a good conscience. As to ourselves, it may doubtless be taken for granted that we observed some degree of moderation, but dinner was polished off very quickly. Seal steak had many ardent adherents already, and it very soon gained more. Seal soup, in which our excellent vegetables showed to advantage, was perhaps even more favourably received.

For the first twenty-four hours after we entered the ice it was so loose that we were able to hold our course and keep up our speed for practically the whole time. On the two following days things did not go quite so smoothly; at times the lines of floes were fairly close, and occasionally we had to go round. We did not meet with any considerable obstruction, however; there were always openings enough to enable us to keep going. In the course of January 6 a change took place, the floes became narrower and the leads broader. By 6 p.m. there was open sea on every side as far as the eye could reach. The day's observations gave our position as lat. 70° S., long. 180° E.

Our passage through the pack had been a four days' pleasure trip, and I have a suspicion that several among us looked back with secret regret to the cruise in smooth water through the ice-floes when the swell of the open Ross Sea gave the *Fram* another chance of showing her rolling capabilities.

But this last part of the voyage was also to be favoured by fortune. These comparatively little-known waters had no terrors to oppose to us. The weather continued surprisingly fine; it could not have been better on a summer trip in the North Sea. Of icebergs there was practically none; a few quite small floebergs were all we met with in the four days we took to cross Ross Sea.

About midday on January 11 a marked brightening of the southern sky announced that it was not far to the goal we had been struggling to reach for five months. At 2.30 p.m. we came in sight of the Great Ice Barrier. Slowly it rose up out of the sea until we were face to face with it in all its imposing majesty. It is difficult with the help of the pen to give any idea of the impression this mighty wall of ice makes on the observer who is confronted with it for the first time. It is altogether a thing which can hardly be described; but one can understand very well that this wall of 100 feet in height was regarded for a generation as an insuperable obstacle to further southward progress.

We knew that the theory of the Barrier's impregnability had long ago been overthrown; there was an opening to the unknown realm beyond it. This opening – the Bay of Whales – ought to lie, according to the descriptions before us, about a hundred miles to the east of the position in which we were. Our course was altered to true east, and during a cruise of twenty-four hours along the Barrier we had every opportunity of marvelling at this gigantic work of Nature. It was not without a certain feeling of suspense that we looked forward to our arrival at the harbour we were seeking What state should we find it in? Would it prove impossible to land at all conveniently?

One point after another was passed, but still our anxious eyes were met by nothing but the perpendicular wall. At last, on the afternoon of January 12, the wall opened. This agreed with our expectations; we were now in long. 164°, the selfsame point where our predecessors had previously found access.

We had before us a great bay, so deep that it was impossible to see the end of it from the crow's-nest; but for the moment there was no chance of getting in. The bay was full of great floes – sea-ice – recently broken up. We therefore went on a little farther to the eastward to await developments. Next morning we returned, and after the lapse of a few hours the floes within the bay began to move. One after another they came sailing out: the passage was soon free.

As we steered up the bay, we soon saw clearly that here we had every chance of effecting a landing. All we had to do was to choose the best place.

CHAPTER 5

ON THE BARRIER

We had thus arrived on January 14 – a day earlier than we had reckoned – at this vast, mysterious, natural phenomenon – the Barrier. One of the most difficult problems of the expedition was solved – that of conveying our draught animals in sound condition to the field of operations. We had taken 97 dogs on board at Christiansand; the number had now increased to 116, and practically all of these would be fit to serve in the final march to the South.

The next great problem that confronted us was to find a suitable place on the Barrier for our station. My idea had been to get everything – equipment and provisions – conveyed far enough into the Barrier to secure us against the unpleasant possibility of drifting out into the Pacific in case the Barrier should be inclined to calve. I had therefore fixed upon ten miles as a suitable distance from the edge of the Barrier. But even our first impression of the conditions seemed to show that we should be spared a great part of this long and troublesome transport. Along its outer edge the Barrier shows an even, flat surface; but here, inside the bay, the conditions were entirely different. Even from the deck of the *Fram* we were able to observe great disturbances of the surface in every direction; huge ridges with hollows between them extended on all sides. The greatest elevation lay to the south in the form of a lofty, arched ridge, which we took to be about 500 feet high on the horizon. But it might be assumed that this ridge continued to rise beyond the range of vision.

Our original hypothesis that this bay was due to underlying land seemed, therefore, to be immediately confirmed. It did not take long to moor the vessel to the fixed ice-foot, which here extended for about a mile and a quarter beyond the edge of the Barrier. Everything had been got ready long before. Bjaaland had put our skis in order, and every man had had his right pairs fitted. Ski-boots had long ago been tried on, time after time, sometimes with one, sometimes with two pairs of stockings. Of course it turned out that the ski-boots were on the small side. To get a bootmaker to make roomy boots is, I believe, an absolute impossibility. However, with two pairs of stockings we could always get along in the neighbourhood of the ship. For longer journeys we had canvas boots, as already mentioned.

Of the remainder of our outfit I need only mention the Alpine ropes, which had also been ready for some time. They were about 30 yards long, and were made of very fine rope, soft as silk, specially suited for use in low temperatures.

After a hurried dinner four of us set out. This first excursion was quite a solemn affair; so much depended on it. The weather was of the very best, calm with brilliant sunshine, and a few light, feathery clouds in the beautiful, pale blue sky. There was warmth in the air which could be felt, even on this immense ice-field. Seals were lying along the ice-foot as far as the eye could reach – great, fat mountains of flesh; food enough to last us and the dogs for years.

The going was ideal; our skis glided easily and pleasantly through the newly fallen loose snow. But none of us was exactly in training after the long five months' sea voyage, so that the pace was not great. After half an hour's march we were already at the first important point – the connection between the sea-ice and the Barrier. This connection had always haunted our brains. What would it be like? A high, perpendicular face of ice, up which we should have to haul our things laboriously with the help of tackles? Or a great and dangerous fissure, which we should not be able to cross without going a long way round? We naturally expected something of the sort. This mighty and terrible monster would, of course, offer resistance in some form or other.

The mystic Barrier! All accounts without exception, from the days of Ross to the present time, had spoken of this remarkable natural formation with apprehensive awe. It was as though one could always read between the lines the same sentence: "Hush, be quiet! the mystic Barrier!"

One, two, three, and a little jump, and the Barrier was surmounted! We looked at each other and smiled; probably the same thought was in the minds of all of us. The monster had begun to lose something of its mystery, the terror something of its force; the incomprehensible was becoming quite easy to understand.

Without striking a blow we had entered into our kingdom. The Barrier was at this spot about 20 feet high, and the junction between it and the sea-ice was completely filled up with driven snow, so that the ascent took the form of a little, gentle slope. This spot would certainly offer us no resistance.

Hitherto we had made our advance without a rope. The sea-ice, we knew, would offer no hidden difficulties; but what would be the condition of things beyond the Barrier was another question. And as we all thought it would be better to have the rope on before we fell into a crevasse than afterwards, our further advance was made with a rope between the first two.

We proceeded in an easterly direction up through a little valley formed by "Mount Nelson" on one side, and "Mount Rönniken" on the other. The reader must not, however, imagine from these imposing names that we were walking between any formidable mountain-ranges. Mounts Nelson and Rönniken were nothing but two old pressure ridges that had been formed in those far-off days when the mighty mass of ice had pushed on with awful force without meeting hindrance or resistance, until at this spot it met a superior power that clove and splintered it, and set a bound to its further advance. It must have been a frightful collision, like the end of a world. But now it was over: peace – an air of infinite peace lay over it all. Nelson and Rönniken were only two pensioned veterans. Regarded as pressure ridges they were huge, raising their highest summits over 100 feet in the air. Here in the valley the surface round Nelson was quite filled up, while Rönniken still showed a deep scar – a fissure or hollow. We approached it cautiously. It was not easy to see how deep it was, and whether it had an invisible connection with Nelson on the other side of the valley. But this was not the case. On a closer examination this deep cleft proved to have a solid, filled-up bottom. Between the ridges the surface was perfectly flat, and offered an excellent site for a dog-camp.

Captain Nilsen and I had worked out a kind of programme of the work to be done, and in this it was decided that the dogs should be brought on to the Barrier as quickly as possible, and there looked after by two men. We chose this place for the purpose. The old pressure ridges told the history of the spot plainly enough; we had no need to fear any kind of disturbance here. The site had the additional advantage that we could see the ship from it, and would always be in communication with those on board.

From here the valley turned slightly to the south. After having marked the spot where our first tent was to be set up, we continued our investigations. The valley sloped gradually upwards, and reached the ridge at a height of 100 feet. From this elevation we had an excellent view over the valley we had been following, and all the other surroundings. On the north the Barrier extended, level and straight, apparently without interruption, and ended on the west in the steep descent of Cape Man's Head, which formed the eastern limit of the inner part of the Bay of Whales, and afforded a snug little corner, where we had found room for our ship. There lay the whole of the inner part of the bay, bounded on all sides by ice, ice and nothing but ice-Barrier as far as we could see, white and blue. This spot would no doubt show a surprising play of colour later on; it promised well in this way.

The ridge we were standing on was not broad – about two hundred yards, I think – and in many places it was swept quite bare by the wind, showing the blue ice itself. We passed over it and made for the pass of Thermopylae, which extended in a southerly direction from the ridge and after a very slight descent was merged in a great plain, surrounded by elevations on all sides – a basin, in fact. The bare ridge we passed over to descend into the basin was a good deal broken up; but the fissures were narrow, and almost entirely filled up again with drift, so that they were not dangerous. The basin gave us the impression of being sheltered and cosy, and, above all, it looked safe and secure. This stretch of ice was – with the exception of a few quite small hummocks of the shape of haycocks – perfectly flat and free from crevasses.

We crossed it, and went up on the ridge that rose very gently on the south. From the top of this all was flat and even as far as we could see; but that was not saying much. For a little while we continued along the ridge in an easterly direction without finding any place that was specially suited for our purpose. Our thoughts returned to the basin as the best sheltered place we had seen.

From the height we were now on, we could look down into the south-eastern part of the Bay of Whales. In contrast to that part of the ice-foot to which we had made fast, the inner bay seemed to consist of ice that had been forced up by pressure. But we had to leave a closer examination of this part till later. We all liked the basin, and agreed to choose it as our future abode, And so we turned and went back again. It did not take long to reach the plain in our own tracks.

On making a thorough examination of the surface and discussing the various possibilities, we came to the conclusion that a site for the hut was to be looked for on the little elevation that rose to the east. It seemed that we should be more snug there than anywhere else, and we were not mistaken. We soon made up our minds that we had chosen the best place the Barrier had to offer. On the spot where the hut was to stand we set up another ski-pole, and then went home.

The good news that we had already found a favourable place for the hut naturally caused great satisfaction on all sides. Everyone had been silently dreading the long and troublesome transport over the Ice Barrier.

There was teeming life on the ice. Wherever we turned we saw great herds of seals – Weddells and crab-eaters. The great sea-leopard, which we had seen occasionally on the floes, was not to be found here. During our whole stay in the Bay of Whales we did not see a single specimen of it. Nor did we ever see the Ross seal. Penguins had not shown themselves particularly often, only a few here and there; but we appreciated them all the more. The few we saw were almost all Adélie penguins. While we were at work making the ship fast, a flock of them suddenly shot up out of the water and on to the ice. They looked about them in surprise for a moment: men and ships do not come their way every day. But it seemed as if their astonishment soon gave way to a desire to see what was happening. They positively sat and studied all our movements. Only now and then they grunted a little and took a turn over the ice. What specially interested them was evidently our work at digging holes in the snow for the grapnels. They flocked about the men who were engaged in this, laid their heads on one side, and looked as if they found it immensely interesting. They did not appear to be the least afraid of us, and for the most part we left them in peace. But some of them had to lose their lives; we wanted them for our collection.

An exciting seal-hunt took place the same day. Three crab-eaters had ventured to approach the ship, and were marked down to increase our store of fresh meat. We picked two mighty hunters to secure the prey for us; they approached with the greatest caution, though this was altogether unnecessary, for the seals lay perfectly motionless. They crept forward in Indian fashion, with their heads down and their backs bent. This looks fine; I chuckle and laugh, but still with a certain decorum. Then there is a report. Two of the sleeping seals give a little spasm, and do not move again. It is otherwise with the third. With snakelike movements it wriggles away through the loose snow with surprising speed. It is no longer target practice, but hunting real game, and the result is in keeping with it. Bang! bang! and bang again. It is a good thing we have plenty of ammunition. One of the hunters uses up all his cartridges and has to go back, but the other sets off in pursuit of the game. Oh, how I laughed! Decorum was no longer possible; I simply shook with laughter. Away they went through the loose snow, the seal first and the hunter after. I could see by the movements of the pursuer that he was furious. He saw that he was in for something which he could not come out of with dignity. The seal made off at such a pace that it filled the air with snow. Although the snow was fairly deep and loose, the seal kept on the surface. Not so the hunter: he sank over the knees at every step, and in a short time was completely outdistanced. From time to time he halted, aimed, and fired. He himself afterwards asserted that every shot had hit. I had my doubts. In any case the seal seemed to take no notice of them, for it went on with undiminished speed. At last the mighty man gave up and turned back. "Beastly hard to kill," I heard him say, as he came on board. I suppressed a smile – did not want to hurt the fellow's feelings.

What an evening! The sun is high in the heavens in spite of the late hour. Over all this mountainous land of ice, over the mighty Barrier running south, there lies a bright, white, shining light, so intense that it dazzles the eyes. But northward lies the night. Leaden grey upon the sea, it passes into deep blue as the eye is raised, and pales by degrees until it is swallowed up in the radiant gleam from the Barrier. What lies behind the night – that smoke-black mass – we know. That part we have explored, and have come off victorious. But what does the dazzling day to the south conceal? Inviting and attractive the fair one lies before us. Yes, we hear you calling, and we shall come. You shall have your kiss, if we pay for it with our lives.

The following day – Sunday – brought the same fine weather. Of course, there could now be no thought of Sunday for us. Not one of us would have cared to spend the day in idleness. We were now divided into two parties: the sea party and the land party. The sea party – ten men – took over the *Fram*, while on this day the land party took up their abode on the Barrier for a year or two, or whatever it might be. The sea party was composed of Nilsen, Gjertsen, Beck, Sundbeck, Ludvig Hansen, Kristensen, Rönne, Nödtvedt, Kutschin, and Olsen. The land party consisted of Prestrud, Johansen, Helmer Hanssen, Hassel, Bjaaland, Stubberud, Lindström, and myself. Lindström was to stay on board for a few days longer, as we still had to take most of our meals on the ship. The plan was that one party, composed of six men, should camp in a sixteen-man tent in the space between Rönniken and Nelson, while another party of two were to live in a tent up at the but site and build the hut. The two last were, of course, our capable carpenters, Bjaaland and Stubberud.

By eleven o'clock in the morning we were at last ready to start. We had one sledge, eight dogs and provisions and equipment weighing altogether 660 pounds. It was my team that was to open the ball. The sea party had all collected on deck to witness the first start. All was now ready; after countless efforts on our part, or, if it is preferred, after a thorough thrashing for every dog, we had at last got them in a line before the sledge in Alaska harness. With a flourish and a crack of the whip we set off. I glanced at the ship. Yes; as I thought – all our comrades were standing in a row, admiring the fine start. I am not quite sure that I did not hold my head rather high and look round with a certain air of triumph. If I did so, it was foolish of me. I ought to have waited; the defeat would have been easier to bear. For defeat it was, and a signal one. The dogs had spent half a year in lying about and eating and drinking, and had got the impression that they would never have anything else to do. Not one of them appeared to understand that a new era of toil had begun. After moving forward a few yards, they all sat down, as though at a word of command, and stared at each other. The most undisguised astonishment could be read in their faces. When at last we had succeeded, with another dose of the whip, in making them understand that we really asked them to work, instead of doing as they were told they flew at each other in a furious scrimmage. Heaven help me! what work we had with those eight dogs that day! If it was going to be like this on the way to the Pole, I calculated in the midst of the tumult that it would take exactly a year to get there, without counting the return journey. During all this confusion I stole another glance at the ship, but the sight that met me made me quickly withdraw my eyes again. They were simply shrieking with laughter, and loud shouts of the most infamous encouragement reached us. "If you go on like that, you'll get there by Christmas," or, "Well done! stick to it. Now you're off." We were stuck faster than ever. Things looked desperate. At last, with the combined strength of all the animals and men, we got the sledge to move again.

So our first sledge trip could not be called a triumph. We then set up our first tent on the Barrier, between Mounts Nelson and

Rönniken – a large, strong tent for sixteen men, with the sheet for the floor sewed on. Round the tent wire ropes were stretched in a triangle, fifty yards on each side. To these the dogs were to be tethered. The tent was furnished with five sleeping-bags and a quantity of provisions. The distance we had come was 1.2 geographical miles, or 2.2 kilometres, measured by sledge-meter. After finishing this work, we went on up to the site selected for the station. Here we set up the tent – a similar tent to the other, for sixteen men – for the use of the carpenters, and marked out the hut site. According to the lie of the ground we elected to make the house face east and west, and not north and south, as one might have been tempted to do, since it was usually supposed that the most frequent and violent winds came from the south. We chose rightly. The prevailing wind was from the east, and thus caught our house on its most protected short wall. The door faced west. When this work was done, we marked out the way from here to the encampment below and thence to the vessel with dark flags at every fifteen paces. In this way we should be able to drive with certainty from one place to another without losing time if a storm should set in. The distance from the hut site to the vessel was 2.2 geographical miles, or 4 kilometres. On Monday, January 16, work began in earnest. About eighty dogs – six teams – drove up to the first encampment with all the provisions and equipment that could be loaded on the sledges, and twenty dogs – Stubberud's and Bjaaland's teams – went with a full load up to the other camp. We had some work indeed, those first days, to get the dogs to obey us. Time after time they tried to take the command from their masters and steer their own course. More than once it cost us a wet shirt to convince them that we really were the masters. It was strenuous work, but it succeeded in the end. Poor dogs! they got plenty of thrashing in those days. Our hours were long; we seldom turned in before eleven at night, and were up again at five. But it did not seem particularly hard; we were all alike eager for the work to be finished as soon as possible, so that the *Fram* might get away. The harbour arrangements were not of the best. The quay she was moored to suddenly broke in pieces, and all hands had to turn out to make her fast to a new quay. Perhaps they had just got to sleep again when the same operation had to be repeated; for the ice broke time after time, and kept the unfortunate "sea-rovers" in constant activity. It is enervating work being always at one's post, and sleeping with one eye open. They had a hard time to contend with, our ten comrades, and the calm way in which they took everything was extraordinary. They were always in a good humour, and always had a joke ready. It was the duty of the sea party to bring up all the provisions and outfit for the wintering party from the hold, and put them on the ice. Then the land party removed them. This work proceeded very smoothly, and it was rare that one party had to wait for the other. During the first few days of sledging all the members of the land party became quite hoarse, some of them so badly that they almost lost their voices. This came from the continual yelling and shouting that we had to do at first to make the dogs go. But this gave the sea party a welcome opportunity of finding us a nickname; we were called "the chatterers."

Apart from the unpleasantness of constantly changing the anchorage, on account of the breaking up and drifting out of the ice, the harbour must in other respects be regarded as very good. A little swell might set in from time to time and cause some disagreeable bumping, but never anything to embarrass the vessel. One very great advantage was that the currents in this corner always set outward, and thus kept off all icebergs. The sledging between the ship and the Barrier was done by five men to begin with, as the carpenters were engaged in building the house. One man had also to be told off as tent guard, for we could not use more than half our teams – six dogs – at a time. If we harnessed the full team of twelve, we only had trouble and fights. The dogs which were thus left behind had to be looked after, and a man was required for this duty. Another of the duties of the tent guard was to cook the day's food and keep the tent tidy. It was a coveted position, and lots were cast for it. It gave a little variety in the continual sledging.

On January 17 the carpenters began to dig the foundations of the house. The effect of all we had heard about the Antarctic storms was that we decided to take every possible precaution to make the house stand on an even keel. The carpenters therefore began by digging a foundation 4 feet down into the Barrier. This was not easy work; 2 feet below the surface they came upon hard, smooth ice, and had to use pickaxes. The same day a stiff easterly breeze sprang up, whirling the snow high into the air, and filling up the foundations as fast as the men dug them. But it would take more than that to stop those fellows in their work. They built a wind-screen of planks, and did it so well that they were able to work all day, unhindered by drifts, until, when evening came, they had the whole foundation dug out. There is no difficulty in doing good work when one has such people to work for one. The stormy weather interfered somewhat with our sledging, and as we found our Alaska harness unsuitable to the conditions, we went on board and began the preparation of Greenland harness for our dogs. All hands worked at it. Our excellent sailmaker, Rönne, sewed forty-six sets of harness in the course of the month. The rest of us spliced the ropes and made the necessary tackles, while others spliced wire-rope shafts to our sledges. When evening came we had an entirely new set of tackle for all our sledges and dogs. This was very successful, and in a few days the whole was working smoothly.

We had now divided ourselves between the two tents, so that five men slept in the lower tent, while the two carpenters and I inhabited the upper one. That evening a rather amusing thing happened to us. We were just turning in when suddenly we heard a penguin's cry immediately outside the tent. We were out in a moment. There, a few yards from the door, sat a big Emperor penguin, making bow after bow. It gave exactly the impression of having come up simply to pay us its respects. We were sorry to repay its attention so poorly, but such is the way of the world. With a final bow it ended its days in the frying-pan.

On January 18 we began bringing up the materials for the hut, and as soon as they arrived the builders began to put them up. It is no exaggeration to say that everything went like a well-oiled machine. One sledge after another drove up to the site and discharged its load. The dogs worked splendidly, and their drivers no less, and as fast as the materials arrived our future home rose into the air. All the parts had been marked before leaving Norway, and were now discharged from the ship in the order in which they were wanted. Besides which, Stubberud himself had built the house, so that he knew every peg of it. It is with gladness and pride that I look back upon those days. With gladness, because no discord was ever heard in the course of this fairly severe labour; with pride, because I was at the head of such a body of men. For men they were, in the true sense of the word. Everyone knew his duty, and did it.

During the night the wind dropped and the morning brought the finest weather, calm and clear. It was a pleasure to work on days like this. Both men and dogs were in the best of spirits. On these journeys between the ship and the station we were constantly hunting seals, but we only took those that came in our way. We never had to go far to find fresh meat. We used to come suddenly upon a herd of them; they were then shot, flayed, and loaded on the sledges with the provisions and building materials. The dogs feasted in those days – they had as much warm flesh as they wanted.

On January 20 we had taken up all the building materials, and could then turn our attention to provisions and stores. The work went merrily, backwards and forwards, and the journey to the *Fram* in the morning with empty sledges was specially enjoyable. The track was now well worn and hard, and resembled a good Norwegian country road more than anything else. The going was splendid. On coming out of the tent at six o'clock in the morning one was instantly greeted with joy by one's own twelve dogs. They barked and howled in emulation, tugged and jerked at their chains to get to their master, and jumped and danced about with joy. Then one would first go down the line and say "Good-morning" to each of them in turn, patting them and saying a few words. Splendid beasts they were. The one who was taken notice of showed every sign of happiness. The most petted of our domestic dogs could not have shown greater devotion than these tamed wolves. All the time the others were yelling and pulling at their chains to get at the one who was being petted, for they are jealous in the extreme. When they had all received their share of attention the harness was brought out, and then the jubilation broke out afresh. Strange as it may seem, I can assert that these animals love their harness. Although they must know that it means hard work, they all show signs of the greatest rapture at the sight of it. I must hasten to add, however, that this only happens at home. Long and fatiguing sledge journeys show a very different state of things. When it came to harnessing, the first trouble of the day began. It was impossible to get them to stand still. The full meal of the previous evening, followed by the night's rest, had given them such a superabundance of energy and joy of life that nothing could make them stand still. They had to have a taste of the whip, and yet it was a pity to start that. After having securely anchored the sledge, one was ready at last with one's team of six dogs harnessed. Now it might be thought that all was plain sailing and that one had only to cast off one's moorings and be taken straight down to the ship. But that was far from being the case. Round about the camp a number of objects had collected in a short time, such as packing-cases, building materials, empty sledges, etc., and to steer clear of these was the great problem of the morning. The dogs' greatest interest was, of course, concentrated upon these objects, and one had to be extremely lucky to avoid a spill.

Let us follow one of these morning drives. The men are all ready and have their dogs well harnessed. One, two, three, and we let them all go at once. We are off like the wind, and before one has time to swing the whip one finds oneself in the middle of a heap of building materials. The dogs have achieved the desire of their lives – to be able to make a thorough investigation of these materials in the way that is so characteristic of the dog and so incomprehensible to us. While this process is going on with the greatest enjoyment, the driver has got clear of the sledge and begins to distentangle the traces, which have wound themselves round planks and posts and whatever else maybe lying handy. He is far from having achieved the desire of his life – to judge from the expressions he uses. At last he is clear again. He looks round first and finds he is not the only one who has met with difficulties in the way. Over there among the cases he sees a performance going on which makes his heart leap with joy. One of the old hands has come to grief, and in so decisive a fashion that it will take him a long time to get clear again. With a triumphant smile he throws himself on the sledge and drives off. So long as he is on the Barrier as a rule everything goes well; there is nothing here to distract the dogs. It is otherwise when he comes down to the sea-ice. Here seals lie scattered about in groups basking in the sunshine, and it may easily happen that his course will be rather crooked. If a team of fresh dogs have made up their minds to turn aside in the direction of a herd of seals, it takes a very experienced driver to get them in the right way again. Personally, on such occasions, I used the only remedy I could see – namely, capsizing the sledge. In loose snow with the sledge upset they soon pulled up. Then, if one was wise, one put them on the right course again quietly and calmly, hoisted the sledge on to an even keel, and went on. But one is not always wise, unfortunately. The desire to be revenged on the disobedient rascals gets the upper hand, and one begins to deal out punishment. But this is not so easy as it seems. So long as you are sitting on the capsized sledge it makes a good anchor, but now – without a load – it is no use, and the dogs know that. So while you are thrashing one the others start off, and the result is not always flattering to the driver. If he is lucky he gets on to the capsized sledge again, but we have seen dogs and sledges arrive without drivers. All this trouble in the early morning sets the blood in active circulation, and one arrives at the ship drenched with perspiration, in spite of a temperature of -5°F. But it sometimes happens that there is no interruption, and then the drive is soon over. The dogs want no encouragement; they are willing enough. The mile and a quarter from the lower camp to the *Fram* is then covered in a few minutes.

When we came out of the tent on the morning of January 21 we were greatly surprised. We thought we must be mistaken, rubbed our eyes, opened them wider; but no, it was no good. The *Fram* was no longer to be seen. It had been blowing pretty strongly during the night, with snow-squalls. Presumably the weather had forced them to put out. We could also hear the roar of the sea dashing against the Barrier. Meanwhile we lost no time. The day before Captain Nilsen and Kristensen had shot forty seals, and of these we had brought in half the same day. We now began to fetch in the rest. During the forenoon, while we were flaying and shooting seals, we heard the old, well-known sound – put, put, put – of the *Fram*'s motor, and presently the crow's-nest appeared above the Barrier. But she did not get into her old berth before evening. A heavy swell had forced her to go outside.

Meanwhile the carpenters were busily constructing the hut. By January 21 the roof was on, and the rest of the work could thus be done under cover. This was a great comfort to the men; at that time their job was undoubtedly the worst of any. Bitterly cold it was for them, but I never heard them talk about it. When I came up to the tent after the day's work, one of them was busy cooking. The meal always consisted of pancakes and pitch-black, strong coffee. How good it tasted! A rivalry soon arose between the two cook-carpenters as to which of them could make the best pancakes. I think they were both clever at it. In the morning we had pancakes again – crisp, hot, delicate pancakes, with the most glorious coffee – before I was even out of my sleeping-bag. That is what the carpenters had to offer me at five o'clock in the morning. No wonder I enjoyed their society. Nor did the men in the lower camp suffer any privation. Wisting showed himself to be possessed of eminent talents as cook for the day. His special dish was penguins and skua gulls in cream sauce. It was served under the name of ptarmigan, of which it really reminded one.

That Sunday we all went on board – with the exception of the necessary tent guards for both camps – and enjoyed life. We had worked hard enough that week.

On Monday, January 23, we began to carry up the provisions. In order to save time, we had decided not to bring the provisions right up to the hut, but to store them for the time being on an elevation that lay on the other side, to the south of Mount Nelson. This spot was not more than 600 yards from the hut, but as the surface was rather rough here, we should save a good deal in the long-run. Afterwards when the *Fram* had sailed, we could take them the rest of the way. As it turned out, we never had time for this, so that our main store remained here. Sledging up to this point offered some difficulties at first. The dogs, who were accustomed to take the road to the lower camp – between Nelson and Rönniken – could not understand why they might not do the same now. The journey with empty sledges down to the ship was often particularly troublesome. From this point the dogs could hear their companions on the other side of Nelson in the lower camp, and then it happened more than once that the dogs took command. If they once got in the humour for playing tricks of that sort, it was by no means easy to get them under control. We all of us had this experience without exception. Not one of us escaped this little extra turn. As the provisions came up each driver took them off his sledge, and laid the cases in the order in which they should lie. We began by placing each sort by itself in small groups over the slope. This plan had the advantage that everything would be easy to find. The load was usually 660 pounds, or 6 cases to each sledge. We had about 900 cases to bring up, and reckoned that we should have them all in place in the course of a week. Everything went remarkably well according to our reckoning.

By noon on Saturday, January 28, the hut was ready, and all the 900 cases were in place. The depot of provisions had quite an imposing appearance. Great rows of cases stood in the snow, all with their numbers outward, so that we could find what we wanted at once. And there was the house, all finished, exactly as it had stood in its native place on Bundefjord. But it would be difficult to imagine more different surroundings: there, green pinewoods and splashing water; here, ice, nothing but ice. But both scenes were beautiful; I stood thinking which I preferred. My thoughts travelled far – thousands of miles in a second. It was the forest that gained the day.

As I have already mentioned, we had everything with us for fastening the but down to the Barrier, but the calm weather we had had all the time led us to suppose that the conditions would not be so bad as we had expected. We were therefore satisfied with the foundation dug in the Barrier. The outside of the but was tarred, and the roof covered with tarred paper, so that it was very visible against the white surroundings. That afternoon we broke up both camps, and moved into our home, "Framheim." What a snug, cosy, and cleanly impression it gave us when we entered the door! Bright, new linoleum everywhere – in the kitchen as well as in our living-room. We had good reason to be happy. Another important point had been got over, and in much shorter time than I had ever hoped. Our path to the goal was opening up; we began to have a glimpse of the castle in the distance. The Beauty is still sleeping, but the kiss is coming, the kiss that shall wake her!

It was a happy party that assembled in the hut the first evening, and drank to the future to the music of the gramophone. All the full-grown dogs were now brought up here, and were fastened to wire ropes stretched in a square, 50 yards on each side. It may be believed that they gave us some music. Collected as they were, they performed under the leadership of some great singer or other daily, and, what was worse, nightly concerts. Strange beasts! what can they have meant by this howling? One began, then two, then a few more, and, finally, the whole hundred. As a rule, during a concert like this they sit well down, stretch their heads as high in the air as they can, and howl to their hearts' content. During this act they seem very preoccupied, and are not easily disturbed. But the strangest thing is the way the concert comes to an end. It stops suddenly along the whole line – no stragglers, no "one cheer more." What is it that imposes this simultaneous stop? I have observed and studied it time after time without result. One would think it was a song that had been learnt. Do these animals possess a power of communicating with each other? The question is extraordinarily interesting. No one among us, who has had long acquaintance with Eskimo dogs, doubts that they have this power. I learned at last to understand their different sounds so well that I could tell by their voices what was going on without seeing them. Fighting, play, love-making, etc., each had its special sound. If they wanted to express their devotion and affection for their master, they would do it in a quite different way. If one of them was doing something wrong – something they knew they were not allowed to do, such as breaking into a meat-store, for example – the others, who could not get in, ran out and gave vent to a sound quite different from those I have mentioned. I believe most of us learned to distinguish these different sounds. There can hardly be a more interesting animal to observe, or one that offers greater variety of study, than the Eskimo dog. From his ancestor the wolf he has inherited the instinct of self-preservation – the right of the stronger – in a far higher degree than our domestic dog. The struggle for life has brought him to early maturity, and given him such qualities as frugality and endurance in an altogether surprising degree. His intelligence is sharp, clear, and well developed for the work he is born to, and the conditions in which he is brought up. We must not call the Eskimo dog slow to learn because he cannot sit up and take sugar when he is told; these are things so widely separated from the serious business of his life that he will never be able to understand them, or only with great difficulty. Among themselves the right of the stronger is the only law. The strongest rules, and does as he pleases undisputedly; everything belongs to him. The weaker ones get the crumbs. Friendship easily springs up between these animals – always combined with respect and fear of the stronger. The weaker, with his instinct of self-preservation, seeks the protection of the stronger. The stronger accepts the position of protector, and thereby secures a trusty helper, always with the thought of one stronger than himself. The instinct of self-preservation is to be found everywhere, and it is so, too, with their relations with man. The dog has learnt to value man as his benefactor, from whom he receives everything necessary for his support. Affection and devotion seem also to have their part in these relations, but no doubt on a closer examination the instinct of self-preservation is at the root of all. As a consequence of this, his respect for his master is far greater than in our domestic dog, with whom respect only exists as a consequence of the fear of a beating. I could without hesitation take the food out of the mouth of any one of my twelve dogs; not one of them would attempt to bite me. And why? Because their respect, as a consequence of the fear of getting nothing next time, was predominant. With my dogs at home I certainly should not try the same thing. They would at once defend their food, and, if necessary, they would not shrink from using their teeth; and this in spite of the fact that these dogs have to all appearance the same respect as the others. What, then, is the reason? It is that this respect is not based on a serious foundation – the instinct of self-preservation – but simply on the fear of a hiding. A case like this proves that the foundation is too weak; the desire of food overcomes the fear of the stick, and the result is a snap.

A few days later the last member of the wintering party – Adolf Henrik Lindström – joined us, and with his arrival our arrangements might be regarded as complete. He had stayed on board hitherto, attending to the cooking there, but now he was no longer necessary. His art would be more appreciated among the "chatterers." The youngest member of the expedition – the cook Karinius Olsen – took over from that day the whole of the cooking on the *Fram,* and performed this work in an extremely conscientious and capable way until the ship reached Hobart in March, 1912, when he again had assistance. This was well done for a lad of twenty. I wish we had many like him.

With Lindström, then, the kitchen and the daily bread were in order. The smoke rose gaily from the shining black chimney, and proclaimed that now the Barrier was really inhabited. How cosy it was, when we came sledging up after the day's work, to see that smoke rising into the air. It is a little thing really, but nevertheless it means so much. With Lindström came not only food, but light and air – both of them his specialities. The Lux lamp was the first thing he rigged up, giving us a light that contributed much to the feeling of comfort and well-being through the long winter. He also provided us with air, but in this he had Stubberud as a partner. These two together managed to give us the finest, purest Barrier air in our room during the whole stay. It is true that this was not done without hard work, but they did not mind that. The ventilation was capricious, and liable to fail now and then. This usually happened when there was a dead calm. Many were the ingenious devices employed by the firm to set the business going again. Generally a Primus stove was used under the exhaust pipe, and ice applied to the supply pipe. While one of them lay on his stomach with the Primus under the exhaust, drawing the air up that way, the other ran up to the roof and dropped big lumps of snow down the supply to get the air in that way. In this fashion they could keep it going by the hour together without giving up.

It finally ended in the ventilation becoming active again without visible cause. There is no doubt that the system of ventilation in a winter-station like ours is of great importance, both to health and comfort. I have read of expeditions, the members of which were constantly suffering from cold and damp and resulting sickness. This is nothing but a consequence of bad ventilation. If the supply of fresh air is sufficient, the fuel will be turned to better account, and the production of warmth will, of course, be greater. If the supply of air is insufficient, a great part of the fuel will be lost in an unconsumed state, and cold and damp will be the result. There must, of course, be a means of regulating the ventilation in accordance with requirements. We used only the Lux lamp in our hut, besides the stove in the kitchen, and with this we kept our room so warm that those of us in the upper berths were constantly complaining of the warmth.

Originally there were places for ten bunks in the room, but as there were only nine of us, one of the bunks was removed and the space used for our chronometer locker. This contained three ordinary ship's chronometers. We had, in addition, six chronometer watches, which we wore continually, and which were compared throughout the whole winter. The meteorological instruments found a place in the kitchen – the only place we had for them. Lindström undertook the position of sub-director of the Framheim meteorological station and instrument-maker to the expedition. Under the roof were stowed all the things that would not stand severe frost, such as medicines, syrup, jam, pickles, and sauces, besides all our sledge-boxes. A place was made for the library under the roof.

The week beginning on Monday, January 30, was spent in

bringing up coal, wood, oil, and our whole supply of dried fish. The temperature this summer varied between +5° and -13°F. – a grand summer temperature. We also shot many seals daily, and we already had a great pile of about a hundred of them lying just outside the door of the hut. One evening as we were sitting at supper Lindström came in to tell us that we need not go down any more to the sea-ice to shoot them, as they were coming up to us. We went out and found he was right. Not far away, and making straight for the hut, came a crab-eater, shining like silver in the sun. He came right up, was photographed, and – shot.

One day I had a rather curious experience. My best dog, Lassesen, had his left hind-paw frozen quite white. It happened while we were all out sledging. Lassesen was a lover of freedom, and had seen his chance of getting loose when unobserved. He used his freedom, like most of these dogs, for fighting. They love fighting, and cannot resist it. He had picked a quarrel with Odin and Thor, and started a battle with them. In the course of the fight the chains that fastened these two had got wound round Lassesen's leg, and twisted so that the circulation was stopped. How long he had been standing so I do not know. But when I came, I saw at once that the dog was in the wrong place. On a closer examination I discovered the frost-bite. I then spent half an hour in restoring the circulation. I succeeded in doing this by holding the paw continuously in my warm hand. At first, while there was no feeling in the limb, it went well; but when the blood began to flow back, of course it was painful, and Lassesen became impatient. He whined, and motioned with his head towards the affected place, as though he wanted to tell me that he found the operation unpleasant. He made no attempt to snap. The paw swelled a good deal after this treatment, but next day Lassesen was as well as ever, though a little lame in that leg.

The entries in my diary at this time are all in telegraphic style, no doubt owing to the amount of work. Thus an entry in February ends with the following words: "An Emperor penguin just come on a visit – soup-kettle." He did not get a very long epitaph.

During this week we relieved the sea party of the last of the dogs – about twenty puppies. There was rejoicing on board when the last of them left the deck, and, indeed, one could not be surprised. With the thermometer about -5°F., as it had been lately, it was impossible to keep the deck clean, as everything froze at once. After they had all been brought on to the ice, the crew went to work with salt and water, and in a short time we recognized the *Fram* again. The puppies were put into boxes and driven up. We had put up a sixteen-man tent to receive them. From the very first moment they declined to stay in it, and there was nothing to be done but to let them out. All these puppies passed a great part of the winter in the open air. So long as the seals' carcasses were lying on the slope, they stayed there; afterwards they found another place. But the tent, despised by the youngsters, came in useful after all. Any bitch that was going to have a litter was put in there, and the tent went by the name of "the maternity hospital." Then one tent after another was put up, and Framheim looked quite an important place. Eight of the sixteen-man tents were set up for our eight teams, two for dried fish, one for fresh meat, one for cases of provisions, and one for coal and wood – fourteen altogether. They were arranged according to a plan drawn up beforehand, and when they were all up they had quite the appearance of a camp.

At this time our dog-harness underwent important alterations, as one of the members of the expedition had the happy idea of combining the Alaska and the Greenland harness. The result satisfied all requirements; in future we always used this construction, and we all agreed that it was much superior to any other harness. The dogs also seemed to be more comfortable in it. That they worked better and more easily is certain, and raw places, so common with Greenland harness, were absolutely unknown.

February 4 was an eventful day. As usual, we all came down to the *Fram,* driving our empty sledges, at half-past six in the morning. When the first man got to the top of the ridge, he began to wave his arms about and gesticulate like a madman. I understood, of course, that he saw something, but what? The next man gesticulated even worse, and tried to shout to me. But it was no use; I could not make anything of it. Then it was my turn to go over the ridge, and, as was natural, I began to feel rather curious. I had only a few yards more to go – and then it was explained. Along the edge of the ice, just to the south of the *Fram,* a large barque lay moored. We had talked of the possibility of meeting the *Terra Nova* – Captain Scott's vessel – when she was on her way to King Edward VII. Land; but it was a great surprise all the same. Now it was my turn to wave my arms, and I am sure I did it no worse than the two first. And the same thing was repeated with all of us, as soon as each one reached the top of the ridge. What the last man did I have never been able to find out for certain – but no doubt he waved his arms too. If a stranger had stood and watched us that morning on the ridge, he would surely have taken us for a lot of incurable lunatics. The way seemed long that day, but at last we got there and heard the full explanation. The *Terra Nova* had come in at midnight. Our watchman had just gone below for a cup of coffee – there was no harm in that – and when he came up again, there was another ship lying off the foot of the Barrier. He rubbed his eyes, pinched his leg, and tried other means of convincing himself that he was asleep, but it was no good. The pinch especially, he told us afterwards, was horribly painful, and all this led him to the conclusion that there really was a second vessel there.

Lieutenant Campbell, the leader of the eastern party, which was to explore King Edward VII. Land, came on board first, and paid Nilsen a visit. He brought the news that they had not been able to reach land, and were now on their way back to McMurdo Sound. From thence it was their intention to go to Cape North and explore the land there. Immediately after my arrival Lieutenant Campbell came on board again and gave me the news himself.

We then loaded our sledges and drove home. At nine o'clock we had the great pleasure of receiving Lieutenant Pennell, the commander of the *Terra Nova*, Lieutenant Campbell, and the surgeon of the expedition, as the first guests in our new home. We spent a couple of very agreeable hours together. Later in the day three of us paid a visit to the *Terra Nova*, and stayed on board to lunch. Our hosts were extremely kind, and offered to take our mail to New Zealand. If I had had time, I should have been glad to avail myself of this friendly offer, but every hour was precious. It was no use to think of writing now.

At two o'clock in the afternoon the *Terra Nova* cast off again, and left the Bay of Whales. We made a strange discovery after this visit. Nearly all of us had caught cold. It did not last long – only a few hours – and then it was over. The form it took was sneezing and cold in the head.

The next day – Sunday, February 5 – the "sea rovers," as we called the *Fram* party, were our guests. We had to have them in two detachments, as they could not all leave the ship at the same time. Four came to dinner and six to supper. We had not much to offer, but we invited them, not so much for the sake of the entertainment as to show them our new home and wish them a successful voyage.

CHAPTER 6

DEPOT JOURNEYS

There was now too little work for eight of us in bringing up stores from the *Fram*, and it became evident that some of us might be more usefully employed elsewhere. It was therefore decided that four men should bring ashore the little that remained, while the other four went southward to lat. 80° S., partly to explore the immediate neighbourhood, and partly to begin the transport of provisions to the south. This arrangement gave us all enough to do. The four who were to continue the work at the station – Wisting, Hassel, Stubberud, and Bjaaland – now had as much as their sledges could carry. The rest of us were busy getting ready. For that matter, everything was prepared in advance, but as yet we had had no experience of a long journey. That was what we were going to get now.

Our departure was fixed for Friday, February 10. On the 9th I went on board to say good-bye, as presumably the *Fram* would have sailed when we came back. I had so much to thank all these plucky fellows for. I knew it was hard for all of them – almost without exception – to have to leave us now, at the most interesting time, and go out to sea to battle for months with cold and darkness, ice and storms, and then have the same voyage over again the next year when they came to fetch us. It was certainly a hard task, but none of them complained. They had all promised to do their best to promote our common object, and therefore all went about their duty without grumbling. I left written orders with the commander of the *Fram*, Captain Nilsen. The substance of these orders may be given in a few words: Carry out our plan in the way you may think best. I knew the man I was giving orders to. A more capable and honourable second in command I could never have had. I knew that the *Fram* was safe in his hands.

Lieutenant Prestrud and I made a trip to the south to find a suitable place for ascending the Barrier on the other side of the bay. The sea-ice was fairly even for this distance; only a few cracks here and there. Farther up the bay there were, curiously enough, long rows of old hummocks. What could this mean? This part was really quite protected from the sea, so that these formations could not be attributed to its action. We hoped to have an opportunity of investigating the conditions more closely later on; there was no time for it now. The shortest and most direct way to the south was the one we were on now. The bay was not wide here. The distance from Framheim to this part of the Barrier was about three miles. The ascent of the Barrier was not difficult; with the exception of a few fissures it was quite easy. It did not take long to get up, except perhaps in the steepest part. The height was 60 feet. It was quite exciting to go up; what should we see at the top? We had never yet had a real uninterrupted view over the Barrier to the south; this was the first time. As it happened, we were not surprised at what we saw when we got up – an endless plain, that was lost in the horizon on the extreme south. Our course, we could see, would take us just along the side of the ridge before mentioned – a capital mark for later journeys. The going was excellent; a thin layer of conveniently loose snow was spread over a hard under-surface, and made it very suitable for skiing. The lie of the ground told us at once that we had the right pattern of skis – the kind for level ground, long and narrow. We had found what we wanted – an ascent for our southern journeys and an open road. This spot was afterwards marked with a flag, and went by the name of "the starting-place." On the way back, as on the way out, we passed large herds of seals, lying asleep. They did not take the least notice of us. If we went up and woke them, they just raised their heads a little, looked at us for a moment, and then rolled over on the other side and went to sleep again. It was very evident that these animals here on the ice have no enemies. They would certainly have set a watch, as their brothers in the North do, if they had had anything to fear.

On this day we used skin clothing for the first time – reindeer-skin clothes of Eskimo cut – but they proved to be too warm. We had the same experience later. In low temperatures these reindeer clothes are beyond comparison the best, but here in the South we did not as a rule have low temperatures on our sledge journeys. On the few occasions when we experienced any cold worth talking about, we were always in skins. When we returned in the evening after our reconnoitring, we had no need of a Turkish bath.

On February 10, at 9.30 a.m., the first expedition left for the South. We were four men, with three sledges and eighteen dogs, six for each sledge. The load amounted to about 550 pounds of provisions per sledge, besides the provisions and outfit for the journey. We could not tell, even approximately, how long the journey would take, as everything was unknown. The chief thing we took on our sledges was dogs' pemmican for the depot, 350 pounds per sledge. We also took a quantity of seal meat cut into steaks, blubber, dried fish, chocolate, margarine, and biscuits. We had ten long bamboo poles, with black flags, to mark the way. The rest of our outfit consisted of two three-man tents, four one-man sleeping-bags, and the necessary cooking utensils.

The dogs were very willing, and we left Framheim at full gallop. Along the Barrier we went well. Going down to the sea-ice we had to pass through a number of big hummocks – a fairly rough surface. Nor was this without consequences; first one sledge, then another, swung round. But no harm was done; we got our gear tested, and that is always an advantage. We also had to pass rather near several large groups of seals, and the temptation was too great. Away went the dogs to one side in full gallop towards the seals. But this time the load was heavy, and they were soon tired of the extra work. In the bay we were in sight of the *Fram*. The ice had now given way entirely, so that she lay close to the Barrier itself. Our four comrades, who were to stay at home, accompanied us. In the first place, they wanted to see us on our way, and in the second, they would be able to lend us a hand in getting up the Barrier, for we were rather apprehensive that it would cost us a wet shirt. Finally, they were to hunt seals. There was plenty of opportunity here; where-ever one looked there were seals – fat heavy beasts.

I had put the home party under Wisting's command, and given them enough work to do. They were to bring up the remainder of the stores from the ship, and to build a large, roomy pent-house against the western wall of the hut, so that we should not have to go directly on to the ice from the kitchen. We also intended to use this as a carpenter's workshop. But they were not to forget the seal-hunting, early and late. It was important to us to get seals enough to enable us all, men and dogs, to live in plenty. And there were enough to be had. If we ran short of fresh meat in the course of the winter, it would be entirely our own fault.

It was a good thing we had help for the climb. Short as it was, it caused us a good deal of trouble; but we had dogs enough, and by harnessing a sufficient number we got the sledges up. I should like to know what they thought on board. They could see we were already hard put to it to get up here. What would it be like when we had to get on to the plateau? I do not know whether they thought of the old saying: Practice makes perfect.

We halted at the starting-place, where we were to separate from our comrades. None of us was particularly sentimental. An honest shake of the hand, and so "Good-bye." The order of our march was as follows: Prestrud first on skis, to show the direction and encourage the dogs. We always went better with someone going in front. Next came Helmer Hanssen. He kept this place on all our journeys – the leading sledge. I knew him well from our previous work together, and regarded him as the most efficient dog-driver I had met. He carried the standard compass on his sledge and checked Prestrud's direction. After him came Johansen, also with a compass. Lastly, I came, with sledge-meter and compass. I preferred to take the last sledge because it enabled me to see what was happening. However careful one may be, it is impossible to avoid dropping things from sledges in making a journey. If the last man keeps a lookout for such things, great inconvenience may often be avoided. I could mention many rather important things that were dropped in the course of our journeys and picked up again by the last man. The hardest work, of course, falls on the first man. He has to open up the road and drive his dogs forward, while we others have only to follow. All honour, then, to the man who performed this task from the first day to the last – Helmer Hanssen.

The position of the "forerunner" is not a very enviable one either. Of course he escapes all bother with dogs, but it is confoundedly tedious to walk there alone, staring at nothing. His only diversion is a shout from the leading sledge: "A little to the right," "A little to the left." It is not so much these simple words that divert him as the tone in which they are called. Now and then the cry comes in a way that makes him feel he is acquitting himself well. But sometimes it sends a cold shiver down his back; the speaker might just as well have added the word "Duffer!" – there is no mistaking his tone. It is no easy matter to go straight on a surface without landmarks. Imagine an immense plain that you have to cross in thick fog; it is dead calm, and the snow lies evenly, without drifts. What would you do? An Eskimo can manage it, but none of us. We should turn to the right or to the left, and give the leading dog-driver with the standard compass endless trouble. It is strange how this affects the mind. Although the man with the compass knows quite well that the man in front cannot do any better, and although he knows that he could not do better himself, he nevertheless gets irritated in time and works himself into the belief that the unsuspecting, perfectly innocent leader only takes these turns to annoy him; and so, as I have said, the words "A little to the left" imply the unspoken addition – perfectly understood on both sides – "Duffer!" I have personal experience of both duties. With the dog-driver time passes far more quickly. He has his dogs to look after, and has to see that all are working and none shirking. Many other points about a team claim his attention, and he must always keep an eye on the sledge itself. If he does not do this, some slight unevenness may throw the runners in the air before he knows where he is. And to right a capsized sledge, weighing about eight hundredweight, is no fun. So, instead of running this risk, he gives his whole attention to what is before him.

From the starting-place the Barrier rises very slightly, until at a cross-ridge it passes into the perfect level. Here on the ridge we halt once more. Our comrades have disappeared and gone to their work, but in the distance the *Fram* lies, framed in shining, blue-white ice. We are but human; uncertainty always limits our prospect. Shall we meet again? And if so, under what conditions? Much lay between that moment and the next time we should see her. The mighty ocean on one side, and the unknown region of ice on the other; so many things might happen. Her flag floats out, waves us a last adieu, and disappears. We are on our way to the South.

This first inland trip on the Barrier was undeniably exciting. The ground was absolutely unknown, and our outfit untried. What kind of country should we have to deal with? Would it continue in this boundless plain without hindrance of any kind? Or would Nature present insurmountable difficulties? Were we right in supposing that dogs were the best means of transport in these regions, or should we have done better to take reindeer, ponies, motor-cars, aeroplanes, or anything else? We went forward at a rattling pace; the going was perfect. The dogs' feet trod on a thin layer of loose snow, just enough to give them a secure hold.

The weather conditions were not quite what we should have wished in an unknown country. It is true that it was calm and mild, and altogether pleasant for travelling, but the light was not good. A grey haze, the most unpleasant kind of light after fog, lay upon the landscape, making the Barrier and the sky merge into one. There was no horizon to be seen. This grey haze, presumably a younger sister of fog, is extremely disagreeable. One can never be certain of one's surroundings. There are no shadows; everything looks the same. In a light like this it is a bad thing to be the forerunner; he does not see the inequalities of the ground until too late – until he is right on them. This often ends in a fall, or in desperate efforts to keep on his feet. It is better for the drivers, they can steady themselves with a hand on the sledge. But they also have to be on the lookout for inequalities, and see that the sledges do not capsize. This light is also very trying to the eyes, and one often hears of snow-blindness after such a day. The cause of this is not only that one strains one's eyes continually; it is also brought about by carelessness. One is very apt to push one's snow-goggles up on to one's forehead, especially if they are fitted with dark glasses. However, we always came through it very well; only a few of us had a little touch of this unpleasant complaint. Curiously enough, snow-blindness has something in common with seasickness. If you ask a man whether he is seasick, in nine cases out of ten he will answer:

"No, not at all – only a little queer in the stomach." It is the same, in a slightly different way, with snow-blindness. If a man comes into the tent in the evening with an inflamed eye and you ask him whether he is snow-blind, you may be sure he will be almost offended. "Snow-blind? Is it likely? No, not at all, only a little queer about the eye."

We did seventeen miles that day without exertion. We had two tents, and slept two in a tent. These tents were made for three men, but were too small for four. Cooking was only done in one, both for the sake of economy, so that we might leave more at the depot, and because it was unnecessary, as the weather was still quite mild.

On this first trip, as on all the depot journeys, our morning arrangements took far too long. We began to get ready at four, but were not on the road till nearly eight. I was always trying some means of remedying this, but without success. It will naturally be asked, What could be the cause of this? and I will answer candidly – it was dawdling and nothing else. On these depot journeys it did not matter so much, but on the main journey we had to banish dawdling relentlessly.

Next day we did the allotted seventeen miles in six hours, and pitched our camp early in the afternoon. The dogs were rather tired, as it had been uphill work all day. To-day, from a distance of twenty-eight miles, we could look down into the Bay of Whales; this shows that we had ascended considerably. We estimated our camp that evening to be 500 feet above the sea. We were astonished at this rise, but ought not to have been so really, since we had already estimated this ridge at 500 feet when we first saw it from the end of the bay. But however it may be, most of us have a strong propensity for setting up theories and inventing something new. What others have seen does not interest us, and on this occasion we took the opportunity – I say we, because I was one of them – of propounding a new theory – that of an evenly advancing ice-slope from the Antarctic plateau. We saw ourselves in our mind's eye ascending gradually to the top, and thus avoiding a steep and laborious climb among the mountains.

The day had been very warm, +12.2° F., and I had been obliged to throw off everything except the most necessary underclothes. My costume may be guessed from the name I gave to the ascent – Singlet Hill. There was a thick fog when we turned out next morning, exceedingly unpleasant. Here every inch was over virgin ground, and we had to do it blindly. That day we had a feeling of going downhill. At one o'clock land was reported right ahead. From the gesticulations of those in front I made out that it must be uncommonly big. I saw absolutely nothing, but that was not very surprising. My sight is not specially good, and the land did not exist.

The fog lifted, and the surface looked a little broken. The imaginary land lasted till the next day, when we found out that it had only been a descending bank of fog. That day we put on the pace, and did twenty-five miles instead of our usual seventeen. We were very lightly clad. There could be no question of skins; they were laid aside at once. Very light wind-clothing was all we wore over our underclothes. On this journey most of us slept barelegged in the sleeping-bags. Next day we were surprised by brilliantly clear weather and a dead calm. For the first time we had a good view. Towards the south the Barrier seemed to continue, smooth and even, without ascending. Towards the east, on the other hand, there was a marked rise – presumably towards King Edward VII. Land, we thought then. In the course of the afternoon we passed the first fissure we had met with. It had apparently been filled up long ago. Our distance that day was twenty-three miles.

On these depot journeys we were always very glad of our Thermos flasks. In the middle of the day we made a halt, and took a cup of scalding hot chocolate, and it was very pleasant to be able to get one without any trouble in the middle of the snow plateau. On the final southern journey we did not take Thermos flasks. We had no lunch then.

On February 14, after a march of eleven and a half miles, we reached 80° S. Unfortunately we did not succeed in getting any astronomical observation on this trip, as the theodolite we had brought with us went wrong, but later observations on several occasions gave 79° 59' S. Not so bad in fog. We had marked out the route up to this point with bamboo poles and flags at every 15 kilometres. Now, as we had not fixed the position by astronomical observation, we found that the flags would not be sufficient, and we had to look for some other means of marking the spot. A few empty cases were broken up and gave a certain number of marks, but not nearly enough. Then our eyes fell upon a bundle of dried fish lying on one of the sledges, and our marking pegs were found. I should like to know whether any road has been marked out with dried fish before; I doubt it. Immediately on our arrival in lat. 80° – at eleven in the morning – we began to erect the depot. It was made quite solid, and was 12 feet high. The going here in 80° was quite different from what we had had all the rest of the way. Deep, loose snow everywhere gave us the impression that it must have fallen in perfectly still weather. Generally when we passed by here – but not always – we found this loose snow.

When the depot was finished and had been photographed, we threw ourselves on the sledges and began the homeward journey. It was quite a treat to sit and be drawn along, a thing that otherwise never happened. Prestrud sat with me. Hanssen drove first, but as he now had the old track to follow, he wanted no one in front. On the last sledge we had the marking pegs. Prestrud kept an eye on the sledge-meter, and sang out at every half-kilometre, while at the same time I stuck a dried fish into the snow. This method of marking the route proved a brilliant one. Not only did the dried fish show us the right way on several occasions, but they also came in very useful on the next journey, when we returned with starving dogs. That day we covered forty-three miles. We did not get to bed till one o'clock at night, but this did not prevent our being up again at four and off at half-past seven. At half-past nine in the evening we drove into Framheim, after covering sixty-two miles that day. Our reason for driving that distance was not to set up any record for the Barrier, but to get home, if possible, before the *Fram* sailed, and thus have an opportunity of once more shaking hands with our comrades and wishing them a good voyage. But as we came over the edge of the Barrier we saw that, in spite of all our pains, we had come too late. The *Fram* was not there. It gave us a strange and melancholy feeling, not easy to understand. But the next moment common sense returned, and our joy at her having got away from the Barrier undamaged after the long stay was soon uppermost. We heard that she had left the bay at noon the same day – just as we were spurting our hardest to reach her.

This depot journey was quite sufficient to tell us what the future had in store. After this we were justified in seeing it in a rosy light. We now had experience of the three important factors – the lie of the ground, the going, and the means of traction – and the result was that nothing could be better. Everything was in the most perfect order. I had always had a high opinion of the dog as a draught animal, but after this last performance my admiration for these splendid animals rose to the pitch of enthusiasm. Let us look at what my dogs accomplished on this occasion: On February 14 they went eleven miles southward with a load of 770 pounds, and on the same day thirty-two miles northward – only four of them, the "Three Musketeers" and Lassesen, as Fix and Snuppesen refused to do any work. The weight they started with from 80°S. was that of the sledge, 165 pounds; Prestrud, 176 pounds; and myself, 182 pounds. Add to this 154 pounds for sleeping-bags, ski, and dried fish, and we have a total weight of 677 pounds, or about 170 pounds per dog. The last day they did sixty-two miles. I think the dogs showed on this occasion that they were well suited for sledging on the Barrier.

In addition to this brilliant result, we arrived at several other conclusions. In the first place, the question of the long time spent in our morning preparations thrust itself on our notice: this could not be allowed to occur on the main journey. At least two hours might be saved, I had no doubt of that – but how? I should have to take time to think it over. What required most alteration was our heavy outfit. The sledges were constructed with a view to the most difficult conditions of ground. The surface here was of the easiest kind, and consequently permitted the use of the lightest outfit. We ought to be able to reduce the weight of the sledges by at least half – possibly more. Our big canvas ski-boots were found to need thorough alteration. They were too small and too stiff, and had to be made larger and softer. Foot-gear had such an important bearing on the success of the whole expedition that we had to do all that could be done to get it right.

The four who had stayed at home had accomplished a fine piece of work. Framheim was hardly recognizable with the big new addition on its western wall. This pent-house was of the same width as the hut – 13 feet – and measured about 10 feet the other way. Windows had been put in – two of them – and it looked quite bright and pleasant when one came in; but this was not to last for long. Our architects had also dug a passage, 5 feet wide, round the whole hut, and this was now covered over, simply by prolonging the sloping roof down to the snow to form a roof over this passage. On the side facing east a plank was fixed across the gable at the required height, and from this boards were brought down to the snow. The lower part of this new extension of the roof was well strengthened, as the weight of snow that would probably accumulate upon it in the course of the winter would be very great. This passage was connected with the pent-house by a side-door in the northern wall. The passage was constructed to serve as a place for storing tinned foods and fresh meat, besides which its eastern end afforded an excellent place to get snow for melting. Here Lindström could be sure of getting as much clean snow as he wanted, which was an impossibility outside the house. We had 120 dogs running about, and they were not particular as to the purpose for which we might want the snow. But here in this snow wall Lindström had no need to fear the dogs. Another great advantage was that he would not have to go out in bad weather, darkness, and cold, every time he wanted a piece of ice.

We now had to turn our attention in the first place, before the cold weather set in, to the arrangement of our dog tents. We could not leave them standing as they were on the snow; if we did so, we should soon find that dogs' teeth are just as sharp as knives; besides which, they would be draughty and cold for the animals. To counteract this, the floor of each tent was sunk 6 feet below the surface of the Barrier. A great part of this excavation had to be done with axes, as we soon came to the bare ice. One of these dog tents, when finished, had quite an important appearance, when one stood at the bottom and looked up. It measured 18 feet from the floor to the peak of the tent, and the diameter of the floor was 15 feet. Then twelve posts were driven into the ice of the floor at equal intervals round the wall of the tent, and the dogs were tethered to them. From the very first day the dogs took a liking to their quarters, and they were right, as they were well off there. I do not remember once seeing frost-rime on the coats of my dogs down in the tent. They enjoyed every advantage there – air, without draughts, light, and sufficient room. Round the tent-pole we left a pillar of snow standing in the middle of the tent to the height of a man. It took us two days to put our eight dog tents in order.

Before the *Fram* sailed one of the whale-boats had been put ashore on the Barrier. One never knew; if we found ourselves in want of a boat, it would be bad to have none, and if we did not have to use it, there was no great harm done. It was brought up on two sledges drawn by twelve dogs, and was taken some distance into the Barrier. The mast stood high in the air, and showed us its position clearly.

Besides all their other work, the four men had found time for shooting seals while we were away, and large quantities of meat were now stowed everywhere. We had to lose no time in getting ready the tent in which we stored our chief supply of seal meat. It would not have lasted long if we had left it unprotected on the ground. To keep off the dogs, we built a wall 7 feet high of large blocks of snow. The dogs themselves saw to its covering with ice, and for the time being all possibility of their reaching the meat was removed.

We did not let the floor grow old under our feet; it was time to be off again to the south with more food. Our departure was fixed for February 22, and before that time we had a great deal to do. All the provisions had first to be brought from the main depot and prepared for the journey. Then we had to open the cases of pemmican, take out the boxes in which it was soldered, four rations in each, cut these open, and put the four rations back in the case without the tin lining. By doing this we saved so much weight, and at the same time avoided the trouble of having this work to do later on in the cold. The tin packing was used for the passage through the tropics, where I was afraid the pemmican might possibly melt and run into the hold of the ship. This opening and repacking took a long time, but we got through it. We used the pent-house as a packing-shed.

Another thing that took up a good deal of our time was our

personal outfit. The question of boots was gone into thoroughly. Most of us were in favour of the big outer boots, but in a revised edition. There were a few – but extremely few – who declared for nothing but soft foot-gear. In this case it did not make so much difference, since they all knew that the big boots would have to be brought on the final journey on account of possible work on glaciers. Those, therefore, who wanted to wear soft foot-gear, and hang their boots on the sledge, might do so if they liked. I did not want to force anyone to wear boots he did not care for; it might lead to too much unpleasantness and responsibility. Everyone, therefore, might do as he pleased. Personally I was in favour of boots with stiff soles, so long as the uppers could be made soft and sufficiently large to give room for as many stockings as one wished to wear. It was a good thing the boot-maker could not look in upon us at Framheim just then – and many times afterwards, for that matter. The knife was mercilessly applied to all his beautiful work, and all the canvas, plus a quantity of the superfluous leather, was cut away. As I had no great knowledge of the shoemaker's craft, I gladly accepted Wisting's offer to operate on mine. The boots were unrecognizable when I got them back from him. As regards shape, they were perhaps just as smart before the alteration, but as that is a very unimportant matter in comparison with ease and comfort, I considered them improved by many degrees. The thick canvas was torn off and replaced by thin weather-proof fabric. Big wedges were inserted in the toes, and allowed room for several more pairs of stockings. Besides this, one of the many soles was removed, thus increasing the available space. It appeared to me that now I had foot-gear that combined all the qualities I demanded – stiff soles, on which Huitfeldt-Höyer Ellefsen ski-bindings could be used, and otherwise soft, so that the foot was not pinched anywhere. In spite of all these alterations, my boots were once more in the hands of the operator before the main journey, but then they were made perfect. The boots of all the others underwent the same transformation, and every day our outfit became more complete. A number of minor alterations in our wardrobe were also carried out. One man was an enthusiast for blinkers on his cap; another did not care for them. One put on a nose-protector; another took his off; and if there was a question of which was right, each was prepared to defend his idea to the last. These were all alterations of minor importance, but being due to individual judgment, they helped to raise the spirits and increase self-confidence. Patents for braces also became the fashion. I invented one myself, and was very proud of it for a time – indeed, I had the satisfaction of seeing it adopted by one of my rivals. But that rarely happened; each of us wanted to make his own inventions, and to be as original as possible. Any contrivance that resembled something already in use was no good. But we found, like the farmer, that the old way often turned out to be the best.

By the evening of February 21 we were again ready to start. The sledges – seven in number – stood ready packed, and were quite imposing in appearance. Tempted by the favourable outcome of our former trip, we put too much on our sledges this time – on some of them, in any case. Mine was overloaded. I had to suffer for it afterwards – or, rather, my noble animals did.

On February 22, at 8.30 a.m., the caravan moved off – eight men, seven sledges, and forty-two dogs – and the most toilsome part of our whole expedition began. As usual, we began well from Framheim. Lindström, who was to stay at home alone and look after things, did not stand and wave farewells to us. Beaming with joy, he made for the hut as soon as the last sledge was in motion. He was visibly relieved. But I knew very well that before long he would begin to take little turns outside to watch the ridge. Would they soon be coming?

There was a light breeze from the south, dead against us, and the sky was overcast. Newly fallen snow made the going heavy, and the dogs had hard work with their loads. Our former tracks were no longer visible, but we were lucky enough to find the first flag, which stood eleven miles inland. From there we followed the dried fish, which stood out sharply against the white snow and were very easy to see. We pitched our camp at six o'-clock in the evening, having come a distance of seventeen miles. Our camp was quite imposing – four tents for three men apiece, with two in each. In two of them the housekeeping arrangements were carried on. The weather had improved during the afternoon, and by evening we had the most brilliantly clear sky.

Next day the going was even heavier, and the dogs were severely tried. We did no more than twelve and a half miles after eight hours' march. The temperature remained reasonable, $+5°$ F. We had lost our dried fish, and for the last few hours were going only by compass.

February 24 began badly – a strong wind from the southeast, with thick driving snow. We could see nothing, and had to steer our course by compass. It was bitter going against the wind, although the temperature was no worse than $-0.4°$ F. We went all day without seeing any mark. The snow stopped falling about noon, and at three o'clock it cleared. As we were looking about for a place to pitch the tents, we caught sight of one of our flags. When we reached it, we found it was flag No. 5 – all our bamboos were numbered, so we knew the exact position of the flag. No. 5 was forty-four and a half miles from Framheim. This agreed well with the distance recorded – forty-four miles.

The next day was calm and clear, and the temperature began to descend, -13° F. But in spite of this lower temperature the air felt considerably milder, as it was quite still. We followed marks and fish the whole way, and at the end of our day's journey we had covered eighteen miles – a good distance for heavy going.

We then had a couple of days of bitter cold with fog, so that we did not see much of our surroundings. We followed the fish and the marks most of the way. We had already begun to find the fish useful as extra food; the dogs took it greedily. The forerunner had to take up each fish and throw it on one side; then one of the drivers went out, took it up, and put it on his sledge. If the dogs had come upon the fish standing in the snow we should soon have had fierce fights. Even now, before we reached the depot in 80° S., the dogs began to show signs of exhaustion, probably as a result of the cold weather (-16.6° F.) and the hard work. They were stiff in the legs in the morning and difficult to set going.

On February 27, at 10.30 a.m., we reached the depot in 80° S. The depot was standing as we had left it, and no snow-drifts had formed about it, from which we concluded that the weather conditions had been quiet. The snow, which we had found very loose when we were there before, was now hardened by the cold. We were lucky with the sun, and got the position of the depot accurately determined.

On our way across these endless plains, where no landmarks of any kind are to be found, we had repeatedly thought of a means of marking our depots so that we might be perfectly sure of finding them again. Our fight for the Pole was entirely dependent on this autumn work, in laying down large supplies of provisions as far to the south as possible in such a way that we could be certain of finding them again. If we missed them, the battle would probably be lost. As I have said, we had discussed the question thoroughly, and come to the conclusion that we should have to try to mark our depots at right angles to the route, in an east and west direction, instead of in a line with the route, north and south. These marks along the line of the route may easily be missed in fog, if they are not close enough together; and if one thus gets out of the line, there is a danger of not picking it up again. According to this new arrangement we therefore marked this depot in 80° S. with high bamboo poles carrying black flags. We used twenty of these – ten on each side of the depot. Between each two flags there was a distance of 984 yards (900 metres), so that the distance marked on each side of the depot was five and a half miles (nine kilometres). Each bamboo was marked with a number, so that we should always be able to tell from this number on which side the depot lay, and how far off. This method was entirely new and untried, but proved afterwards to work with absolute certainty. Our compasses and sledge-meters had, of course, been carefully adjusted at the station, and we knew that we could rely on them.

Having put this in order, we continued our journey on the following day. The temperature fell steadily as we went inland; if it continued in this way it would be cold before one got to the Pole. The surface remained as before – flat and even. We ourselves had a feeling that we were ascending, but, as the future will show, this was only imagination. We had had no trouble with fissures, and it almost looked as if we should avoid them altogether, since, of course, it might be supposed that the part of the Barrier nearest the edge would be the most fissured, and we had already left that behind us. South of 80° we found the going easier, but the dogs were now beginning to be stiff and sore-footed, and it was hard work to get them started in the morning. The sore feet I am speaking of here are not nearly so bad as those the dogs are liable to on the sea-ice of the Arctic regions. What caused sore feet on this journey was the stretches of snow-crust we had to cross; it was not strong enough to bear the dogs, and they broke through and cut their paws. Sore feet were also caused by the snow caking and sticking between the toes. But the dog that has to travel on sea-ice in spring and summer is exposed to worse things – the sharp ice cuts the paws and the salt gets in. To prevent this kind of sore feet one is almost obliged to put socks on the dogs. With the kind of foot-trouble our dogs experienced it is not necessary to take any such precautions. As a result of the long sea voyage their feet had become unusually tender and could not stand much. On our spring journey we noticed no sore-footedness, in spite of the conditions being worse rather than better; probably their feet had got into condition in the course of the winter.

On March 3 we reached 81° S. The temperature was then -45.4° F., and it did not feel pleasant. The change had come too rapidly; this could be seen both in men and in dogs. We pitched our camp at three in the afternoon, and went straight into the tents. The following day was employed in building and marking the depot. That night was the coldest we observed on the trip, as the temperature was -49° F. when we turned out in the morning. If one compares the conditions of temperature in the Arctic and Antarctic regions, it will be seen that this temperature is an exceptionally low one. The beginning of March corresponds, of course, to the beginning of September in the northern hemisphere – a time of year when summer still prevails. We were astonished to find this low temperature while summer ought still to have lasted, especially when I remembered the moderate temperatures Shackleton had observed on his southern sledge journey. The idea at once occurred to me of the existence of a local pole of maximum cold extending over the central portion of the Ross Barrier. A comparison with the observations recorded at Captain Scott's station in McMurdo Sound might to some extent explain this. In order to establish it completely one would require to have information about the conditions in King Edward Land as well. The observations Dr. Mawson is now engaged upon in Adélie Land and on the Barrier farther west will contribute much to the elucidation of this question.

In 81° S. we laid down a depot consisting of fourteen cases of dogs' pemmican – 1,234 pounds. For marking this depot we had no bamboo poles, so there was nothing to be done but to break up some cases and use the pieces as marks; this was, at any rate, better than nothing. Personally, I considered these pieces of wood, 2 feet high, good enough, considering the amount of precipitation I had remarked since our arrival in these regions. The precipitation we had observed was very slight, considering the time of year – spring and summer. If, then, the snowfall was so inconsiderable at this time of the year and along the edge of the Barrier, what might it not be in autumn and winter in the interior? As I have said, something was better than nothing, and Bjaaland, Hassel, and Stubberud, who were to return to Lindström's flesh-pots on the following day, were given the task of setting up these marks. As with the former depot, this one was marked for nine kilometres on each side from east to west. So that we might know where the depot was, in case we should come upon one of these marks in a fog, all those on the east were marked with a little cut of an axe. I must confess they looked insignificant, these little bits of wood that were soon lost to sight on the boundless plain, and the idea that they held the key of the castle where the fair one slept made me smile. They looked altogether too inconsiderable for such an honour. Meanwhile, we others, who were to go on to the south, took it easy. The rest was good for the dogs especially, though the cold prevented their enjoying it as they should have done.

At eight o'clock next morning we parted company with the three who went north. I had to send home one of my dogs, Odin, who had got an ugly raw place – I was using Greenland harness on him – and I went on with five dogs. These were very thin, and apparently worn out; but in any case we had to reach 82° S. before we gave up. I had had some hope that we might have got to 83°, but it began to look as if we had a poor chance of that. After 81° S. the Barrier began to take on a slightly different appearance instead of the absolutely flat surface, we saw on the first day a good many small formations of the shape of haycocks. At that time we did not pay much attention to these apparently insignificant irregularities, but later on we learned to keep our eyes open and our feet active when passing in their vicinity. On this first day southward from 81° S. we noticed nothing; the going was excellent, the temperature not so bad as it had been, -27.4° F., and the distance covered very creditable. The next day we got our first idea of the meaning of these little mounds, as the surface was cut up by crevasse after crevasse. These fissures were not particularly wide, but were bottomless, as far as we could see. About noon Hanssen's three leading dogs, Helge, Mylius, and Ring, fell into one of them, and remained hanging by their harness; and it was lucky the traces held, as the loss of these three would have been severely felt. When the rest of the team saw these three disappear, they stopped short. Fortunately, they had a pronounced fear of these fissures, and always stopped when anything happened. We understood now that the haycock formations were the result of pressure, and that crevasses were always found in their neighbourhood.

That day was for the most part thick and hazy, with a northerly wind, and snow-showers from time to time. Between the showers we caught sight of lofty – very lofty – pressure ridges, three or four of them, to the eastward. We estimated their distance at about six miles. Next day, March 7, we had the same experience that Shackleton mentions on several occasions. The morning began clear and fine, with a temperature of -40° F. In the course of the forenoon a breeze sprang up from the south-east, and increased to a gale during the afternoon.

The temperature rose rapidly, and when we pitched our camp at three in the afternoon it was only -0.4° F. At our camping-place that morning we left a case of dogs' pemmican, for use on the homeward journey, and marked the way to the south with splinters of board at every kilometre. Our distance that day was only twelve and a half miles. Our dogs, especially mine, looked miserable – terribly emaciated. It was clear that they could only reach 82° S. at the farthest. Even then the homeward journey would be a near thing.

We decided that evening to be satisfied with reaching 82°, and then return. During this latter part of the trip we put up our two tents front to front, so that the openings joined; in this way we were able to send the food direct from one tent to the other without going outside, and that was a great advantage. This circumstance led to a radical alteration in our camping system, and gave us the idea of the best five-man tent that has probably yet been seen in the Polar regions. As we lay dozing that evening in our sleeping-bags, thinking of everything and nothing, the idea suddenly occurred to us that if the tents were sewed together as they now stood – after the fronts had been cut away – we should get one tent that would give us far more room for five than the two separate tents as they were. The idea was followed up, and the fruit of it was the tent we used on the journey to the Pole – an ideal tent in every way. Yes, circumstances work wonders; for I suppose one need not make Providence responsible for these trifles?

On March 8 we reached 82° S., and it was the utmost my five dogs could manage. Indeed, as will shortly be seen, it was already too much. They were completely worn out, poor beasts.

218

This is the only dark memory of my stay in the South – the over-taxing of these fine animals – I had asked more of them than they were capable of doing. My consolation is that I did not spare myself either. To set this sledge, weighing nearly half a ton, in motion with tired-out dogs was no child's play. And setting it in motion was not always the whole of it: sometimes one had to push it forward until one forced the dogs to move. The whip had long ago lost its terrors. When I tried to use it, they only crowded together, and got their heads as much out of the way as they could; the body did not matter so much. Many a time, too, I failed altogether to get them to go, and had to have help. Then two of us shoved the sledge forward, while the third used the whip, shouting at the same time for all he was worth. How hard and unfeeling one gets under such conditions; how one's whole nature may be changed! I am naturally fond of all animals, and try to avoid hurting them. There is none of the "sportsman's" instinct in me; it would never occur to me to kill an animal – rats and flies excepted – unless it was to support life. I think I can say that in normal circumstances I loved my dogs, and the feeling was undoubtedly mutual. But the circumstances we were now in were not normal – or was it, perhaps, myself who was not normal? I have often thought since that such was really the case. The daily hard work and the object I would not give up had made me brutal, for brutal I was when I forced those five skeletons to haul that excessive load. I feel it yet when I think of Thor – a big, fine, smooth-haired dog – uttering his plaintive howls on the march, a thing one never hears a dog do while working. I did not understand what it meant – would not understand, perhaps. On he had to go – on till he dropped. When we cut him open we found that his whole chest was one large abscess.

The altitude at noon gave us 81° 54' 30", and we therefore went the other six miles to the south, and pitched our camp at 3.30 p.m. in 82° S. We had latterly had a constant impression that the Barrier was rising, and in the opinion of all of us we ought now to have been at a height of about 1,500 feet and a good way up the slope leading to the Pole. Personally I thought the ground continued to rise to the south. It was all imagination, as our later measurements showed.

We had now reached our highest latitude that autumn, and had reason to be well satisfied. We laid down 1,370 pounds here, chiefly dogs' pemmican. We did nothing that afternoon, only rested a little. The weather was brisk, clear and calm, -13° F. The distance this last day was thirteen and a half miles.

Next day we stayed where we were, built our depot, and marked it. The marking was done in the same way as in 81° S., with this difference, that here the pieces of packing-case had small, dark blue strips of cloth fastened to the top, which made them easier to see. We made this depot very secure, so that we could be certain it would stand bad weather in the course of the winter. I also left my sledge behind, as I saw the impossibility of getting it home with my team; besides which, an extra sledge at this point might possibly be useful later. This depot − 12 feet high − was marked with a bamboo and a flag on the top, so that it could be seen a great way off.

On March 10 we took the road for home. I had divided my dogs between Wisting and Hanssen, but they got no assistance from these bags of bones, only trouble. The other three teams had held out well. There was hardly anything wrong to be seen with Hanssen's. Wisting's team was looked upon as the strongest, but his dogs had got very thin; however, they did their work well. Wisting's sledge had also been overloaded; it was even heavier than mine. Johansen's animals had originally been re-garded as the weakest, but they proved themselves very tough in the long-run. They were no racers, but always managed to scramble along somehow. Their motto was: "If we don't get there to-day, we'll get there to-morrow." They all came home.

Our original idea was that the homeward journey should be a sort of pleasure trip, that we should sit on the sledges and take it easy; but in the circumstances this was not to be thought of. The dogs had quite enough to do with the empty sledges. The same day we reached the place where we had left a case of dogs' pemmican, and camped there, having done twenty-nine and three-quarter miles. The weather was cold and raw; tempera-ture, -25.6° F. This weather took the last remnant of strength out of my dogs; instead of resting at night, they lay huddled to-gether and freezing. It was pitiful to see them. In the morning they had to be lifted up and put on their feet; they had not strength enough to raise themselves. When they had staggered on a little way and got some warmth into their bodies, they seemed to be rather better – at any rate, they could keep up with us. The following day we did twenty-four and three-quar-ter miles; temperature, -32.8° F.

On the 12th we passed the depot in 81° S. The big pressure ridges to the east were easily visible, and we got a good bearing, which would possibly come in useful later for fixing the posi-tion of the depot. That day we did twenty-four and three-quarter miles; temperature, -39° F. March 13 began calm and fine, but by half-past ten in the morning a strong wind had sprung up from the east-south-east with thick driving snow. So as not to lose the tracks we had followed so far, we pitched our camp, to wait till the storm was over. The wind howled and took hold of the tents, but could not move them. The next day it blew just as hard from the same quarter, and we decided to wait. The temperature was as usual, with the wind in this quarter; -11.2° F. The wind did not moderate till 10.30 a.m. on the 15th, when we were able to make a start.

What a sight there was outside! How were we going to begin to bring order out of this chaos? The sledges were completely snowed up; whips, ski-bindings, and harness largely eaten up. It was a nice predicament. Fortunately we were well supplied with Alpine rope, and that did for the harness; spare straps came in for ski-bindings, but the whips were not so easy to make good. Hanssen, who drove first, was bound to have a fairly serviceable whip; the others did not matter so much, though it was rather awkward for them. In some way or other he provided himself with a whip that answered his purpose. I saw one of the others armed with a tent-pole, and he used it till we reached Framheim. At first the dogs were much afraid of this monster of a whip, but they soon found out that it was no easy matter to reach them with the pole, and then they did not care a scrap for it.

At last everything seemed to be in order, and then we only had to get the dogs up and in their places. Several of them were so indifferent that they had allowed themselves to be completely snowed under, but one by one we got them out and put them on their feet. Thor, however, refused absolutely. It was impossible to get him to stand up; he simply lay and whined. There was nothing to be done but to put an end to him, and as we had no firearms, it had to be done with an axe. It was quite successful; less would have killed him. Wisting took the carcass on his sledge to take it to the next camp, and there cut it up. The day was bitterly cold – fog and snow with a southerly breeze; temperature, -14.8° F. We were lucky enough to pick up our old tracks of the southern journey, and could follow them. Lurven, Wisting's best dog, fell down on the march, and died on the spot. He was one of those dogs who had to work their hardest the whole time; he never thought of shirking for a moment; he pulled and pulled until he died.

All sentimental feeling had vanished long ago; nobody thought of giving Lurven the burial he deserved. What was left of him, skin and bones, was cut up and divided among his companions.

On March 16 we advanced seventeen miles; temperature, -29.2° F. Jens, one of my gallant "Three Musketeers," had been given a ride all day on Wisting's sledge; he was too weak to walk any longer. Thor was to have been divided among his companions that evening, but, on account of the abscess in his chest, we changed our minds. He was put into an empty case and buried. During the night we were wakened by a fearful noise. The dogs were engaged in a fierce fight, and it was easy to guess from their howls that it was all about food. Wisting, who always showed himself quickest in getting out of the bag, was instantly on the spot, and then it was seen that they had dug up Thor, and were now feasting on him. It could not be said that they were hard to please in the way of food. Associations of ideas are curious things; "sauce hollandaise" suddenly occurred to my mind. Wisting buried the carcass again, and we had peace for the rest of the night.

On the 17th it felt bitterly cold, with -41.8° F, and a sharp snowstorm from the south-east. Lassesen, one of my dogs, who had been following the sledges loose, was left behind this morning at the camping-place; we did not miss him till late in the day. Rasmus, one of the "Three Musketeers," fell to-day. Like Lurven, he pulled till he died. Jens was very ill, could not touch food, and was taken on Wisting's sledge. We reached our depot in 80° S. that evening, and were able to give the dogs a double ration. The distance covered was twenty-one and three-quarter miles. The surface about here had changed in our absence; great, high snow-waves were now to be seen in all directions. On one of the cases in the depot Bjaaland had written a short message, besides which we found the signal arranged with Hassel – a block of snow on the top of the depot to show that they had gone by, and that all was well. The cold continued persistently. The following day we had -41.8° F. Ola and Jens, the two survivors of the "Three Musketeers," had to be put an end to that day; it was a shame to keep them alive any longer. And with them the "Three Musketeers" disappear from this history. They were inseparable friends, these three; all of them almost entirely black. At Flekkerö, near Christiansand, where we kept our dogs for several weeks before taking them on board, Rasmus had got loose, and was impossible to catch. He always came and slept with his two friends, unless he was being hunted. We did not succeed in catching him until a few days before we took them on board, and then he was practically wild. They were all three tied up on the bridge on board, where I was to have my team, and from that day my closer acquaintance with the trio is dated. They were not very civilly disposed for the first month. I had to make my advances with a long stick – scratch them on the back. In this way I insinuated myself into their confidence, and we became very good friends. But they were a terrible power on board; wherever these three villains showed themselves, there was always a row. They loved fighting. They were our fastest dogs. In our races with empty sledges, when we were driving around Framheim, none of the others could beat these three. I was always sure of leaving the rest behind when I had them in my team.

I had quite given up Lassesen, who had been left behind that morning, and I was very sorry for it, as he was my strongest and most willing beast. I was glad, therefore, when he suddenly appeared again, apparently fit and well. We presumed that he had dug up Thor again, and finished him. It must have been food that had revived him. From 80° S. home he did remarkably good work in Wisting's team.

That day we had a curious experience, which was useful for the future. The compass on Hanssen's sledge, which had always been reliability itself, suddenly began to go wrong; at any rate, it did not agree with the observations of the sun, which we fortunately had that day. We altered our course in accordance with our bearings. In the evening, when we took our things into the tent, the housewife, with scissors, pins, needles, etc., had lain close against the compass. No wonder it turned rebellious.

On March 19 we had a breeze from the south-east and -45.4° F. "Rather fresh," I find noted in my diary. Not long after we had started that morning, Hanssen caught sight of our old tracks. He had splendid eyesight – saw everything long before anyone else. Bjaaland also had good sight, but he did not come up to Hanssen. The way home was now straightforward, and we could see the end of our journey. Meanwhile a gale sprang up from the south-east, which stopped us for a day; temperature, -29.2° F. Next day the temperature had risen, as usual, with a south-east wind; we woke up to find it +15.8° F. on the morning of the 21st. That was a difference that could be felt, and not an unpleasant one; we had had more than enough of -40°. It was curious weather that night: violent gusts of wind from the east and south-east, with intervals of dead calm – just as if they came off high land. On our way northward that day we passed our flag No. 6, and then knew that we were fifty-three miles from Framheim. Pitched our camp that evening at thirty-seven miles from the station. We had intended to take this stretch of the way in two days, seeing how tired the dogs were; but it turned out otherwise, for we lost our old tracks during the forenoon, and in going on we came too far to the east, and high up on the ridge mentioned before. Suddenly Hanssen sang out that he saw something funny in front – what it was he did not know. When that was the case, we had to apply to the one who saw even better than Hanssen, and that was my glass. Up with the glass, then – the good old glass that has served me for so many years. Yes, there was certainly something curious. It must be the Bay of Whales that we were looking down into, but what were those black things moving up and down? They are our fellows hunting seals, someone suggested, and we all agreed. Yes, of course, it was so clear that there was no mistaking it. "I can see a sledge – and there's another – and there's a third." We nearly had tears in our eyes to see how industrious they were. "Now they're gone. No; there they are again. Strange how they bob up and down, those fellows!" It proved to be a mirage; what we saw was Framheim with all its tents. Our lads, we were sure, were just taking a comfortable midday nap, and the tears we were nearly shedding were withdrawn. Now we could survey the situation calmly. There lay Framheim, there was Cape Man's Head, and there West Cape, so that we had come too far to the east. "Hurrah for Framheim! half-past seven this evening," shouted one. "Yes, that's all we can do," cried another; and away we went. We set our course straight for the middle of the bay. We must have got pretty high up, as we went down at a terrific pace. This was more than the forerunner could manage; he flung himself on a sledge as it went by. I had a glimpse of Hanssen, who was busy making a whip-handle, as I passed; the soles of his feet were then very prominent. I myself was lying on Hanssen's sledge, shaking with laughter; the situation was too comical. Hanssen picked himself up again just as the last sledge was passing and jumped on. We all collected in a mass below the ridge – sledges and dogs mixed up together.

The last part of the way was rather hard work. We now found the tracks that we had lost early in the day; one dried fish after another stuck up out of the snow and led us straight on. We reached Framheim at seven in the evening, half an hour earlier than we had thought. It was a day's march of thirty-seven miles – not so bad for exhausted dogs. Lassesen was the only one I brought home out of my team. Odin, whom I had sent home from 81° S., died after arriving there. We lost altogether eight dogs on this trip; two of Stubberud's died immediately after coming home from 81° S. Probably the cold was chiefly responsible; I feel sure that with a reasonable temperature they would have come through.

The three men who came home from 81° S. were safe and sound. It is true that they had run short of food and matches the last day, but if the worst came to the worst, they had the dogs. Since their return they had shot, brought in, cut up, and stowed away, fifty seals – a very good piece of work.

Lindström had been untiring during our absence; he had put everything in splendid order. In the covered passage round the hut he had cut out shelves in the snow and filled them with slices of seal meat. Here alone there were steaks enough for the whole time we should spend here. On the outer walls of the hut, which formed the other side of the passage, he had put up shelves, and there all kinds of tinned foods were stored. All was in such perfect order that one could put one's hand on what one wanted in the dark. There stood salt meat and bacon by themselves, and there were fish-cakes. There you read the label on a tin of caramel pudding, and you could be sure that the rest of the caramel puddings were in the vicinity. Quite right; there they stood in a row, like a company of soldiers. Oh, Lindström, how long will this order last?

Well, that was, of course, a question I put to myself in the strictest secrecy. Let me turn over my diary. On Thursday, July 27, I find the following entry: "The provision passage turns our days into chaotic confusion. How my mind goes back to the time when one could find what one wanted without a light of any kind! If you put out your hand to get a plum-pudding and shut it again, you could be sure it was a plum-pudding you had hold of. And so it was throughout Lindström's department. But now – good Heavens! I am ashamed to put down what happened to me yesterday. I went out there in the most blissful ignorance of the state of things now prevailing, and, of course, I had no light with me, for everything had its place. I put out my hand and grasped. According to my expectation I ought to have been in possession of a packet of candles, but the experiment had failed. That which I held in my hand could not possibly be a packet of candles. It was evident from the feel that it was something of a woollen nature. I laid the object down, and had recourse to the familiar expedient of striking a match. Do you know what it was? A dirty old – pair of pants! and do you want to know where I found it? Well, it was between the butter and the sweetmeats. That was mixing things up with a vengeance."

But Lindström must not have all the blame. In this passage everyone was running backwards and forwards, early and late, and as a rule in the dark. And if they knocked something down on the way, I am not quite sure that they always stopped to pick it up again.

Then he had painted the ceiling of the room white. How cosy it looked when we put our heads in that evening! He had seen us a long way off on the Barrier, the rascal, and now the table was laid with all manner of dainties. But seal-steaks and the smell of coffee were what attracted us, and it was no small quantity that disappeared that evening. Home! – that word has a good sound, wherever it may be, at sea, on land, or on – the Barrier. How comfortable we made ourselves that night! The first thing we did now was to dry all our reindeer-skin clothes; they were wet through. This was not to be done in a hurry. We had to stretch the garments that were to be dried on lines under the ceiling of the room, so that we could not dry very much at a time.

We got everything ready, and made some improvements in our outfit for a last depot journey before the winter set in. This time the destination was 80° S., with about a ton and a quarter of fresh seal meat. How immensely important it would be on the main journey if we could give our dogs as much seal meat as they could eat at 80° S.; we all saw the importance of this, and were eager to carry it out. We set to work once more at the outfit; the last trip had taught us much that was new. Thus Prestrud and Johansen had come to the conclusion that a double sleeping-bag was preferable to two single ones. I will not enter upon the discussion that naturally arose on this point. The double bag has many advantages, and so has the single bag; let it therefore remain a matter of taste. Those two were, however, the only ones who made this alteration. Hanssen and Wisting were busy carrying out the new idea for the tents, and it was not long before they had finished. These tents are as much like a snow hut in form as they can be; instead of being entirely round, they have a more oblong form, but there is no flat side, and the wind has no point of attack. Our personal outfit also underwent some improvements.

The Bay of Whales – the inner part of it, from Man's Head to West Cape – was now entirely frozen over, but outside the sea lay immense and dark. Our house was now completely covered with snow. Most of this was Lindström's work; the blizzard had not helped him much. This covering with snow has a great deal to do with keeping the hut snug and warm. Our dogs – 107 in number – mostly look like pigs getting ready for Christmas; even the famished ones that made the last trip are beginning to recover. It is an extraordinary thing how quickly such an animal can put on flesh.

It was interesting to watch the home-coming of the dogs from the last trip. They showed no sign of surprise when we came into camp; they might have been there all the time. It is true they were rather more hungry than the rest. The meeting between Lassesen and Fix was comic. These two were inseparable friends; the first-named was boss, and the other obeyed him blindly. On this last trip I had left Fix at home, as he did not give me the impression of being quite up to the work; he had therefore put on a lot of flesh, big eater as he was. I stood and watched their meeting with intense curiosity. Would not Fix take advantage of the occasion to assume the position of boss? In such a mass of dogs it took some little time before they came across each other. Then it was quite touching. Fix ran straight up to the other, began to lick him, and showed every sign of the greatest affection and joy at seeing him again. Lassesen, on his part, took it all with a very superior air, as befits a boss. Without further ceremony, he rolled his fat friend in the snow and stood over him for a while – no doubt to let him know that he was still absolute master, beyond dispute. Poor Fix! – he looked quite crestfallen. But this did not last long; he soon avenged himself on the other, knowing that he could tackle him with safety.

In order to give a picture of our life as it was at this time, I will quote a day from my diary. March 25 – Saturday: "Beautiful mild weather, +6.8° F. all day. Very light breeze from the south-east. Our seal-hunters – the party that came home from 81° S. – were out this morning, and brought back three seals. This makes sixty-two seals altogether since their return on March 11. We have now quite enough fresh meat both for ourselves and for all our dogs. We get to like seal-steak more and more every day. We should all be glad to eat it at every meal, but we think it safer to make a little variety. For breakfast – eight o'clock – we now have regularly hot cakes with jam, and Lindström knows how to prepare them in a way that could not be surpassed in the best American houses. In addition, we have bread, butter, cheese, and coffee. For dinner we mostly have seal meat (we introduced rather more tinned meat into the menu in the course of the winter), and sweets in the form of tinned Californian fruit, tarts, and tinned puddings. For supper, seal-steak, with whortleberry jam, cheese, bread, butter, and coffee. Every Saturday evening a glass of toddy and a cigar. I must frankly confess that I have never lived so well. And the consequence is that we are all in the best of health, and I feel certain that the whole enterprise will be crowned with success.

"It is strange indeed here to go outside in the evening and see the cosy, warm lamp-light through the window of our little snow-covered hut, and to feel that this is our snug, comfortable home on the formidable and dreaded Barrier. All our little puppies – as round as Christmas pigs – are wandering about outside, and at night they lie in crowds about the door. They never take shelter under a roof at night. They must be hardy beasts. Some of them are so fat that they waddle just like geese."

The *aurora australis* was seen for the first time on the evening of March 28. It was composed of shafts and bands, and extended from the south-west to the north-east through the zenith. The light was pale green and red. We see many fine sunsets here, unique in the splendour of their colour. No doubt the surroundings in this fairyland of blue and white do much to increase their beauty.

The departure of the last depot journey was fixed for Friday, March 31. A few days before, the seal-hunting party went out on the ice and shot six seals for the depot. They were cleaned and all superfluous parts removed, so that they should not be too heavy. The weight of these six seals was then estimated at about 2,400 pounds.

On March 31, at 10 a.m., the last depot party started. It consisted of seven men, six sledges, and thirty-six dogs. I did not go myself this time. They had the most beautiful weather to begin their journey – dead calm and brilliantly clear. At seven o'clock that morning, when I came out of the hut, I saw a sight so beautiful that I shall never forget it. The whole surroundings of the station lay in deep, dark shadow, in lee of the ridge to the east. But the sun's rays reached over the Barrier farther to the north, and there the Barrier lay golden red, bathed in the morning sun. It glittered and shone, red and gold, against the jagged row of mighty masses of ice that bounds our Barrier on the north. A spirit of peace breathed over all. But from Framheim the smoke ascended quietly into the air, and proclaimed that the spell of thousands of years was broken.

The sledges were heavily loaded when they went southward. I saw them slowly disappear over the ridge by the starting-place. It was a quiet time that followed after all the work and hurry of preparation. Not that we two who stayed at home sat still doing nothing. We made good use of the time. The first thing to be done was to put our meteorological station in order. On April 1 all the instruments were in use. In the kitchen were hung our two mercury barometers, four aneroids, barograph, thermograph, and one thermometer. They were placed in a well-protected corner, farthest from the stove. We had no house as yet for our outside instruments, but the sub-director went to work to prepare one as quickly as possible, and so nimble were his hands that when the depot party returned there was the finest instrument-screen standing ready on the hill, painted white so that it shone a long way off: The wind-vane was a work of art, constructed by our able engineer, Sundbeck. No factory could have supplied a more handsome or tasteful one. In the in-strument-screen we had a thermograph, hygrometer, and ther-mometers. Observations were made at 8 a.m., 2 p.m., and 8 p.m. When I was at home I took them, and when I was away it was Lindström's work.

On the night before April 11 something or other fell down in the kitchen – according to Lindström, a sure sign that the trav-ellers might be expected home that day. And, sure enough, at noon we caught sight of them up at the starting-place. They came across at such a pace that the snow was scattered all round them, and in an hour's time we had them back. They had much to tell us. In the first place, that everything had been duly tak-en to the depot in 80°S. Then they surprised me with an ac-count of a fearfully crevassed piece of surface that they had come upon, forty-six and a half miles from the station, where they had lost two dogs. This was very strange; we had now traversed this stretch of surface four times without being particularly troubled with anything of this sort, and then, all of a sudden, when they thought the whole surface was as solid as a rock, they found themselves in danger of coming to grief altogether. In thick weather they had gone too far to the west; then, instead of arriving at the ridge, as we had done before, they came down into the valley, and there found a surface so dangerous that they nearly had a catastrophe. It was a precisely similar piece of surface to that already mentioned to the south of 81° S., but full of small hummocks everywhere. The ground was apparently solid enough, and this was just the most dangerous thing about it; but, as they were crossing it, large pieces of the surface fell away just in rear of them, disclosing bottomless crevasses, big enough to swallow up everything – men, dogs, and sledges. With some difficulty they got out of this ugly place by steering to the east. Now we knew of it, and we should certainly be very careful not to come that way again. In spite of this, however, we afterwards had an even more serious encounter with this nasty trap.

One dog had also been left behind on the way; it had a wound on one of its feet, and could not be harnessed in the sledge. It had been let loose a few miles to the north of the depot, doubtless with the idea that it would follow the sledges. But the dog seemed to have taken another view of the matter, and was never seen again. There were some who thought that the dog had probably returned to the depot, and was now passing its days in ease and luxury among the laboriously transported seals' carcasses. I must confess that this idea was not very attractive to me; there was, indeed, a possibility that such a thing had happened, and that the greater part of our seal meat might be missing when we wanted it. But our fears proved groundless; Cook – that was the name of the dog; we had a Peary as well, of course – was gone for ever.

The improved outfit was in every way successful. Praises of the new tent were heard on every hand, and Prestrud and Johansen were in the seventh heaven over their double sleeping-bag. I fancy the others were very well satisfied with their single ones.

And with this the most important part of the autumn's work came to an end. The foundation was solidly laid; now we had only to raise the edifice. Let us briefly sum up the work accomplished between January 14 and April 11: The complete erection of the station, with accommodation for nine men for several years; provision of fresh meat for nine men and a hundred and fifteen dogs for half a year – the weight of the seals killed amounted to about 60 tons; and, finally, the distribution of 3 tons of supplies in the depots in latitudes 80°, 81°, and 82°S. The depot in 80°S. contained seal meat, dogs' pemmican, biscuits, butter, milk-powder, chocolate, matches, and paraffin, besides a quantity of outfit. The total weight of this depot was 4,200 pounds. In 81°S., 1/2 ton of dogs' pemmican. In 82°S., pemmican, both for men and dogs, biscuits, milk-powder, chocolate, and paraffin, besides a quantity of outfit. The weight of this depot amounted to 1,366 pounds.

CHAPTER 7

PREPARING FOR WINTER

Winter! I believe most people look upon winter as a time of storms, cold, and discomfort. They look forward to it with sadness, and bow before the inevitable – Providence ordains it so. The prospect of a ball or two cheers them up a little, and makes the horizon somewhat brighter; but, all the same – darkness and cold – ugh, no! let us have summer, they say. What my comrades thought about the winter that was approaching I cannot say; for my part, I looked forward to it with pleasure. When I stood out there on the snow hill, and saw the light shining out of the kitchen window, there came over me an indescribable feeling of comfort and well-being. And the blacker and more stormy the winter night might be, the greater would be this feeling of well-being inside our snug little house. I see the reader's questioning look, and know what he will say: "But weren't you awfully afraid the Barrier would break off, and float you out to sea?" I will answer this question as frankly as possible. With one exception, we were all at this time of the opinion that the part of the Barrier on which the hut stood rested on land, so that any fear of a sea voyage was quite superfluous. As to the one who thought we were afloat, I think I can say very definitely that he was not afraid. I believe, as a matter of fact, that he gradually came round to the same view as the rest of us.

If a general is to win a battle, he must always be prepared. If his opponent makes a move, he must see that he is able to make a counter-move; everything must be planned in advance, and nothing unforeseen. We were in the same position; we had to consider beforehand what the future might bring, and make our arrangements accordingly while there was time. When the sun had left us, and the dark period had set in, it would be too late. What first of all claimed our attention and set our collective brain-machinery to work was the female sex. There was no peace for us even on the Barrier. What happened was that the entire feminine population – eleven in number – had thought fit to appear in a condition usually considered "interesting," but which, under the circumstances, we by no means regarded in that light. Our hands were indeed full enough without this. What was to be done? Great deliberation. Eleven maternity hospitals seemed rather a large order, but we knew by experience that they all required first aid. If we left several of them in the same place there would be a terrible scene, and it would end in their eating up each other's pups. For what had happened only a few days before? Kaisa, a big black-and-white bitch, had taken a three-months-old pup when no one was looking, and made a meal off it. When we arrived we saw the tip of its tail disappearing, so there was not much to be done. Now, it fortunately happened that one of the dog-tents became vacant, as Prestrud's team was divided among the other tents; as "forerunner," he had no use for dogs. Here, with a little contrivance, we could get two of them disposed of; a dividing wall could be put up. When first laying out the station, we had taken this side of life into consideration, and a "hospital" in the shape of a sixteen-man tent had been erected; but this was not nearly enough. We then had recourse to the material of which there is such superabundance in these parts of the earth-snow. We erected a splendid big snow-hut. Besides this, Lindström in his leisure hours had erected a little building, which was ready when we returned from the second depot journey. We had none of us asked what it was for, but now we knew Lindström's kind heart. With these arrangements at our disposal we were able to face the winter.

Camilla, the sly old fox, had taken things in time; she knew what it meant to bring up children in the dark, and, in truth, it was no pleasure. She had therefore made haste, and was ready as soon as the original "hospital" was prepared. She could now look forward to the future with calmness in the last rays of the disappearing sun; when darkness set in, her young ones would be able to look after themselves. Camilla, by the way, had her own views of bringing up her children. What there was about the hospital that she did not like I do not know, but it is certain that she preferred any other place. It was no rare thing to come across Camilla in a tearing gale and a temperature twenty below zero with one of her offspring in her mouth. She was going out to look for a new place. Meanwhile, the three others, who had to wait, were shrieking and howling. The places she chose were not, as a rule, such as we should connect with the idea of comfort; a case, for instance, standing on its side, and fully exposed to the wind, or behind a stack of planks, with a draught coming through that would have done credit to a factory chimney.

But if she liked it, there was nothing to be said. If the family were left alone in such a place, she would spend some days there before moving on again. She never returned to the hospital voluntarily, but it was not a rare thing to see Johansen, who was guardian to the family, hauling off the lady and as many of her little ones as he could get hold of in a hurry. They then disappeared into the hospital with words of encouragement.

At the same time we introduced a new order of things with our dogs. Hitherto we had been obliged to keep them tied up on account of seal-hunting; otherwise they went off by themselves and ravaged. There were certain individuals who specially distinguished themselves in this way, like Wisting's Major. He was a born hunter, afraid of nothing. Then there was Hassel's Svarten; but a good point about him was that he went off alone, while the Major always had a whole staff with him. They usually came back with their faces all covered with blood. To put a stop to this sport we had been obliged to keep them fast; but now that the seals had left us, we could let them loose. Naturally the first use to which they put their liberty was fighting. In the course of time – for reasons impossible to discover – bitter feelings and hatred had arisen between certain of the dogs, and now they were offered an opportunity of deciding which was the stronger, and they seized upon it with avidity. But after a time their manners improved, and a regular fight became a rarity. There were, of course, a few who could never see each other without flying at one another's throats, like Lassesen and Hans, for instance; but we knew their ways, and could keep an eye on them. The dogs soon knew their respective tents, and their places in them. They were let loose as soon as we came out in the morning, and were chained up again in the evening when they were to be fed. They got so used to this that we never had much trouble; they all reported themselves cheerfully when we came in the evening to fasten them up, and every animal knew his own master and tent, and knew at once what was expected of him. With howls of delight the various dogs collected about their masters, and made for the tents in great jubilation. We kept up this arrangement the whole time. Their food consisted of seal's flesh and blubber one day, and dried fish the next; as a rule, both disappeared without any objection, though they certainly preferred the seal. Throughout the greater part of the winter we had carcasses of seals lying on the slope, and these were usually a centre of great interest. The spot might be regarded as the market-place of Framheim, and it was not always a peaceful one. The customers were many and the demand great, so that sometimes lively scenes took place. Our own store of seal's flesh was in the "meat-tent." About a hundred seals had been cut up and stacked there. As already mentioned, we built a wall of snow, two yards high, round this tent, as a protection against the dogs. Although they had as much to eat as they wanted, and although they knew they were not allowed to try to get in – or possibly this prohibition was just the incentive – they were always casting longing eyes in that direction, and the number of claw-marks in the wall spoke eloquently of what went on when we were not looking. Snuppesen, in particular, could not keep herself away from that wall, and she was extremely light and agile, so that she had the best chance. She never engaged in this sport by herself, but always enticed out her attendant cavaliers, Fix and Lasse; these, however, were less active, and had to be content with looking on. While she jumped inside the wall – which she only succeeded in doing once or twice – they ran round yelling. As soon as we heard their howls, we knew exactly what was happening, and one of us went out, armed with a stick. It required some cunning to catch her in the act, for as soon as one approached, her cavaliers stopped howling, and she understood that something was wrong. Her red fox's head could then be seen over the top, looking round. It need scarcely be said that she did not jump into the arms of the man with the stick, but, as a rule, he did not give up until he had caught and punished her. Fix and Lasse also had their turns; it was true they had done nothing wrong, but they might. They knew this, and watched Snuppesen's chastisement at a distance. The tent where we kept the dried fish stood always open; none of them attempted to take fish.

The sun continued its daily course, lower and lower. We did not see much of it after the return from the last depot journey; on April 11 it came, and vanished again at once. Easter came round on the Barrier, as in other parts of the globe, and had to be kept. Holidays with us were marked by eating a little more than usual; there was no other sign. We did not dress differently, nor did we introduce any other change. In the evening of a holiday we generally had a little gramophone, a glass of toddy, and a cigar; but we were careful with the gramophone. We knew we should soon get tired of it if we used it too often; therefore we only brought it out on rare occasions, but we enjoyed its music all the more when we heard it. When Easter was over, a sigh of relief escaped us all; these holidays are always tiring. They are tedious enough in places which have more amusements to offer than the Barrier, but here they were insufferably long.

Our manner of life was now completely in order, and everything worked easily and well. The chief work of the winter would be the perfecting of our outfit for the coming sledge journey to the South. Our object was to reach the Pole – everything else was secondary. The meteorological observations were in full swing and arranged for the winter. Observations were made at 8 a.m., 2 p.m., and 8 p.m. We were so short-handed that I could not spare anyone for night duty, besides which, living as we did in a small space, it would have a disturbing effect if there were always someone moving about; there would never be any peace. My special aim was that everyone should be happy and comfortable, so that, when the spring came, we might all be fresh and well and eager to take up the final task. It was not my intention that we should spend the winter in idleness – far from it. To be contented and well, a man must always be occupied. I therefore expected everyone to be busy during the hours that were set apart for work. At the end of the day each man was free to do what he pleased. We had also to keep some sort of order and tidiness, as well as circumstances permitted. It was therefore decided that each of us should take a week's duty as "orderly." This duty consisted in sweeping the floor every morning, emptying ash-trays, etc. To secure plenty of ventilation – especially in our sleeping-places – a rule was made that no one might have anything under his bunk except the boots he had in wear. Each man had two pegs to hang his clothes on, and this was sufficient for what he was wearing every day; all superfluous clothing was stuffed into our kit-bags and put out. In this way we succeeded in maintaining some sort of tidiness; in any case, the worst of the dirt was got rid of. Whether a fastidious housekeeper would have found everything in order is doubtful.

Everyone had his regular work. Prestrud, with the assistance of Johansen, looked after the astronomical observations and the pendulum observations. Hassel was set in authority over coal, wood, and paraffin; he was responsible for the supply lasting out. As manager of the Framheim coal and wood business, he, of course, received the title of Director, and this dignity might possibly have gone to his head if the occupation of errand-boy had not been combined with it. But it was. Besides receiving the orders, he had to deliver the goods, and he discharged his duties with distinction. He succeeded in hoodwinking his largest customer – Lindström – to such an extent that, in the course of the winter, he saved a good deal of coal. Hanssen had to keep the depot in order and bring in everything we required. Wisting had charge of the whole outfit, and was responsible that nothing was touched without permission. Bjaaland and Stubberud were to look after the pent-house and the passage round the hut. Lindström was occupied in the kitchen – the hardest and most thankless work on an expedition like this. No one says anything so long as the food is good; but let the cook be unlucky and burn the soup one day, and he will hear something. Lindström had the excellent disposition of a man who is never put out; whatever people might say, it was "all the same" to him.

On April 19 we saw the sun for the last time, since it then went below our horizon – the ridge to the north. It was intensely red, and surrounded by a sea of flame, which did not disappear altogether until the 21st. Now everything was well. As far as the hut was concerned, it could not be better; but the pent-house, which it was originally intended to use as a work-room, soon proved too small, dark, and cold, besides which all the traffic went through that room, so that work would be constantly interrupted or stopped altogether at times. Except this dark hole we had no workroom, and we had a lot of work to do. Of course, we might use our living-room, but then we should be in each other's way all day long; nor would it be a good plan to give up the only room where we could sometimes find peace and comfort to be a workshop. I know it is the usual custom to do so, but I have always found it a bad arrangement. Now, indeed, we were at our wits' end, but circumstances once more came to our aid. For we may just as well confess it: we had forgotten to bring out a tool which is a commonplace necessity on a Polar expedition – namely, a snow-shovel. A well-equipped expedition, as ours was to a certain extent, ought to have at least twelve strong, thick iron spades. We had none. We had two remnants, but they did not help us very far. Fortunately, however, we had a very good, solid iron plate with us, and now Bjaaland stepped into the breach, and made a whole dozen of the very best spades. Stubberud managed the handles, and they might all have been turned out by a big factory. This circumstance had very important results for our future well-being, as will be seen. If we had had the shovels with us from the start, we should have cleared the snow away from our door every morning, like tidy people. But as we had none, the snow had increased daily before our door, and, before Bjaaland was ready with the spades, had formed a drift extending from the

245

entrance along the western side of the house. This snow-drift, which was as big as the house itself, naturally caused some frowns, when one morning all hands turned out, armed with the new shovels, to make a clearance. As we stood there, afraid to begin, one of us – it must have been Lindström, or Hanssen perhaps, or was it myself? well, it doesn't matter – one of us had the bright idea of taking Nature in hand, and working with her instead of against her. The proposal was that we should dig out a carpenter's shop in the big snow-drift, and put it in direct communication with the hut. This was no sooner suggested than adopted unanimously. And now began a work of tunnelling which lasted a good while, for one excavation led to another, and we did not stop until we had a whole underground village – probably one of the most interesting works ever executed round a Polar station. Let us begin with the morning when we thrust the first spade into the drift; it was Thursday, April 20. While three men went to work to dig right into the drift from the hut door westward, three more were busy connecting it with the hut. This was done by stretching boards – the same that we had used on the *Fram* as a false deck for the dogs – from the drift up to the roof of the pent-house. The open part between the drift and the pent-house on the northern side was filled up entirely into a solid wall, which went up to join the roof that had just been put on. The space between the pent-house and the drift on the south wall was left open as an exit. But now we had the building fever on us, and one ambitious project succeeded another. Thus we agreed to dig a passage the whole length of the drift, and terminate it by a large snow-hut, in which we were to have a vapour bath. That was something like a plan – a vapour bath in 79°S. Hanssen, snow-hut builder by profession, went to work at it. He built it quite small and solid, and extended it downward, so that, when at last it was finished, it measured 12 feet from floor to roof. Here we should have plenty of room to fit up a vapour bath. Meanwhile the tunnellers were advancing; we could hear the sound of their pickaxes and spades coming nearer and nearer. This was too much for Hanssen. As he had now finished the hut, he set to work to dig his way to the others; and when he begins a thing, it does not take him very long. We could hear the two parties continually nearing each other. The excitement increases. Will they meet? Or are they digging side by side on different lines? The Simplon, Mont Cenis, and other engineering works, flashed through my brain. If they were going to hit it off, we must be – hullo! I was interrupted in my studies by a glistening face, which was thrust through the wall just as I was going to dig my spade into it. It was Wisting, pioneer of the Framheim tunnel. He had good reason to be glad he escaped with his nose safe and sound. In another instant I should have had it on my spade. It was a fine sight, this long, white passage, ending in the high, shining dome. As we dug forward, we dug down at the same time so as not to weaken the roof. There was plenty to take down below; the Barrier was deep enough.

When this was finished, we began to work on the carpenter's shop. This had to be dug considerably deeper, as the drift was rounded off a little to the side. We therefore dug first into the drift, and then right down; as far as I remember, we went 6 feet down into the Barrier here. The shop was made roomy, with space enough for both carpenters and length enough for our sledges. The planing-bench was cut out in the wall and covered with boards. The workshop terminated at its western end in a little room, where the carpenters kept their smaller tools. A broad stairway, cut in the snow and covered with boards, led from the shop into the passage. As soon as the workshop was finished, the workmen moved in, and established themselves under the name of the Carpenters' Union. Here the whole sledging outfit for the Polar journey was remodelled. Opposite the carpenters came the smithy, dug to the same depth as the other; this was less used. On the other side of the smithy, nearer to the hut, a deep hole was dug to receive all the waste water from the kitchen. Between the Carpenters' Union and the entrance to the pent-house, opposite the ascent to the Barrier, we built a little room, which, properly speaking, deserves a very detailed explanation; but, for want of space, this must be deferred till later. The ascent to the Barrier, which had been left open while all these works were in progress, was now closed by a contrivance which is also worth mentioning. There are a great many people who apparently have never learnt to shut a door after them; where two or three are gathered together, you generally find at least one who suffers from this defect. How many would there be among us, who numbered nine? It is no use asking a victim of this complaint to shut the door after him; he is simply incapable of doing it. I was not yet well enough acquainted with my companions as regards the door-shutting question, and in order to be on the safe side we might just as well put up a self-closing door. This was done by Stubberud, by fixing the door-frame into the wall in an oblique position just like a cellar-door at home. Now the door could not stay open;

it had to fall to. I was glad when I saw it finished; we were secured against an invasion of dogs. Four snow steps covered with boards led from the door down into the passage. In addition to all these new rooms, we had thus gained an extra protection for our house.

While this work was in progress, our instrument-maker had his hands full; the clockwork mechanism of the thermograph had gone wrong: the spindle was broken, I believe. This was particularly annoying, because this thermograph had been working so well in low temperatures. The other thermograph had evidently been constructed with a view to the tropics; at any rate, it would not go in the cold. Our instrument-maker has one method of dealing with all instruments – almost without exception. He puts them in the oven, and stokes up the fire. This time it worked remarkably well, since it enabled him to ascertain beyond a doubt that the thing was useless. The thermograph would not work in the cold. Meanwhile he got it cleared of all the old oil that stuck to it everywhere, on wheels and pins, like fish-glue; then it was hung up to the kitchen ceiling. The temperature there may possibly revive it, and make it think it is in the tropics. In this way we shall have the temperature of the "galley" registered, and later on we shall probably be able to reckon up what we have had for dinner in the course of the week. Whether Professor Mohn will be overjoyed with this result is another question, which the instrument-maker and director did not care to go into. Besides these instruments we have a hygrograph – we are well supplied; but this takes one of us out of doors once in the twenty-four hours. Lindström has cleaned it and oiled it and set it going. In spite of this, at three in the morning it comes to a stop. But I have never seen Lindström beaten yet. After many consultations he was given the task of trying to construct a thermograph out of the hygrograph and the disabled thermograph; this was just the job for him. The production he showed me a few hours later made my hair stand on end. What would Steen say? Do you know what it was? Well, it was an old meat-tin circulating inside the thermograph case. Heavens! what an insult to the self-registering meteorological instruments! I was thunderstruck, thinking, of course, that the man was making a fool of me. I had carefully studied his face all the time to find the key to this riddle, and did not know whether to laugh or weep. Lindström's face was certainly serious enough; if it afforded a measure of the situation, I believe tears would have been appropriate. But when my eye fell upon the thermograph and read, "Stavanger Preserving Co.'s finest rissoles," I could contain myself no longer. The comical side of it was too much for me, and I burst into a fit of laughter. When my laughter was subdued, I heard the explanation. The cylinder did not fit, so he had tried the tin, and it went splendidly. The rissole-thermograph worked very well as far as -40° C., but then it gave up.

Our forces were now divided into two working parties. One of them was to dig out some forty seals we had lying about 3 feet under the snow; this took two days. The heavy seals' carcasses, hard as flint, were difficult to deal with. The dogs were greatly interested in these proceedings. Each carcass, on being raised to the surface, was carefully inspected; they were piled up in two heaps, and would provide food enough for the dogs for the whole winter. Meanwhile the other party were at work under Hassel's direction on a petroleum cellar. The barrels which had been laid up at the beginning of February were now deep below the snow. They now dug down at both ends of the store, and made a passage below the surface along the barrels; at the same time they dug far enough into the Barrier to give the requisite height for the barrels. When the snow had been thrown out, one hole was walled up again, while a large entrance was constructed over the other. Stubberud's knowledge of vaulting came in useful here, and he has the credit of having built the splendid arched entrance to the oil-store. It was a pleasure to go down into it; probably no one has had so fine a storehouse for petroleum before. But Hassel did not stop here; he had the building fever on him in earnest. His great project of connecting the coal and wood store with the house below the surface nearly took my breath away; it seemed to me an almost superhuman labour, but they did it. The distance from the coal-tent to the house was about ten yards. Here Hassel and Stubberud laid out their line so that it would strike the passage round the house at the south-east angle. When they had done this, they dug a gigantic hole down into the Barrier half-way between the tent and the house, and then dug in both directions from here and soon finished the work. But now Prestrud had an idea. While the hole remained open he wished to avail himself of the opportunity of arranging an observatory for his pendulum apparatus, and he made a very good one. He did it by digging at right angles to the passage, and had his little observatory between the coal-tent and the house. When all the snow was cleared out, the big hole was covered over again, and now we could go from the kitchen direct to the coal-store without going out. First we followed the passage round the house – you remember where all the tinned provisions stood in such perfect order – then, on reaching the south-east angle of the house, this new passage opened out and led across to the coal-tent. In the middle of the passage, on the right-hand side, a door led into the pendulum observatory. Continuing along the passage, one came first to some steps leading down, and then the passage ended in a steep flight of steps which led up through a hole in the snow surface. On going up this one suddenly found oneself in the middle of the coal-tent. It was a fine piece of work, and did all honour to its designers. It paid, too – Hassel could now fetch coal at any time under cover, and escaped having to go out of doors.

But this was not the end of our great underground works. We wanted a room where Wisting could store all the things in his charge; he was specially anxious about the reindeer-skin clothing, and wished to have it under a roof. We therefore decided upon a room sufficiently large to house all these articles, and at the same time to provide working-space for Wisting and Hanssen, who would have to lash all the sledges as fast as they came from Bjaaland. Wisting elected to build this room in a big snow-drift that had formed around the tent in which he had kept all his stuff; the spot lay to the north-east of the house. The Clothing Store, as this building was called, was fairly large, and provided space not only for all our equipment, but also for a workshop. From it a door led into a very small room, where Wisting set up his sewing-machine and worked on it all through the winter. Continuing in a north-easterly direction, we came to another big room, called the Crystal Palace, in which all the ski and sledging cases were stored. Here all the provisions for the sledge journey were packed. For the time being this room remained separate from the others, and we had to go out of doors to reach it. Later, when Lindström had dug out an enormous hole in the Barrier at the spot where he took all the snow and ice for cooking, we connected this with the two rooms last mentioned, and were thus finally able to go everywhere under the snow.

The astronomical observatory had also arisen; it lay right alongside the Crystal Palace. But it had an air of suffering from debility, and before very long it passed peacefully away. Prestrud afterwards invented many patents; he used an empty barrel for a time as a pedestal, then an old block of wood. His experience of instrument-stands is manifold.

All these undertakings were finished at the beginning of May. One last piece of work remained, and then at last we should be ready. This was the rebuilding of the depot. The small heaps in which the cases were piled proved unsatisfactory, as the passages between the different piles offered a fine site for snow-drifts. All the cases were now taken out and laid in two long rows, with sufficient intervals between them to prevent their offering resistance to the drifting snow. This work was carried out in two days.

The days were now fairly short, and we were ready to take up our indoor work. The winter duties were assigned as follows: Prestrud, scientific observations; Johansen, packing of sledging provisions; Hassel had to keep Lindström supplied with coal, wood, and paraffin, and to make whip-lashes – an occupation he was very familiar with from the *Fram*'s second expedition;

Stubberud was to reduce the weight of the sledge cases to a minimum, besides doing a lot of other things. There was nothing he could not turn his hand to, so the programme of his winter work was left rather vague. I knew he would manage a great deal more than the sledge cases, though it must be said that it was a tiresome job he had. Bjaaland was allotted the task which we all regarded with intense interest – the alteration of the sledges. We knew that an enormous amount of weight could be saved, but how much? Hanssen and Wisting had to lash together the different parts as they were finished; this was to be done in the Clothing Store. These two had also a number of other things on their programme for the winter.

There are many who think that a Polar expedition is synonymous with idleness. I wish I had had a few adherents of this belief at Framheim that winter; they would have gone away with a different opinion. Not that the hours of work were excessively long, the circumstances forbade that. But during those hours the work was brisk.

On several previous sledge journeys I had made the experience that thermometers are very fragile things. It often happens that at the beginning of a journey one breaks all one's thermometers, and is left without any means of determining the temperature. If in such circumstances one had accustomed oneself to guess the temperature, it would have given the mean temperature for the month with a fair degree of accuracy. The guesses for single days might vary somewhat from reality on one side or the other, but, as I say, one would arrive at a fair estimate of the mean temperature. With this in my mind I started a guessing competition. As each man came in in the morning he gave his opinion of the temperature of the day, and this was entered in a book. At the end of the month the figures were gone through, and the one who had guessed correctly the greatest number of times won the prize – a few cigars. Besides giving practice in guessing the temperature, it was a very good diversion to begin the day with. When one day is almost exactly like another, as it was with us, the first hour of the morning is often apt to be a little sour, especially before one has had one's cup of coffee. I may say at once that this morning grumpiness very seldom showed itself with us. But one never knows – one cannot always be sure. The most amiable man may often give one a surprise before the coffee has had its effect. In this respect the guessing was an excellent thing; it took up everyone's attention, and diverted the critical moments. Each man's entrance was awaited with excitement, and one man was not allowed to make his guess in the hearing of the next – that would undoubtedly have exercised an influence. Therefore they had to speak as they came in, one by one.

"Now, Stubberud, what's the temperature to-day ?" Stubberud had his own way of calculating, which I never succeeded in getting at. One day, for instance, he looked about him and studied the various faces.

"It isn't warm to-day," he said at last, with a great deal of conviction. I could immediately console him with the assurance that he had guessed right. It was -69°F. The monthly results were very interesting. So far as I remember, the best performance the competition could show in any month was eight approximately correct guesses. A man might keep remarkably close to the actual temperature for a long time, and then suddenly one day make an error of 25°. It proved that the winner's mean temperature agreed within a few tenths of a degree with the actual mean temperature of the month, and if one took the mean of all the competitors' mean temperatures, it gave a result which, practically speaking, agreed with the reality. It was especially with this object in view that this guessing was instituted. If later on we should be so unlucky as to lose all our thermometers, we should not be entirely at a loss. It may be convenient to mention here that on the southern sledge journey we had four thermometers with us. Observations were taken three times daily, and all four were brought home in undamaged condition. Wisting had charge of this scientific branch, and I think the feat he achieved in not breaking any thermometers is unparalleled.

CHAPTER 8

A DAY AT FRAMHEIM

In order to understand our daily life better, we will now make a tour of Framheim. It is June 23, early in the morning. Perfect stillness lies over the Barrier – such stillness as no one who has not been in these regions has any idea of. We come up the old sledge road from the place where the *Fram* used to lie. You will stop several times on the way and ask whether this can be real; anything so inconceivably beautiful has never yet been seen. There lies the northern edge of the *Fram* Barrier, with Mounts Nelson and Rönniken nearest; behind them, ridge after ridge, peak after peak, the venerable pressure masses rise, one higher than another. The light is so wonderful; what causes this strange glow? It is clear as daylight, and yet the shortest day of the year is at hand. There are no shadows, so it cannot be the moon. No; it is one of the few really intense appearances of the *aurora australis* that receives us now. It looks as though Nature wished to honour our guests, and to show herself in her best attire. And it is a gorgeous dress she has chosen. Perfectly calm, clear with a starry sparkle, and not a sound in any direction. But wait: what is that? Like a stream of fire the light shoots across the sky, and a whistling sound follows the movement. Hush! can't you hear? It shoots forward again, takes the form of a band, and glows in rays of red and green. It stands still for a moment, thinking of what direction it shall take, and then away again, followed by an intermittent whistling sound. So Nature has offered us on this wonderful morning one of her most mysterious, most incomprehensible, phenomena – the audible southern light. "Now you will be able to go home and tell your friends that you have personally seen and heard the southern lights, for I suppose you have no doubt that you have really done so?" "Doubt? How can one be in doubt about what one has heard with one's own ears and seen with one's own eyes? "And yet you have been deceived, like so many others! The whistling northern and southern lights have never existed. They are only a creation of your own yearning for the mystical, accompanied by your own breath, which freezes in the cold air. Goodbye, beautiful dream! It vanishes from the glorious landscape." Perhaps it was stupid of me to call attention to that; my guests have now lost much of the beautiful mystery, and the landscape no longer has the same attraction.

Meanwhile we have come up past Nelson and Rönniken, and are just climbing the first ridge. Not far away a big tent rises before us, and in front of it we see two long, dark lines. It is our main depot that we are coming to, and you can see that we keep our things in good order, case upon case, as if they had been placed in position by an expert builder. And they all point the same way; all the numbers face the north. "What made you choose that particular direction?" is the natural question. "Had you any special object?" "Oh yes, we had. If you will look towards the east, you will notice that on the horizon the sky has a rather lighter, brighter colour there than in any other part.

That is the day as we see it now. At present we cannot see to do anything by its light. It would have been impossible to see that these cases were lying with their numbers to the north if it had not been for the brilliant *aurora australis*. But that light colour will rise and grow stronger. At nine o'clock it will be in the north-east, and we shall be able to trace it ten degrees above the horizon. You would not then think it gave so much light as it really does, but you would be able without an effort to read the numbers. What is more, you would be able to read the makers' names which are marked on several of the cases, and when the flush of daylight has moved to the north, you will be able to see them even more clearly. No doubt these figures and letters are big – about 2 inches high and 14 inches broad – but it shows, nevertheless, that we have daylight here at the darkest time of the year, so there is not the absolute darkness that people think. The tent that stands behind there contains dried fish; we have a great deal of that commodity, and our dogs can never suffer hunger. But now we must hurry on, if we are to see how the day begins at Framheim.

"What we are passing now is the mark-flag. We have five of them standing between the camp and the depot; they are useful on dark days, when the east wind is blowing and the snow falling. And there on the slope of the hill you see Framheim. At present it looks like a dark shadow on the snow, although it is not far away. The sharp peaks you see pointing to the sky are all our dog tents. The but itself you cannot see; it is completely snowed under and hidden in the Barrier.

"But I see you are getting warm with walking. We will go a little more slowly, so that you won't perspire too much. It is not more than -51°, so you have every reason to be warm walking. With that temperature and calm weather like to-day one soon feels warm if one moves about a little .... The flat place we have now come down into is a sort of basin; if you bend down and look round the horizon, you will be able with an effort to follow the ridges and hummocks the whole way round. Our house lies on the slope we are now approaching. We chose that particular spot, as we thought it would offer the best protection, and it turned out that we were right. The wind we have had has nearly always come from the east, when there was any strength in it, and against such winds the slope provides an excellent shelter. If we had placed our house over there where the depot stands, we should have felt the weather much more severely. But now you must be careful when we come near to the house, so that the dogs don't hear us. We have now about a hundred and twenty of them, and if they once start making a noise, then good-bye to the peaceful Polar morning. Now we are there, and in such daylight as there is, you can see the immediate surroundings. You can't see the house, you say. No; I can quite believe it. That chimney sticking out of the snow is all there is left above the Barrier. This trap-door we are coming to you might take for a loose piece of boarding thrown out on the snow, but that is not the case: it is the way down into our home. You must stoop a bit when you go down into the Barrier. Everything is on a reduced scale here in the Polar regions; we can't afford to be extravagant. Now you have four steps down; take care, they are rather high. Luckily we have come in time to see the day started. I see the passage-lamp is not yet lighted, so Lindström has not turned out. Take hold of the tail of my anorak and follow me. This is a passage in the snow that we are in, leading to the pent-house. Oh! I'm so sorry; you must forgive me! Did you hurt yourself? I quite forgot to tell you to look out for the threshold of the pent-house door. It is not the first time some-one has fallen over it. That's a trap we have all fallen into; but now we know it, and it doesn't catch us any more.

"If you will wait a second I'll strike a match, and then we shall see our way. Here we are in the kitchen. Now make your-self invisible and follow me all day, and you will see what our life is like. As you know, it is St. John's Eve, so we shall only work during the forenoon; but you will be able to see how we spend a holiday evening. When you send your account home, you must promise me not to paint it in too strong colours. Good-bye for the present."

Br-r-r-r-r! There's the alarm-clock. I wait and wait and wait. At home I am always accustomed to hear that noise followed by the passage of a pair of bare feet across the floor, and a yawn or so. Here – not a sound. When Amundsen left me he forgot to say where I could best put myself. I tried to follow him into the room, but the atmosphere there – no thanks! I could easily guess that nine men were sleeping in a room 19 feet by 13 feet; it did not require anyone to tell me that. Still not a sound. I sup-pose they only keep that alarm-clock to make themselves imag-ine they are turning out. Wait a minute, though. "Lindtrom! Lindtrom!" He went by the name of Lindtrom, not Lindström. "Now, by Jove! you've got to get up! The clock's made row enough." That's Wisting; I know his voice – I know him at home. He was always an early bird. A frightful crash! That's Lindström slipping out of his bunk. But if he was late in turn-

261

ing out, it did not take him long to get into his clothes. One! two! three! and there he stood in the doorway, with a little lamp in his hand. It was now six o'clock. He looked well; round and fat, as when I saw him last. He is in dark blue clothes, with a knitted helmet over his head. I should like to know why; it is certainly not cold in here. For that matter, I have often felt it colder in kitchens at home in the winter, so that cannot be the reason. Oh, I have it! He is bald, and doesn't like to show it. That is often the way with bald men; they hate anyone seeing it. The first thing he does is to lay the fire. The range is under the window, and takes up half the 6 feet by 13 feet kitchen. His method of laying a fire is the first thing that attracts my attention. At home we generally begin by splitting sticks and laying the wood in very carefully. But Lindström just shoves the wood in anyhow, all over the place. Well, if he can make that barn, he's clever. I am still wondering how he will manage it, when he suddenly stoops down and picks up a can. Without the slightest hesitation, as though it were the most natural thing in the world, he pours paraffin over the wood. Not one or two drops – oh no; he throws on enough to make sure. A match – and then I understood how Lindström got it to light. It was smartly done, I must say – but Hassel ought to have seen it! Amundsen had told me something of their arrangements on the way up, and I knew Hassel was responsible for coal, wood, and oil.

The water-pot had been filled the evening before, and he had only to push it to one side to make room for the kettle, and this did not take long to boil with the heat he had set going. The fire burned up so that it roared in the chimney – this fellow is not short of fuel. Strange, what a hurry he is in to get that coffee ready! I thought breakfast was at eight, and it is now not more than a quarter past six. He grinds the coffee till his cheeks shake to and fro – incessantly. If the quality is in proportion to the quantity, it must be good enough. "Devil take it" – Lindström's morning greeting – "this coffee-mill is not worth throwing to the pigs! Might just as well chew the beans. It wouldn't take so long." And he is right; after a quarter of an hour's hard work he has only ground just enough. Now it is half-past six. On with the coffee! Ah, what a perfume! I would give something to know where Amundsen got it from. Meanwhile the cook has taken out his pipe, and is smoking away gaily on an empty stomach; it does not seem to do him any harm. Hullo! There's the coffee boiling over.

While the coffee was boiling and Lindström smoked, I was still wondering why he was in such a hurry to get the coffee ready. You ass! I thought; can't you see? Of course, he is going to give himself a drink of fresh, hot coffee before the others are up; that's clear enough. When the coffee was ready, I sat down on a camp-stool that stood in a corner, and watched him. But I must say he surprised me again. He pushed the coffee-kettle away from the fire and took down a cup from the wall; then went to a jug that stood on the bench and poured out – would you believe it? – a cup of cold tea! If he goes on in this way, we shall have surprises enough before evening, I thought to myself. Then he began to be deeply interested in an enamelled iron bowl, which stood on a shelf above the range. The heat, which was now intense (I looked at the thermograph which hung from the ceiling; it registered 84°F.), did not seem to be sufficient for its mysterious contents. It was also wrapped up in towels and cloths, and gave me the impression of having caught a severe cold. The glances he threw into it from time to time were anxious; he looked at the clock, and seemed to have something on his mind. Then suddenly I saw his face brighten; he gave a long, not very melodious whistle, bent down, seized a dust-pan, and hurried out into the pent-house. Now I was really excited. What was coming next? He came back at once with a happy smile all over his face, and the dust-pan full of – coal! If I had been curious before, I was now anxious. I withdrew as far as possible from the range, sat down on the floor itself, and fixed my eyes on the thermograph. As I thought, the pen began to move upward with rapid steps. This was too bad. I made up my mind to pay a visit to the Meteorological Institute as soon as I got home, and tell them what I had seen with my own eyes. But now the heat seemed intolerable down on the floor, where I was sitting; what must it be like – heavens above, the man was sitting on the stove! He must have gone out of his mind. I was just going to give a cry of terror, when the door opened, and in came Amundsen from the room. I gave a deep sigh. Now it would be all right the time was ten minutes past seven. "'Morning, Fatty!" – "'Morning." – "What's it like outside?" – "Easterly breeze and thick when I was out; but that's a good while ago." This fairly took my breath away He stood there with the coolest air in the world and talked about the weather, and I could take my oath he had not been outside the door that morning. "How's it getting on to-day – is it coming?" Amundsen looks with interest at the mysterious bowl. Lindström takes another peep under the cloth. "Yes, it's coming at last; but I've had to give it a lot to-day." – " Yes, it feels like it," answers the other, and goes out. My interest is now divided between "it " in the bowl and Amundsen's return, with the meteorological discussion that will ensue. It is not long before he reappears; evidently the temperature outside is not inviting. "Let's hear again, my friend " – he seats himself on the camp-stool beside which I am sitting on the floor – "what kind of weather did you say it was?" I prick up my ears; there is going to be fun. "It was an easterly breeze and thick as a wall, when I was out at six o'clock." – "Hm! then it has cleared remarkably quickly. It's a dead calm now, and quite clear." – "Ah, that's just what I should have thought! I could see it was falling light, and it was getting brighter in the east." He got out of that well. Meanwhile it was again the turn of the bowl. It was taken down from the shelf over the range and put on the bench; the various cloths were removed one by one until it was left perfectly bare. I could not resist any longer; I had to get up and look. And indeed it was worth looking at. The bowl was filled to the brim with golden-yellow dough, full of air-bubbles, and showing every sign that he had got it to rise. Now I began to respect Lindström; he was a devil of a fellow. No confectioner in our native latitudes could have shown a finer dough. It was now 7.25; everything seems to go by the clock here.

Lindström threw a last tender glance at his bowl, picked up a little bottle of spirit, and went into the next room. I saw my chance of following him in. There was not going to be any fun out there with Amundsen, who was sitting on the camp-stool half asleep. In the other room it was pitch-dark, and an atmosphere – no, ten atmospheres at least! I stood still in the doorway and breathed heavily. Lindström stumbled forward in the darkness, felt for and found the matches. He struck one, and lighted a spirit-holder that hung beneath a hanging lamp. There was not much to be seen by the light of the spirit flame; one could still only guess. Hear too, perhaps. They were sound sleepers, those boys. One grunted here and another there; they were snoring in every corner. The spirit might have been burning for a couple of minutes, when Lindström had to set to work in a hurry. He was off just as the flame went out, leaving the room in black darkness. I heard the spirit bottle and the nearest stool upset, and what followed I don't know, as I was unfamiliar with the surroundings – but there was a good deal of it. I heard a click – had no idea what it was – and then the same movement back again to the lamp. Of course, he now fell over the stool he had upset before. Meanwhile there was a hissing sound, and a stifling smell of paraffin. I was thinking of making my escape through the door, when suddenly, just as I suppose it happened on the first day of Creation, in an instant there was light. But it was a light that defies description; it dazzled and hurt the eyes, it was so bright. It was perfectly white and extremely agreeable – when one was not looking at it. Evidently it was one of the 200-candle Lux lamps. My admiration for Lindström had now risen to enthusiasm. What would I not have given to be able to make myself visible, embrace him, and tell him what I thought of him! But that could not be; I should not then be able to see life at Framheim as it really was. So I stood still. Lindström first tried to put straight what he had upset in his struggle with the lamp. The spirit had, of course, run out of the bottle when it fell, and was now flowing all over the table. This did not seem to make the slightest impression on him; a little scoop with his hand, and it all landed on Johansen's clothes, which were lying close by. This fellow seemed to be as well off for spirit as for paraffin. Then he vanished into the kitchen, but reappeared immediately with plates, cups, knives and forks. Lindström's laying of the breakfast-table was the finest clattering performance I have ever heard. If he wanted to put a spoon into a cup, he did not do it in the ordinary way; no, he put down the cup, lifted the spoon high in the air, and then dropped it into the cup. The noise he made in this way was infernal. Now I began to see why Amundsen had got up so early; he wanted to escape this process of laying the table, I expect. But this gave me at once an insight into the good-humour of the gentlemen in bed: if this had happened anywhere else, Lindström would have had a boot at his head. But here – they must have been the most peaceable men in the world.

Meanwhile I had had time to look around me. Close to the door where I was standing a pipe came down to the floor. It struck me at once that this was a ventilating-pipe. I bent down and put my hand over the opening; there was not so much as a hint of air to be felt. So this was the cause of the bad atmosphere. The next things that caught my eye were the bunks – nine of them: three on the right hand and six on the left. Most of the sleepers – if they could be regarded as such while the table was being laid – slept in bags – sleeping-bags. They must have been warm enough. The rest of the space was taken up by a long table, with small stools on two sides of it. Order appeared to reign; most of the clothes were hung up. Of course, a few lay on the floor, but then Lindström had been running about in the dark, and perhaps he had pulled them down. On the table, by the window, stood a gramophone and some tobacco-boxes and ash-trays. The furniture was not plentiful, nor was it in the style of Louis Quinze or Louis Seize, but it was sufficient. On the wall with the window hung a few paintings, and on the other portraits of the King, Queen, and Crown Prince Olav, apparently cut out of an illustrated paper, and pasted on blue cardboard. In the corner nearest the door on the right, where there was no bunk, the space seem to be occupied by clothes, some hanging on the wall, some on lines stretched across. So that was the drying-place, modest in its simplicity. Under the table were some varnished boxes – Heaven knows what they were for!

Now there seemed to be life in one of the bunks. It was Wisting, who was getting tired of the noise that still continued. Lindström took his time, rattling the spoons, smiling maliciously to himself, and looking up at the bunks. He did not make all this racket for nothing. Wisting, then, was the first to respond, and apparently the only one; at any rate, there was not a sign of movement in any of the others. "Good-morning, Fatty!" "Thought you were going to stop there till dinner." This is Lindström's greeting. "Look after yourself, old 'un. If I hadn't got you out, you'd have been asleep still." That was paying him in his own coin: Wisting was evidently not to be trifled with. However, they smiled and nodded to each other in a way that showed that there was no harm meant. At last Lindström had got rid of the last cup, and brought down the curtain on that act with the dropping of the final spoon. I thought now that he would go back to his work in the kitchen; but it looked as if he had something else to do first. He straightened himself, thrust his chin in the air and put his head back – reminding me very forcibly of a young cockerel preparing to crow – and roared with the full force of his lungs: "Turn out, boys, and look sharp!" Now he had finished his morning duty there. The sleeping-bags seemed suddenly to awake to life, and such remarks as, "That's a devil of a fellow!" or "Shut up, you old chatterbox!" showed that the inhabitants of Framheim were now awake. Beaming with joy, the cause of the trouble disappeared into the kitchen.

And now, one after the other they stick their heads out, followed by the rest of them. That must be Helmer Hanssen, who was on the Gjöa; he looks as if he could handle a rope. Ah, and there we have Olav Olavson Bjaaland! I could have cried aloud for joy – my old friend from Holmenkollen. The great long-distance runner, you remember. And he managed the jump, too – 50 metres, I think – standing. If Amundsen has a few like him, he will get to the Pole all right. And there comes Stubberud, the man the Aftenpost said was so clever at double-entry book-keeping. As I see him now, he does not give me the impression of being a book-keeper – but one can't tell. And here come Hassel, Johansen, and Prestrud; now they are all up, and will soon begin the day's work.

"Stubberud!" It is Lindström putting his head in at the door. "If you want any hot cakes, you must get some air down." Stubberud merely smiles; he looks as if he felt sure of getting them, all the same. What was it he talked about? Hot cakes? They must be connected with the beautiful dough and the delicate, seductive smell of cooking that is now penetrating through the crack of the door. Stubberud is going, and I must go with him. Yes, as I thought – there stands Lindström in all his glory before the range, brandishing the weapon with which he turns the cakes; and in a pan lie three brownish-yellow buckwheat cakes quivering with the heat of the fire. Heavens, how hungry it made me! I take up my old position, so as not to be in anyone's way, and watch Lindström. He's the man – he produces hot cakes with astonishing dexterity; it almost reminds one of a juggler throwing up balls, so rapid and regular is the process. The way he manipulates the cake-slice shows a fabulous proficiency. With the skimmer in one hand he dumps fresh dough into the pan, and with the cake-slice in the other he removes those that are done, all at the same time; it seems almost more than human!

There comes Wisting, salutes, and holds out a little tin mug. Flattered by the honour, the cook fills his mug with boiling water, and he disappears into the pent-house. But this interruption puts Lindström off his jugglery with the hot cakes-one of them rolls down on to the floor. This fellow is extraordinarily phlegmatic; I can't make out whether he missed that cake or not. I believe the sigh that escaped him at the same instant meant something like: "Well, we must leave some for the dogs."

And now they all come in single file with their little mugs, and get each a drop of boiling water. I get up, interested in this proceeding, and slip out with one of them into the pent-house and so on to the Barrier. You will hardly believe me, when I tell you what I saw – all the Polar explorers standing in a row, brushing their teeth! What do you say to that? So they are not such absolute pigs, after all. There was a scent of Stomatol everywhere.

Here comes Amundsen. He has evidently been out taking the meteorological observations, as he holds the anemometer in one hand. I follow him through the passage, and, when no one is looking, take the opportunity of slapping him on the shoulder and saying "A grand lot of boys." He only smiled; but a smile may often say more than many words. I understood what it meant; he had known that a long while and a good deal more.

It was now eight o'clock. The door from the kitchen to the room was left wide open, and the warmth streamed in and mixed with the fresh air that Stubberud had now forced to come down the right way. Now it was pleasanter inside – fresh, warm air everywhere. Then came a very interesting scene. As the tooth-brushing gentlemen returned, they had to guess the temperature, one by one. This gave occasion for much joking and fun, and, amid laughter and chat, the first meal of the day was taken. In after-dinner speeches, amid toasts and enthusiasm, our Polar explorers are often compared with our forefathers, the bold vikings. This comparison never occurred to me for a moment when I saw this assemblage of ordinary, everyday men-brushing their teeth. But now that they were busy with the dishes, I was bound to acknowledge its aptitude; for our forefathers the vikings could not possibly have attacked their food with greater energy than these nine men did.

One pile of "hot-chek" after another disappeared as if they had been made of air – and I, in my simplicity, had imagined that one of them was a man's ration! Spread with butter and surmounted with jam, these cakes slipped down with fabulous rapidity. With a smile I thought of the conjurer, holding an egg in his hand one minute and making it disappear the next. If it is a cook's best reward to see his food appreciated, then, indeed, Lindström had good wages. The cakes were washed down with big bowls of strong, aromatic coffee. One could soon trace the effect, and conversation became general. The first great subject was a novel, which was obviously very popular, and was called "The Rome Express." It appeared to me, from what was said – I have unfortunately never read this celebrated work – that a murder had been committed in this train, and a lively discussion arose as to who had committed it. I believe the general verdict was one of suicide. I have always supposed that subjects of conversation must be very difficult to find on expeditions like these, where the same people mix day after day for years; but there was certainly no sign of any such difficulty here. No sooner had the express vanished in the distance than in steamed – the language question. And it came at full steam, too. It was clear that there were adherents of both camps present. For fear of hurting the feelings of either party, I shall abstain from setting down what I heard: but I may say as much as this – that the party of reform ended by declaring the maal to be the only proper speech of Norway, while their opponents maintained the same of their language.

After a while pipes came out, and the scent of "plug" soon struggled with the fresh air for supremacy. Over the tobacco the work for the day was discussed. "Well, I'll have enough to do supplying that woodswallower over the holiday," said Hassel. I gave a chuckle. If Hassel had known of the way the paraffin was used that morning, he would have added something about the "oil-drinker," I expect. It was now half-past eight, and Stubberud and Bjaaland got up. From the number of different garments they took out and put on, I guessed they were going out. Without saying anything, they trudged out. Meanwhile the others continued their morning smoke, and some even began to read, but by about nine they were all on the move. They put on their skin clothing and made ready to go out. By this time Bjaaland and Stubberud had returned from a walk, as I understood from such remarks as "Beastly cold," "Sharp snow by the depot," and the like. Prestrud was the only one who did not get ready to go out; he went to an open space underneath the farthest bunk, where there was a box. He raised the lid of this, and three chronometers appeared; at the same moment three of the men produced their watches, and a comparison was made and entered in a book. After each watch had been compared, its owner went outside, taking his watch with him. I took the opportunity of slipping out with the last man – Prestrud and his chronometers were too serious for me; I wanted to see what the others were about.

There was plenty of life outside; dogs' howls in every key came from the tents. Some of those who had left the house before us were out of sight, so they had probably gone to their respective tents, and presently one could see by the lights that they were in the act of letting their dogs loose. How well the lighted-up tents looked against the dark, star-strewn sky! Though it could no longer be called dark: the little flush of dawn had spread and overpowered the glow of the *aurora australis*, which had greatly decreased since I last saw it; evidently it was near its end. Now the four-footed band began to swarm out, darting like rockets from the tents. Here were all colours-grey, black, red, brown, white, and a mixture of all of them. What surprised me was that they were all so small; but otherwise they looked splendid. Plump and round, well kept and groomed, bursting with life. They instantly collected into little groups of from two to five, and it was easy to see that these groups consisted of intimate friends – they absolutely petted each other. In each of these clusters there was one in particular who was made much of; all the others came round him, licked him, fawned upon him, and gave him every sign of deference.

They all run about without a sign of unfriendliness. Their chief interest seems to be centred in two large black mounds that are visible in the foreground of the camp; what they are I am unable to make out – there is not light enough for that – but I am probably not far wrong in guessing that they are seals. They are rather hard eating, anyhow, for I can hear them crunching under the dogs' teeth. Here there is an occasional disturbance of the peace; they do not seem to agree so well over their food, but there is never a regular battle. A watchman is present, armed with a stick, and when he shows himself and makes his voice heard, they soon separate. They appear to be well disciplined.

What appealed to me most was the youngsters and the youngest of all. The young ones, to judge from their appearance, were about ten months old. They were perfect in every way; one could see they had been well cared for from their birth. Their coats were surprisingly thick – much more so than those of the older dogs. They were remarkably plucky, and would not give in to anyone.

And there are the smallest of all – like little balls of wool; they roll themselves in the snow and have great fun. I am astonished that they can stand the cold as they do; I should never have thought that such young animals could live through the winter.

Afterwards I was told that they not only bore the cold well, but were far more hardy than the older ones. While the grown-up dogs were glad to go into their tents in the evening, the little ones refused to do so; they preferred to sleep outside. And they did so for a great part of the winter.

Now all the men have finished unchaining their dogs, and, with their lanterns in their hands, they move in various directions and disappear – apparently into the Barrier surface. There will be many interesting things to see here in the course of the day – I can understand that. What on earth became of all these people? There we have Amundsen; he is left alone, and appears to be in charge of the dogs. I go up to him and make myself known.

"Ah, I'm glad you came," he says; "now I can introduce you to some of our celebrities. To begin with, here is the trio – Fix, Lasse, and Snuppesen. They always behave like this when I am out – could not think of leaving me in peace for an instant. Fix, that big grey one that looks like a wolf, has many a snap on his conscience. His first exploit was on Flekkerö, near Christiansand, where all the dogs were kept for a month after they arrived from Greenland; there he gave Lindström a nasty bite when his back was turned. What do you think of a bite of a mouth like that?"

Fix is now tame, and without a growl allows his master to take hold of his upper and under jaws and open his mouth – ye gods, what teeth! I inwardly rejoice that I was not in Lindström's trousers that day.

"If you notice," he continues, with a smile, "you will see that Lindström still sits down cautiously. I myself have a mark on my left calf, and a good many more of us have the same. There are several of us who still treat him with respect. And here we have Lassesen – that's his pet name; he was christened Lasse – almost pure black, as you see. I believe he was the wildest of the lot when they came on board. I had him fastened up on the bridge with my other dogs, beside Fix – those two were friends from their Greenland days. But I can tell you that when I had to pass Lasse, I always judged the distance first. As a rule, he just stood looking down at the deck – exactly like a mad bull. If I tried to make overtures, he didn't move – stood quite still; but I could see how he drew back his upper lip and showed a row of teeth, with which I had no desire to become acquainted. A fortnight passed in this way. Then at last the upper lip sank and the head was raised a little, as though he wanted to see who it was that brought him food and water every day. But the way from that to friendship was long and tortuous. In the time that followed, I used to scratch him on the back with a stick; at first he jumped round, seized the stick, and crushed it between his teeth. I thought myself lucky that it was not my hand. I came a little nearer to him every day, until one day I risked my hand. He gave me an ugly look, but did nothing; and then came the beginning of our friendship. Day by day we became better friends, and now you can see what footing we are on. The third is Snuppesen, a dark red lady; she is their sworn friend, and never leaves them. She is the quickest and most active of our dogs. You can see that she is fond of me; she is generally on her hind legs, and makes every effort to get at my face. I have tried to get her out of the way of that, but in vain; she will have her own way. I have no other animals for the moment that are worth showing – unless you would care to hear a song. If so, there is Uranus, who is a professional singer. We'll take the trio with us, and you shall hear."

We made for two black-and-white dogs that were lying by themselves on the snow a little way off, while the three jumped and danced about us. As we approached the other two, and they caught sight of the trio, they both jumped up as though at a word of command, and I guessed that we had found the singer. Lord save us, what an awful voice! I could see that the concert was for Lasse's benefit, and Uranus kept it up as long as we stood in his vicinity. But then my attention was suddenly aroused by the appearance of another trio, which made an extraordinary favourable impression. I turned to my companion for information.

"Yes," he continued, "those are three of Hanssen's team; probably some of our best animals. The big black-and-white one is called Zanko – he appears to be rather old; the two others, which look like sausages with matches underneath, are Ring and Mylius. As you see, they are not very big, rather on the small side, but they are undoubtedly among our best workers. From their looks we have concluded that they are brothers – they are as like as two drops of water. Now we will go straight through the mass and see whether we come across any more celebrities. There we have Karenius, Sauen, Schwartz, and Lucy; they belong to Stubberud, and are a power in the camp. Bjaaland's tent is close by; his favourites are lying there – Kvaen, Lap, Pan, Gorki, and Jaala. They are small, all of them, but fine dogs. There, in the south-east corner, stands Hassel's tent, but we shall not see any of his dogs here now. They are all lying outside the entrance to the oil-store, where he is generally to be found. The next tent is Wisting's. We must take a turn round there and see if we can find his lot. There they are – those four playing there. The big, reddish-brown one on the right is the Colonel, our handsomest animal. His three companions are Suggen, Arne, and Brun. I must tell you a little story about the Colonel when he was on Flekkerö. He was perfectly wild then, and he broke loose and jumped into the sea. He wasn't discovered till he was half-way between Flekkerö and the mainland, where he was probably going in search of a joint of mutton. Wisting and Lindström, who were then in charge of the dogs, put off in a boat, and finally succeeded in overtaking him, but they had a hard tussle before they managed to get him on board. Afterwards Wisting had a swimming-race with the Colonel, but I don't remember what was the result. We can expect a great deal of these dogs. There's Johansen's tent over in the corner; there is not much to be said about his dogs. The most remarkable of them is Camilla. She is an excellent mother, and brings up her children very well; she usually has a whole army of them, too.

"Now I expect you have seen dogs enough, so, if you have no objection, I will show you underground Framheim and what goes on there. I may just as well add that we are proud of this work, and you will probably find that we have a right to be. We'll begin with Hassel, as his department is nearest."

We now went in the direction of the house, passed its western end, and soon arrived at an erection that looked like a derrick. Underneath it was a large trap-door. Where the three legs of the derrick met, there was made fast a small block, and through the block ran a rope, made fast at one end to the trap-door. A weight hung at the other end, some feet above the surface of the snow.

"Now we are at Hassel's," said my companion. It was a good thing he could not see me, for I must have looked rather foolish. At Hassel's? I said to myself. What in the world does the man mean? We were standing on the bare Barrier.

"Do you hear that noise? That's Hassel sawing wood."

Now he bent down and raised the heavy trap-door easily with the help of the weight. Broad steps of snow led down, deep down, into the Barrier. We left the trap-door open, so as to have the benefit of the little daylight there was. My host went first; I followed. After descending four or five steps, we came to a doorway which was covered with a woollen curtain. We pushed this aside. The sound that had first reached me as a low rumbling now became sharper, and I could plainly hear that it was caused by sawing. We went in. The room we entered was long and narrow, cut out of the Barrier. On a solid shelf of snow there lay barrel after barrel arranged in exemplary order; if they were all full of paraffin, I began to understand Lindström's extravagance in lighting his fire in the morning: here was paraffin enough for several years. In the middle of the room a lantern was hanging, an ordinary one with wire netting round the glass. In a dark room it certainly would not have given much light, but in these white surroundings it shone like the sun. A Primus lamp was burning on the floor. The thermometer, which hung a little way from the Primus, showed -5° F., so Hassel could hardly complain of the heat, but he had to saw, so it did not matter. We approached Hassel. He looked as if he had plenty to do, and was sawing away so that the sawdust was flying. "'Morning." – "'Morning." The sawdust flew faster and faster. "You seem to be busy to-day." – "Oh yes!" – the saw was now working with dangerous rapidity – "if I'm to get finished for the holiday, I must hurry up." – How's the coal-supply getting on?" That took effect. The saw stopped instantly, was raised, and put down by the wall. I waited for the next step in suppressed excitement; something hitherto undreamt of must be going to happen. Hassel looked round – one can never be careful enough – approached my host, and whispered, with every sign of caution "I did him out of twenty-five kilos last week." I breathed again; I had expected something much worse than that. With a smile of satisfaction Hassel resumed his interrupted work, and I believe nothing in the world would have stopped him again. The last I saw as we returned through the doorway was Hassel surrounded by a halo of sawdust.

We were back on the Barrier surface; a touch of the finger, and the trap-door swung over and fell noiselessly into its place. I could see that Hassel was capable of other things besides sawing birchwood. Outside lay his team, guarding all his movements – Mikkel, Ræven, Masmas, and Else. They all looked well. Now we were going to see the others.

We went over to the entrance of the hut and raised the trapdoor; a dazzling light met my eyes. In the wall of the steps leading down from the surface a recess had been cut to hold a wooden case lined with bright tin; this contained a little lamp which produced this powerful light. But it was the surroundings that made it so bright – ice and snow everywhere. Now I could look about me for the first time; it had been dark when I came in the morning. There was the snow-tunnel leading to the pent-house; I could see that by the threshold that grinned at me. But there, in the opposite direction, what was there? I could see that the passage was continued, but where did it lead? Standing in the bright light, it looked quite dark in the tunnel.

"Now we will go and see Bjaaland first." With these words my companion bent down, and set off through the dark passage. "Look there, in the snow-wall – just under our feet – can you see the light?" By degrees my eyes had accustomed themselves to the darkness of the tunnel, and I could see a greenish light shining through the snow-wall where he pointed. And now another noise fell on my ears – a monotonous sound – coming from below.

"Look out for the steps!" Yes, he could be sure of that; I had come one cropper that day, and it was enough. We once more descended into the Barrier by broad, solid snow-steps covered with boards. Suddenly a door was opened – a sliding-door in the snow-wall – and I stood in Bjaaland's and Stubberud's premises. The place might be about 6 feet high, 15 feet long, and 7 feet wide. On the floor lay masses of shavings, which made it warm and cosy. At one end stood a Primus lamp with a large tin case over it, from which steam was issuing. "How is it going?" – "All right. We're just bending the runners. I've made a rough estimate of the weight, and find I can bring it down to 48 pounds." This seemed to me almost incredible. Amundsen had told me on the way up this morning of the heavy sledges they had – 165 pounds each. And now Bjaaland was going to bring them down to 48 pounds, less than a third of their original weight. In the snow-walls of the room were fixed hooks and shelves, where the tools were kept. Bjaaland's carpenter's bench was massive enough – cut out in the snow and covered with boards. Along the opposite wall was another planing-bench, equally massive, but somewhat shorter than the first. This was evidently Stubberud's place. He was not here to-day, but I could see that he was engaged in planing down the sledge cases and making them lighter. One of them was finished; I leaned forward and looked at it. On the top, where a little round aluminium lid was let in, was written: "Original weight, 9 kilos; reduced weight, 6 kilos." I could understand what this saving of weight meant to men who were going on such a journey as these had before them. One lamp provided all the illumination, but it gave an excellent light. We left Bjaaland. I felt sure that the sledging outfit was in the best of hands.

We then made our way into the pent-house, and here we met Stubberud. He was engaged in cleaning up and putting things straight for the holiday. All the steam that came out of the kitchen, when the door was opened, had condensed on the roof and walls in the form of rime several inches thick, and Stubberud was now clearing this off with a long broom. Everything was going to be shipshape for Midwinter Eve; I could see that. We went in. Dinner was on, humming and boiling. The kitchen floor was scrubbed clean, and the linoleum with which it was covered shone gaily. It was the same in the living-room; everything was cleaned. The linoleum on the floor and the American cloth on the table were equally bright. The air was pure – absolutely pure. All the bunks were made tidy, and the stools put in their places. There was no one here.

"You have only seen a fraction of our underground palaces,

but I thought we would take a turn in the loft first and see what it is like. Follow me." We went out into the kitchen, and then up some steps fastened in the wall, and through the trap-door to the loft. With the help of a little electric lamp, we were able to look about us. The first thing that met my eyes was the library. There stood the Framheim library, and it made the same good impression as everything else – books numbered from 1 to 80 in three shelves. The catalogue lay by the side of them, and I cast my eye over it. Here were books to suit all tastes; "Librarian, Adolf Henrik Lindström," I read at the end. So he was librarian, too-truly a many-sided man. Long rows of cases stood here, full of whortleberry jam, cranberries, syrup, cream, sugar, and pickles. In one corner I saw every sign of a dark-room; a curtain was hung up to keep the light off, and there was an array of developing-dishes, measuring-glasses, etc. This loft was made good use of. We had now seen everything, and descended again to continue our inspection.

Just as we reached the pent-house, Lindström came in with a big bucket of ice; I understood that it was to be used in the manufacture of water. My companion had armed himself with a large and powerful lantern, and I saw that we were going to begin our underground travels. In the north wall of the pent-house there was a door, and through this we went, entering a passage built against the house, and dark as the grave. The lantern had lost its power of illumination; it burned with a dull, dead light, which did not seem to penetrate beyond the glass. I stretched my hands in front of me. My host stopped and gave me a lecture on the wonderful order and tidiness they had succeeded in establishing among them. I was a willing listener, for

I had already seen enough to be able to certify the truth of what he told me without hesitation. But in the place we were now in, I had to take his word for it, for it was all as black as bilge-water. We had just started to move on again, and I felt so secure, after all he had told me about the orderly way things were kept, that I let go my guide's anorak, which I had been holding. But that was foolish of me. Smack! I went down at full length. I had trodden on something round – something that brought me down. As I fell, I caught hold of something – also round – and I lay convulsively clutching it. I wanted to convince myself of what it was that lay about on the floor of such a tidy house. The glimmer of the lantern, though not particularly strong, was enough to show me what I held in my arms – a Dutch cheese! I put it back in the same place – for the sake of tidiness – sat up, and looked down at my feet. What was it I had stumbled over? A Dutch cheese – if it wasn't another of the same family! I began to form my own opinion of the tidiness now, but said nothing. But I should like to know why he didn't fall over the cheeses, as he was walking in front. Oh, I answered myself, I guess he knew what sort of order the place was in.

At the eastern end of the house the passage was brilliantly lighted up by the window that looked out on this side; I could now see more clearly where I was. Opposite the window, in the part of the Barrier that here formed the other wall of the passage, a great hole had been dug; nothing was to be seen in it but black darkness. My companion knew his way, so I could rely upon him, but I should have hesitated to go in there alone. The hole extended into the Barrier, and finally formed a fairly large room with a vaulted roof. A spade and an axe on the floor were all I saw. What in the world was this hall used for? "You see, all the ice and snow from here has gone to our water-supply." So this was Lindström's quarry, from which he had hewn out ice and snow all these months for cooking, drinking, and washing. In one of the walls, close to the floor, there was a little hole just big enough for a man to crawl through.

"Now you must make yourself small and follow me; we are going to visit Hanssen and Wisting." And my companion disappeared like a snake into the hole. I threw myself down, quick as lightning, and followed. I would not have cared to be left alone there in pitch-darkness. I managed to get hold of one of his calves, and did not let go until I saw light on the other side. The passage we crept through was equally narrow all the way, and forced one to crawl on hands and knees; fortunately, it was not long. It ended in a fairly large, square room. A low table stood in the middle of the floor, and on it Helmer Hanssen was engaged in lashing sledges. The room gave one the impression of being badly lighted, though it had a lamp and candles. On a closer examination, I found that this was due to the number of dark objects the place contained. Against one of the walls there was clothing – immense piles of skin – clothing. Over this were spread blankets to protect it from the rime that was formed on the roof and fell down. Against the opposite wall was a stack of sledges, and at the end, opposite the door, were piles of woollen underclothing. Any outfitter in Christiania might have envied this stock; here one saw Iceland jackets, sweaters, underclothes of immense thickness and dimensions, stockings, mits, etc. In the corner formed by this wall and the one where the sledges stood was the little hole by which we had entered. Beyond the sledges, in the same wall, there was a door with a curtain in front of it, and from within it came a strange humming. I was much interested to know what this might be, but had to hear first what these two had to say.

"What do you think of the lashings now, Hanssen?"

"Oh, they'll hold right enough; at any rate, they'll be better than they were before. Look here, how they've pointed the ends!"

I leaned forward to see what was wrong with the sledge-lashings, and, I must say, what I saw surprised me. Is such a thing possible? The pointing of a lashing is a thing a sailor is very careful about. He knows that if the end is badly pointed, it does not matter how well the lashing is put on; therefore it is an invariable rule that lashings must be pointed as carefully as possible. When I looked at this one, what do you think I saw? Why, the end of the lashing was nailed down with a little tack, such as one would use to fasten labels. "That would be a nice thing to take to the Pole!" This final observation of Hanssen's was doubtless the mildest expression of what he thought of the work. I saw how the new lashings were being put on, and I was quite ready to agree with Hanssen that they would do the work. It was, by the way, no easy job, this lashing at -15°F., as the thermometer showed, but Hanssen did not seem to mind it.

I had heard that Wisting also took part in this work, but he was not to be seen. Where could he be? My eyes involuntarily sought the curtain, behind which the humming sound was audible. I was now ready to burst with curiosity. At last the lashing question appears to be thrashed out, and my companion shows signs of moving on. He leaves his lantern and goes up to the curtain. "Wisting!" – "Yes!" The answer seems to come from a far distance. The humming ceases, and the curtain is thrust aside. Then I am confronted by the sight that has impressed me most of all on this eventful day. There sits Wisting, in the middle of the Barrier, working a sewing-machine. The temperature outside is now -60°F. This seems to me to require some explanation; I slink through the opening to get a closer view. Then – ugh! I am met by a regular tropical blast. I glance at the thermometer; it shows +50° F. But how can this be? Here he is, sewing in an ice-cellar at +50°. I was told in my school-days that ice melts at about +32°. If the same law is still in operation, he ought to be sitting in a shower-bath. I go right in; the sewing-room is not large, about 6 feet each way. Besides the sewing-machine – a modern treadle-machine – the room contains a number of instruments, compasses, and so forth, besides the large tent he is now working on. But what interests me most is the way in which he circumvents the shower-bath. I see it now; it is very cleverly contrived. He has covered the roof and walls with tin and canvas, so arranged that all the melting ice goes the same way, and runs into a wash-tub that stands below. In this manner he collects washing water, which is such a precious commodity in these regions – wily man! I afterwards hear that nearly all the outfit for the Polar journey is being made in this little ice-cabin. Well, with men like these I don't think Amundsen will deserve any credit for reaching the Pole. He ought to be thrashed if he doesn't.

Now we have finished here, and must in all probability have seen everything. My guide goes over to the wall where the clothing is lying and begins to rummage in it. A clothing inspection, I say to myself; there's no great fun in that. I sit down on the pile of sledges by the opposite wall, and am going over in my mind all I have seen, when suddenly he thrusts his head forward – like a man who is going to make a dive – and disappears among the bundles of skins. I jump up and make for the piles of clothing; I am beginning to feel quite lost in this mysterious world. In my hurry I collide with Hanssen's sledge, which falls off the table; he looks round furiously. It is a good thing he could not see me; he looked like murder. I squeeze in between the bundles of clothing, and what do I see? Another hole in the wall; another low, dark passage. I pluck up courage and plunge in. This tunnel is rather higher than the other, and I can walk, bending double. Fortunately, the light at the other end shows up at once, so that my journey in the dark is not a long one this time. I come out into another large room of about the same size as the last, and afterwards learn that it is known as the Crystal Palace. The name is appropriate, as crystals sparkle on every side. Against one wall a number of pairs of ski are resting; elsewhere there are cases, some yellow and some black. I guess the meaning of this at once, after my visit to Stubberud. The yellow cases are the original ones, and the black the improved ones. They think of everything here. Of course, in snow black is a far better colour than light yellow; the cases will be pleasanter to look at, and very much easier to see at a distance. And if they happen to run short of marks, all they need do will be to break up a case and make as many black marks as they want; they will be easily seen in the snow. The lids of these cases surprise me. They are no bigger than ordinary large milk-can lids, and of the same form; they are loose, as with a milk-can, and are put on in the same way. Then it suddenly occurs to me. When I was sitting on the sledges in Hanssen's workshop, I noticed little pieces of wire rope fixed to both ribs of the sledge. There were eight of them on each side – just the right number. They are lashings for four cases, and they will hardly take more than that on a sledge. On one rib all the wire ropes ended in eyes; on the other they ended in thin lashings. Obviously there were four of them to each case – two forward and two aft of the lid. If these were reeved and drawn taut, the cases would be held as in a vice, and the lids could be taken off freely at any time. It was an ingenious idea, which would save a lot of work.

But there sits Johansen in the middle of the Palace, packing. He seems to have a difficult problem to solve; he looks so profoundly thoughtful. Before him is a case half packed, marked "Sledge No. V., Case No. 4." More singular contents I have never seen – a mixture of pemmican and sausage. I have never heard of sausages on a sledge journey; it must be something quite new. The pieces of pemmican are cylindrical in shape, about 2 inches high and 4 and 3/4 inches in diameter; when they are packed, there will be large star-shaped openings between every four of them. Each of these openings is filled up with a sausage, which stands straight up and down, and is of exactly the height of the case. But sausage – let me see. Ah! there's a sausage with a tear in its skin; I run across and look at it. Oh, the cunning rascals! if it isn't milk-powder they are smuggling in like this! So every bit of space is utilized. The gaps left by these round pieces of pemmican at the sides of the cases are, of course, only half as large as the rest, and so cannot take a milk-sausage; but don't imagine that the space is wasted. No;

chocolate is broken up into small pieces and stowed in there. When all these cases are packed, they will be as full as if they were of solid wood. There is one ready packed; I must see what it contains. Biscuits – 5,400 biscuits is marked on the lid. They say that angels are specially gifted with patience, but theirs must be a trifle compared with Johansen's. There was absolutely not a fraction of an inch left in that case.

The Crystal Palace at present reminds one strongly of a grocer's and chandler's store – pemmican, biscuits, chocolate, and milk-sausage, lie about everywhere. In the other wall, opposite the ski, there is an opening. I see my companion making for it, but this time I intend to keep an eye on him. He goes up two steps, pushes a trap-door, and there he stands on the Barrier – but I am there, too. The trap-door is replaced, and I see that we are close to another door in the Barrier, but this is a modern sliding-door. It leads into the clothing store. I turn to my host and give him my best thanks for the interesting circular trip through the Barrier, expressing my admiration of all the fine engineering works I have seen, and so on. He cuts me short with the remark that we are not nearly done yet. He has only brought me up this way to save my having to crawl back again. "We are going in now," he adds, "to continue our journey under the surface." I see that there is no getting out of it, although I am beginning to have enough of these underground passages. My host seems to guess my thoughts, as he adds: "We must see them now when the men are working. Afterwards they will not have the same interest." I see that he is right, pull myself together, and follow him.

But Fate wills it otherwise. As we come out on the Barrier, Hanssen is standing there with his sledge and six fresh dogs harnessed. My companion has just time to whisper to me, " Jump on; I'll wait here," when the sledge starts off at a terrific pace with me as a passenger, unsuspected by Hanssen.

We went along so that the snow dashed over us. He had his dogs well in hand, this fellow, I could see that; but they were a wild lot of rascals he had to deal with. I heard the names of Hok and Togo in particular; they seemed inclined for mischief. All of a sudden they darted back on their companions under the traces, and got the whole team in a tangle; but they were not able to do very much, as the whip, which was wielded with great dexterity, constantly sang about their ears. The two sausages I had noticed on the slope – Ring and Mylius – were leaders; they, too, were full of pranks, but kept their places. Hai and Rap were also in the team. Rap, whose ear was split, would have liked very much to get his friend Hai to join in a little fight with Hok and Togo, but for the whip. It swished to and fro, in and out, among them without mercy, and made them behave like good boys. After us, some yards behind, came Zanko. He seemed to be put out because he had not been harnessed. Meanwhile we went at a gallop up the hill to the depot, and the last flag was passed. There was a marked difference in the daylight here now. It was eleven o'clock, and the flush of dawn had risen a good way in the sky and was approaching the north. The numbers and marks on the cases were easily visible.

Hanssen drew up smartly by the rows of cases and halted. We stepped off the sledge. He stood still for a moment and looked round, then turned the sledge over, with the runners in the air. I supposed he did this to prevent the dogs making off when his back was turned; personally, I thought it was a poor safeguard. I jumped up on a case, and sat there to await what developments might come. And they came in the form of Zanko. Hanssen had moved off a little way with a piece of paper in his hand, and seemed to be examining the cases as he went along. Zanko had now reached his friends, Ring and Mylius, and the meeting was a very cordial one on both sides. This was too much for Hok; he was on to them like a rocket, followed by his friend Togo. Hai and Rap never let such an opportunity escape them, and they eagerly flung themselves into the thick of the fight. "Stop that, you blackguards!" It was Hanssen who threw this admonition in advance, as he came rushing back. Zanko, who was free, had kept his head sufficiently to observe the approaching danger; without much hesitation, he cut away and made for Framheim with all possible speed. Whether the others missed their sixth combatant, or whether they, too, became aware of Hanssen's threatening approach, I am unable to determine; certain it is that they all got clear of each other, as though at a given signal, and made off the same way. The capsized sledge made no difference to them; they went like the wind over the slope, and disappeared by the flagstaff. Hanssen did not take long to make up his mind, but what was the use? He went as fast as he could, no doubt, but had reached no farther than to the flagstaff, when the dogs, with the capsized sledge behind them, ran into Framheim and were stopped there.

I went quietly back, well pleased with the additional experience. Down on the level I met Hanssen on his way to the depot a second time; he looked extremely angry, and the way in which he used the whip did not promise well for the dogs' backs.

Zanko was now harnessed in the team. On my return to Framheim I saw no one, so I slipped into the pent-house, and waited for an opportunity of getting into the kitchen. This was not long in coming. Puffing and gasping like a small locomotive, Lindström swung in from the passage that led round the house. In his arms he again carried the big bucket full of ice, and an electric lamp hung from his mouth. In order to open the kitchen-door, he had only to give it a push with his knee; I slipped in. The house was empty. Now, I thought, I shall have a good chance of seeing what Lindström does when he is left alone. He put down the bucket of ice, and gradually filled up the water-pot which was on the fire. Then he looked at the clock: a quarter-past eleven – good; dinner will be ready in time. He drew a long, deep sigh, then went into the room, filled and lit his pipe. Thereupon he sat down and took up a doll that was sitting on a letter-weight. His whole face lighted up; one could see how pleased he was. He wound up the doll and put it on the table; as soon as he let it go, it began to turn somersaults, one after another, endlessly. And Lindström? Well, he laughed till he must have been near convulsions, crying out all the while: "That's right, Olava; go it again!" I then looked at the doll carefully, and it was certainly something out of the common. The head was that of an old woman – evidently a disagreeable old maid – with yellow hair, a hanging under-jaw, and a love-sick expression. She wore a dress of red-and-white check, and when she turned head over heels it caused, as might be expected, some disturbance of her costume. The figure, one could see, had originally been an acrobat, but these ingenious Polar explorers had transformed it into this hideous shape.

293

When the experiment was repeated, and I understood the situation, I could not help roaring, too, but Lindström was so deeply occupied that he did not hear me. After amusing himself for about ten minutes with this, he got tired of Olava, and put her up on the weight again. She sat there nodding and bowing until she was forgotten.

Meanwhile Lindström had gone to his bunk, and was lying half in it. Now, I thought to myself, he is going to take a little nap before dinner. But no; he came out again at once, holding a tattered old pack of cards in his hand. He went back to his place, and began a quiet and serious game of patience. It did not take long, and was probably not very complicated, but it served its purpose. One could see what a pleasure it was to him whenever a card came in its right place. Finally, all the cards were in order; he had finished the game. He sat a little while longer, enjoying the sight of the finished packs; then he picked them all up with a sigh, and rose, mumbling: "Yes, he'll get to the Pole, that's sure; and, what's more, he'll get there first." He put the cards back on the shelf in his bunk, and looked well pleased with himself.

Then the process of laying the table began once more, but with far less noise than in the morning; there was nobody to be annoyed by it now. At five minutes to twelve a big ship's bell was rung, and not long after the diners began to arrive. They did not make any elaborate toilet, but sat down to table at once. The dishes were not many: a thick, black seal soup, with all manner of curious things in it – seal meat cut into " small dice" is no doubt the expression, but it would be misleading here; "large dice" we had better call them – with potatoes, carrots, cabbage, turnips, peas, celery, prunes, and apples. I should like to know what our cooks at home would call that dish. Two large jugs of syrup and water stood on the table. Now I had another surprise; I was under the impression that a dinner like this passed off in silence, but that was by no means the case here. They talked the whole time, and the conversation chiefly turned on what they had been doing during the forenoon. For dessert they had some green plums. Pipes and books soon made their appearance.

By about two o'clock the boys gave fresh signs of life. I knew they were not going to work that afternoon – St. Hans' Eve – but habit is a strange thing. Bjaaland rose in a peremptory fashion, and asked who was going to have the first turn. After a lot of questions and answers, it was decided that Hassel should be the first. What it was I could not make out. I heard them talk about one or two Primuses, and say that half an hour was the most one could stand, but that did not mean anything to me. I should have to stick to Hassel; he was going first. If there should be no second man, I should, at any rate, have seen what the first one did. Everything became quiet again; it was only in the kitchen that one could tell that the Barrier was inhabited.

At half-past two Bjaaland, who had been out, came in and announced that now it was all a mass of steam. I watched Hassel anxiously. Yes; this announcement seemed to put life into him. He got up and began to undress. Very strange, I thought; what can this be? I tried the Sherlock Holmes method – first Bjaaland goes out; that is fact number one. Then he comes back; that I could also make sure of. So far the method worked well. But then comes the third item "It is all a mass of steam." What in the world does that mean? The man has gone out – if not out on to the Barrier, then certainly into it – into snow-ice, and then he comes back and says that it is all a mass of steam. It seems ridiculous – absurd. I send Sherlock Holmes to the deuce, and watch Hassel with increasing excitement; if he takes any more off – I felt I was blushing, and half turned my head, but there he stopped. Then he picked up a towel, and away we went: out through the pent-house door – it was all I could do to follow him – along the snow tunnel in nothing but – Here steam really began to meet us, getting thicker and thicker as we came into the Barrier. The tunnel became so full of steam that I could see nothing. I thought with longing of the tail of Amundsen's anorak that was so useful on such occasions, but here there was nothing to take hold of. Far away in the fog I could see a light, and made my way to it with caution. Before I knew where I was, I stood at the other end of the passage, which led into a large room, covered with rime, and closed overhead by a mighty dome of ice. The steam was troublesome, and spoilt my view of the room. But what had become of Hassel? I could only see Bjaaland. Then suddenly the fog seemed to clear for an instant, and I caught sight of a bare leg disappearing into a big black box, and a moment later I saw Hassel's smiling face on the top of the box. A shudder passed through my frame – he looked as if he had been decapitated. On further consideration, his features were too smiling; the head could not be severed from the body yet. Now the steam began to clear away little by little, and at last one could see clearly what was going on. I had to laugh; it was all very easy to understand now. But I think Sherlock Holmes would have found it a hard-nut to crack if he had been set down blindfold on the Antarctic Barrier, as I was, so to speak, and asked to explain the situation. It was one of those folding American vapour-baths that Hassel sat in. The bathroom, which had looked so spacious and elegant in the fog, reduced itself to a little snow-hut of insignificant appearance. The steam was now collected in the bath, and one could see by the face above that it was beginning to be warm there. The last thing I saw Bjaaland do was to pump two Primus lamps that were placed just under the bath up to high pressure, and then disappear. What a lesson an actor might have had in watching the face before me! It began with such a pleasant expression – well-being was written upon it in the brightest characters – then by degrees the smile wore off, and gave place to seriousness. But this did not last long; there was a trembling of the nostrils, and very soon it could clearly be seen that the bath was no longer of a pleasant nature. The complexion, from being normal, had changed to an ultra-violet tint; the eyes opened wider and wider, and I was anxiously awaiting a catastrophe.

It came, but in a very different form from that I had expected. Suddenly and noiselessly the bath was raised, and the steam poured out, laying a soft white curtain over what followed. I could see nothing; only heard that the two Primuses were turned down. I think it took about five minutes for the steam to disappear, and what did I see then? – Hassel, bright as a new shilling, dressed in his best for St. Hans' Eve. I availed myself of the opportunity to examine the first, and probably the only, vapour-bath on the Antarctic Barrier. It was, like everything else I had seen, very ingeniously contrived. The bath was a high box without bottom, and with a hole, large enough for the head, in the top. Ail the walls were double and were made of windproof material, with about an inch between for the air to circulate. This box stood on a platform, which was raised a couple of feet above the snow surface. The box fitted into a groove, and was thus absolutely tight. In the platform immediately under the bath a rectangular opening was cut, lined round with rubber packing, and into this opening a tin box fitted accurately. Under the tin box stood two Primus lamps, and now everyone will be able to understand why Hassel felt warm. A block hung from the top of the hut, with a rope reeved in it; one end was made fast to the upper edge of the bath, and the other went down into the bath. In this way the bather himself could raise the bath without assistance, and free himself when the heat became too great. The temperature outside the snow-wall was -65° F. Cunning lads! I afterwards heard that Bjaaland and Hassel had constructed this ingenious bath.

I now went back to the house, and saw how they all – almost – made use of the vapour-bath. By a quarter-past five all the bathing was concluded, and everyone put on his furs; it was evident that they were going out. I followed the first man who left the hut; he was provided with a lantern, and indeed it was wanted. The weather had changed: a south-west wind had sprung up suddenly, and now the air was thick with snow. It was not a fall of snow, for one could see the stars in the zenith, but snow caught up by the wind and whirled along. A man had to know the surroundings well to find his way now; one had to feel – it was impossible to keep one's eyes open. I took up a position in lee of a snow-drift, and waited to see what would happen. The dogs did not seem to be inconvenienced by the change of weather; some of them lay curled up in a ring, with their nose under their tail, on the snow, while others were running about. One by one the men came out; each had a lantern in his hand. As they arrived at the place where the dogs were, each was surrounded by his team, who followed him to the tents with joyous howls. But everything did not pass off peacefully; I heard – I think it was in Bjaaland's tent – a deafening noise going on, and looked in at the door. Down there, deep below the surface, they were having a warm time. All the dogs were mixed up together in one mass: some were biting, some shrieking, some howling. In the midst of this mass of raging dogs I saw a human figure swinging round, with a bunch of dog-collars in one hand, while he dealt blows right and left with the other, and blessed the dogs all the time. I thought of my calves and withdrew. But the human figure that I had seen evidently won the mastery, as the noise gradually subsided and all became quiet. As each man got his dogs tied up, he went over to the meat-tent and took a box of cut-up seal meat, which stood on the wall out of the dogs' reach. This meat had been cut up earlier in the day by two men. They took it in turns, I heard; two men had this duty daily. The dogs were then fed, and half an hour after this was done the camp again lay as I had found it in the morning, quiet and peaceful. With a temperature of -65° F., and a velocity of twenty-two miles an hour, the south-wester swept over the Barrier, and whirled the snow high into the air above Framheim; but in their tents the dogs lay, full-fed and contented, and felt nothing of the storm.

In the hut preparations for a feast were going on, and now one could really appreciate a good house. The change from the howling wind, the driving snow, the intense cold, and the absolute darkness, was great indeed when one came in. Everything was newly washed, and the table was gaily decorated. Small Norwegian flags were everywhere, on the table and walls. The festival began at six, and all the "vikings" came merrily in. Lindström had done his best, and that is not saying a little. I specially admired his powers and his liberality – and I think, even in the short time I have observed him, he has shown no sign of being stingy – when he appeared with the "Napoleon" cakes. Now I must tell you that these cakes were served after every man had put away a quarter of a plum-pudding. The cakes were delightful to look at – the finest puff-pastry, with layers of vanilla custard and cream. They made my mouth water. But the size of them! – there could not be one of those mountains of cake to every man? One among them all, perhaps – if they could be expected to eat Napoleon cakes at all after plum-pudding. But why had he brought in eight – two enormous dishes with four on each? Good heavens! – one of the vikings had just started, and was making short work of his mountain. And one after another they all walked into them, until the whole eight had disappeared. I should have nothing to say about hunger, misery, and cold, when I came hone. My head was going round; the temperature must have been as many degrees above zero in here as it was below zero outside. I looked up at Wisting's bunk, where a thermometer was hanging: +95° F. The vikings did not seem to take the slightest notice of this trifle; their work with the "Napoleons" continued undisturbed.

Soon the gorgeous cake was a thing of the past, and cigars came out. Everyone, without exception, allowed himself this luxury. Up to now they had not shown much sign of abstinence; I wanted to know what was their attitude with regard to strong drinks. I had heard, of course, that indulgence in alcohol on Polar expeditions was very harmful, not to say dangerous. "Poor boys!" I thought to myself; "that must be the reason of your fondness for cake. A man must have one vice, at least. Deprived of the pleasure of drinking, they make up for it in gluttony." Yes, now I could see it quite plainly, and I was heartily sorry for them. I wondered how the "Napoleons" felt now; they looked rather depressed. No doubt the cake took some time to settle down.

Lindström, who now seemed unquestionably the most wideawake of them all, came in and began to clear the table. I expected to see every man roll into his bunk to digest. But no; that side of the question did not appear to trouble them much. They remained seated, as though expecting more. Oh yes, of course; there was coffee to come. Lindström was already in the doorway with cups and jugs. A cup of coffee would be just the thing after such a meal.

"Stubberud!" – this was Lindström's voice, calling from some place in the far distance – "hurry up, before they get warm!" I rushed after Stubberud to see what the things were that were not to get warm; I thought it might possibly be something that was to be taken outside. Great Heaven! there was Lindström lying on his stomach up in the loft, and handing down through the trap-door – what do you think? – a bottle of Benedictine and a bottle of punch, both white with frost! Now I could see that the fish were to swim – what's more, they were to be drowned. A happier smile than that with which Stubberud received the bottles, or more careful and affectionate handling than they received on their way through the kitchen, I have never seen. I was touched. Ah, these boys knew how a liqueur should be served! "Must be served cold," was on the label of the punch bottle. I can assure P. A. Larsen that his prescription was followed to the letter that evening. Then the gramophone made its appearance, and it did me good to see the delight with which it was received. They seemed to like this best, after all, and every man had music to suit his taste. All agreed to honour the cook for all his pains, and the concert therefore began with "Tararaboom-de-ay," followed by the "Apache" waltz. His part of the programme was concluded with a humorous recitation. Meanwhile he stood in the doorway with a beatific smile; this did him good. In this way the music went the round, and all had their favourite tunes. Certain numbers were kept to the last; I could see that they were to the taste of all. First came an air from "The Huguenots," sung by Michalowa; this showed the vikings to be musical. It was beautifully sung. "But look here," cried an impatient voice: "aren't we going to have Borghild Bryhn to-night?" "Yes," was the answer; "here she comes." And Solveig's Song followed. It was a pity Borghild Bryhn was not there; I believe the most rapturous applause would not have moved her so much as the way her song was received here that evening. As the notes rang clear and pure through the room, one could see the faces grow serious. No doubt the words of the poem affected them all as they sat there in the dark winter night on the vast wilderness of ice, thousands and thousands of miles from all that was dear to them. I think that was so; but it was the lovely melody, given with perfect finish and rich natural powers, that opened their hearts. One could see how it did them good; it was as though they were afraid of the sound of their own voices afterwards. At last one of them could keep silence no longer. "My word, how beautifully she sings!" he exclaimed; "especially the ending. I was a little bit afraid that she would give the last note too sharp, in spite of the masterly way in which she controls her voice. And it is outrageously high, too. But instead of that, the note came so pure and soft and full that it alone was enough to make a better man of one." And then this enthusiastic listener tells them how he once heard the same song, but with a very different result. "It went quite well," he says, "until it came to the final note. Then you could see the singer fill her mighty bosom for the effort, and out came a note so shrill that – well, you remember the walls of Jericho." After this the gramophone is put away. No one seems to want any more.

Now it is already half-past eight, it must be nearly bed-time. The feast has lasted long enough, with food, drink, and music. Then they all get on their feet, and there is a cry of "Bow and arrows." Now, I say to myself, as I withdraw into the corner where the clothes are hanging – now the alcohol is beginning to take effect. It is evident that something extraordinarily interesting is going to take place, as they are all so active. One of them goes behind the door and fetches out a little cork target, and another brings out of his bunk a box of darts. So it is dart-throwing – the children must be amused. The target is hung up on the door of the kitchen leading to the pent-house, and the man who is to throw first takes up his position at the end of the table at a distance of three yards. And now the shooting competition begins, amid laughter and noise. There are marksmen of all kinds, good, bad, and indifferent. Here comes the champion – one can see that by the determined way in which he raises the dart and sends it flying; his will, no doubt, be the top score. That is Stubberud; of the five darts he throws, two are in the bull's-eye and three close to it. The next is Johansen; he is not bad, either, but does not equal the other's score. Then comes Bjaaland; I wonder whether he is as smart at this game as he is on ski? He places himself at the end of the table, like the others, but takes a giant's stride forward. He is a leery one, this; now he is not more than a yard and a half from the target. He throws well; the darts describe a great round arch. This is what is known as throwing "with a high trajectory," and it is received with great applause. The trajectory turns out to be too high, and all his darts land in the wall above the door. Hassel throws with "calculation." What he calculates it is not easy to understand. Not on hitting the target, apparently; but if his calculations have to do with the kitchen-door, then they are more successful. Whether Amundsen "calculates" or not makes very little difference; his are all misses in any case. Wisting's form is the same. Prestrud is about half-way between the good shots and the bad. Hanssen throws like a professional, slinging his dart with great force. He evidently thinks he is hunting walrus. All the scores are carefully entered in a book, and prizes will be given later on.

Meanwhile Lindström is playing patience; his day's work is now done. But, besides his cards, he is much interested in what is going on round the target, and puts in a good word here and there. Then he gets up with a determined look; he has one more duty to perform. This consists of changing the light from the big lamp under the ceiling to two small lamps, and the reason for the change is that the heat of the big lamp would be too strongly felt in the upper bunks. This operation is a gentle hint that the time has come for certain people to turn in. The room looks dark now that the great sun under the ceiling is extinguished; the two lamps that are now alight are good enough, but one seems, nevertheless, to have made a retrograde step towards the days of pine-wood torches.

By degrees, then, the vikings began to retire to rest. My description of the day's life at Framheim would be incomplete if I did not include this scene in it. Lindström's chief pride, I had been told, was that he was always the first man in bed; he would willingly sacrifice a great deal to hold this record. As a rule, he had no difficulty in fulfilling his desire, as nobody tried to be before him; but this evening it was otherwise. Stubberud was far advanced with his undressing when Lindström came in, and, seeing a chance at last of being "first in bed," at once challenged the cook. Lindström, who did not quite grasp the situation, accepted the challenge, and then the race began, and was followed by the others with great excitement. Now Stubberud is ready, and is just going to jump into his bunk, which is over Lindström's, when he suddenly feels himself clutched by the leg and held back. Lindström hangs on to the leg with all his force, crying out, in the most pitiable voice: "Wait a bit, old man, till I'm undressed too!" It reminded me rather of the man who was going to fight, and called out: "Wait till I get a hold of you!" But the other was not to be persuaded; he was determined to win. Then Lindström let go, tore off his braces – he had no time for more – and dived head first into his bunk. Stubberud tried to protest; this was not fair, he was not undressed, and so on.

"That doesn't matter," replied the fat man; "I was first, all the same."

The scene was followed with great amusement and shouts of encouragement, and ended in a storm of applause when Lindström disappeared into his bunk with his clothes on. But that was not the end of the business, for his leap into the bunk was followed by a fearful crash, to which no one paid any attention in the excitement of the moment, himself least of all. But now the consequences appeared. The shelf along the side of his bunk, on which he kept a large assortment of things, had fallen down, and filled the bunk with rifles, ammunition, gramophone-discs, tool-boxes, sweetmeat-boxes, pipes, tins of tobacco, ash-trays, boxes of matches, etc., and there was no room left for the man himself. He had to get out again, and his defeat was doubly hard. With shame he acknowledged Stubberud as the victor; "but," he added, "you shan't be first another time." One by one the others turned in; books were produced – here and there a pipe as well – and in this way the last hour was passed. At eleven o'clock precisely the lamps were put out, and the day was at an end.

Soon after, my host goes to the door, and I follow him out. I had told him I had to leave again this evening, and he is going to see me off. "I'll take you as far as the depot," he says; "the rest of the way you can manage by yourself." The weather has improved considerably, but it is dark – horribly dark. "So that we may find the way more easily," he says, "I'll take my trio. If they don't see the way, they'll smell it out." Having let loose the three dogs, who evidently wonder what the meaning of it may be, he puts a lantern on a stack of timber – to show him the way back,

I suppose – and we go off. The dogs are evidently accustomed to go this way, for they set off at once in the direction of the depot.

"Yes," says my companion, "it's not to be wondered at that they know the way. They have gone it every day – once at least, often two or three times – since we came here. There are three of us who always take our daily walk in this direction – Bjaaland, Stubberud, and I. As you saw this morning, those two went out at half-past eight. They did that so as to be back to work at nine. We have so much to do that we can't afford to lose any time. So they take their walk to the depot and back; at nine I generally do the same. The others began the winter with the same good resolution; they were all so enthusiastic for a morning walk. But the enthusiasm didn't last long, and now we three are the only enthusiasts left. But, short as the way is – about 650 yards – we should not venture to go without those marks that you saw, and without our dogs. I have often hung out a lantern, too; but when it is as cold as this evening, the paraffin freezes and the light goes out. Losing one's way here might be a very serious matter, and I don't want to run the risk of it.

" Here we have the first mark-post; we were lucky to come straight upon it. The dogs are on ahead, making for the depot. Another reason for being very careful on the way to the depot is that there is a big hole, 20 feet deep, just by a hummock on that slope where, you remember, the last flag stands. If one missed one's way and fell into it, one might get hurt." We passed close to the second mark. "The next two marks are more difficult to hit off – they are so low; and I often wait and call the dogs to me to find the way – as I am going to do now, for instance. It is impossible to see anything unless you come right on it, so we must wait and let the dogs help us. I know exactly the number of paces between each mark, and when I have gone that number, I stop and first examine the ground close by. If that is no good, I whistle for the dogs, who come at once. Now you'll see" – a long whistle – "it won't be long before they are here. I can hear them already." He was right; the dogs came running out of the darkness straight towards us. "To let them see that we want to find the way to the depot, we must begin to walk on." We did so. As soon as the dogs saw this, they went forward again, but this time at a pace that allowed us to keep up with them at a trot, and soon after we were at the last mark.

"As you see, my lantern over at the camp is just going out, so I hope you will excuse my accompanying you farther. You know your way, anyhow."

With these words we parted, and my host went back, followed by the faithful trio, whilst I ...

CHAPTER 9

THE END OF THE WINTER

After Midwinter Day the time began to pass even more quickly than before. The darkest period was over, and the sun was daily drawing nearer. In the middle of the darkest time, Hassel came in one morning and announced that Else had eight puppies. Six of these were ladies, so their fate was sealed at once; they were killed and given to their elder relations, who appreciated them highly. It could hardly be seen that they chewed them at all; they went down practically whole. There could be no doubt of their approval, as the next day the other two had also disappeared.

The weather conditions we encountered down here surprised us greatly. In every quarter of the Antarctic regions of which we had any information, the conditions had always proved very unsettled. On the *Belgica*, in the drift-ice to the west of Graham Land, we always had rough, unpleasant weather. Nordenskjöld's stay in the regions to the east of same land gave the same report – storm after storm the whole time. And from the various English expeditions that have visited McMurdo Sound we hear of continual violent winds. Indeed, we know now that while we were living on the Barrier in the most splendid weather – calms or light breezes – Scott at his station some four hundred miles to the west of us was troubled by frequent storms, which greatly hindered his work.

I had expected the temperature to remain high, as throughout the winter we could very clearly see the dark sky over the sea. Whenever the state of the air was favourable, the dark, heavy water-sky was visible in a marked degree, leaving no doubt that a large extent of Ross Sea was open the whole year round. Nevertheless, the temperature went very low, and without doubt the mean temperature shown by our observations for the year is the lowest that has ever been recorded. Our lowest temperature, on August 13, 1911, was -74.2°F. For five months of the year we were able to record temperatures below -58°F. The temperature rose with every wind, except the south-west; with that it more usually went down.

We observed the *aurora australis* many times, but only a few of its appearances were specially powerful. They were of all possible forms, though the form of ribbon-like bands seemed to be commonest. Most of the *aurorœ* were multicoloured – red and green.

My hypothesis of the solidity of the Barrier – that is, of its resting upon underlying land – seems to be confirmed at all points by our observations during our twelve months' stay on it. In the course of the winter and spring the pack-ice is forced up against the Barrier into pressure-ridges of as much as 40 feet in height. This took place only about a mile and a quarter from our hut, without our noticing its effect in the slightest degree. In my opinion, if this Barrier had been afloat, the effect of the violent shock which took place at its edge would not merely have been noticeable, but would have shaken our house. While building the house, Stubberud and Bjaaland heard a loud noise a long way off, but could feel nothing. During our whole stay we never heard a sound or felt a movement on this spot. Another very good proof seems to be afforded by the large theodolite that Prestrud used. It would take next to nothing to disturb its level – a slight change of temperature might be enough. So delicate an instrument would have soon shown an inclination if the Barrier had been afloat.

The day we entered the bay for the first time, a small piece of its western cape broke away. During the spring the drift-ice pressed in an insignificant part of one of the many points on the outer edge of the Barrier. With these exceptions, we left the Barrier as we found it, entirely unaltered. The soundings, which showed a rapid rise in the bottom as the *Fram* changed her position southward along the Barrier, are also a clear sign that land is close at hand. Finally, the formations of the Barrier appear to be the best proof. It could not rise to 1,100 feet – which we measured as the rise from Framheim to a point about thirty-one miles to the south – without subjacent land.

Work now proceeded on the sledging outfit with feverish haste. We had for a long time been aware that we should have to do our utmost and make the best use of our time if we were to have the general outfit for our common use ready by the middle of August. For preparing our personal outfit we had to use our leisure time. By the first half of August we could begin to see the end of our labour. Bjaaland had now finished the four sledges. It was a masterly piece of work that he had carried out in the course of the winter; they were extremely lightly constructed, but very strong. They were of the same length as the original sledges – about 12 feet – and were not shod. We should have a couple of the old *Fram* sledges with us, and these were shod with strong steel plates, so that they could be used if the surface and going rendered it necessary. The average weight of the new sledges was 53 pounds. We had thus saved as much as 110 pounds per sledge.

When Bjaaland had finished them, they were taken into the "Clothing Store." The way in which Hanssen and Wisting lashed the various parts together was a guarantee of their soundness; in fact, the only way in which one can expect work to be properly and carefully carried out is to have it done by the very men who are to use the things. They know what is at stake. They do it so that they may reach their destination; more than that, they do it so that they may come back again. Every piece of binding is first carefully examined and tested; then it is put on, cautiously and accurately. Every turn is hauled taut, taking care that it is in its right place. And, finally, the lashing is pointed in such a way that one would do best to use a knife or an axe if it has to be undone again; there is no danger of jerking it out with the fingers. A sledge journey of the kind we had before us is a serious undertaking, and the work has to be done seriously.

It was no warm and comfortable workshop that they had for doing this. The Clothing Store was always the coldest place, probably because there was always a draught through it. There was a door out on to the Barrier, and an open passage leading to the house. Fresh air was constantly passing through, though not in any very great quantity; but it does not take much to make itself felt when the air is at a temperature of about -75°F., and when one is working with bare fingers. There were always some degrees of frost here. In order to keep the lashings pliable while they were being put on, they used a Primus lamp on a stone close to where they were working. I often admired their patience when I stood watching them; I have seen them more than once working bare-handed by the hour together in a temperature of about -22°F. This may pass for a short time; but through the coldest and darkest part of the winter, working day after day, as they did, it is pretty severe, and a great trial of patience. Nor were their feet very well off either; it makes hardly any difference what one puts on them if one has to stay still. Here, as elsewhere in the cold, it was found that boots with wooden soles were the best for sedentary work; but for some reason or other the occupants of the Clothing Store would not give their adherence to the wooden-sole principle, and continued to work all through the winter in their reindeer-skin and sealskin boots. They preferred stamping their feet to acknowledging the incontestable superiority of wooden soles in such conditions.

As the sledges were finished, they were numbered from one to seven, and stored in the clothing department. The three old sledges we should have to use were made for the *Fram's* second expedition. They were extremely strong, and, of course, heavier than the new ones. They were all carefully overhauled; all the bindings and lashings were examined, and replaced wherever necessary. The steel shoes were taken off one, but retained on the other two, in case we should meet with conditions where they would be required.

In addition to this work of lashing, these two had plenty of other occupation. Whenever Wisting was not taken up by the work on the sledges, one could hear the hum of his sewing-machine. He had a thousand different things to do in his sewing-room, and was in there nearly every day till late in the evening. It was only when the target and darts came out at half-past eight that he showed himself, and if it had not been that he had undertaken the position of marker at these competitions, we should hardly have seen him even then. His first important piece of work was making four three-man tents into two. It was not easy to manage these rather large tents in the little hole that went by the name of the sewing-room; of course, he used the table in the Clothing Store for cutting out, but, all the same, it is a mystery how he contrived to get hold of the right seams when he sat in his hole. I was prepared to see the most curious-looking tents when once they were brought out and set up in daylight; one might imagine that the floor of one would be sewed on to the side of another. But nothing of the sort happened. When the tents were brought out for the first time and set up, they proved to be perfect. One would have thought they had been made in a big sail-loft instead of in a snow-drift. Neat-fingered fellows like this are priceless on such an expedition as ours.

On the second *Fram* expedition they used double tents, and as, of course, nothing is so good and serviceable as the thing one has not got, the praises of double tents were now sung in every key. Well, I naturally had to admit that a house with double walls is warmer than one with single walls, but, at the same time, one must not lose sight of the fact that the double-walled house is also twice as heavy; and when one has to consider the weight of a pocket-handkerchief, it will be understood that the question of the real advantages of the double-walled house had to be thoroughly considered before taking the step of committing oneself to it. I had thought that with double walls one would possibly avoid some of the rime that is generally so troublesome in the tents, and often becomes a serious matter. If, then, the double walls would in any way prevent or improve this condition of things, I could see the advantage of having them; for the increased weight caused by the daily deposit of rime would in a short time be equal to, if not greater than, the additional weight of the double tent. These double tents are made so that the outer tent is fast and the inner loose. In the course of our discussion, it appeared that the deposit of rime occurred just as quickly on a double tent as on a single one, and thus the utility of the double tent appeared to me to be rather doubtful. If the object was merely to have it a few degrees warmer in the tent, I thought it best to sacrifice this comfort to the weight we should thereby save. Moreover, we were so plentifully supplied with warm sleeping things that we should not have to suffer any hardship.

But another question cropped up as a result of this discussion – the question of what was the most useful colour for a tent. We were soon agreed that a dark-coloured tent was best, for several reasons: In the first place, as a relief to the eyes. We knew well enough what a comfort it would be to come into a dark tent after travelling all day on the glistening Barrier surface. In the next place, the dark colour would make the tent a good deal warmer when the sun was up – another important consideration. One may easily prove this by walking in dark clothes in a hot sun, and afterwards changing to white ones. And, finally, a dark tent would be far easier to see on the white surface than a light one. When all these questions had been discussed, and the superiority of a dark tent admitted, we were doubly keen on it, since all our tents happened to be light, not to say white, and the possibility of getting dark ones was not very apparent. It is true that we had a few yards of darkish " gabardine," or light windproof material, which would have been extremely suitable for this purpose, but every yard of it had long ago been destined for some other use, so that did not get us out of the difficulty. "But," said somebody – and he had a very cunning air as he uttered that "but" – "but haven't we got ink and ink-powder that we can dye our tents dark with?" Yes, of course! We all smiled indulgently; the thing was so plain that it was almost silly to mention it, but all the same – the man was forgiven his silliness, and dye-works were established. Wisting accepted the position of dyer, in addition to his other duties, and succeeded so well that before very long we had two dark blue tents instead of the white ones.

These looked very well, no doubt, freshly dyed as they were, but the question was, What would they look like after a couple of months' use? The general opinion was that they would probably, to a great extent, have reverted to their original colour – or lack of colour. Some better patent had to be invented. As we were sitting over our coffee after dinner one day, someone suddenly suggested: "But look here – suppose we took our bunk – curtains and made an outer tent of them?" This time the smile that passed over the company, as they put down their cups, was almost compassionate. Nothing was said, but the silence meant something like: "Poor chap! – as if we hadn't all thought of that long ago!" The proposal was adopted without discussion, and Wisting had another long job, in addition to all the rest. Our bunk-curtains were dark red, and made of very light material; they were sewed together, curtain to curtain, and finally the whole was made into an outer tent. The curtains only sufficed for one tent, but, remembering that half a loaf is better than no bread, we had to be satisfied with this. The red tent, which was set up a few days after, met with unqualified approval; it would be visible some miles away in the snow. Another important advantage was that it would protect and preserve the main tent. Inside, the effect of the combination of red and blue was to give an agreeably dark shade. Another question was how to protect the tent from a hundred loose dogs, who were no better behaved than others of their kind. If the tent became stiff and brittle, it might be spoilt in a very short time. And the demands we made on our tents were considerable; we expected them to last at least 120 days. I therefore got Wisting to make two tent-protectors, or guards. These guards consisted simply of a piece of gabardine long enough to stretch all round the tent, and to act as a fence in preventing the dogs from coming in direct contact with the tents. The guards were made with loops, so that they could be stretched upon ski-poles. They looked very fine when they were finished, but they never came to be used; for, as soon as we began the journey, we found a material that was even more suitable and always to be had – snow. Idiots! – of course, we all knew that, only we wouldn't say so. Well, that was one against us. However, the guards came in well as reserve material on the trip, and many were the uses they were put to.

In the next place, Wisting had to make wind-clothing for every man. That we had brought out proved to be too small, but the things he made were big enough. There was easily room for two more in my trousers; but they have to be so. In these regions one soon finds out that everything that is roomy is warm and comfortable, while everything that is tight – foot-gear, of course, excepted – is warm and uncomfortable. One quickly gets into a perspiration, and spoils the clothes. Besides the breeches and anorak of light wind-cloth, he made stockings of the same material. I assumed that these stockings – worn among the other stockings we had on – would have an insulating effect. Opinions were greatly divided on this point; but I must confess – in common with my four companions on the Polar journey – that I would never make a serious trip without them. They fulfilled all our expectations. The rime was deposited on them freely, and was easily brushed off. If they got wet, it was easy to dry them in almost all weathers; I know of no material that dries so quickly as this windproof stuff. Another thing was that they protected the other stockings against tears, and made them last much longer than would otherwise have been the case.

As evidence of how pleased we who took part in the long sledge journey were with these stockings, I may mention that when we reached the depot in 80°S. – on the homeward trip, be it noted; that is, when we looked upon the journey as over – we found there some bags with various articles of clothing. In one of these were two pairs of windproof stockings – the bag presumably belonged to an opponent of the idea – and it may be imagined that there was some fun. We all wanted them – all, without exception. The two lucky ones each seized his pair and hid it, as if it was the most costly treasure. What they wanted with them I cannot guess, as we were at home; but this example shows how we had learnt to appreciate them.

I recommend them most warmly to men who are undertaking similar expeditions. But – I must add – they must give themselves the trouble of taking off their foot-gear every evening, and brushing the rime off their stockings; if one does not do this, of course, the rime will thaw in the course of the night, and everything will be soaking wet in the morning. In that case you must not blame the stockings, but yourself.

After this it was the turn of the underclothing; there was nothing in the tailoring and outfitting department that Wisting could not manage. Among our medical stores we had two large rolls of the most beautiful fine light flannel, and of this he made underclothing for all of us. What we had brought out from home was made of extremely thick woollen material, and we were afraid this would be too warm. Personally, I wore Wisting's make the whole trip, and have never known anything so perfect. Then he had covers for the sleeping-bags to sew and patch, and one thing and another. Some people give one the impression of being able to make anything, and to get it done in no time – others not.

Hanssen had his days well occupied, industrious and handy as he was. He was an expert at anything relating to sledges, and knew exactly what had to be done. Whatever he had a hand in, I could feel sure of; he never left anything to chance. Besides lashing the sledges, he had a number of other things to do. Amongst them, he was to prepare all the whips we required – two for each driver, or fourteen altogether. Stubberud was to supply the handles. In consultation with the "Carpenters' Union," I had chosen a handle made of three narrow strips of hickory. I assumed that if these were securely lashed together, and the lashings covered with leather, they would make as strong a handle as one could expect to get. The idea of the composite handle of three pieces of wood was that it would give and bend instead of breaking. We knew by experience that a solid whip-handle did not last very long. It was arranged, then, that the handles were to be made by Stubberud, and passed on to Hanssen.

The whip-lashes were made by Hassel, in the course of the winter, on the Eskimo model. They were round and heavy – as they should be – and dangerous to come near, when they were wielded by an experienced hand. Hanssen received these different parts to join them together and make the whip. As usual, this was done with all possible care. Three strong lashings were put on each handle, and these again were covered with leather. Personally, Hanssen was not in favour of the triple hickory handle, but he did the work without raising any objection. We all remarked, it is true, that at this time, contrary to his habit, he spent the hours after supper with Wisting. I wondered a little at this, as I knew Hanssen was very fond of a game of whist after supper, and never missed it unless he had work to do. I happened one evening to express my surprise at this, and Stubberud answered at once: "He's making handles." – "What sort of handles?" – "Whip-handles; but," Stubberud added, "I'll guarantee those hickory handles I'm making. You can't have anything tougher and stronger than those." He was rather sore about it, that was easy to see; the idea was his own, too. Then – talk of the devil – in walked Hanssen, with a fine big whip in his hand. I, of course, appeared extremely surprised. "What," I said, "more whips?" – "Yes," said he; "I don't believe in those I'm making in the daytime. But here's a whip that I can trust." I must admit that it looked well. The whole handle was covered, so that one could not see what it was made of. "But," I ventured to object, "are you sure it is as strong as the others?" – "Oh, as to that," he answered, "I'm quite ready to back it against any of those – " He did not say the word, nor was there

320

any need. His meaning was unmistakable, and "rotten whips" sounded in our ears as plainly as if he had shouted it. I had no time to observe the effect of this terrible utterance, for a determined voice called out: "We'll see about that!" I turned round, and there was Stubberud leaning against the end of the table, evidently hurt by Hanssen's words, which he took as a personal affront. "If you dare risk your whip, come on." He had taken down one of the insulted triple-handled whips from the shelf in his bunk, and stood in a fighting attitude. This promised well. We all looked at Hanssen. He had gone too far to be able to draw back; he had to fight. He took his weapon in his hand, and entered the "ring." The conditions were arranged and accepted by both parties; they were to fight until one of the handles was broken. And then the whip duel began. The opponents were very serious over it. One, two, three – the first blow fell, handle against handle. The combatants had shut their eyes and awaited the result; when they opened them again, they shone with happy surprise – both handles were as whole as before. Now each of them was really delighted with his own handle, and the blows fell faster. Stubberud, who was standing with his back to the table, got so excited over the unexpected result that, every time he raised his weapon, he gave the edge of the table a resounding smack without knowing it. How many rounds had been fought I do not know, when I heard a crack, followed by the words: "There you can see, old man!" As Stubberud left the ring, I was able to see Hanssen. He stood on the battle-field, eyeing his whip; it looked like a broken lily. The spectators had not been silent; they had followed the fight with excitement, amid laughter and shouts. "That's right, Stubberud. Don't give in!" "Bravo, Hanssen! that's a good one!"

The whips afterwards turned out remarkably well – not that they lasted out the trip, but they held together for a long while. Whip-handles are a very perishable commodity; if one used nothing but the lash, they would be everlasting, but, as a rule, one is not long satisfied with that. It is when one gives a "confirmation," as we call it, that the handle breaks. A confirmation is generally held when some sinner or other has gone wrong and refuses to obey. It consists in taking the first opportunity, when the sledge stops, of going in among the dogs, taking out the defiant one, and laying into him with the handle. These confirmations, if they occur frequently, may use up a lot of handles.

It was also arranged that Hanssen should prepare goggles in the Eskimo fashion, and he began this work; but it soon appeared that everyone had some patent of his own which was much better. Therefore it was given up, and every man made his own goggles.

Stubberud's chief work was making the sledge cases lighter, and he succeeded in doing this, but not without hard work. It took far longer than one would have thought. The wood had a good many knots, and he often had to work against the grain; the planing was therefore rather difficult and slow. He planed a good deal off them, but could "guarantee them," as he said. Their sides were not many millimetres thick; to strengthen them in the joints, corners of aluminium were put on.

In addition to remaking the sledges, Bjaaland had to get the skis ready. To fit the big, broad boots we should wear, the Huitfeldt fittings had to be much broader than usual, and we had such with us, so that Bjaaland had only to change them. The ski-bindings were like the snow-goggles; everyone had his own patent. I found the bindings that Bjaaland had put on for himself so efficient that

I had no hesitation in ordering similar ones for myself; and it may be said to their honour, and to the honour of him who made them, that they were first-rate, and served me well during the whole trip. They were, after all, only a retention of the old system, but, with the help of hooks and eyes, they could be put on and taken off in an instant. And those were the conditions we demanded of our bindings – that they should hold the foot as firmly as a vice, and should be easy to hook on and take off. For we always had to take them off on the journey; if one left one's bindings out for a night, they were gone in the morning. The dogs looked upon them as a delicacy. The toe-strap also had to be removed in the evening; in other words, the ski had to be left absolutely bare.

Johansen, besides his packing, was occupied in making weights and tent-pegs. The weights were very ingeniously made; the steelyard system was adopted. If they were never used, it was not the fault of the weights – they were good enough. But the reason was that we had all our provisions so arranged that they could be taken without being weighed. We were all weighed on August 6, and it then appeared that Lindström was the heaviest, with 13 st. 8 lbs. On that occasion he was officially christened "Fatty." The tent-pegs Johansen made were the opposite of what such pegs usually are; in other words, they were flat instead of being high. We saw the advantage at once. Besides being so much lighter, they were many times stronger. I do not know that we ever broke a peg on the trip; possibly we lost one or two. Most of them were brought home undamaged.

Hassel worked at his whip-lashes down in the petroleum store. It was an uncomfortable place for him – always cold; but he had the lashes ready by the time he had promised them.

Prestrud made charts and copied out tables. Six of us were to have these copies. In each sledge there was a combined provision and observation book, bearing the same number as the sledge. It contained, first, an exact list of the provisions contained in each case on that sledge, and, in addition, the necessary tables for our astronomical observations. In these books each man kept a daily account of every scrap of provisions he took out; in this way we could always check the contents of the cases, and know what quantity of provisions we had. Farther on in the book the observations were entered, and the distance covered for the day, course, and so on.

That is a rough outline of what we were doing in the course of the winter in "working hours." Besides this there were, of course, a hundred things that every man had to do for his personal equipment. During the winter each man had his outfit served out to him, so that he might have time to make whatever alterations he found necessary. Every man received a heavy and a lighter suit of reindeer-skin, as well as reindeer-skin mits and stockings. He also had dogskin stockings and sealskin kamiks. In addition, there was a complete outfit of underclothing and wind-clothes. All were served alike; there was no priority at all. The skin clothing was the first to be tackled, and here there was a good deal to be done, as nothing had been made to measure. One man found that the hood of his anorak came too far down over his eyes, another that it did not come down far enough; so both had to set to work at alterations, one cutting off, the other adding a piece. One found his trousers too long, another too short, and they had to alter those. However, they managed it; the needle was always at work, either for sewing a piece on, or for hemming the shortened piece. Although we began this work in good time, it looked as if we should never have finished. The room orderly had to sweep out huge piles of strips and reindeer-hair every morning, but the next morning there were just as many. If we had stayed there, I am sure we should still be sitting and sewing away at our outfit.

A number of patents were invented. Of course, the everlasting mask for the face was to the fore, and took the form of nose-protectors. I, too, allowed myself to be beguiled into experimenting, with good reason, as I thought, but with extremely poor results. I had hit upon something which, of course, I thought much better than anything that had been previously tried. The day I put on my invention, I not only got my nose frozen, but my forehead and cheek as well. I never tried it again. Hassel was great at new inventions; he wore nose-protectors all over him. These patents are very good things for passing the time; when one actually takes the field, they all vanish. They are useless for serious work.

The sleeping-bags were also a great source of interest. Johansen was at work on the double one he was so keen on. Heaven knows how many skins he put into it! I don't, nor did I ever try to find out. Bjaaland was also in full swing with alterations to his. He found the opening at the top inconvenient, and preferred to have it in the middle; his arrangement of a flap, with buttons and loops, made it easy to mistake him for a colonel of dragoons when he was in bed. He was tremendously pleased with it; but so he was with his snow-goggles, in spite of the fact that he could not see with them, and that they allowed him to become snow-blind. The rest of us kept our sleeping-bags as they were, only lengthening or shortening them as required. We were all greatly pleased with the device for closing them – on the plan of a sack.

Outside our bags we had a cover of very thin canvas; this was extremely useful, and I would not be without it for anything. In the daytime the sleeping-bag was always well protected by this cover; no snow could get in. At night it was perhaps even more useful, as it protected the bag from the moisture of the breath. Instead of condensing on the skin and making it wet, this settled on the cover, forming in the course of the night a film of ice, which disappeared again during the day, breaking off while the bag ay stretched on the sledge. This cover ought to be of ample size; it is important that it should be rather longer than the sleeping-bag, so that one may have plenty of it round the neck, and thus prevent the breath from penetrating into the bag. We all had double bags – an inner and an outer one. The inner one was of calf-skin or thin female reindeer-skin, and quite light; the outer one was of heavy buck reindeer-skin, and weighed about 13 pounds. Both were open at the end, like a sack, and were laced together round the neck. I have always found this pattern the easiest, simplest, most comfortable, and best. We recommend it to all.

Novelties in the way of snow-goggles were many. This was, of course, a matter of the greatest importance and required study – it was studied, too! The particular problem was to find good goggles without glass. It is true that I had worn nothing but a pair of ordinary spectacles, with light yellow glasses, all the autumn, and that they had proved excellent; but for the long journey I was afraid these would give insufficient protection. I therefore threw myself into the competition for the best patent. The end of it was that we all went in for leather goggles, with a little slit for the eyes. The Bjaaland patent won the prize, and was most adopted. Hassel had his own invention, combined with a nose-protector;

when spread out it reminded me of the American eagle. I never saw him use it. Nor did any of us use these new goggles, except Bjaaland. He used his own goggles the whole way, but then, he was the only one who became snow-blind. The spectacles I wore – Hanssen had the same; they were the only two pairs we had – gave perfect protection; not once did I have a sign of snow-blindness. They were exactly like other spectacles, without any gauze at all round the glasses; the light could penetrate everywhere. Dr. Schanz, of Dresden, who sent me these glasses, has every right to be satisfied with his invention; its beats anything I have ever tried or seen.

The next great question was our boots. I had expressly pointed out that boots must be taken, whether the person concerned intended to wear them or not; for boots were indispensable, in case of having to cross any glacier, which was a contingency we had to reckon with, from the descriptions we had read of the country. With this proviso everyone might do as he pleased, and all began by improving their boots in accordance with our previous experience. The improvement consisted in making them larger. Wisting took mine in hand again, and began once more to pull them to pieces. It is only by tearing a thing to pieces that one can see what the work is like. We gained a good insight into the way our boots had been made; stronger or more conscientious work it would be impossible to find. It was hard work pulling them to pieces. This time mine lost a couple more soles. How many that made altogether I do not remember, but now I got what I had always called for – room enough. Besides being able to wear all the foot-coverings I had, I could also find room for a wooden sole. That made me happy; my great object was achieved. Now the temperature could be as low as it liked; it would not get through the wooden soles and my various stockings – seven pairs, I think, in all. I was pleased that evening, as the struggle had been a long one; it had taken me nearly two years to arrive at this result.

And then there was the dog-harness, which we must all have in order. The experience of the last depot journey, when two dogs fell into a crevasse through faulty harness, must not be allowed to repeat itself, We therefore devoted great care and attention to this gear, and used all the best materials we had. The result rewarded our pains; we had good, strong harness for every team.

This description will, perhaps, open the eyes of some people, and show them that the equipment of an expedition such as we were about to enter upon is not the affair of a day. It is not money alone that makes for the success of such an expedition – though, Heaven knows, it is a good thing to have – but it is in a great measure – indeed, I may say that this is the greatest factor – the way in which the expedition is equipped – the way in which every difficulty is foreseen, and precautions taken for meeting or avoiding it. Victory awaits him who has everything in order – luck, people call it. Defeat is certain for him who has neglected to take the necessary precautions in time; this is called bad luck. But pray do not think this is an epitaph I wish to have inscribed on my own tomb. No; honour where honour is due – honour to my faithful comrades, who, by their patience, perseverance and experience, brought our equipment to the limit of perfection, and thereby rendered our victory possible.

On August 16 we began to pack our sledges; two were placed in the Crystal Palace and two in the Clothing Store. It was a great advantage to be able to do this work under cover; at this time the temperature was dancing a cancan between -58° and -75°F., with an occasional refreshing breeze of thirteen or fourteen miles an hour. It would have been almost an impossibility to pack the sledges out of doors under these conditions if it was to be done carefully and firmly; and, of course, it had to be so done. Our fixed wire-rope lashings had to be laced together with lengths of thin rope, and this took time; but when properly done, as it was now, the cases were held as though in a vice, and could not move. The zinc plates we had had under the sledges to keep them up in loose snow had been taken off; we could not see that we should have any use for them. In their place we had lashed a spare ski under each sledge, and these were very useful later. By August 22 all the sledges were ready, waiting to be driven away.

The dogs did not like the cold weather we had now had for so long; when the temperature went down between -58° and -75° F., one could see by their movements that they felt it. They stood still and raised their feet from the ground in turn, holding each foot up for a while before putting it down again on the cold surface. They were cunning and resourceful in the extreme. They did not care very much for fish, and some of them were difficult to get into the tents on the evenings when they knew there was fish. Stubberud, especially, had a great deal of trouble with one of the young dogs – Funcho was his name. He was born at Madeira during our stay there in September, 1910. On meat evenings each man, after fastening up his dogs, went, as has been described, up to the wall of the meat-tent and took his box of chopped-up meat, which was put out there. Funcho used to watch for this moment. When he saw Stubberud take the box, he knew there was meat, and then he came quietly into the tent, as though there was nothing the matter. If, on the other hand, Stubberud showed no sign of fetching the box, the dog would not come, nor was it possible to get hold of him. This happened a few times, but then Stubberud hit upon a stratagem. When Funcho, as usual – even on a fish evening – watched the scene of chaining up the other dogs from a distance, Stubberud went calmly up to the wall, took the empty box that lay there, put it on his shoulder, and returned to the tent. Funcho was taken in. He hurried joyfully into the tent, delighted, no doubt, with Stubberud's generosity in providing meat two evenings running. But there, to his great surprise, a very different reception awaited him from that he expected. He was seized by the neck and made fast for the night. After an ugly scowl at the empty box, he looked at Stubberud; what he thought, I am not sure. Certain it is that the ruse was not often successful after that. Funcho got a dried fish for supper, and had to be content with it.

We did not lose many dogs in the course of the winter. Two – Jeppe and Jakob – died of some disease or other. Knægten was shot, as he lost almost all his hair over half his body. Madeiro, born at Madeira, disappeared early in the autumn; Tom disappeared later – both these undoubtedly fell into crevasses. We had a very good opportunity – twice – of seeing how this might happen; both times we saw the dog disappear into the crevasse, and could watch him from the surface. He went quite quietly backwards and forwards down below without uttering a sound. These crevasses were not deep, but they were steep-sided, so that the dog could not get out without help. The two dogs I have mentioned undoubtedly met their death in this way: a slow death it must be, when one remembers how tenacious of life a dog is. It

330

happened several times that dogs disappeared, were absent for some days, and then came back; possibly they had been down a crevasse, and had finally succeeded in getting out of it again. Curiously enough, they did not pay much attention to the weather when they went on trips of this kind. When the humour took them, they would disappear, even if the temperature was down in the fifties below zero, with wind and driving snow. Thus Jaala, a lady belonging to Bjaaland, took it into her head to go off with three attendant cavaliers. We came upon them later; they were then lying quietly behind a hummock down on the ice, and seemed to be quite happy. They had been away for about eight days without food, and during that time the temperature had seldom been above -58° F.

August 23 arrived: calm, partly overcast, and -43.6°F. Finer weather for taking out our sledges and driving them over to the starting-point could not be imagined. They had to be brought up through the door of the Clothing Store; it was the largest and the easiest to get through. We had first to dig away the snow, which latterly had been allowed to collect there, as the inmates of this department had for some time past used the inner passage. The snow had blotted out everything, so that no sign of the entrance could be seen; but with a couple of strong shovels, and a couple of strong men to use them, the opening was soon laid bare. To get the sledges up was a longer business; they weighed 880 pounds apiece, and the way up to the surface was steep. A tackle was rigged, and by hauling and shoving they slowly, one by one, came up into daylight. We dragged them away to a place near the instrument-screen, so as to get a clear start away from the house. The dogs were fresh and wild, and wanted plenty of room; a case, not to mention a post, still less the instrument-screen, would all have been objects of extreme interest, to which, if there had been the slightest opportunity, their course would infallibly have been directed. The protests of their drivers would have been of little avail. The dogs had not been let loose that morning, and every man was now in his tent harnessing them. Meanwhile I stood contemplating the packed sledges that stood there ready to begin the long journey.

I tried to work up a little poetry – "the ever-restless spirit of man " – "the mysterious, awe-inspiring wilderness of ice" – but it was no good; I suppose it was too early in the morning. I abandoned my efforts, after coming to the conclusion that each sledge gave one more the idea of a coffin than of anything else, all the cases being painted black.

It was as we had expected: the dogs were on the verge of exploding. What a time we had getting them all into the traces! They could not stand still an instant; either it was a friend they wanted to wish good-morning, or it was an enemy they were longing to fly at. There was always something going on; when they kicked out with their hind-legs, raising a cloud of snow, or glared defiantly at each other, it often caused their driver an anxious moment. If he had his eye on them at this stage, he might, by intervening quickly and firmly, prevent the impending battle; but one cannot be everywhere at once, and the result was a series of the wildest fights. Strange beasts! They had been going about the place comparatively peacefully the whole winter, and now, as soon as they were in harness, they must needs fight as if their lives depended on it. At last we were all ready and away. It was the first time we had driven with teams of twelve, so that we were anxious to see the result.

It went better than we had expected; of course, not like an express train, but we could not expect that the first time. Some of the dogs had grown too fat in the course of the winter, and had difficulty in keeping up; for them this first trip was a stiff pull. But most of them were in excellent condition – fine, rounded bodies, not lumpish. It did not take long to get up the hill this time; most of them had to stop and get their wind on the slope, but there were some that did it without a halt. Up at the top everything looked just as we had left it in April. The flag was still standing where we had planted it, and did not look much the worse for wear. And, what was still stranger, we could see our old tracks southward. We drove all our sledges well up, unharnessed the dogs, and let them go. We took it for granted that they would all rush joyfully home to the flesh-pots, nor did the greater number disappoint us. They set off gaily homewards, and soon the ice was strewn with dogs. They did not behave altogether like good children. In some places there was a sort of mist over the ice; this was the cloud of snow thrown up by the combatants. But on their return they were irreproachable; one could not take any notice of a halt here and there. At the inspection that evening, it appeared that ten of them were missing. That was strange – could all ten have gone down crevasses? It seemed unlikely.

Next morning two men went over to the starting-point to look for the missing dogs. On the way they crossed a couple of crevasses, but there was no dog to be seen. When they arrived at the place where the sledges stood, there lay all ten curled up asleep. They were lying by their own sledges, and did not seem to take the slightest notice of the men's arrival. One or two of them may have opened an eye, but that was all. When they were roused and given to understand by unmistakable signs that their presence was desired at home, they seemed astonished beyond all bounds. Some of them simply declined to believe it; they merely turned round a few times and lay down again on the same spot. They had to be flogged home. Can anything more inexplicable be imagined? There they lay, three miles from their comfortable home, where they knew that abundance of food awaited them – in a temperature of -40°F. Although they had now been out for twenty-four hours, none of them gave a sign of wanting to leave the spot. If it had been summer, with warm sunshine, one might have understood it; but as it was – no!

That day – August 24 – the sun appeared above the Barrier again for the first time in four months. He looked very smiling, with a friendly nod for the old pressure-ridges he had seen for so many years; but when his first beams reached the starting-point, his face might well show surprise. "Well, if they're not first, after all! And I've been doing all I could to get here!" It could not be denied; we had won the race, and reached the Barrier a day before him.

The day for our actual start could not be fixed; we should have to wait until the temperature moderated somewhat. So long as it continued to grovel in the depths, we could not think of setting out. All our things were now ready up on the Barrier, and nothing remained but to harness the dogs and start. When I say all our things were ready, this is not the impression anyone would have gained who looked in on us; the cutting out and sewing were going on worse than ever. What had previously occurred to one as a thing of secondary importance, which might be done if there was time, but might otherwise quite well be dropped, now suddenly appeared as the most important part of the whole outfit; and then out came the knife and cut away, until great heaps of offcuts and hair lay about the floor; then the needle was produced, and seam after seam added to those there were already.

The days went by, and the temperature would give no sign of spring; now and then it would make a jump of about thirty degrees, but only to sink just as rapidly back to -58° F. It is not at all pleasant to hang about waiting like this; I always have the idea that I am the only one who is left behind, while all the others are out on the road. And I could guess that I was not the only one of us who felt this.

"I'd give something to know how far Scott is to-day."

"Oh, he's not out yet, bless you! It's much too cold for his ponies."

"Ah, but how do you know they have it as cold as this? I expect it's far warmer where they are, among the mountains; and you can take your oath they're not lying idle. Those boys have shown what they can do."

This was the sort of conversation one could hear daily. The uncertainty was worrying many of us – not all – and, personally, I felt it a great deal. I was determined to get away as soon as it was at all possible, and the objection that much might be lost by starting too early did not seem to me to have much force. If we saw that it was too cold, all we had to do was to turn back; so that I could not see there was any risk.

September came, with -43.6° F. That is a temperature that one can always stand, but we had better wait and see what it is going to do; perhaps it will only play its old tricks again. The next day, -63.4° F.; calm and clear. September 6, -20.2° F. At last the change had come, and we thought it was high time. The next day, -7.6° F. The little slant of wind that came from the east felt quite like a mild spring breeze. Well, at any rate, we now had a good temperature to start in. Every man ready; to-morrow we are off.

September 8 arrived. We turned out as usual, had breakfast, and were then on the move. We had not much to do. The empty sledges we were to use for driving up to the starting-point were ready; we only had to throw a few things on to them. But it turned out that the mere fact of having so few things was the cause of its taking a long time. We were to harness twelve dogs to the empty sledges, and we had an idea that it would cost us a struggle to get away. We helped each other, two and two, to bring the dogs to the sledges and harness them. Those who were really careful had anchored their sledges to a peg firmly fixed in the snow; others had contented themselves with capsizing their sledges; and others, again, were even more reckless. We all had to be ready before the first man could start; otherwise, it would have been impossible for those who were behind to hold in their dogs, and the result would have been a false start.

Our dogs were in a fearful state of excitement and confusion that morning, but at last everything was ready, barring one or two trifles. Then I suddenly heard a wild yell, and, spinning round, I saw a team tearing off without a driver. The next driver rushed forward to help, with the result that his dogs made off after the others. The two sledges were on ahead, and the two drivers after them in full gallop; but the odds were too unequal – in a few moments the drivers were beaten. The two runaway teams had made off in a south-westerly direction, and were going like the wind. The men had hard work; they had long ago stopped running, and were now following in the tracks of the sledges. The dogs had disappeared behind the ridges, which the men did not reach till much later.

Meanwhile the rest of us waited. The question was, what would those two do when at last they had come up with their sledges? Would they turn and go home, or would they drive up to the starting-point? Waiting was no fun under any circumstances, and so we decided to go on to the starting-point, and, if necessary, wait there. No sooner said than done, and away we went. Now we should see what command the fellows had over their dogs, for, in all canine probability, these teams would now try to follow the same course that the runaways had taken. This fear turned out not to be groundless; three managed to turn their dogs and put them in the right direction, but the other two were off on the new course. Afterwards, of course, they tried to make out that they thought we were all going that way. I smiled, but said nothing. It had happened more than once that my own dogs had taken charge; no doubt I had felt rather foolish at the time, but after all ....

It was not till noon that we all assembled with our sledges. The drivers of the runaways had had stiff work to catch them, and were wet through with their exertions. I had some thoughts of turning back, as three young puppies had followed us; if we went on, we should have to shoot them. But to turn back after all this work, and then probably have the same thing over again next morning, was not a pleasant prospect. And, above all, to see Lindström standing at the door, shaking with laughter – no, we had better go on. I think we were all agreed in this. The dogs were now harnessed to the loaded sledges, and the empty ones were stacked one above another. At 1.30 p.m. we were off. The old tracks were soon lost sight of, but we immediately picked up the line of flags that had been set up at every second kilometre on the last depot journey. The going was splendid, and we went at a rattling pace to the south. We did not go very far the first day – eleven and three-quarter miles – and pitched our camp at 3.30 p.m. The first night out is never very pleasant, but this time it was awful. There was such a row going on among our ninety dogs that we could not close our eyes. It was a blessed relief when four in the morning came round, and we could begin to get up. We had to shoot the three puppies when we stopped for lunch that day. The going was the same; nothing could be better. The flags we were following stood just as we had left them; they showed no trace of there having been any snowfall in the interval. That day we did fifteen and a half miles. The dogs were not yet in training, but were picking up every hour.

By the 10th they seemed to have reached their full vigour; that day none of us could hold in his team. They all wanted to get forward, with the result that one team ran into another, and confusion followed. This was a tiresome business; the dogs wore themselves out to no purpose, and, of course, the time spent in extricating them from one another was lost. They were perfectly wild that day. When Lassesen, for instance, caught sight of his enemy Hans, who was in another team, he immediately encouraged his friend Fix to help him. These two then put on all the speed they could, with the result that the others in the same team were excited by the sudden acceleration, and joined in the spurt. It made no difference how the driver tried to stop them; they went on just as furiously, until they reached the team that included the object of Lassesen's and Fix's endeavours. Then the two teams dashed into each other, and we had ninety-six dogs' legs to sort out. The only thing that could be done was to let those who could not hold in their teams unharness some of the dogs and tie them on the sledge. In this way we got things to work satisfactorily at last. We covered eighteen and a half miles that day.

On Monday, the 11th, we woke up to a temperature of -67.9° F. The weather was splendid, calm, and clear. We could see by the dogs that they were not feeling happy, as they had kept comparatively quiet that night. The cold affected the going at once; it was slow and unyielding. We came across some crevasses, and Hanssen's sledge was nearly in one; but it was held up, and he came out of it without serious consequences. The cold caused no discomfort on the march; on the contrary, at times it was too warm. One's breath was like a cloud, and so thick was the vapour over the dogs that one could not see one team from the next, though the sledges were being driven close to one another.

On the 12th it was -61.6° F., with a breeze dead against us. This was undeniably bitter. It was easy to see that the temperature was too much for the dogs; in the morning, especially, they were a pitiful sight. They lay rolled up as tightly as possible, with their noses under their tails, and from time to time one could see a shiver run through their bodies; indeed, some of them were constantly shivering. We had to lift them up and put them into their harness. I had to admit that with this temperature it would not pay to go on; the risk was too great. We therefore decided to drive on to the depot in 80° S., and unload our sledges there. On that day, too, we made the awkward discovery that the fluid in our compasses had frozen, rendering them useless. The weather had become very thick, and we could only guess vaguely the position of the sun. Our progress under these circumstances was very doubtful; possibly we were on the right course, but it was just as probable – nay, more so – that we were off it. The best thing we could do, therefore, was to pitch our camp, and wait for a better state of things. We did not bless the instrument-maker who had supplied those compasses.

It was 10 a.m. when we stopped. In order to have a good shelter for the long day before us, we decided to build two snow-huts. The snow was not good for this purpose, but, by fetching blocks from all sides, we managed to put up the huts. Hanssen built one and Wisting the other. In a temperature such as we now had, a snow-hut is greatly preferable to a tent, and we felt quite comfortable when we came in and got the Primus going. That night we heard a strange noise round us. I looked under my bag to see whether we had far to drop, but there was no sign of a disturbance anywhere. In the other but they had heard nothing. We afterwards discovered that the sound was only due to snow "settling." By this expression I mean the movement that takes place when a large extent of the snow surface breaks and sinks (settles down). This movement gives one the idea that the ground is sinking under one, and it is not a pleasant feeling. It is followed by a dull roar, which often makes the dogs jump into the air – and their drivers, too, for that matter. Once we heard this booming on the plateau so loud that it seemed like the thunder of cannon. We soon grew accustomed to it.

Next day the temperature was -62.5° F., calm, and perfectly clear. We did eighteen and a half miles, and kept our course as well as we could with the help of the sun. It was -69.3° F. when we camped. This time I had done a thing that I have always been opposed to: I had brought spirits with me in the form of a bottle of Norwegian aquavit and a bottle of gin. I thought this a suitable occasion to bring in the gin. It was as hard as flint right through. While we were thawing it the bottle burst, and we threw it out into the snow, with the result that all the dogs started to sneeze. The next bottle – "Aquavit, No. 1" – was like a bone, but we had learnt wisdom by experience, and we succeeded with care in thawing it out. We waited till we were all in our bags, and then we had one. I was greatly disappointed; it was not half so good as I had thought. But I am glad I tried it, as I shall never do so again. The effect was nil; I felt nothing, either in my head or my feet.

The 14th was cool – the temperature remained at -68.8° F. Fortunately it was clear, so that we could see where we were going. We had not gone far before a bright projection appeared on the level surface. Out with the glasses – the depot! There it lay, right in our course. Hanssen, who had driven first the whole way, without a forerunner, and for the most part without a compass, had no need to be ashamed of his performance. We agreed that it was well done, and that, no doubt, was all the thanks he got. We reached it at 10.15 a.m., and unloaded our sledges at once. Wisting undertook the far from pleasant task of getting us a cup of warm milk at -68.8° F. He put the Primus behind one of the cases of provisions, and set it going; strangely enough, the paraffin was still liquid in the vessel, but this was no doubt because it had been well protected in the case. A cup of Horlick's Malted Milk tasted better that day than the last time I had tried it – in a restaurant in Chicago.

Having enjoyed that, we threw ourselves on the almost empty

sledges, and set our course for home. The going was difficult, but, with the light weight they now had to pull, the dogs went along well. I sat with Wisting, as I considered his team the strongest. The cold held on unchanged, and I was often surprised that it was possible to sit still on the sledges, as we did, without freezing; but we got on quite well. One or two I saw off their sledges all day, and most of us jumped off from time to time and ran by the side to get warm. I myself took to my ski and let myself be pulled along. This so-called sport has never appealed to me, but under the circumstances it was permissible; it warmed my feet, and that was the object of it. I again had recourse to this "sport" of ski-driving later on, but that was for another reason.

On the 15th, as we sat in the tent cooking and chatting, Hanssen suddenly said: "Why, I believe my heel's gone!" Off came his stockings, and there was a big, dead heel, like a lump of tallow. It did not look well. He rubbed it until he thought he "could feel something again," and then put his feet back in his stockings and got into his bag. Now it was Stubberud's turn. "Blest if I don't think there's something wrong with mine, too." Same proceeding – same result. This was pleasant – two doubtful heels, and forty-six miles from Framheim! When we started next morning it was fortunately milder – "almost summer": -40° F. It felt quite pleasant. The difference between -40° and -60° is, in my opinion, very perceptible. It may perhaps be thought that when one gets so far down, a few degrees one way or the other do not make any difference, but they do.

While driving that day we were obliged to let loose several of the dogs, who could not keep up; we supposed that they would follow our tracks. Adam and Lazarus were never seen again. Sara fell dead on the way without any previous symptom. Camilla was also among those let loose.

On the way home we kept the same order as on the previous days. Hanssen and Wisting, as a rule, were a long way ahead, unless they stopped and waited. We went at a tearing pace. We had thought of halting at the sixteen-mile flag, as we called it – the mark at thirty kilometres from Framheim – and waiting for the others to come up, but as the weather was of the best, calm and clear, and with our tracks on the way south perfectly plain, I decided to go on. The sooner we got the bad heels into the house, the better. The two first sledges arrived at 4 p.m.; the next at 6, and the two following ones at 6.30. The last did not come in till 12.30 a.m. Heaven knows what they had been doing on the way!

With the low temperatures we experienced on this trip, we noticed a curious snow-formation that I had never seen before. Fine – extremely fine – drift-snow collected, and formed small cylindrical bodies of an average diameter of 1 1/4 inches, and about the same height; they were, however, of various sizes. They generally rolled over the surface like a wheel, and now and then collected into large heaps, from which again, one by one, or several together, they continued their rolling. If you took one of these bodies in the hand, there was no increase of weight to be felt – not the very slightest. If you took one of the largest and crushed it, there was, so to speak, nothing left. With the temperature in the -40's, we did not see them.

As soon as we came home, we attended to the heels. Prestrud had both his heels frozen, one slightly, the other more severely, though, so far as I could determine, not so badly as the other two. The first thing we did was to lance the big blisters that had formed and let out the fluid they contained; afterwards we put on boracic compresses, night and morning. We kept up this treatment for a long time; at last the old skin could be removed, and the new lay there fresh and healthy. The heel was cured.

Circumstances had arisen which made me consider it necessary to divide the party into two. One party was to carry out the march to the south; the other was to try to reach King Edward VII. Land, and see what was to be done there, besides exploring the region around the Bay of Whales. This party was composed of Prestrud, Stubberud, and Johansen, under the leadership of the first-named.

The advantages of this new arrangement were many. In the first place, a smaller party could advance more rapidly than a larger one. Our numbers, both of men and dogs, on several of the previous trips had clearly shown the arrangement to be unfortunate. The time we took to get ready in the morning – four hours – was one of the consequences of being a large party. With half the number, or only one tent full, I hoped to be able to reduce this time by half. The importance of the depots we had laid down was, of course, greatly increased, since they would now only have to support five members of the party originally contemplated, and would thus be able to furnish them with supplies for so much more time. From a purely scientific point of view, the change offered such obvious advantages that it is unnecessary to insist upon them. Henceforward, therefore, we worked, so to speak, in two parties. The Polar party was to leave as soon as spring came in earnest. I left it to Prestrud himself to fix the departure of the party he was to lead; there was no such hurry for them – they could take things more easily.

Then the same old fuss about the outfit began all over again, and the needles were busy the whole time. Two days after our return, Wisting and Bjaaland went out to the thirty-kilometre mark with the object of bringing in the dogs that had been let loose on that part of the route and had not yet returned. They made the trip of sixty kilometres (thirty-seven and a half miles) in six hours, and brought all the stragglers – ten of them – back with them. The farthest of them were found lying by the flag; none of them showed a sign of getting up when the sledges came. They had to be picked up and harnessed, and one or two that had sore feet were driven on the sledges. In all probability most of them would have returned in a few days. But it is incomprehensible that healthy, plucky dogs, as many of them were, should take it into their heads to stay behind like that.

On September 24 we had the first tidings of spring, when Bjaaland came back from the ice and told us he had shot a seal. So the seals had begun to come up on to the ice; this was a good sign. The next day we went out to bring it in, and we got another at the same time. There was excitement among the dogs when they got fresh meat, to say nothing of fresh blubber. Nor were we men inclined to say no to a fresh steak.

On September 27 we removed the roof that had covered over the window of our room. We had to carry the light down through a long wooden channel, so that it was considerably reduced by the time it came in; but it was light – genuine daylight – and it was much appreciated.

On the 26th Camilla came back, after an absence of ten days. She had been let loose sixty-eight miles from Framheim on the last trip. When she came in, she was as fat as ever; probably she had been feasting in her solitude on one of her comrades. She was received with great ovations by her many admirers.

On September 29 a still more certain sign of spring appeared – a flight of Antarctic petrels. They came flying up to us to bring the news that now spring had come – this time in earnest. We were delighted to see these fine, swift birds again. They flew round the house several times to see whether we were all there still; and we were not long in going out to receive them. It was amusing to watch the dogs: at first the birds flew pretty near the ground; when the dogs caught sight of them, they rushed out – the whole lot of them – to catch them. They tore along, scouring the ground, and, of course, all wanted to be first. Then the birds suddenly rose into the air, and presently the dogs lost sight of them. They stood still for a moment, glaring at each other, evidently uncertain of what was the best thing to do. Such uncertainty does not, as a rule, last long. They made up their minds with all desirable promptitude and flew at each other's throats.

So now spring had really arrived; we had only to cure the frost-bitten heels and then away.

CHAPTER 10

THE START FOR THE POLE

At last we got away, on October 19. The weather for the past few days had not been altogether reliable; now windy, now calm – now snowing, now clear: regular spring weather, in other words. That day it continued unsettled; it was misty and thick in the morning, and did not promise well for the day, but by 9.30 there was a light breeze from the east, and at the same time it cleared.

There was no need for a prolonged inquiry into the sentiments of the party. – What do you think? Shall we start?" – Yes, of course. Let's be jogging on." There was only one opinion about it. Our coursers were harnessed in a jiffy, and with a little nod – as much as to say, "See you to-morrow" – we were off. I don't believe Lindström even came out of doors to see us start. "Such an every-day affair: what's the use of making a fuss about it?"

There were five of us – Hanssen, Wisting, Hassel, Bjaaland, and myself. We had four sledges, with thirteen dogs to each. At the start our sledges were very light, as we were only taking supplies for the trip to 80° S., where all our cases were waiting for us; we could therefore sit on the sledges and flourish our whips with a jaunty air. I sat astride on Wisting's sledge, and anyone who had seen us would no doubt have thought a Polar journey looked very inviting.

Down on the sea-ice stood Prestrud with the cinematograph, turning the crank as fast as he could go as we went past. When we came up on to the Barrier on the other side, he was there again, turning incessantly. The last thing I saw, as we went over the top of the ridge and everything familiar disappeared, was a cinematograph; it was coming inland at full speed. I had been engaged in looking out ahead, and turned round suddenly to throw a last glance in the direction of the spot that to us stood for all that was beautiful on earth, when I caught sight of – what do you think? A cinematograph. "He can't be taking anything but air now, can he?" – "Hardly that." The cinematograph vanished below the horizon.

The going was excellent, but the atmosphere became thicker as we went inland. For the first twelve miles from the edge of the Barrier I had been sitting with Hassel, but, seeing that Wisting's dogs could manage two on the sledge better than the others, I moved. Hanssen drove first; he had to steer by compass alone, as the weather had got thicker. After him came Bjaaland, then Hassel, and, finally, Wisting and I. We had just gone up a little slope, when we saw that it dropped rather steeply on the other side; the descent could not be more than 20 yards long. I sat with my back to the dogs, looking aft, and was enjoying the brisk drive. Then suddenly the surface by the side of the sledge dropped perpendicularly, and showed a yawning black abyss, large enough to have swallowed us all, and a little more. A few inches more to one side, and we should have taken no part in the Polar journey. We guessed from this broken surface that we had come too far to the east, and altered our course more westerly. When we had reached safer ground, I took the opportunity of putting on my skis and driving so; in this way the weight was more distributed. Before very long it cleared a little, and we saw one of our mark-flags straight ahead. We went up to it; many memories clung to the spot – cold and slaughter of dogs. It was there we had killed the three puppies on the last trip.

We had then covered seventeen miles, and we camped, well pleased with the first day of our long journey. My belief that, with all in one tent, we should manage our camping and preparations much better than before was fully justified. The tent went up as though it arose out of the ground, and everything was done as though we had had long practice. We found we had ample room in the tent, and our arrangements worked splendidly the whole time. They were as follows: as soon as we halted, all took a hand at the tent. The pegs in the valance of the tent were driven in, and Wisting crept inside and planted the pole, while the rest of us stretched the guy-ropes. When this was done, I went in, and all the things that were to go inside were handed in to me – sleeping-bags, kit-bags, cookers, provisions. Everything was put in its place, the Primus lighted, and the cooker filled with snow. Meanwhile the others fed their dogs and let them loose. Instead of the "guard," we shovelled loose snow round the tent; this proved to be sufficient protection – the dogs respected it. The bindings were taken off all our ski, and either stowed with other loose articles in a provision-case, or hung up together with the harness on the top of the ski, which were lashed upright to the front of the sledge. The tent proved excellent in every way; the dark colour subdued the light, and made it agreeable.

Neptune, a fine dog, was let loose when we had come six miles over the plain; he was so fat that he could not keep up. We felt certain that he would follow us, but he did not appear. We then supposed that he had turned back and made for the flesh-pots, but, strangely enough, he did not do that either. He never arrived at the station; it is quite a mystery what became of him. Rotta, another fine animal, was also set free; she was not fit for the journey, and she afterwards arrived at home. Ulrik began by having a ride on the sledge; he picked up later. Björn went limping after the sledge. Peary was incapacitated; he was let loose and followed for a time, but then disappeared. When the eastern party afterwards visited the depot in 80° S., they found him there in good condition. He was shy at first, but by degrees let them come near him and put the harness on. He did very good service after that. Uranus and Fuchs were out of condition. This was pretty bad for the first day, but the others were all worth their weight in gold.

During the night it blew a gale from the east, but it moderated in the morning, so that we got away at 10 a.m. The weather did not hold for long; the wind came again with renewed force from the same quarter, with thick driving snow. However, we went along well, and passed flag after flag. After going nineteen and a quarter miles, we came to a snow beacon that had been erected at the beginning of April, and had stood for seven months; it was still quite good and solid. This gave us a good deal to think about: so we could depend upon these beacons; they would not fall down. From the experience thus gained, we afterwards erected the whole of our extensive system of beacons on the way south. The wind went to the south-east during the day; it blew, but luckily it had stopped snowing. The temperature was -11.5° F., and bitter enough against the wind. When we stopped in the evening and set our tent, we had just found our tracks from the last trip; they were sharp and clear, though six weeks old. We were glad to find them, as we had seen no flag for some time, and were beginning to get near the ugly trap, forty-six and a half miles from the house, that had been found on the last depot journey, so we had to be careful.

The next day, the 21st, brought very thick weather: a strong breeze from the south-east, with thick driving snow. It would not have been a day for crossing the trap if we had not found our old tracks. It was true that we could not see them far, but we could still see the direction they took. So as to be quite safe, I now set our course north-east by east – two points east was the original course. And compared with our old tracks, this looked right, as the new course was considerably more easterly than the direction of the tracks. One last glance over the camping-ground to see whether anything was forgotten, and then into the blizzard. It was really vile weather, snowing from above and drifting from below, so that one was quite blinded. We could not see far; very often we on the last sledge had difficulty in seeing the first. Bjaaland was next in front of us. For a long time we had been going markedly downhill, and this was not in accordance with our reckoning; but in that weather one could not make much of a reckoning. We had several times passed over crevasses, but none of any size. Suddenly we saw Bjaaland's sledge sink over. He jumped off and seized the trace. The sledge lay on its side for a few seconds, then began to sink more and more, and finally disappeared altogether. Bjaaland had got a good purchase in the snow, and the dogs lay down and dug their claws in. The sledge sank more and more – all this happened in a few moments.

"Now I can't hold it any longer." We – Wisting and I – had just come up. He was holding on convulsively, and resisting with all his force, but it was no use – inch by inch the sledge sank deeper. The dogs, too, seemed to understand the gravity of the situation; stretched out in the snow, they dug their claws in, and resisted with all their strength. But still, inch by inch, slowly and surely, it went down into the abyss. Bjaaland was right enough when he said he couldn't hold on any longer. A few seconds more, and his sledge and thirteen dogs would never have seen the light of day again. Help came at the last moment. Hanssen and Hassel, who were a little in advance when it happened, had snatched an Alpine rope from a sledge and came to his assistance. They made the rope fast to the trace, and two of us – Bjaaland and I – were now able, by getting a good purchase, to hold the sledge suspended. First the dogs were taken out; then Hassel's sledge was drawn back and placed across the narrowest part of the crevasse, where we could see that the edges were solid. Then by our combined efforts the sledge, which was dangling far below, was hoisted up as far as we could get it, and made fast to Hassel's sledge by the dogs' traces. Now we could slack off and let go: one sledge hung securely enough by the other. We could breathe a little more freely.

The next thing to be done was to get the sledge right, up, and before we could manage that it had to be unloaded. A man would have to go down on the rope, cast off the lashings of the cases, and attach them again for drawing up. They all wanted this job, but Wisting had it; he fastened the Alpine rope round his body and went down. Bjaaland and I took up our former positions, and acted as anchors; meanwhile Wisting reported what he saw down below. The case with the cooker was hanging by its last thread; it was secured, and again saw the light of day. Hassel and Hanssen attended to the hauling up of the cases, as Wisting had them ready. These two fellows moved about on the brink of the chasm with a coolness that I regarded at first with approving eyes. I admire courage and contempt for danger. But the length to which they carried it at last was too much of a good thing; they were simply playing hide-and-seek with Fate. Wisting's information from below – that the cornice they were standing on was only a few inches thick – did not seem to have the slightest effect on them; on the contrary, they seemed to stand all the more securely.

"We've been lucky," said Wisting; "this is the only place where the crevasse is narrow enough to put a sledge across. If we had gone a little more to the left" – Hanssen looked eagerly in that direction – "none of us would have escaped. There is no surface there; only a crust as thin as paper. It doesn't look very inviting down below, either; immense spikes of ice sticking up everywhere, which would spit you before you got very far down."

This description was not attractive; it was well we had found "such a good place." Meanwhile Wisting had finished his work, and was hauled up. When asked whether he was not glad to be on the surface again, he answered with a smile that "it was nice and warm down there." We then hauled the sledge up, and for the time being all was well. "But," said Hassel, "we must be careful going along here, because I was just on the point of going in when Hanssen and I were bringing up the sledge." He smiled as though at a happy memory. Hassel had seen that it was best to be careful. There was no need to look for crevasses; there was literally nothing else to be seen.

There could be no question of going farther into the trap, for we had long ago come to the conclusion that, in spite of our precautions, we had arrived at this ugly place. We should have to look about for a place for the tent, but that was easier said than done. There was no possibility of finding a place large enough for both the tent and the guy-ropes; the tent was set up on a small, apparently solid spot, and the guys stretched across crevasses in all directions. We were beginning to be quite familiar with the place. That crevasse ran there and there, and it had a side-fissure that went so and so – just like schoolboys learning a lesson.

Meanwhile we had brought all our things as far as possible into a place of safety; the dogs lay harnessed to reduce the risk of losing them. Wisting was just going over to his sledge – he had gone the same way several times before – when suddenly I saw nothing but his head, shoulders and arms above the snow. He had fallen through, but saved himself by stretching his arms out as he fell. The crevasse was bottomless, like the rest. We went into the tent and cooked lobscouse. Leaving the weather to take care of itself, we made ourselves as comfortable as we could. It was then one o'clock in the afternoon. The wind had fallen considerably since we came in, and before we knew what was happening, it was perfectly calm. It began to brighten a little about three, and we went out to look at it.

The weather was evidently improving, and on the northern horizon there was a sign of blue sky. On the south it was thick. Far off, in the densest part of the mist, we could vaguely see the outline of a dome-like elevation, and Wisting and Hanssen went off to examine it. The dome turned out to be one of the small haycock formations that we had seen before in this district. They struck at it with their poles, and just as they expected – it was hollow, and revealed the darkest abyss. Hanssen was positively chuckling with delight when he told us about it; Hassel sent him an envious glance.

By 4 p.m. it cleared, and a small reconnoitring party, composed of three, started to find a way out of this. I was one of the three, so we had a long Alpine rope between us; I don't like tumbling in, if I can avoid it by such simple means. We set out to the east – the direction that had brought us out of the same broken ground before – and we had not gone more than a few paces when we were quite out of it. It was now clear enough to look about us. Our tent stood at the north-eastern corner of a tract that was full of hummocks; we could decide beyond a doubt that this was the dreaded trap. We continued a little way to the east until we saw our course clearly, and then returned to camp. We did not waste much time in getting things ready and leaving the place. It was a genuine relief to find ourselves once more on good ground, and we resumed our journey southward at a brisk pace.

That we were not quite out of the dangerous zone was shown by a number of small hummocks to the south of us. They extended across our course at right angles. We could also see from some long but narrow crevasses we crossed that we must keep a good look-out. When we came into the vicinity of the line of hummocks that lay in our course, we stopped and discussed our prospects. "We shall save a lot of time by going straight on through here instead of going round," said Hanssen. I had to admit this; but, on the other hand, the risk was much greater. "Oh, let's try it," he went on; "if we can't do it, we can't." I was weak, and allowed myself to be persuaded, and away we went among the haycocks. I could see how Hanssen was enjoying himself; this was just what he wanted. We went faster and faster. Curiously enough, we passed several of these formations without noticing anything, and began to hope that we should get through. Then suddenly Hanssen's three leading dogs disappeared, and the others stopped abruptly. He got them hauled up without much trouble and came over. We others, who were following, crossed without accident, but our further progress seemed doubtful, for after a few more paces the same three dogs fell in again. We were now in exactly the same kind of place as before; crevasses ran in every direction, like a broken pane of glass. I had had enough, and would take no more part in this death-ride. I announced decisively that we must turn back, follow our tracks, and go round it all. Hanssen looked quite disappointed. "Well," he said, "but we shall be over it directly." "I dare say we shall," I replied; "but we must go back first." This was evidently hard on him; there was one formation in particular that attracted him, and he wanted to try his strength with it. It was a pressure-mass that, as far as appearance went, might just as well have been formed out in the drift-ice. It looked as if it was formed of four huge lumps of ice raised on end against each other. We knew what it contained without examination – a yawning chasm. Hanssen cast a last regretful glance upon it, and then turned back.

We could now see all our surroundings clearly. This place lay, as we had remarked before, in a hollow; we followed it round, and came up the rise on the south without accident. Here we caught sight of one of our flags; it stood to the east of us, and thus confirmed our suspicion that we had been going too far to the west. We had one more contact with the broken ground, having to cross some crevasses and pass a big hole; but then it was done, and we could once more rejoice in having solid ice beneath us.

Hanssen, however, was not satisfied till he had been to look into the hole. In the evening we reached the two snow-huts we had built on the last trip, and we camped there, twenty-six miles from the depot. The huts were drifted up with snow, so we left them in peace, and as the weather was now so mild and fine, we preferred the tent.

It had been an eventful day, and we had reason to be satisfied that we had come off so easily. The going had been good, and it had all gone like a game. When we started the next morning it was overcast and thick, and before we had gone very far we were in the midst of a south-wester, with snow so thick that we could hardly see ten sledge-lengths ahead of us. We had intended to reach the depot that day, but if this continued, it was more than doubtful whether we should find it.

Meanwhile we put on the pace. It was a long way on, so there was no danger of driving past it. During this while it had remained clear in the zenith, and we had been hoping that the wind and snow would cease; but we had no such luck – it increased rather than dropped. Our best sledge-meter – one we knew we could depend on – was on Wisting's sledge; therefore he had to check the distance. At 1.30 p.m. he turned round to me, and pointed out that we had gone the exact distance; I called out to Hanssen to use his eyes well. Then, at that very moment, the depot showed up a few sledge-lengths to the left of us, looking like a regular palace of snow in the thick air. This was a good test both for the sledge-meter and the compass. We drove up to it and halted. There were three important points to be picked up on our way south, and one of them was found; we were all glad and in good spirits.

The ninety-nine miles from Framheim to this point had been covered in four marches, and we could now rest our dogs, and give them as much seal's flesh as they were capable of eating. Thus far the trip had been a good one for the animals; with one exception, they were all in the best condition. This exception was Uranus. We had never been able to get any fat on his bones; he remained thin and scraggy, and awaited his death at the depot, a little later, in 82° S. If Uranus was lanky to look at, the same could not be said of Jaala, poor beast! In spite of her condition, she struggled to keep up; she did her utmost, but unless her dimensions were reduced before we left 82° S., she would have to accompany Uranus to another world.

The cases of provisions and outfit that we had left here on the last trip were almost entirely snowed under, but it did not take long to dig them out. The first thing to be done was to cut up the seals for the dogs. These grand pieces of meat, with the blubber attached, did not have to be thrown at the dogs; they just helped themselves as long as there was any meat cut up, and when that was finished, they did not hesitate to attack the "joint." It was a pleasure to see them, as they lay all over the place, enjoying their food; it was all so delightfully calm and peaceful, to begin with. They were all hungry, and thought of nothing but satisfying their immediate cravings; but when this was done there was an end of the truce. Although Hai had only half finished his share, he must needs go up to Rap and take away the piece he was eating. Of course, this could not happen without a great row, which resulted in the appearance of Hanssen; then Hai made himself scarce. He was a fine dog, but fearfully obstinate; if he had once taken a thing into his head, it was not easy to make him give it up. On one of our depot journeys it happened that I was feeding Hanssen's dogs. Hai had made short work of his pemmican, and looked round for more. Ah! there was Rap enjoying his – that would just do for him. In a flash Hai was upon him, forced him to give up his dinner, and was about to convert it to his own use. Meanwhile I had witnessed the whole scene, and before Hai knew anything about it, I was upon him in turn. I hit him over the nose with the whip-handle, and tried to take the pemmican from him, but it was not so easy. Neither of us would give in, and soon we were both rolling over and over in the snow struggling for the mastery. I came off victorious after a pretty hot fight, and Rap got his dinner again. Any other dog would have dropped it at once on being hit over the nose, but not Hai.

It was a treat to get into the tent; the day had been a bitter one. During the night the wind went round to the north, and all the snow that had been blown northward by the wind of the previous day had nothing to do but to come back again; the road was free. And it made the utmost use of its opportunity; nothing could be seen for driving snow when we turned out next morning. We could only stay where we were, and console ourselves with the thought that it made no difference, as it had been decided that we were to remain here two days. But staying in a tent all day is never very amusing, especially when one is compelled to keep to one's sleeping-bag the whole time. You soon get tired of talking, and you can't write all day long, either. Eating is a good way of passing the time, if you can afford it, and so is reading, if you have anything to read; but as the menu is limited, and the library as a rule somewhat deficient on a sledging trip, these two expedients fall to the ground. There is, however, one form of entertainment that may be indulged in under these circumstances without scruple, and that is a good nap. Happy the man who can sleep the clock round on days like these; but that is a gift that is not vouchsafed to all, and those who have it will not own up to it. I have heard men snore till I was really afraid they would choke, but as for acknowledging that they had been asleep – never! Some of them even have the coolness to assert that they suffer from sleeplessness, but it was not so bad as that with any of us.

In the course of the day the wind dropped, and we went out to do some work. We transferred the old depot to the new one. We now had here three complete sledge-loads, for which there would be little use, and which, therefore, were left behind. The eastern party availed themselves of part of these supplies on their journey, but not much. This depot is a fairly large one, and might come in useful if anyone should think of exploring the region from King Edward Land southward. As things were, we had no need of it. At the same time the sledges were packed, and when evening came everything was ready for our departure. There had really been no hurry about this, as we were going to stay here on the following day as well; but one soon learns in these regions that it is best to take advantage of good weather when you have it – you never know how long it will last. There was, however, nothing to be said about the day that followed; we could doze and doze as much as we liked. The work went on regularly, nevertheless. The dogs gnawed and gnawed, storing up strength with every hour that went by.

We will now take a trip out to our loaded sledges, and see what they contain. Hanssen's stands first, bow to the south; behind it come Wisting's, Bjaaland's and Hassel's. They all look pretty much alike, and as regards provisions their loads are precisely similar.

Case No. 1 contains about 5,300 biscuits, and weighs 111 pounds.

Case No. 2: 112 rations of dogs' pemmican; 11 bags of dried milk, chocolate, and biscuits. Total gross weight, 177 pounds.

Case No. 3: 124 rations of dogs' pemmican; 10 bags of dried milk and biscuits. Gross weight, 161 pounds.

Case No. 4: 39 rations of dogs' pemmican; 86 rations of men's pemmican; 9 bags of dried milk and biscuits. Gross weight, 165 pounds.

Case No. 5: 96 rations of dogs' pemmican. Weight, 122 pounds.

Total net weight of provisions per sledge, 668 pounds.

With the outfit and the weight of the sledge itself, the total came to pretty nearly 880 pounds.

Hanssen's sledge differed from the others, in that it had aluminium fittings instead of steel and no sledge-meter, as it had to be free from iron on account of the steering-compass he carried. Each of the other three sledges had a sledge-meter and compass. We were thus equipped with three sledge-meters and four compasses. The instruments we carried were two sextants and three artificial horizons – two glass and one mercury – a hypsometer for measuring heights, and one aneroid. For meteorological observations, four thermometers. Also two pairs of binoculars. We took a little travelling case of medicines from Burroughs Wellcome and Co. Our surgical instruments were not many: a dental forceps and – a beard-clipper. Our sewing outfit was extensive. We carried a small, very light tent in reserve; it would have to be used if any of us were obliged to turn back. We also carried two Primus lamps. Of paraffin we had a good supply: twenty-two and a half gallons divided among three sledges. We kept it in the usual cans, but they proved too weak; not that we lost any paraffin, but Bjaaland had to be constantly soldering to keep them tight. We had a good soldering outfit. Every man carried his own personal bag, in which he kept reserve clothing, diaries and observation books. We took a quantity of loose straps for spare ski-bindings. We had double sleeping-bags for the first part of the time; that is to say, an inner and an outer one. There were five watches among us, of which three were chronometer watches.

We had decided to cover the distance between 80° and 82° S. in daily marches of seventeen miles. We could easily have done twice this, but as it was more important to arrive than to show great speed, we limited the distance; besides which, here between the depots we had sufficient food to allow us to take our time. We were interested in seeing how the dogs would manage the loaded sledges. We expected them to do well, but not so well as they did.

On October 25 we left 80° S. with a light north-westerly breeze, clear and mild. I was now to take up my position in advance of the sledges, and placed myself a few paces in front of Hanssen's, with my skis pointing in the right direction. A last look behind me: "All ready?" and away I went. I thought – no; I didn't have time to think. Before I knew anything about it, I was sent flying by the dogs. In the confusion that ensued they stopped, luckily, so that I escaped without damage, as far as that went. To tell the truth, I was angry, but as I had sense enough to see that the situation, already sufficiently comic, would be doubly ridiculous if I allowed my annoyance to show itself, I wisely kept quiet. And, after all, whose fault was it? I was really the only one to blame; why in the world had I not got away faster? I now changed my plan entirely – there is nothing to be ashamed of in that, I hope – and fell in with the awkward squad; there I was more successful. "All ready? Go!" And go they did. First Hanssen went off like a meteor; close behind him came Wisting, and then Bjaaland and Hassel. They all had skis on, and were driving with a line. I had made up my mind to follow in the rear, as I thought the dogs would not keep this up for long, but I soon had enough of it. We did the first six and a quarter miles in an hour. I thought that would do for me, so I went up to Wisting, made a rope fast to his sledge, and there I stood till we reached 85° 5' S. – three hundred and forty miles. Yes; that was a pleasant surprise. We had never dreamed of anything of the sort – driving on skis to the Pole! Thanks to Hanssen's brilliant talents as a dog-driver, we could easily do this. He had his dogs well in hand, and they knew their master. They knew that the moment they failed to do their duty they would be pulled up, and a hiding all round would follow. Of course, as always happens, Nature occasionally got the better of discipline; but the "confirmation" that resulted checked any repetition of such conduct for a long while. The day's march was soon completed in this way, and we camped early.

On the following day we were already in sight of the large pressure-ridges on the east, which we had seen for the first time on the second depot journey between 81° and 82° S., and this showed that the atmosphere must be very clear. We could not see any greater number than the first time, however. From our experience of beacons built of snow, we could see that if we built such beacons now, on our way south, they would be splendid marks for our return journey; we therefore decided to adopt this system of landmarks to the greatest possible extent. We built in all 150 beacons, 6 feet high, and used in their construction 9,000 blocks, cut out of the snow with specially large snow-knives. In each of them was deposited a paper, giving the number and position of the beacon, and indicating the distance and the direction to be taken to reach the next beacon to the north. It may appear that my prudence was exaggerated, but it always seemed to me that one could not be too careful on this endless, uniform surface. If we lost our way here, it would be difficult enough to reach home. Besides which, the building of these beacons had other advantages, which we could all see and appreciate. Every time we stopped to build one, the dogs had a rest, and they wanted this, if they were to keep up the pace.

We erected the first beacon in 80° 23' S. To begin with, we contented ourselves with putting them up at every thirteenth or fifteenth kilometre. On the 29th we shot the first dog, Hanssen's Bone. He was too old to keep up, and was only a hindrance. He was placed in depot under a beacon, and was a great joy to us – or rather to the dogs – later on.

On the same day we reached the second important point – the depot in 81° S. Our course took us very slightly to the east of it. The small pieces of packing-case that had been used as marks on each side of the depot could be seen a long way off. On a subsequent examination they showed no sign of snowfall; they stood just as they had been put in. In the neighbourhood of the depot we crossed two quite respectable crevasses; they were apparently filled up, and caused us no trouble. We reached the depot at 2 p.m.; everything was in the best of order. The flag was flying, and hardly looked as if it had been up a day, although it had now been waving there for nearly eight months. The drifts round the depot were about 1 1/2 feet high.

The next day was brilliant – calm and clear. The sun really baked the skin of one's face. We put all our skin clothing out to dry; a little rime will always form at the bottom of a sleeping-bag. We also availed ourselves of this good opportunity to determine our position and check our compasses; they proved to be correct. We replaced the provisions we had consumed on the way, and resumed our journey on October 31.

There was a thick fog next morning, and very disagreeable weather; perhaps we felt it more after the previous fine day. When we passed this way for the first time going south, Hanssen's dogs had fallen into a crevasse, but it was nothing to speak of; otherwise we had no trouble. Nor did we expect any this time; but in these regions what one least expects frequently happens. The snow was loose and the going heavy; from time to time we crossed a narrow crevasse. Once we saw through the fog a large open hole; we could not have been very far from it, or we should not have seen it, the weather was so thick. But all went well till we had come thirteen and a half miles. Then Hanssen had to cross a crevasse a yard wide, and in doing it he was unlucky enough to catch the point of his skis in the traces of the hindmost dogs, and fall right across the crevasse. This looked unpleasant. The dogs were across, and a foot or two on the other side, but the sledge was right over the crevasse, and had twisted as Hanssen fell, so that a little more would bring it into line with the crevasse, and then, of course, down it would go. The dogs had quickly scented the fact that their lord and master was for the moment incapable of administering a "confirmation," and they did not let slip the golden opportunity. Like a lot of roaring tigers, the whole team set upon each other and fought till the hair flew. This naturally produced short, sharp jerks at the traces, so that the sledge worked round more and more, and at the same time the dogs, in the heat of the combat, were coming nearer and nearer to the brink. If this went on, all was irretrievably lost. One of us jumped the crevasse, went into the middle of the struggling team, and, fortunately, got them to stop. At the same time, Wisting threw a line to Hanssen and hauled him out of his unpleasant position – although, I thought to myself, as we went on: I wonder whether Hanssen did not enjoy the situation? Stretched across a giddy abyss, with the prospect of slipping down it at any moment – that was just what he would like. We secured the sledge, completed our seventeen miles, and camped.

From 81° S. we began to erect beacons at every nine kilometres. The next day we observed the lowest temperature of the whole of this journey: -30.1° F The wind was south-south-east, but not very strong. It did not feel like summer, all the same. We now adopted the habit which we kept up all the way to the south – of taking our lunch while building the beacon that lay half-way in our day's march. It was nothing very luxurious – three or four dry oatmeal biscuits, that was all. If one wanted a drink, one could mix snow with the biscuit – "bread and water." It is a diet that is not much sought after in our native latitudes, but latitude makes a very great difference in this world. It anybody had offered us more "bread and water," we should gladly have accepted it.

That day we crossed the last crevasse for a long time to come, and it was only a few inches wide. The surface looked grand ahead of us; it went in very long, almost imperceptible undulations. We could only notice them by the way in which the beacons we put up often disappeared rather rapidly.

On November 2 we had a gale from the south, with heavy snow. The going was very stiff, but the dogs got the sledges along better than we expected. The temperature rose, as usual, with a wind from this quarter: +14° F. It was a pleasure to be out in such a temperature, although it did blow a little. The day after we had a light breeze from the north. The heavy going of the day before had completely disappeared; instead of it we had the best surface one could desire, and it made our dogs break into a brisk gallop. That was the day we were to reach the depot in 82° S., but as it was extremely thick, our chances of doing so were small. In the course of the afternoon the distance was accomplished, but no depot was visible. However, our range of vision was nothing to boast of – ten sledge-lengths; not more. The most sensible thing to do, under the circumstances, was to camp and wait till it cleared.

At four o'clock next morning the sun broke through. We let it get warm and disperse the fog, and then went out. What a morning it was – radiantly clear and mild. So still, so still lay the mighty desert before us, level and white on every side. But, no; there in the distance the level was broken: there was a touch of colour on the white. The third important point was reached, the extreme outpost of civilization. Our last depot lay before us; that was an unspeakable relief. The victory now seemed half won. In the fog we had come about three and a half miles too far to the west; but we now saw that if we had continued our march the day before, we should have come right into our line of flags. There they stood, flag after flag, and the little strip of black cloth seemed to wave quite proudly, as though it claimed credit for the way in which it had discharged its duty. Here, as at the depot in 81° S., there was hardly a sign of snowfall. The drift round the depot had reached the same height as there – 1 1/2 feet. Clearly the same conditions of weather had prevailed all over this region. The depot stood as we had made it, and the sledge as we had left it. Falling snow and drift had not been sufficient to cover even this. The little drift that there was offered an excellent place for the tent, being hard and firm. We at once set about the work that had to be done. First, Uranus was sent into the next world, and although he had always given us the impression of being thin and bony, it was now seen that there were masses of fat along his back; he would be much appreciated when we reached here on the return. Jaala did not look as if she would fulfil the conditions, but we gave her another night. The dogs' pemmican in the depot was just enough to give the dogs a good feed and load up the sledges again. We were so well supplied with all other provisions that we were able to leave a considerable quantity behind for the return journey.

Next day we stayed here to give the dogs a thorough rest for the last time. We took advantage of the fine weather to dry our outfit and check our instruments. When evening came we were all ready, and now we could look back with satisfaction to the good work of the autumn; we had fully accomplished what we aimed at – namely, transferring our base from 78° 38' to 82° S. Jaala had to follow Uranus; they were both laid on the top of the depot, beside eight little ones that never saw the light of day. During our stay here we decided to build beacons at every fifth kilometre, and to lay down depots at every degree of latitude. Although the dogs were drawing the sledges easily at present, we knew well enough that in the long-run they would find it hard work if they were always to have heavy weights to pull. The more we could get rid of, and the sooner we could begin to do so, the better.

On November 6, at 8 a.m., we left 82° S. Now the unknown lay before us; now our work began in earnest. The appearance of the Barrier was the same everywhere – flat, with a splendid surface. At the first beacon we put up we had to shoot Lucy. We were sorry to put an end to this beautiful creature, but there was nothing else to be done. Her friends – Karenius, Sauen, and Schwartz – scowled up at the beacon where she lay as they passed, but duty called, and the whip sang dangerously near them, though they did not seem to hear it. We had now extended our daily march to twenty-three miles; in this way we should do a degree in three days.

On the 7th we decided to stop for a day's rest. The dogs had been picking up wonderfully every day, and were now at the top of their condition, as far as health and training went. With the greatest ease they covered the day's march at a pace of seven and a half kilometres (four miles and two-thirds) an hour. As for ourselves, we never had to move a foot; all we had to do was to let ourselves be towed. The same evening we had to put an end to the last of our ladies – Else. She was Hassel's pride and the ornament of his team; but there was no help for it. She was also placed at the top of a beacon.

When we halted that evening in 82° 20′ S., we saw on the south-western horizon several heavy masses of drab-coloured cloud, such as are usually to be seen over land. We could make out no land that evening, however; but when we came out next

369

morning and directed our glasses to that quarter, the land lay there, lofty and clear in the morning sun. We were now able to distinguish several summits, and to determine that this was the land extending south-eastward from Beardmore Glacier in South Victoria Land. Our course had been true south all the time; at this spot we were about 250 miles to the east of Beardmore Glacier. Our course would continue to be true south.

The same evening – November 8 – we reached 83° S. by dead reckoning. The noon altitude next day gave 83° 1' S. The depot we built here contained provisions for five men and twelve dogs for four days; it was made square – 6 feet each way – of hard, solid blocks of snow. A large flag was placed on the top. That evening a strange thing happened – three dogs deserted, going northward on our old tracks. They were Lucy's favourites, and had probably taken it into their heads that they ought to go back and look after their friend. It was a great loss to us all, but especially to Bjaaland; they were all three first-rate animals, and among the best we had. He had to borrow a dog from Hanssen's team, and if he did not go quite so smoothly as before, he was still able to keep up.

On the 10th we got a bearing of the mountain chain right down in south by west true. Each day we drew considerably nearer the land, and could see more and more of its details: mighty peaks, each loftier and wilder than the last, rose to heights of 15,000 feet. What struck us all were the bare sides that many of these mountains showed; we had expected to see them far more covered with snow. Mount Fridtjof Nansen, for example, had quite a blue-black look. Only quite at the summit was it crowned by a mighty hood of ice that raised its shining top to some 15,000 feet. Farther to the south rose Mount Don Pedro Christophersen;

it was more covered with snow, but the long, gabled summit was to a great extent bare. Still farther south Mounts Alice Wedel Jarlsberg, Alice Gade, and Ruth Gade, came in sight; all snow-clad from peak to base. I do not think I have ever seen a more beautiful or wilder landscape. Even from where we were, we seemed to be able to see a way up from several places. There lay Liv's Glacier for instance, which would undoubtedly afford a good and even ascent, but it lay too far to the north. It is of enormous extent, and would prove interesting to explore. Crown Prince Olav's Mountains looked less promising, but they also lay too far to the north. A little to the west of south lay an apparently good way up. The mountains nearest to the Barrier did not seem to offer any great obstruction. What one might find later, between Mounts Pedro Christophersen and Fridtjof Nansen, was not easy to say.

On the 12th we reached 84° S. On that day we made the interesting discovery of a chain of mountains running to the east; this, as it appeared from the spot where we were, formed a semicircle, where it joined the mountains of South Victoria Land. This semicircle lay true south, and our course was directed straight towards it.

In the depot in 84° S. we left, besides the usual quantity of provisions for five men and twelve dogs for four days, a can of paraffin, holding 17 litres (about 34 gallons). We had abundance of matches, and could therefore distribute them over all the depots. The Barrier continued as flat as before, and the going was as good as it could possibly be. We had thought that a day's rest would be needed by the dogs for every degree of latitude, but this proved superfluous; it looked as if they could no longer be tired. One or two had shown signs of bad feet, but were now perfectly well; instead of losing strength, the dogs seemed to become stronger and more active every day. Now they, too, had sighted the land, and the black mass of Mount Fridtjof Nansen seemed specially to appeal to them; Hanssen often had hard work to keep them in the right course. Without any longer stay, then, we left 84° S. the next day, and steered for the bay ahead.

That day we went twenty-three miles in thick fog, and saw nothing of the land. It was hard to have to travel thus blindly off an unknown coast, but we could only hope for better weather. During the previous night we had heard, for a change, a noise in the ice. It was nothing very great, and sounded like scattered infantry fire – a few rifle-shots here and there underneath our tent; the artillery had not come up yet. We took no notice of it, though I heard one man say in the morning: "Blest if I didn't think I got a whack on the ear last night." I could witness that it had not cost him his sleep, as that night he had very nearly snored us all out of the tent.

During the forenoon we crossed a number of apparently newly-formed crevasses; most of them only about an inch wide. There had thus been a small local disturbance occasioned by one of the numerous small glaciers on land. On the following night all was quiet again, and we never afterwards heard the slightest sound.

On November 14 we reached 84° 40' S. We were now rapidly approaching land; the mountain range on the east appeared to turn north-eastward. Our line of ascent, which we had chosen long ago and now had our eyes fixed upon as we went, would take us a trifle to the west of south, but so little that the digression was of no account. The semicircle we saw to the south made a more disquieting impression, and looked as if it would offer great irregularities. On the following day the character of the surface began to change; great wave-like formations seemed to roll higher and higher as they approached the land, and in one of the troughs of these we found the surface greatly disturbed. At some bygone time immense fissures and chasms would have rendered its passage practically impossible, but now they were all drifted up, and we had no difficulty in crossing.

That day – November 15 – we reached 85° S., and camped at the top of one of these swelling waves. The valley we were to cross next day was fairly broad, and rose considerably on the other side. On the west, in the direction of the nearest land, the undulation rose to such a height that it concealed a great part of the land from us. During the afternoon we built the usual depot, and continued our journey on the following day. As we had seen from our camping-ground, it was an immense undulation that we had to traverse; the ascent on the other side felt uncomfortably warm in the powerful sun, but it was no higher than 300 feet by the aneroid. From the top of this wave the Barrier stretched away before us, flat at first, but we could see disturbances of the surface in the distance. Now we are going to have some fun in getting to land, I thought, for it seemed very natural that the Barrier, hemmed in as it was here, would be much broken up. The disturbances we had seen consisted of some big, old crevasses, which were partly filled up; we avoided them easily. Now there was another deep depression before us; with a correspondingly high rise on the other side. We went over it capitally; the surface was absolutely smooth, without a sign of fissure or hole anywhere. Then we shall get them when we are on the top, I thought. It was rather stiff work uphill, unaccustomed as we were to slopes. I stretched my neck more and more to get a view. At last we were up; and what a sight it was that met us! Not an irregularity, not a sign of disturbance; quietly and evenly the ascent continued. I believe that we were then already above land; the large crevasses that we had avoided down below probably formed the boundary. The hypsometer gave 930 feet above the sea.

We were now immediately below the ascent, and made the final decision of trying it here. This being settled, we pitched our camp. It was still early in the day, but we had a great deal to arrange before the morrow. Here we should have to overhaul our whole supply of provisions, take with us what was absolutely necessary for the remainder of the trip, and leave the rest behind in depot. First, then, we camped, worked out our position, fed the dogs and let them loose again, and then went into our tent to have something to eat and go through the provision books.

We had now reached one of the most critical points of our journey. Our plan had now to be laid so that we might not only make the ascent as easily as possible, but also get through to the end. Our calculations had to be made carefully, and every possibility taken into account. As with every decision of importance, we discussed the matter jointly. The distance we had before us, from this spot to the Pole and back, was 683 miles. Reckoning with the ascent that we saw before us, with other unforeseen obstructions, and finally with the certain factor that the strength of our dogs would be gradually reduced to a fraction of what it now was, we decided to take provisions and equipment for sixty days on the sledges, and to leave the remaining supplies – enough for thirty days – and outfit in depot. We calculated, from the experience we had had, that we ought to be able to reach this point again with twelve dogs left. We now had forty-two dogs. Our plan was to take all the forty-two up to the plateau; there twenty-four of them were to be slaughtered, and the journey continued with three sledges and eighteen dogs. Of these last eighteen, it would be necessary, in our opinion, to slaughter six in order to bring the other twelve back to this point. As the number of dogs grew less, the sledges would become lighter and lighter, and when the time came for reducing their number to twelve, we should only have two sledges left. This time again our calculations came out approximately right; it was only in reckoning the number of days that we made a little mistake – we took eight days less than the time allowed. The number of dogs agreed exactly; we reached this point again with twelve.

After the question had been well discussed and each had given his opinion, we went out to get the repacking done. It was lucky the weather was so fine, otherwise this taking stock of provisions might have been a bitter piece of work. All our supplies were in such a form that we could count them instead of weighing them. Our pemmican was in rations of 2 kilogram (1 pound 12 ounces). The chocolate was divided into small pieces, as chocolate always is, so that we knew what each piece weighed. Our milk-powder was put up in bags of 102 ounces just enough for a meal. Our biscuits possessed the same property – they could be counted, but this was a tedious business, as they were rather small. On this occasion we had to count 6,000 biscuits. Our provisions consisted only of these four kinds, and the combination turned out right enough. We did not suffer from a craving either for fat or sugar, though the want of these substances is very commonly felt on such journeys as ours. In our biscuits we had an excellent product, consisting of oatmeal, sugar, and dried milk. Sweetmeats, jam, fruit, cheese, etc., we had left behind at Framheim.

We took our reindeer-skin clothing, for which we had had no use as yet, on the sledges. We were now coming on to the high ground, and it might easily happen that it would be a good thing to have. We did not forget the temperature of -40° F. that Shackleton had experienced in 88° S., and if we met with the same, we could hold out a long while if we had the skin clothing. Otherwise, we had not very much in our bags. The only change we had with us was put on here, and the old clothes hung out to air. We reckoned that by the time we came back, in a couple of months, they would be sufficiently aired, and we could put them on again. As far as I remember, the calculation proved correct. We took more foot-gear than anything else: if one's feet are well shod, one can hold out a long time.

When all this was finished, three of us put on our skis and made for the nearest visible land. This was a little peak, a mile and three-quarters away – Mount Betty. It did not look lofty or imposing, but was, nevertheless, 1,000 feet above the sea. Small as it was, it became important to us, as it was there we got all our geological specimens. Running on skis felt quite strange, although I had now covered 385 miles on them; but we had driven the whole way, and were somewhat out of training. We could feel this, too, as we went up the slope that afternoon. After Mount Betty the ascent became rather steep, but the surface was even, and the going splendid, so we got on fast. First we came up a smooth mountain-side, about 1,200 feet above the sea, then over a little plateau; after that another smooth slope like the first, and then down a rather long, flat stretch, which after a time began to rise very gradually, until it finally passed into small glacier formations. Our reconnaissance extended to these small glaciers. We had ascertained that the way was practicable, as far as we were able to see; we had gone about five and a half miles from the tent, and ascended 2,000 feet. On the way back we went gloriously; the last two slopes down to the Barrier gave us all the speed we wanted. Bjaaland and I had decided to take a turn round by Mount Betty for the sake of having real bare ground under our feet; we had not felt it since Madeira in September, 1910, and now we were in November, 1911. No sooner said than done. Bjaaland prepared for an elegant "Telemark swing," and executed it in fine style. What I prepared to do, I am still not quite sure. What I did was to roll over, and I did it with great effect. I was very soon on my feet again, and glanced at Bjaaland; whether he had seen my tumble, I am not certain. However, I pulled myself together after this unfortunate performance, and remarked casually that it is not so easy to forget what one has once learnt. No doubt he thought that I had managed the "Telemark swing"; at any rate, he was polite enough to let me think so.

Mount Betty offered no perpendicular crags or deep precipices to stimulate our desire for climbing; we only had to take off our ski, and then we arrived at the top. It consisted of loose screes, and was not an ideal promenade for people who had to be careful of their boots. It was a pleasure to set one's foot on bare ground again, and we sat down on the rocks to enjoy the scene. The rocks very soon made themselves felt, however, and brought us to our feet again. We photographed each other in "picturesque attitudes," took a few stones for those who had not yet set foot on bare earth, and strapped on our skis. The dogs, after having been so eager to make for bare land when they first saw it, were now not the least interested in it; they lay on the snow, and did not go near the top. Between the bare ground and the snow surface there was bright, blue-green ice, showing that at times there was running water here. The dogs did what they could to keep up with us on the way down, but they were soon left behind. On our return, we surprised our comrades with presents from the country, but I fear they were not greatly appreciated. I could hear such words as, "Norway-stones – heaps of them," and I was able to put them together and understand what was meant. The "presents" were put in depot, as not absolutely indispensable on the southern journey.

By this time the dogs had already begun to be very voracious. Everything that came in their way disappeared; whips, ski-bindings, lashings, etc., were regarded as delicacies. If one put down anything for a moment, it vanished. With some of them this voracity went so far that we had to chain them.

CHAPTER 11

THROUGH THE MOUNTAINS

On the following day – November 17 – we began the ascent. To provide for any contingency, I left in the depot a paper with information of the way we intended to take through the mountains, together with our plan for the future, our outfit, provisions, etc. The weather was fine, as usual, and the going good. The dogs exceeded our expectations; they negotiated the two fairly steep slopes at a jog-trot. We began to think there was no difficulty they could not surmount; the five miles or so that we had gone the day before, and imagined would be more than enough for this day's journey, were now covered with full loads in shorter time. The small glaciers higher up turned out fairly steep, and in some places we had to take two sledges at a time with double teams. These glaciers had an appearance of being very old, and of having entirely ceased to move. There were no new crevasses to be seen; those that there were, were large and wide, but their edges were rounded off everywhere, and the crevasses themselves were almost entirely filled with snow. So as not to fall into these on the return, we erected our beacons in such a way that the line between any two of them would take us clear of any danger. It was no use working in Polar clothing among these hills; the sun, which stood high and clear, was uncomfortably warm, and we were obliged to take off most of our things. We passed several summits from 3,000 to 7,000 feet high; the snow on one of them had quite a reddish-brown tint.

Our distance this first day was eleven and a half miles, with a rise of 2,000 feet. Our camp that evening lay on a little glacier among huge crevasses; on three sides of us were towering summits. When we had set our tent, two parties went out to explore the way in advance. One party – Wisting and Hanssen – took the way that looked easiest from the tent – namely, the course of the glacier; it here rose rapidly to 4,000 feet, and disappeared in a south-westerly direction between two peaks. Bjaaland formed the other party. He evidently looked upon this ascent as too tame, and started up the steepest part of the mountain – side. I saw him disappear up aloft like a fly. Hassel and I attended to the necessary work round about and in the tent.

We were sitting inside chatting, when we suddenly heard someone come swishing down towards the tent. We looked at each other; that fellow had some pace on. We had no doubt as to who it was – Bjaaland, of course. He must have gone off to refresh old memories. He had a lot to tell us; amongst other things, he had found "the finest descent" on the other side. What he meant by "fine" I was not certain. If it was as fine as the ascent he had made, then I asked to be excused. We now heard the others coming, and these we could hear a long way off. They had also seen a great deal, not to mention "the finest descent." But both parties agreed in the mournful intelligence that we should have to go down again. They had both observed the immense glacier that stretched beneath us running east and west. A lengthy discussion took place between the two parties, who mutually scorned each other's "discoveries." "Yes; but look here, Bjaaland, we could see that from where you were standing there's a sheer drop ..." "... You couldn't see me at all. I tell you I was to the west of the peak that lies to the south of the peak that" I gave up trying to follow the discussion any longer. The way in which the different parties had disappeared and come in sight again gave me every reason to decide in favour of the route the last arrivals had taken. I thanked these keen gentlemen for their strenuous ramble in the interests of the expedition, and went straight off to sleep. I dreamed of mountains and precipices all night, and woke up with Bjaaland whizzing down from the sky. I announced once more that I had made up my mind for the other course, and went to sleep again.

We debated next morning whether it would not be better to take the sledges two by two to begin with; the glacier before us looked quite steep enough to require double teams. It had a rise of 2,000 feet in quite a short distance. But we would try first with the single teams. The dogs had shown that their capabilities were far above our expectation; perhaps they would be able to do even this. We crept off: The ascent began at once – good exercise after a quart of chocolate. We did not get on fast, but we won our way. It often looked as if the sledge would stop, but a shout from the driver and a sharp crack of the whip kept the dogs on the move. It was a fine beginning to the day, and we gave them a well-deserved rest when we got up. We then drove in through the narrow pass and out on the other side. It was a magnificent panorama that opened before us. From the pass we had come out on to a very small flat terrace, which a few yards farther on began to drop steeply to a long valley. Round about us lay summit after summit on every side. We had now come behind the scenes, and could get our bearings better. We now saw the southern side of the immense Mount Nansen; Don Pedro Christophersen we could see in his full length. Between these two mountains we could follow the course of a glacier that rose in terraces along their sides. It looked fearfully broken and disturbed, but we could follow a little connected line among the many crevasses; we saw that we could go a long way, but we also saw that the glacier forbade us to use it in its full extent. Between the first and second terraces the ice was evidently impassable. But we could see that there was an unbroken ledge up on the side of the mountain; Don Pedro would help us out. On the north along the Nansen Mountain there was nothing but chaos, perfectly impossible to get through. We put up a big beacon where we were standing, and took bearings from it all round the compass.

I went back to the pass to look out over the Barrier for the last time. The new mountain chain lay there sharp and clear; we could see how it turned from the east up to east-north-east, and finally disappeared in the north-east – as we judged, about 84° S. From the look of the sky, it appeared that the chain was continued farther. According to the aneroid, the height of the terrace on which we stood was 4,000 feet above the sea. From here there was only one way down, and we began to go. In making these descents with loaded sledges, one has to use the greatest care, lest the speed increase to such a degree that one loses command over the sledge. If this happens, there is a danger, not only of running over the dogs, but of colliding with the sledge in front and smashing it. This was all the more important in our case, as the sledges carried sledge-meters. We therefore put brakes of rope under our runners when we were to go downhill. This was done very simply by taking a few turns with a thin piece of rope round each runner; the more of these turns one took, the more powerful, of course, was the brake. The art consisted in choosing the right number of turns, or the right brake; this was not always attained, and the consequence was that, before we had come to the end of these descents, there were several collisions. One of the drivers, in particular, seemed to have a supreme contempt for a proper brake; he would rush down like a flash of lightning, and carry the man in front with him. With practice we avoided this, but several times things had an ugly look.

The first drop took us down 800 feet; then we had to cross a wide, stiff piece of valley before the ascent began again. The snow between the mountains was loose and deep, and gave the dogs hard work. The next ascent was up very steep glaciers, the last of which was the steepest bit of climbing we had on the whole journey – stiff work even for double teams. Going in front of the dogs up these slopes was, I could see, a business that Bjaaland would accomplish far more satisfactorily than I, and I gave up the place to him. The first glacier was steep, but the second was like the side of a house. It was a pleasure to watch Bjaaland use his skis up there; one could see that he had been up a hill before. Nor was it less interesting to see the dogs and the drivers go up. Hanssen drove one sledge alone; Wisting and Hassel the other. They went by jerks, foot by foot, and ended by reaching the top. The second relay went somewhat more easily in the tracks made by the first.

Our height here was 4,550 feet, the last ascent having brought us up 1,250 feet; we had arrived on a plateau, and after the dogs had rested we continued our march. Now, as we advanced, we had a better view of the way we were going; before this the nearest mountains had shut us in. The mighty glacier opened out before us, stretching, as we could now see, right up from the Barrier between the lofty mountains running east and west. It was by this glacier that we should have to gain the plateau; we could see that. We had one more descent to make before reaching it, and from above we could distinguish the edges of some big gaps in this descent, and found it prudent to examine it first. As we thought, there was a side-glacier coming down into it, with large, ugly crevasses in many places; but it was not so bad as to prevent our finally reaching, with caution and using good brakes, the great main ice-field – Axel Heiberg Glacier.

The plan we had proposed to ourselves was to work our way up to the place where the glacier rose in abrupt masses between the two mountains. The task we had undertaken was greater than we thought. In the first place, the distance was three times as great as any of us had believed; and, in the second place, the snow was so loose and deep that it was hard work for the dogs after all their previous efforts. We set our course along the white line that we had been able to follow among the numerous crevasses right up to the first terrace. Here tributary glaciers came down on all sides from the mountains and joined the main one; it was one of these many small arms that we reached that evening, directly under Don Pedro Christophersen.

The mountain below which we had our camp was covered

with a chaos of immense blocks of ice. The glacier on which we were was much broken up, but, as with all the others, the fissures were of old date, and, to a large extent, drifted up. The snow was so loose that we had to trample a place for the tent, and we could push the tent-pole right down without meeting resistance; probably it would be better higher up. In the evening Hanssen and Bjaaland went out to reconnoitre, and found the conditions as we had seen them from a distance. The way up to the first terrace was easily accessible; what the conditions would be like between this and the second terrace we had still to discover.

It was stiff work next day getting up to the first terrace. The arm of the glacier that led up was not very long, but extremely steep and full of big crevasses; it had to be taken in relays, two sledges at a time. The state of the going was, fortunately, better than on the previous day, and the surface of the glacier was fine and hard, so that the dogs got a splendid hold. Bjaaland went in advance up through this steep glacier, and had his work cut out to keep ahead of the eager animals. One would never have thought we were between 85° and 86° S.; the heat was positively disagreeable, and, although lightly clad, we sweated as if we were running races in the tropics. We were ascending rapidly, but, in spite of the sudden change of pressure, we did not yet experience any difficulty of breathing, headache, or other unpleasant results. That these sensations would make their appearance in due course was, however, a matter of which we could be certain. Shackleton's description of his march on the plateau, when headache of the most violent and unpleasant kind was the order of the day, was fresh in the memory of all of us.

In a comparatively short time we reached the ledge in the glacier that we had noticed a long way off; it was not quite flat, but sloped slightly towards the edge. When we came to the place to which Hanssen and Bjaaland had carried their reconnaissance on the previous evening, we had a very fine prospect of the further course of the glacier. To continue along it was an impossibility; it consisted here – between the two vast mountains – of nothing but crevasse after crevasse, so huge and ugly that we were forced to conclude that our further advance that way was barred. Over by Fridtjof Nansen we could not go; this mountain here rose perpendicularly, in parts quite bare, and formed with the glacier a surface so wild and cut up that all thoughts of crossing the ice-field in that direction had to be instantly abandoned. Our only chance lay in the direction of Don Pedro Christophersen; here, so far as we could see, the connection of the glacier and the land offered possibilities of further progress. Without interruption the glacier was merged in the snow-clad mountain-side, which rose rapidly towards the partially bare summit. Our view, however, did not extend very far. The first part of the mountain-side was soon bounded by a lofty ridge running east and west, in which we could see huge gaps here and there. From the place where we were standing, we had the impression that we should be able to continue our course up there under the ridge between these gaps, and thus come out beyond the disturbed tract of glacier. We might possibly succeed in this, but we could not be certain until we were up on the ridge itself.

We took a little rest – it was not a long one – and then started. We were impatient to see whether we could get forward up above. There could be no question of reaching the height without double teams; first we had to get Hanssen's and Wisting's sledges up, and then the two others. We were not particularly keen on thus covering the ground twice, but the conditions made it imperative. We should have been pleased just then if we had known that this was to be the last ascent that would require double teams; but we did not know this, and it was more than any of us dared to hope. The same hard work, and the same trouble to keep the dogs at an even pace, and then we were up under the ridge amongst the open chasms. To go farther without a careful examination of the ground was not to be thought of. Doubtless, our day's march had not been a particularly long one, but the piece we had covered had indeed been fatiguing enough. We therefore camped, and set our tent at an altitude of 5,650 feet above the sea.

We at once proceeded to reconnoitre, and the first thing to be examined was the way we had seen from below. This led in the right direction – that is, in the direction of the glacier, east and west – and was thus the shortest. But it is not always the shortest way that is the best; here, in any case, it was to be hoped that another and longer one would offer better conditions. The shortest way was awful – possibly not altogether impracticable, if no better was to be found. First we had to work our way across a hard, smooth slope, which formed an angle of 45 degrees, and ended in a huge, bottomless chasm. It was no great pleasure to cross over here on ski, but with heavily-laden sledges the enjoyment would be still less. The prospect of seeing sledge, driver, and dogs slide down sideways and disappear into the abyss was a great one. We got across with whole skins on ski, and continued our exploration. The mountain-side along which we were advancing gradually narrowed between vast fissures above and vaster fissures below, and finally passed by a very narrow bridge – hardly broader than the sledges – into the glacier. On each side of the bridge, one looked down into a deep blue chasm. To cross here did not look very inviting; no doubt we could take the dogs out and haul the sledges over, and thus manage it – presuming the bridge held – but our further progress, which would have to be made on the glacier, would apparently offer many surprises of an unpleasant kind. It was quite possible that, with time and patience, one would be able to tack through the apparently endless succession of deep crevasses; but we should first have to see whether something better than this could not be found in another direction. We therefore returned to camp.

Here in the meantime everything had been put in order, the tent set up, and the dogs fed. Now came the great question: What was there on the other side of the ridge? Was it the same desperate confusion, or would the ground offer better facilities? Three of us went off to see. Excitement rose as we neared the saddle; so much depended on finding a reasonable way. One more pull and we were up; it was worth the trouble. The first glance showed us that this was the way we had to go. The mountain-side ran smooth and even under the lofty summit-like a gabled church tower – of Mount Don Pedro Christophersen, and followed the direction of the glacier. We could see the place where this long, even surface united with the glacier; to all appearance it was free from disturbance. We saw some crevasses, of course, but they were far apart, and did not give us the idea that they would be a hindrance. But we were still too far from the spot to be able to draw any certain conclusions as to the character of the ground; we therefore set off towards the bottom to examine the conditions more closely. The surface was loose up here, and the snow fairly deep; our skis slipped over it well, but it would be heavy for dogs. We advanced rapidly, and soon came to the huge crevasses. They were big enough and deep enough, but so scattered that, without much trouble, we could find a way between them. The hollow between the two mountains, which was filled by the Heiberg Glacier, grew narrower and narrower towards the end, and, although appearances were still very pleasant, I expected to find some disturbance when we arrived at the point where the mountain-side passed into the glacier. But my fears proved groundless; by keeping right under Don Pedro we went clear of all trouble, and in a short time, to our great joy, we found ourselves above and beyond that chaotic part of the Heiberg Glacier which had completely barred our progress.

Up here all was strangely peaceful; the mountain-side and the glacier united in a great flat terrace – a plain, one might call it – without disturbance of any kind. We could see depressions in the surface where the huge crevasses had formerly existed, but now they were entirely filled up, and formed one with the surrounding level. We could now see right to the end of this mighty glacier, and form some idea of its proportions. Mount Wilhelm Christophersen and Mount Ole Engelstad formed the end of it; these two beehive-shaped summits, entirely covered with snow, towered high into the sky. We understood now that the last of the ascent was before us, and that what we saw in the distance between these two mountains was the great plateau itself. The question, then, was to find a way up, and to conquer this last obstruction in the easiest manner. In the radiantly clear air we could see the smallest details with our excellent prismatic glasses, and make our calculations with great confidence. It would be possible to clamber up Don Pedro himself; we had done things as difficult before. But here the side of the mountain was fairly steep, and full of big crevasses and a fearful quantity of gigantic blocks of ice. Between Don Pedro and Wilhelm Christophersen an arm of the glacier went up on to the plateau, but it was so disturbed and broken up that it could not be used. Between Wilhelm Christophersen and Ole Engelstad there was no means of getting through. Between Ole Engelstad and Fridtjof Nansen, on the other hand, it looked more promising, but as yet the first of these mountains obstructed our view so much that we could not decide with certainty. We were all three rather tired, but agreed to continue our excursion, and find out what was here concealed. Our work to-day would make our progress to-morrow so much the easier. We therefore went on, and laid our course straight over the topmost flat terrace of the Heiberg Glacier. As we advanced, the ground between Nansen and Engelstad opened out more and more, and without going any farther we were able to decide from the formations that here we should undoubtedly find the best way up. If the final ascent at the end of the glacier, which was only partly visible, should present difficulties, we could make out from where we stood that it would be possible, without any great trouble, to work our way over the upper end of the Nansen Mountain itself, which here passed into the plateau by a not too difficult glacier. Yes, now we were certain that it was indeed the great plateau and nothing else that we saw before us. In the pass between the two mountains, and some little distance within the plateau, Helland Hansen showed up, a very curious peak to look at. It seemed to stick its nose up through the plateau, and no more; its shape was long, and it reminded one of nothing so much as the ridge of a roof. Although this peak was thus only just visible, it stood 11,000 feet above the sea.

After we had examined the conditions here, and found out that on the following day – if the weather permitted – we should reach the plateau, we turned back, well satisfied with the result of our trip. We all agreed that we were tired, and longing to reach camp and get some food. The place where we turned was, according to the aneroid, 8,000 feet above the sea; we were therefore 2,500 feet higher than our tent down on the hill-side. Going down in our old tracks was easier work, though the return journey was somewhat monotonous. In many places the slope was rapid, and not a few fine runs were made. On approaching our camping-ground we had the sharpest descent, and here, reluctant as we might be, we found it wiser to put both our poles together and form a strong brake. We came down smartly enough, all the same. It was a grand and imposing sight we had when we came out on the ridge under which – far below – our tent stood. Surrounded on all sides by huge crevasses and gaping chasms, it could not be said that the site of our camp looked very inviting. The wildness of the landscape seen from this point is not to be described; chasm after chasm, crevasse after crevasse, with great blocks of ice scattered promiscuously about, gave one the impression that here Nature was too powerful for us. Here no progress was to be thought of.

It was not without a certain satisfaction that we stood there and contemplated the scene. The little dark speck down there – our tent – in the midst of this chaos, gave us a feeling of strength and power. We knew in our hearts that the ground would have to be ugly indeed if we were not to manoeuvre our way across it and find a place for that little home of ours. Crash upon crash, roar upon roar, met our ears. Now it was a shot from Mount Nansen, now from one of the others; we could see the clouds of snow rise high into the air. It was evident that these mountains were throwing off their winter mantles and putting on a more spring-like garb.

We came at a tearing pace down to the tent, where our companions had everything in most perfect order. The dogs lay snoring in the heat of the sun, and hardly condescended to move when we came scudding in among them. Inside the tent a regular tropical heat prevailed; the sun was shining directly on to the red cloth and warming it. The Primus hummed and hissed, and the pemmican-pot bubbled and spurted. We desired nothing better in the world than to get in, fling ourselves down, eat, and drink. The news we brought was no trifling matter – the plateau to-morrow. It sounded almost too good to be true; we had reckoned that it would take us ten days to get up, and now we should do it in four. In this way we saved a great deal of dog food, as we should be able to slaughter the superfluous animals six days earlier than we had calculated. It was quite a little feast that evening in the tent; not that we had any more to eat than usual – we could not allow ourselves that – but the thought of the fresh dog cutlets that awaited us when we got to the top made our mouths water. In course of time we had so habituated ourselves to the idea of the approaching slaughter that this event did not appear to us so horrible as it would otherwise have done. Judgment had already been pronounced, and the selection made of those who were worthy of prolonged life and those who were to be sacrificed. This had been, I may add, a difficult problem to solve, so efficient were they all.

The rumblings continued all night, and one avalanche after another exposed parts of the mountain-sides that had been concealed from time immemorial. The following day, November 20, we were up and away at the usual time, about 8 a.m. The weather was splendid, calm and clear. Getting up over the saddle was a rough beginning of the day for our dogs, and they gave a good account of themselves, pulling the sledges up with single teams this time. The going was heavy, as on the preceding day, and our advance through the loose snow was not rapid. We did not follow our tracks of the day before, but laid our course directly for the place where we had decided to attempt the ascent. As we approached Mount Ole Engelstad, under which we had to pass in order to come into the arm of the glacier between it and Mount Nansen, our excitement began to rise. What does the end look like? Does the glacier go smoothly on into the plateau, or is it broken up and impassable? We rounded Mount Engelstad more and more; wider and wider grew the opening. The surface looked extremely good as it gradually came into view, and it did not seem as though our assumption of the previous day would be put to shame. At last the whole landscape opened out, and without obstruction of any kind whatever the last part of the ascent lay before us. It was both long and steep from the look of it, and we agreed to take a little rest before beginning the final attack.

We stopped right under Mount Engelstad in a warm and sunny place, and allowed ourselves on this occasion a little lunch, an indulgence that had not hitherto been permitted. The cooking-case was taken out, and soon the Primus was humming in a way that told us it would not be long before the chocolate was ready. It was a heavenly treat, that drink. We had all walked ourselves warm, and our throats were as dry as tinder. The contents of the pot were served round by the cook – Hanssen. It was no use asking him to share alike; he could not be persuaded to take more than half of what was due to him – the rest he had to divide among his comrades. The drink he had prepared this time was what he called chocolate, but I had some difficulty in believing him. He was economical, was Hanssen, and permitted no extravagance; that could be seen very well by his chocolate. Well, after all, to people who were accustomed to regard "bread and water" as a luxury, it tasted, as I have said, heavenly. It was the liquid part of the lunch that was served extra; if anyone wanted something to eat, he had to provide it himself – nothing was offered him. Happy was he who had saved some biscuits from his breakfast! Our halt was not a very long one. It is a queer thing that, when one only has on light underclothing and windproof overalls, one cannot stand still for long without feeling cold. Although the temperature was no lower than -4° F., we were glad to be on the move again. The last ascent was fairly hard work, especially the first half of it. We never expected to do it with single teams, but tried it all the same. For this last pull up I must give the highest praise both to the dogs and their drivers; it was a brilliant performance on both sides. I can still see the situation clearly before me. The dogs seemed positively to understand that this was the last big effort that was asked of them; they lay flat down and hauled, dug their claws in and dragged themselves forward. But they had to stop and get breath pretty often, and then the driver's strength was put to the test. It is no child's play to set a heavily-laden sledge in motion time after time. How they toiled, men and beasts, up that slope! But they got on, inch by inch, until the steepest part was behind them. Before them lay the rest of the ascent in a gentle rise, up which they could drive without a stop. It was stiff, nevertheless, and it took a long time before we were all up on the plateau on the southern side of Mount Engelstad.

We were very curious and anxious to see what the plateau looked like. We had expected a great, level plain, extending boundlessly towards the south; but in this we were disappointed. Towards the south-west it looked very level and fine, but that was not the way we had to go. Towards the south the ground continued to rise in long ridges running east and west, probably a continuation of the mountain chain running to the south-east, or a connection between it and the plateau. We stubbornly continued our march; we would not give in until we had the plain itself before us. Our hope was that the ridge projecting from Mount Don Pedro Christophersen would be the last; we now had it before us. The going changed at once up here; the loose snow disappeared, and a few wind-waves (sastrugi) began to show themselves. These were specially unpleasant to deal with on this last ridge; they lay from south-east to north-west, and were as hard as flints and as sharp as knives. A fall among them might have had very serious consequences. One would have thought the dogs had had enough work that day to tire them, but this last ridge, with its unpleasant snow-waves, did not seem to trouble them in the least. We all drove up gaily, towed by the sledges, on to what looked to us like the final plateau, and halted at 8 p.m. The weather had held fine, and we could apparently see a very long way. In the far distance, extending to the north-west, rose peak after peak; this was the chain of mountains running to the south-east, which we now saw from the other side. In our own vicinity, on the other band, we saw nothing but the backs of the mountains so frequently mentioned. We afterwards learned how deceptive the light can be. I consulted the aneroid immediately on our arrival at the camping-ground, and it showed 10,920 feet above the sea, which the hypsometer afterwards confirmed. All the sledge-meters gave seventeen geographical miles, or thirty-one kilometres (nineteen and a quarter statute miles). This day's work – nineteen and a quarter miles, with an ascent of 5,750 feet – gives us some idea of what can be performed by dogs in good training. Our sledges still had what might be considered heavy loads; it seems superfluous to give the animals any other testimonial than the bare fact.

It was difficult to find a place for the tent, so hard was the snow up here. We found one, however, and set the tent. Sleeping-bags and kit-bags were handed in to me, as usual, through the tent-door, and I arranged everything inside. The cooking-case and the necessary provisions for that evening and the next morning were also passed in; but the part of my work that went more quickly than usual that night was getting the Primus started, and pumping it up to high-pressure. I was hoping thereby to produce enough noise to deaden the shots that I knew would soon be heard – twenty-four of our brave companions and faithful helpers were marked out for death. It was hard – but it had to be so. We had agreed to shrink from nothing in order to reach our goal. Each man was to kill his own dogs to the number that had been fixed.

The pemmican was cooked remarkably quickly that evening, and I believe I was unusually industrious in stirring it. There went the first shot – I am not a nervous man, but I must admit that I gave a start. Shot now followed upon shot – they had an uncanny sound over the great plain. A trusty servant lost his life each time. It was long before the first man reported that he had finished; they were all to open their dogs, and take out the entrails to prevent the meat being contaminated. The entrails were for the most part devoured warm on the spot by the victims' comrades, so voracious were they all. Suggen, one of Wisting's dogs, was especially eager for warm entrails; after enjoying this luxury, he could be seen staggering about in a quite misshapen condition. Many of the dogs would not touch them at first, but their appetite came after a while.

The holiday humour that ought to have prevailed in the tent that evening – our first on the plateau – did not make its appearance; there was depression and sadness in the air – we had grown so fond of our dogs. The place was named the "Butcher's Shop." It had been arranged that we should stop here two days to rest and eat dog. There was more than one among us who at first would not hear of taking any part in this feast; but as time went by, and appetites became sharper, this view underwent a change, until, during the last few days before reaching the Butcher's Shop, we all thought and talked of nothing but dog cutlets, dog steaks, and the like. But on this first evening we put a restraint on ourselves; we thought we could not fall upon our four-footed friends and devour them before they had had time to grow cold.

We quickly found out that the Butcher's Shop was not a hospitable locality. During the night the temperature sank, and violent gusts of wind swept over the plain; they shook and tore at the tent, but it would take more than that to get a hold of it. The dogs spent the night in eating; we could hear the crunching and grinding of their teeth whenever we were awake for a moment. The effect of the great and sudden change of altitude made itself felt at once; when I wanted to turn round in my bag, I had to do it a bit at a time, so as not to get out of breath. That my comrades were affected in the same way, I knew without asking them; my ears told me enough.

It was calm when we turned out, but the weather did not look altogether promising; it was overcast and threatening. We occupied the forenoon in flaying a number of dogs. As I have said, all the survivors were not yet in a mood for dog's flesh, and it therefore had to be served in the most enticing form. When flayed and cut up, it went down readily all along the line; even the most fastidious then overcame their scruples. But with the skin on we should not have been able to persuade them all to eat that morning; probably this distaste was due to the smell clinging to the skins, and I must admit that it was not appetizing. The meat itself, as it lay there cut up, looked well enough, in all conscience; no butcher's shop could have exhibited a finer sight than we showed after flaying and cutting up ten dogs. Great masses of beautiful fresh, red meat, with quantities of the most tempting fat, lay spread over the snow. The dogs went round and sniffed at it. Some helped themselves to a piece; others were digesting. We men had picked out what we thought was the youngest and tenderest one for ourselves. The whole arrangement was left to Wisting, both the selection and the preparation of the cutlets. His choice fell upon Rex, a beautiful little animal – one of his own dogs, by the way. With the skill of an expert, he hacked and cut away what he considered would be sufficient for a meal. I could not take my eyes off his work; the delicate little cutlets had an absolutely hypnotizing effect as they were spread out one by one over the snow. They recalled memories of old days, when no doubt a dog cutlet would have been less tempting than now – memories of dishes on which the cutlets were elegantly arranged side by side, with paper frills on the bones, and a neat pile of petits pois in the middle. Ah, my thoughts wandered still farther afield – but that does not concern us now, nor has it anything to do with the South Pole.

I was aroused from my musings by Wisting digging his axe into the snow as a sign that his work was done, after which he picked up the cutlets, and went into the tent. The clouds had dispersed somewhat, and from time to time the sun appeared, though not in its most genial aspect. We succeeded in catching it just in time to get our latitude determined – 85° 36' S. We were lucky, as not long after the wind got up from the east-south-east, and, before we knew what was happening, everything was in a cloud of snow. But now we snapped our fingers at the weather; what difference did it make to us if the wind howled in the guy-ropes and the snow drifted? We had, in any case, made up our minds to stay here for a while, and we had food in abundance. We knew the dogs thought much the same so long as we have enough to eat, let the weather go hang. Inside the tent Wisting was getting on well when we came in after making these observations. The pot was on, and, to judge by the savoury smell, the preparations were already far advanced. The cutlets were not fried; we had neither frying-pan nor butter. We could, no doubt, have got some lard out of the pemmican, and we might have contrived some sort of a pan, so that we could have fried them if it had been necessary; but we found it far easier and quicker to boil them, and in this way we got excellent soup into the bargain. Wisting knew his business surprisingly well; he had put into the soup all those parts of the pemmican that contained most vegetables, and now he served us the finest fresh meat soup with vegetables in it. The clou of the repast was the dish of cutlets. If we had entertained the slightest doubt of the quality of the meat, this vanished instantly on the first trial. The meat was excellent, quite excellent, and one cutlet after another disappeared with lightning-like rapidity. I must admit that they would have lost nothing by being a little more tender, but one must not expect too much of a dog. At this first meal I finished five cutlets myself, and looked in vain in the pot for more. Wisting appeared not to have reckoned on such a brisk demand.

We employed the afternoon in going through our stock of provisions, and dividing the whole of it among three sledges;

the fourth – Hassel's – was to be left behind. The provisions were thus divided. Sledge No.1 (Wisting's) contained

Biscuits, 3,700 (daily ration, 40 biscuits per man).

Dogs' pemmican, 277 3/4 pounds (1/2 kilogram, or 1 pound 1 1/2 ounces per dog per day).

Men's pemmican, 59 1/2 pounds (350 grams, or 12.34 ounces per man per day).

Chocolate, 12 3/4 pounds (40 grams, or 1.4 ounces per man per day).

Milk-powder, 13 1/4 pounds (60 grams, or 2.1 ounces per man per day).

The other two sledges had approximately the same supplies, and thus permitted us on leaving this place to extend our march over a period of sixty days with full rations. Our eighteen surviving dogs were divided into three teams, six in each. According to our calculation, we ought to be able to reach the Pole from here with these eighteen, and to leave it again with sixteen. Hassel, who was to leave his sledge at this point, thus concluded his provision account, and the divided provisions were entered in the books of the three others.

All this, then, was done that day on paper. It remained to make the actual transfer of provisions later, when the weather permitted. To go out and do it that afternoon was not advisable. Next day, November 23, the wind had gone round to the north-east, with comparatively manageable weather, so at seven in the morning we began to repack the sledges. This was not an altogether pleasant task; although the weather was what I have called "comparatively manageable," it was very far from being suitable for packing provisions. The chocolate, which by this time consisted chiefly of very small pieces, had to be taken out, counted, and then divided among the three sledges. The same with the biscuits; every single biscuit had to be taken out and counted, and as we had some thousands of them to deal with, it will readily be understood what it was to stand there in about -4° F. and a gale of wind, most of the time with bare hands, fumbling over this troublesome occupation. The wind increased while we were at work, and when at last we had finished, the snow was so thick that we could scarcely see the tent.

Our original intention of starting again as soon as the sledges were ready was abandoned. We did not lose very much by this; on the contrary, we gained on the whole. The dogs – the most important factor of all – had a thorough rest, and were well fed. They had undergone a remarkable change since our arrival at the Butcher's Shop; they now wandered about, fat, sleek, and contented, and their former voracity had completely disappeared. As regards ourselves, a day or two longer made no difference; our most important article of diet, the pemmican, was practically left untouched, as for the time being dog had completely taken its place. There was thus no great sign of depression to be noticed when we came back into the tent after finishing our work, and had to while away the time. As I went in, I could descry Wisting a little way off kneeling on the ground, and engaged in the manufacture of cutlets. The dogs stood in a ring round him, and looked on with interest. The north-east wind whistled and howled, the air was thick with driving snow, and Wisting was not to be envied. But he managed his work well, and we got our dinner as usual. During the evening the wind moderated a little, and went more to the east; we went to sleep with the best hopes for the following day.

Saturday, November 25, came; it was a grand day in many respects. I had already seen proofs on several occasions of the kind of men my comrades were, but their conduct that day was such that I shall never forget it, to whatever age I may live. In the course of the night the wind had gone back to the north, and increased to a gale. It was blowing and snowing so that when we came out in the morning we could not see the sledges; they were half snowed under. The dogs had all crept together, and protected themselves as well as they could against the blizzard. The temperature was not so very low (-16.6° F), but low enough to be disagreeably felt in a storm. We had all taken a turn outside to look at the weather, and were sitting on our sleeping-bags discussing the poor prospect. "It's the devil's own weather here at the Butcher's," said one; "it looks to me as if it would never get any better. This is the fifth day, and it's blowing worse than ever." We all agreed. "There's nothing so bad as lying weather-bound like this," continued another; "it takes more out of you than going from morning to night." Personally, I was of the same opinion. One day may be pleasant enough, but two, three, four, and, as it now seemed, five days – no, it was awful. "Shall we try it?" No sooner was the proposal submitted than it was accepted unanimously and with acclamation. When I think of my four friends of the southern journey, it is the memory of that morning that comes first to my mind. All the qualities that I most admire in a man were clearly shown at that juncture: courage and dauntlessness, without boasting or big words. Amid joking and chaff, everything was packed, and then – out into the blizzard.

It was practically impossible to keep one's eyes open; the fine drift-snow penetrated everywhere, and at times one had a feeling of being blind. The tent was not only drifted up, but covered with ice, and in taking it down we had to handle it with care. so as not to break it in pieces. The dogs were not much inclined to start, and it took time to get them into their harness, but at last we were ready. One more glance over the camping-ground to see that nothing we ought to have with us had been forgotten. The fourteen dogs' carcasses that were left were piled up in a heap, and Hassel's sledge was set up against it as a mark. The spare sets of dog-harness, some Alpine ropes, and all our crampons for ice-work, which we now thought would not be required, were left behind. The last thing to be done was planting a broken ski upright by the side of the de-pot. It was Wisting who did this, thinking, presumably, that an extra mark would do no harm. That it was a happy thought the future will show.

And then we were off: It was a hard pull to begin with, both for men and beasts, as the high sastrugi continued towards the south, and made it extremely difficult to advance. Those who had sledges to drive had to be very attentive, and support them so that they did not capsize on the big waves, and we who had no sledges found great difficulty in keeping our feet, as we had nothing to lean against. We went on like this, slowly enough, but the main thing was that we made progress. The ground at first gave one the impression of rising, though not much. The going was extremely heavy; it was like dragging oneself through sand. Meanwhile the sastrugi grew smaller and smaller, and finally they disappeared altogether, and the surface became quite flat. The going also improved by degrees, for what reason it is difficult to say, as the storm continued unabated, and the drift – now combined with falling snow – was thicker than ever. It was all the driver could do to see his own dogs. The surface, which had become perfectly level, had the appearance at times of sinking; in any case, one would have thought so from the pace of the sledges. Now and again the dogs would set off suddenly at a gallop. The wind aft, no doubt, helped the pace somewhat, but it alone could not account for the change.

I did not like this tendency of the ground to fall away. In my opinion, we ought to have done with anything of that sort after reaching the height at which we were; a slight slope upward, possibly, but down – no, that did not agree with my reckoning. So far the incline had not been so great as to cause uneasiness, but if it seriously began to go downhill, we should have to stop and camp. To run down at full gallop, blindly and in complete ignorance of the ground, would be madness. We might risk falling into some chasm before we had time to pull up.

Hanssen, as usual, was driving first. Strictly speaking, I should now have been going in advance, but the uneven surface at the start and the rapid pace afterwards had made it impossible to walk as fast the dogs could pull. I was therefore following by the side of Wisting's sledge, and chatting with him. Suddenly I saw Hanssen's dogs shoot ahead, and downhill they went at the wildest pace, Wisting after them. I shouted to Hanssen to stop, and he succeeded in doing so by twisting his sledge. The others, who were following, stopped when they came up to him. We were in the middle of a fairly steep descent; what there might be below was not easy to decide, nor would we try to find out in that weather. Was it possible that we were on our way down through the mountains again? It seemed more probable that we lay on one of the numerous ridges; but we could be sure of nothing before the weather cleared. We trampled down a place for the tent in the loose snow, and soon got it up. It was not a long day's march that we had done – eleven and three-quarter miles – but we had put an end to our stay at the Butcher's Shop, and that was a great thing. The boiling-point test that evening showed that we were 10,300 feet above the sea, and that we had thus gone down 620 feet from the Butcher's. We turned in and went to sleep. As soon as it brightened, we should have to be ready to jump out and look at the weather; one has to seize every opportunity in these regions. If one neglects to do so, it may mean a long wait and much may be lost. We therefore all slept with one eye open, and we knew well that nothing could happen without our noticing it.

At three in the morning the sun cut through the clouds and we through the tent-door. To take in the situation was more than the work of a moment. The sun showed as yet like a pat of butter, and had not succeeded in dispersing the thick mists; the wind had dropped somewhat, but was still fairly strong. This is, after all, the worst part of one's job – turning out of one's good, warm sleeping-bag, and standing outside for some time in thin clothes, watching the weather. We knew by experience that a gleam like this, a clearing in the weather, might come suddenly, and then one had to be on the spot. The gleam came; it did not last long, but long enough. We lay on the side of a ridge that

406

fell away pretty steeply. The descent on the south was too abrupt, but on the south-east it was better and more gradual, and ended in a wide, level tract. We could see no crevasses or unpleasantness of any kind. It was not very far that we could see, though; only our nearest surroundings. Of the mountains we saw nothing, neither Fridtjof Nansen nor Don Pedro Christophersen. Well content with our morning's work, we turned in again and slept till 6 a.m., when we began our morning preparations. The weather, which had somewhat improved during the night, had now broken loose again, and the north-easter was doing all it could. However, it would take more than storm and snow to stop us now, since we had discovered the nature of our immediate surroundings; if we once got down to the plain, we knew that we could always feel our way on.

After putting ample brakes on the sledge-runners, we started off downhill in a south-easterly direction. The slight idea of the position that we had been able to get in the morning proved correct. The descent was easy and smooth, and we reached the plain without any adventure. We could now once more set our faces to the south, and in thick driving snow we continued our way into the unknown, with good assistance from the howling north-easterly gale. We now recommenced the erection of beacons, which had not been necessary during the ascent. In the course of the forenoon we again passed over a little ridge, the last of them that we encountered. The surface was now fine enough, smooth as a floor and without a sign of sastrugi. If our progress was nevertheless slow and difficult, this was due to the wretched going, which was real torture to all of us. A sledge journey through the Sahara could not have offered a worse surface to move over. Now the forerunners came into their own, and from here to the Pole Hassel and I took it in turns to occupy the position.

The weather improved in the course of the day, and when we camped in the afternoon it looked quite smiling. The sun came through and gave a delightful warmth after the last few bitter days. It was not yet clear, so that we could see nothing of our surroundings. The distance according to our three sledge-meters was eighteen and a half miles; taking the bad going into consideration, we had reason to be well satisfied with it. Our altitude came out at 9,475 feet above the sea, or a drop of 825 feet in the course of the day. This surprised me greatly. What did it mean? Instead of rising gradually, we were going slowly down. Something extraordinary must await us farther on, but, what? According to dead reckoning our latitude that evening was 86° S.

November 27 did not bring us the desired weather; the night was filled with sharp gusts from the north; the morning came with a slack wind, but accompanied by mist and snowfall. This was abominable; here we were, advancing over absolutely virgin ground, and able to see nothing. The surface remained about the same – possibly rather more undulating. That it had been blowing here at some time, and violently too, was shown by the under-surface, which was composed of sastrugi as hard as iron. Luckily for us, the snowfall of the last few days had filled these up, so as to present a level surface. It was heavy going, though better than on the previous day.

As we were advancing, still blindly, and fretting at the persistently thick weather, one of us suddenly called out: "Hullo, look there!" A wild, dark summit rose high out of the mass of fog to the east-south-east. It was not far away – on the contrary, it seemed threateningly near and right over us. We stopped and looked at the imposing sight, but Nature did not expose her objects of interest for long. The fog rolled over again, thick, heavy and dark, and blotted out the view. We knew now that we had to be prepared for surprises. After we had gone about ten miles the fog again lifted for a moment, and we saw quite near – a mile or so away – two long, narrow mountain ridges to the west of us, running north and south, and completely covered with snow. These – Helland Hansen's Mountains – were the only ones we saw on our right hand during the march on the plateau; they were between 9,000 and 10,000 feet high, and would probably serve as excellent landmarks on the return journey. There was no connection to be traced between these mountains and those lying to the east of them; they gave us the impression of being entirely isolated summits, as we could not make out any lofty ridge running east and west. We continued our course in the constant expectation of finding some surprise or other in our line of route. The air ahead of us was as black as pitch, as though it concealed something. It could not be a storm, or it would have been already upon us. But we went on and on, and nothing came. Our day's march was eighteen and a half miles.

I see that my diary for November 28 does not begin very promisingly: "Fog, fog – and again fog. Also fine falling snow, which makes the going impossible. Poor beasts, they have toiled hard to get the sledges forward to-day." But the day did not turn out so badly after all, as we worked our way out of this uncertainty and found out what was behind the pitch-dark clouds. During the forenoon the sun came through and thrust aside the fog for a while; and there, to the south-east, not many miles away, lay an immense mountain mass. From this mass, right across our course, ran a great, ancient glacier; the sun shone down upon it and showed us a surface full of huge irregularities. On the side nearest to the mountain these disturbances were such that a hasty glance was enough to show us the impossibility of advancing that way. But right in our line of route – straight on to the glacier – it looked, as far as we could see, as though we could get along. The fog came and went, and we had to take advantage of the clear intervals to get our bearings. It would, no doubt, have been better if we could have halted, set up our tent, and waited for decently clear weather, so that we might survey the ground at our ease and choose the best way. Going forward without an idea of what the ground was like, was not very pleasant. But how long should we have to wait for clear weather? That question was unanswerable; possibly a week, or even a fortnight, and we had no time for that. Better go straight on, then, and take what might come.

What we could see of the glacier appeared to be pretty steep; but it was only between the south and south-east, under the new land, that the fog now and again lifted sufficiently to enable us to see anything. From the south round to the west the fog lay as thick as gruel. We could see that the big crevasses lost themselves in it, and the question of what the glacier looked like on the west had to be put aside for the moment. It was to the south we had to go, and there it was possible to go forward a little way. We continued our march until the ground began to show signs of the glacier in the form of small crevasses, and then we halted. It was our intention to lighten our sledges before tackling the glacier; from the little we could see of it, it was plain enough that we should have stiff work. It was therefore important to have as little as possible on the sledges.

We set to work at once to build the depot; the snow here was excellent for this purpose – as hard as glass. In a short time an immense erection of adamantine blocks of snow rose into the air, containing provisions for five men for six days and for eighteen dogs for five days. A number of small articles were also left behind.

While we were thus occupied, the fog had been coming and going; some of the intervals had been quite clear, and had given me a good view of the nearest part of the range. It appeared to be quite isolated, and to consist of four mountains; one of these – Mount Helmer Hanssen – lay separated from the rest. The other three – Mounts Oscar Wisting, Sverre Hassel, and Olav Bjaaland – lay closer together. Behind this group the air had been heavy and black the whole time, showing that more land must be concealed there. Suddenly, in one of the brightest intervals, there came a rift in this curtain, and the summits of a colossal mountain mass appeared. Our first impression was that this mountain – Mount Thorvald Nilsen – must be something over 20,000 feet high; it positively took our breath away, so formidable did it appear. But it was only a glimpse that we had, and then the fog enclosed it once more. We had succeeded in taking a few meagre bearings of the different summits of the nearest group; they were not very grand, but better ones were not to be obtained. For that matter, the site of the depot was so well marked by its position under the foot of the glacier that we agreed it would be impossible to miss it.

Having finished the edifice, which rose at least 6 feet into the air, we put one of our black provision cases on the top of it, so as to be able to see it still more easily on the way back. An observation we had contrived to take while the work was in progress gave us our latitude as 86° 21' S. This did not agree very well with the latitude of our dead reckoning – 86° 23' S. Meanwhile the fog had again enveloped everything, and a fine, light snow was falling. We had taken a bearing of the line of glacier that was most free of crevasses, and so we moved on again. It was some time before we felt our way up to the glacier. The crevasses at its foot were not large, but we had no sooner entered upon the ascent than the fun began. There was something uncanny about this perfectly blind advance among crevasses and chasms on all sides. We examined the compass from time to time, and went forward cautiously.

Hassel and I went in front on a rope; but that, after all, was not much of a help to our drivers. We naturally glided lightly on our ski over places where the dogs would easily fall through. This lowest part of the glacier was not entirely free from danger, as the crevasses were often rendered quite invisible by a thin overlying layer of snow. In clear weather it is not so bad to have to cross such a surface, as the effect of light and shade is usually to show up the edges of these insidious pitfalls, but on a day like this, when everything looked alike, one's advance is doubtful. We kept it going, however, by using the utmost caution. Wisting came near to sounding the depth of one of these dangerous crevasses with sledge, dogs and all, as the bridge he was about to cross gave way. Thanks to his presence of mind and a lightning-like movement – some would call it luck – he

412

managed to save himself. In this way we worked up about 200 feet, but then we came upon such a labyrinth of yawning chasms and open abysses that we could not move. There was nothing to be done but to find the least disturbed spot, and set the tent there.

As soon as this was done Hanssen and I set out to explore. We were roped, and therefore safe enough. It required some study to find a way out of the trap we had run ourselves into. Towards the group of mountains last described – which now lay to the east of us – it had cleared sufficiently to give us a fairly good view of the appearance of the glacier in that direction. What we had before seen at a distance, was now confirmed. The part extending to the mountains was so ground up and broken that there was positively not a spot where one could set one's foot. It looked as if a battle had been fought here, and the ammunition had been great blocks of ice. They lay pell-mell, one on the top of another, in all directions, and evoked a picture of violent confusion. Thank God we were not here while this was going on, I thought to myself, as I stood looking out over this battlefield; it must have been a spectacle like doomsday, and not on a small scale either. To advance in that direction, then, was hopeless, but that was no great matter, since our way was to the south. On the south we could see nothing; the fog lay thick and heavy there. All we could do was to try to make our way on, and we therefore crept southward.

On leaving our tent we had first to cross a comparatively narrow snow-bridge, and then go along a ridge or saddle, raised by pressure, with wide open crevasses on both sides. This ridge led us on to an icewave about 25 feet high – a formation which was due to the pressure having ceased before the wave had been forced to break and form hummocks. We saw well enough that this would be a difficult place to pass with sledges and dogs, but in default of anything better it would have to be done. From the top of this wave-formation we could see down on the other side, which had hitherto been hidden from us. The fog prevented our seeing far, but the immediate surroundings were enough to convince us that with caution we could beat up farther. From the height on which we stood, every precaution would be required to avoid going down on the other side; for there the wave ended in an open crevasse, specially adapted to receive any drivers, sledges or dogs that might make a slip.

This trip that Hanssen and I took to the south was made entirely at random, as we saw absolutely nothing; our object was to make tracks for the following day's journey. The language we used about the glacier as we went was not altogether complimentary; we had endless tacking and turning to get on. To go one yard forward, I am sure we had to go at least ten to one side. Can anyone be surprised that we called it the Devil's Glacier? At any rate, our companions acknowledged the justness of the name with ringing acclamations when we told them of it.

At Hell's Gate Hanssen and I halted. This was a very remarkable formation; the glacier had here formed a long ridge about 20 feet high; then, in the middle of this ridge, a fissure had opened, making a gateway about 6 feet wide. This formation – like every – thing else on the glacier-was obviously very old, and for the most part filled with snow. From this point the glacier, as far as our view extended to the south, looked better and better; we therefore turned round and followed our tracks in the comforting conviction that we should manage to get on.

Our companions were no less pleased with the news we brought of our prospects. Our altitude that evening was 8,650 feet above the sea – that is to say, at the foot of the glacier we had reached an altitude of 8,450 feet, or a drop from the Butcher's of 2,570 feet. We now knew very well that we should have this ascent to make again, perhaps even more; and this idea did not arouse any particular enthusiasm. In my diary I see that I conclude the day with the following words "What will the next surprise be, I wonder?"

It was, in fact, an extraordinary journey that we were undertaking, through new regions, new mountains, glaciers, and so on, without being able to see. That we were prepared for surprises was perhaps quite natural. What I liked least about this feeling one's way forward in the dark was that it would be difficult – very difficult indeed – to recognize the ground again on the way back. But with this glacier lying straight across our line of route, and with the numerous beacons we had erected, we reassured ourselves on this score. It would take a good deal to make us miss them on the return. The point for us, of course, was to find our descent on to the Barrier again – a mistake there might be serious enough. And it will appear later in this narrative that my fear of our not being able to recognize the way was not entirely groundless. The beacons we had put up came to our aid, and for our final success we owe a deep debt of gratitude to our prudence and thoughtfulness in adopting this expedient.

Next morning, November 29, brought considerably clearer weather, and allowed us a very good survey of our position. We could now see that the two mountain ranges uniting in 86° S. were continued in a mighty chain running to the south-east, with summits from 10,000 to 15,000 feet. Mount Thorvald Nilsen was the most southerly we could see from this point. Mounts Hanssen, Wisting, Bjaaland, and Hassel formed, as we had thought the day before, a group by themselves, and lay separated from the main range.

The drivers had a warm morning's work. They had to drive with great circumspection and patience to grapple with the kind of ground we had before us; a slight mistake might be enough to send both sledge and dogs with lightning rapidity into the next world. It took, nevertheless, a remarkably short time to cover the distance we had explored on the previous evening; before we knew it, we were at Hell's Gate.

Bjaaland took an excellent photograph here, which gives a very good idea of the difficulties this part of the journey presented. In the foreground, below the high snow-ridge that forms one side of a very wide but partly filled-up crevasse, the marks of ski can be seen in the snow. This was the photographer, who, in passing over this snow-bridge, struck his ski into it to try the strength of the support. Close to the tracks can be seen an open piece of the crevasse; it is a pale blue at the top, but ends in the deepest black – in a bottomless abyss. The photographer got over the bridge and back with a whole skin, but there could be no question of risking sledges and dogs on it, and it can be seen in the photograph that the sledges have been turned right round to try another way. The two small black figures in the distance, on the right, are Hassel and I, who are reconnoitring ahead.

It was no very great distance that we put behind us that day-nine and a quarter miles in a straight line. But, taking into account all the turns and circuits we had been compelled to make, it was not so short after all. We set our tent on a good, solid foundation, and were well pleased with the day's work. The altitude was 8,960 feet above the sea. The sun was now in the west, and shining directly upon the huge mountain masses. It was a fairy landscape in blue and white, red and black, a play of colours that defies description. Clear as it now appeared to be, one could understand that the weather was not all that could be wished, for the south-eastern end of Mount Thorvald Nilsen lost itself in a dark, impenetrable cloud, which led one to suspect a continuation in that direction, though one could not be certain.

Mount Nilsen – ah! anything more beautiful, taking it altogether, I have never seen. Peaks of the most varied forms rose high into the air, partly covered with driving clouds. Some were sharp, but most were long and rounded. Here and there one saw bright, shining glaciers plunging wildly down the steep sides, and merging into the underlying ground in fearful confusion. But the most remarkable of them all was Mount Helmer Hanssen; its top was as round as the bottom of a bowl, and covered by an extraordinary ice-sheet, which was so broken up and disturbed that the blocks of ice bristled in every direction like the quills of a porcupine. It glittered and burned in the sunlight – a glorious spectacle. There could only be one such mountain in the world, and as a landmark it was priceless. We knew that we could not mistake that, however the surroundings might appear on the return journey, when possibly the conditions of lighting might be altogether different.

After camping, two of us went out to explore farther. The prospect from the tent was not encouraging, but we might possibly find things better than we expected. We were lucky to find the going so fine as it was on the glacier; we had left our crampons behind at the Butcher's Shop, and if we had found smooth ice, instead of a good, firm snow surface, such as we now had, it would have caused us much trouble. Up – still up, among monsters of crevasses, some of them hundreds of feet wide and possibly thousands of feet deep. Our prospects of advancing were certainly not bright; as far as we could see in the line of our route one immense ridge towered above another, concealing on their farther sides huge, wide chasms, which all had to be avoided. We went forward – steadily forward – though the way round was both long and troublesome. We had no rope on this time, as the irregularities were so plain that it would have been difficult to go into them. It turned out, however, at several points, that the rope would not have been out of place. We were just going to cross over one of the numerous ridges – the surface here looked perfectly whole – when a great piece broke right under the back half of Hanssen's ski. We could not deny ourselves the pleasure of glancing down into the hole. The sight was not an inviting one, and we agreed to avoid this place when we came on with our dogs and sledges. Every day we had occasion to bless our skis. We often used to ask each other where we should now have been without these excellent appliances. The usual answer was: Most probably at the bottom of some crevasse. When we first read the different accounts of the aspect and nature of the Barrier, it was clear to all of us, who were born and bred with skis on our feet, that these must be regarded as indispensable. This view was confirmed and strengthened every day, and I am not giving too much credit to our excellent skis when I say that they not only played a very important part, but possibly the most important of all, on our journey to the South Pole. Many a time we traversed stretches of surface so cleft and disturbed that it would have been an impossibility to get over them on foot. I need scarcely insist on the advantages of skis in deep, loose snow.

After advancing for two hours, we decided to return. From the raised ridge on which we were then standing, the surface ahead of us looked more promising than ever; but we had so often been deceived on the glacier that we had now become definitely sceptical. How often, for instance, had we thought that beyond this or that undulation our trials would be at an end, and that the way to the south would lie open and free; only to reach the place and find that the ground behind the ridge was, if possible, worse than what we had already been struggling with. But this time we seemed somehow to feel victory in the air. The formations appeared to promise it, and yet – had we been so often deceived by these formations that we now refused to offer them a thought? Was it possibly instinct that told us this? I do not know, but certain it is that Hanssen and I agreed, as we stood there discussing our prospects, that behind the farthest ridge we saw, we should conquer the glacier. We had a feverish desire to go and have a look at it; but the way round the many crevasses was long, and – I may as well admit it – we were beginning to get tired. The return, downhill as it was, did not take long, and soon we were able to tell our comrades that the prospects for the morrow were very promising.

While we had been away, Hassel had measured the Nilsen Mountain, and found its height to be 15,500 feet above the sea. How well I remember that evening, when we stood contemplating the glorious sight that Nature offered, and believing the air to be so clear that anything within range of vision must have shown itself; and how well, too, I remember our astonishment on the return journey on finding the whole landscape completely transformed! If it had not been for Mount Helmer Hanssen, it would have been difficult for us to know where we were. The atmosphere in these regions may play the most awkward tricks. Absolutely clear as it seemed to us that evening, it nevertheless turned out later that it had been anything but clear. One has, therefore, to be very careful about what one sees or does not see. In most cases it has proved that travellers in the Polar regions have been more apt to see too much than too little; if, however, we had charted this tract as we saw it the first time, a great part of the mountain ranges would have been omitted.

During the night a gale sprang up from the south-east, and blew so that it howled in the guy-ropes of the tent; it was well that the tent-pegs had a good hold. In the morning, while we were at breakfast, it was still blowing, and we had some thoughts of waiting for a time; but suddenly, without warning, the wind dropped to such an extent that all our hesitation vanished. What a change the south-east wind had produced! The splendid covering of snow that the day before had made ski-running a pleasure, was now swept away over great stretches of surface, exposing the hard substratum. Our thoughts flew back; the crampons we had left behind seemed to dance before my eyes, backwards and forwards, grinning and pointing fingers at me. It would be a nice little extra trip back to the Butcher's to fetch them.

Meanwhile, we packed and made everything ready. The tracks of the day before were not easy to follow; but if we lost them now and again on the smooth ice surface, we picked them up later on a snow-wave that had resisted the attack of the wind. It was hard and strenuous work for the drivers. The sledges were difficult to manage over the smooth, sloping ice; sometimes they went straight, but just as often cross-wise, requiring sharp attention to keep them from capsizing. And this had to be prevented at all costs, as the thin provision cases would not stand many bumps on the ice; besides which, it was such hard work righting the sledges again that for this reason alone the drivers exercised the greatest care.

The sledges were put to a severe test that day, with the many great and hard irregularities we encountered on the glacier; it is a wonder they survived it, and is a good testimonial for Bjaaland's work.

The glacier that day presented the worst confusion we had yet had to deal with. Hassel and I went in front, as usual, with the rope on. Up to the spot Hanssen and I had reached the evening before our progress was comparatively easy; one gets on so much quicker when one knows that the way is practicable. After this point it became worse; indeed, it was often so bad that we had to stop for a long time and try in various directions, before finding a way. More than once the axe had to be used to hack away obstructions. At one time things looked really serious; chasm after chasm, hummock after hummock, so high and steep that they were like mountains. Here we went out and explored in every direction to find a passage; at last we found one, if, indeed, it deserved the name of a passage. It was a bridge so narrow that it scarcely allowed room for the width of the sledge; a fearful abyss on each side. The crossing of this place reminded me of the tight-rope walker going over Niagara. It was a good thing none of us was subject to giddiness, and that the dogs did not know exactly what the result of a false step would be.

On the other side of this bridge we began to go downhill, and our course now lay in a long valley between lofty undulations on each side. It tried our patience severely to advance here, as the line of the hollow was fairly long and ran due west. We tried several times to lay our course towards the south and clamber up the side of the undulation, but these efforts did not pay us. We could always get up on to the ridge, but we could not come down again on the other side; there was nothing to be done but to follow the natural course of the valley until it took us into the tract lying to the south. It was especially the drivers whose patience was sorely tried, and I could see them now and then take a turn up to the top of the ridge, not satisfied with the exploration Hassel and I had made. But the result was always the same; they had to submit to Nature's caprices and follow in our tracks.

Our course along this natural line was not entirely free from obstruction; crevasses of various dimensions constantly crossed our path. The ridge or undulation, at the top of which we at last arrived, had quite an imposing effect. It terminated on the east in a steep drop to the underlying surface, and attained at this point a height of over 100 feet. On the west it sloped gradually into the lower ground and allowed us to advance that way. In order to have a better view of the surroundings we ascended the eastern and highest part of the ridge, and from here we at once had a confirmation of our supposition of the day before. The ridge we had then seen, behind which we hoped to find better conditions, could now be seen a good way ahead. And what we then saw made our hearts beat fast with joy. Could that great white, unbroken plain over there be real, or was it only an illusion? Time would show.

Meanwhile Hassel and I jogged on, and the others followed. We had to get through a good many difficulties yet before we reached that point, but, compared with all the breakneck places we had already crossed, these were of a comparatively tame description. It was with a sigh of relief that we arrived at the plain that promised so well; its extent was not very great, but we were not very exacting either in this respect, after our last few days' march over the broken surface. Farther to the south we could still see great masses piled up by pressure, but the intervals between them were very great and the surface was whole. This was, then, the first time since we tackled the Devil's Glacier that we were able to steer true south for a few minutes.

As we progressed, it could be seen that we had really come upon another kind of ground; for once we had not been made fools of. Not that we had an unbroken, level surface to go upon – it would be a long time before we came to that – but we were able to keep our course for long stretches at a time. The huge crevasses became rarer, and so filled up at both ends that we were able to cross them without going a long way round. There was new life in all of us, both dogs and men, and we went rapidly southward. As we advanced, the conditions improved more and more. We could see in the distance some huge dome-shaped formations, that seemed to tower high into the air: these turned out to be the southernmost limit of the big crevasses and to form the transition to the third phase of the glacier.

It was a stiff climb to get up these domes, which were fairly high and swept smooth by the wind. They lay straight in our course, and from their tops we had a good view. The surface we were entering upon was quite different from that on the northern side of the domes. Here the big crevasses were entirely filled with snow and might be crossed anywhere. What specially attracted one's attention here was an immense number of small formations in the shape of haycocks. Great stretches of the surface were swept bare, exposing the smooth ice.

It was evident that these various formations or phases in the glacier were due to the underlying ground. The first tract we had passed, where the confusion was so extreme, must be the part that lay nearest the bare land; in proportion as the glacier left the land, it became less disturbed: In the haycock district the disturbance had not produced cracks in the surface to any extent, only upheaval here and there. How these haycocks were formed and what they looked like inside we were soon to find out. It was a pleasure to be able to advance all the time, instead of constantly turning and going round; only once or twice did we have to turn aside for the larger haycocks, otherwise we kept our course. The great, clean-swept stretches of surface that we came upon from time to time were split in every direction, but the cracks were very narrow – about half an inch wide.

We had difficulty in finding a place for the tent that evening;

the surface was equally hard everywhere, and at last we had to set it on the bare ice. Luckily for our tent-pegs, this ice was not of the bright, steely variety; it was more milky in appearance and not so hard, and we were thus able to knock in the pegs with the axe.

When the tent was up, Hassel went out as usual to fetch snow for the cooker. As a rule he performed this task with a big knife, specially made for snow; but this evening he went out armed with an axe. He was very pleased with the abundant and excellent material that lay to his hand; there was no need to go far. Just outside the tent door, two feet away, stood a fine little haycock, that looked as if it would serve the purpose well. Hassel raised his axe and gave a good sound blow; the axe met with no resistance, and went in up to the haft. The haycock was hollow. As the axe was pulled out the surrounding part gave way, and one could hear the pieces of ice falling down through the dark hole. It appeared, then, that two feet from our door we had a most convenient way down into the cellar. Hassel looked as if he enjoyed the situation. "Black as a sack," he smiled; "couldn't see any bottom." Hanssen was beaming; no doubt he would have liked the tent a little nearer. The material provided by the haycock was of the best quality, and well adapted for cooking purposes.

The next day, December 1, was a very fatiguing one for us all. From early morning a blinding blizzard raged from the southeast, with a heavy fall of snow. The going was of the very worst kind – polished ice. I stumbled forward on ski, and had comparatively easy work. The drivers had been obliged to take off their skis and put them on the loads, so as to walk by the side, support the sledges, and give the dogs help when they came to a difficult place; and that was pretty often, for on this smooth ice surface there were a number of small scattered sastrugi, and these consisted of a kind of snow that reminded one more of fish-glue than of anything else when the sledges came in contact with it. The dogs could get no hold with their claws on the smooth ice, and when the sledge came on to one of these tough little waves, they could not manage to haul it over, try as they might. The driver then had to put all his strength into it to prevent the sledge stopping. Thus in most cases the combined efforts of men and dogs carried the sledge on.

In the course of the afternoon the surface again began to be more disturbed, and great crevasses crossed our path time after time. These crevasses were really rather dangerous; they looked very innocent, as they were quite filled up with snow, but on a nearer acquaintance with them we came to understand that they were far more hazardous than we dreamed of at first. It turned out that between the loose snow-filling and the firm ice edges there was a fairly broad, open space, leading straight down into the depths. The layer of snow which covered it over was in most cases quite thin. In driving out into one of these snow-filled crevasses nothing happened as a rule; but it was in getting off on the other side that the critical moment arrived. For here the dogs came up on to the smooth ice surface, and could get no hold for their claws, with the result that it was left entirely to the driver to haul the the sledge up. The strong pull he then had to give sent him through the thin layer of snow. Under these circumstances he took a good, firm hold of the sledge-lashing, or of a special strap that had been made with a view to these accidents. But familiarity breeds contempt, even with the most cautious, and some of the drivers were often within an ace of going down into "the cellar."

If this part of the journey was trying for the dogs, it was certainly no less so for the men. If the weather had even been fine, so that we could have looked about us, we should not have minded it so much, but in this vile weather it was, indeed, no pleasure. Our time was also a good deal taken up with thawing noses and cheeks as they froze – not that we stopped; we had no time for that. We simply took off a mit, and laid the warm hand on the frozen spot as we went; when we thought we had restored sensation, we put the hand back into the mit. By this time it would want warming. One does not keep one's hands bare for long with the thermometer several degrees below zero and a storm blowing. In spite of the unfavourable conditions we had been working in, the sledge-meters that evening showed a distance of fifteen and a half miles. We were well satisfied with the day's work when we camped.

Let us cast a glance into the tent this evening. It looks cosy enough. The inner half of the tent is occupied by three sleeping-bags, whose respective owners have found it both comfortable and expedient to turn in, and may now be seen engaged with their diaries. The outer half – that nearest the door – has only two sleeping-bags, but the rest of the space is taken up with the whole cooking apparatus of the expedition. The owners of these two bags are still sitting up. Hanssen is cook, and will not turn in until the food is ready and served. Wisting is his sworn comrade and assistant, and is ready to lend him any aid that may be required. Hanssen appears to be a careful cook; he evidently does not like to burn the food, and his spoon stirs the contents of the pot incessantly. "Soup!" The effect of the word is instantaneous. Everyone sits up at once with a cup in one hand and a spoon in the other. Each one in his turn has his cup filled with what looks like the most tasty vegetable soup. Scalding hot it is, as one can see by the faces, but for all that it disappears with surprising rapidity. Again the cups are filled, this time with more solid stuff pemmican. With praiseworthy despatch their contents are once more demolished, and they are filled for the third time. There is nothing the matter with these men's appetites. The cups are carefully scraped, and the enjoyment of bread and water begins. It is easy to see, too, that it is an enjoyment – greater, to judge by the pleasure on their faces, than the most skilfully devised menu could afford. They positively caress the biscuits before they eat them. And the water – ice-cold water they all call for – this also disappears in great quantities, and procures, I feel certain from their expression, a far greater pleasure and satisfaction than the finest wine that was ever produced. The Primus hums softly during the whole meal, and the temperature in the tent is quite pleasant.

When the meal is over, one of them calls for scissors and looking-glass, and then one may see the Polar explorers dressing their hair for the approaching Sunday. The beard is cut quite short with the clipper every Saturday evening; this is done not so much from motives of vanity as from considerations of utility and comfort. The beard invites an accumulation of ice, which may often be very embarrassing. A beard in the Polar regions seems to me to be just as awkward and unpractical as – well, let us say, walking with a tall hat on each foot. As the beard-clipper and the mirror make their round, one after the other disappears into his bag, and with five "Good-nights," silence falls upon the tent. The regular breathing soon announces that the day's work demands its tribute. Meanwhile the south-easter howls, and the snow beats against the tent. The dogs have curled themselves up, and do not seem to trouble themselves about the weather.

The storm continued unabated on the following day, and on account of the dangerous nature of the ground we decided to wait awhile. In the course of the morning – towards noon, perhaps – the wind dropped a little, and out we went. The sun peeped through at times, and we took the welcome opportunity of getting an altitude – 86° 47' S. was the result.

At this camp we left behind all our delightful reindeer-skin clothing, as we could see that we should have no use for it, the temperature being far too high. We kept the hoods of our reindeer coats, however; we might be glad of them in going against the wind. Our day's march was not to be a long one; the little slackening of the wind about midday was only a joke. It soon came on again in earnest, with a sweeping blizzard from the same quarter – the south-east. If we had known the ground, we should possibly have gone on; but in this storm and driving snow, which prevented our keeping our eyes open, it was no use. A serious accident might happen and ruin all. Two and half miles was therefore our whole distance. The temperature when we camped was -5.8° F. Height above the sea, 9,780 feet.

In the course of the night the wind veered from south-east to north, falling light, and the weather cleared. This was a good chance for us, and we were not slow to avail ourselves of it. A gradually rising ice surface lay before us, bright as a mirror. As on the preceding days, I stumbled along in front on ski, while the others, without their ski, had to follow and support the sledges. The surface still offered filled crevasses, though perhaps less frequently than before. Meanwhile small patches of snow began to show themselves on the polished surface, and soon increased in number and size, until before very long they united and covered the unpleasant ice with a good and even layer of snow. Then ski were put on again, and we continued our way to the south with satisfaction.

We were all rejoicing that we had now conquered this treacherous glacier, and congratulating ourselves on having at last arrived on the actual plateau. As we were going along, feeling pleased about this, a ridge suddenly appeared right ahead, telling us plainly that perhaps all our sorrows were not yet ended. The ground had begun to sink a little, and as we came nearer we could see that we had to cross a rather wide, but not deep, valley before we arrived under the ridge. Great lines of hummocks and haycock-shaped pieces of ice came in view on every side; we could see that we should have to keep our eyes open.

And now we came to the formation in the glacier that we called the Devil's Ballroom. Little by little the covering of snow that we had praised in such high terms disappeared, and before us lay this wide valley, bare and gleaming. At first it went well enough; as it was downhill, we were going at a good pace on the smooth ice. Suddenly Wisting's sledge cut into the surface, and turned over on its side. We all knew what had happened – one of the runners was in a crevasse. Wisting set to work, with the assistance of Hassel, to raise the sledge, and take it out of its dangerous position; meanwhile Bjaaland had got out his camera and was setting it up. Accustomed as we were to such incidents, Hanssen and I were watching the scene from a point a little way in advance, where we had arrived when it happened. As the photography took rather a long time, I assumed that the crevasse was one of the filled ones and presented no particular danger, but that Bjaaland wanted to have a souvenir among his photographs of the numerous crevasses and ticklish situations we had been exposed to. As to the crack being filled up, there was of course no need to inquire. I hailed them, and asked how they were getting on. "Oh, all right," was the answer; "we've just finished." – "What does the crevasse look like?" – "Oh, as usual," they shouted back; "no bottom." I mention this little incident just to show how one can grow accustomed to anything in this world. There were these two – Wisting and Hassel – lying over a yawning, bottomless abyss, and having their photograph taken; neither of them gave a thought to the serious side of the situation. To judge from the laughter and jokes we heard, one would have thought their position was something quite different.

When the photographer had quietly and leisurely finished his work – he got a remarkably good picture of the scene – the other two together raised the sledge, and the journey was continued. It was at this crevasse that we entered his Majesty's Ballroom. The surface did not really look bad. True, the snow was blown away, which made it difficult to advance, but we did not see many cracks. There were a good many pressure-masses, as already mentioned, but even in the neighbourhood of these we could not see any marked disturbance. The first sign that the surface was more treacherous than it appeared to be was when Hanssen's leading dogs went right through the apparently solid floor. They remained hanging by their harness, and were easily pulled up again. When we looked through the hole they had made in the crust, it did not give us the impression of being very dangerous, as, 2 or 3 feet below the outer crust, there lay another surface, which appeared to consist of pulverized ice. We assumed that this lower surface was the solid one, and that therefore there was no danger in falling through the upper one. But Bjaaland was able to tell us a different story. He had, in fact, fallen through the outer crust, and was well on his way through the inner one as well, when he got hold of a loop of rope on his sledge and saved himself in the nick of time. Time after time the dogs now fell through, and time after time the men went in. The effect of the open space between the two crusts was that the ground under our feet sounded unpleasantly hollow as we went over it. The drivers whipped up their dogs as much as they could, and with shouts and brisk encouragement they went rapidly over the treacherous floor. Fortunately this curious formation was not of great extent, and we soon began to observe a change for the better as we came up the ridge. It soon appeared that the Ballroom was the glacier's last farewell to us. With it all irregularities ceased, and both surface and going improved by leaps and bounds, so that before very long we had the satisfaction of seeing that at last we had really conquered all these unpleasant difficulties. The surface at once became fine and even, with a splendid covering of snow everywhere, and we went rapidly on our way to the south with a feeling of security and safety.

CHAPTER 12

AT THE POLE

In lat. 87° S. – according to dead reckoning – we saw the last of the land to the north-east. The atmosphere was then apparently as clear as could be, and we felt certain that our view covered all the land there was to be seen from that spot. We were deceived again on this occasion, as will be seen later. Our distance that day (December 4) was close upon twenty-five miles; height above the sea, 10,100 feet.

The weather did not continue fine for long. Next day (December 5) there was a gale from the north, and once more the whole plain was a mass of drifting snow. In addition to this there was thick falling snow, which blinded us and made things worse, but a feeling of security had come over us and helped us to advance rapidly and without hesitation, although we could see nothing. That day we encountered new surface conditions – big, hard snow-waves (sastrugi). These were anything but pleasant to work among, especially when one could not see them. It was of no use for us "forerunners" to think of going in advance under these circumstances, as it was impossible to keep on one's feet. Three or four paces was often the most we managed to do before falling down. The sastrugi were very high, and often abrupt; if one came on them unexpectedly, one required to be more than an acrobat to keep on one's feet. The plan we found to work best in these conditions was to let Hanssen's dogs go first; this was an unpleasant job for Hanssen, and for his dogs too, but it succeeded, and succeeded well. An upset here and there was, of course, unavoidable, but with a little patience the sledge was always righted again. The drivers had as much as they could do to support their sledges among these sastrugi, but while supporting the sledges, they had at the same time a support for themselves. It was worse for us who had no sledges, but by keeping in the wake of them we could see where the irregularities lay, and thus get over them. Hanssen deserves a special word of praise for his driving on this surface in such weather. It is a difficult matter to drive Eskimo dogs forward when they cannot see; but Hanssen managed it well, both getting the dogs on and steering his course by compass. One would not think it possible to keep an approximately right course when the uneven ground gives such violent shocks that the needle flies several times round the compass, and is no sooner still again than it recommences the same dance; but when at last we got an observation, it turned out that Hanssen had steered to a hair, for the observations and dead reckoning agreed to a mile. In spite of all hindrances, and of being able to see nothing, the sledge-meters showed nearly twenty-five miles. The hypsometer showed 11,070 feet above the sea; we had therefore reached a greater altitude than the Butcher's.

December 6. brought the same weather: thick snow, sky and plain all one, nothing to be seen. Nevertheless we made splendid progress. The sastrugi gradually became levelled out, until the surface was perfectly smooth; it was a relief to have even ground to go upon once more. These irregularities that one was constantly falling over were a nuisance; if we had met with them in our usual surroundings it would not have mattered so much; but up here on the high ground, where we had to stand and gasp for breath every time we rolled over, it was certainly not pleasant.

That day we passed 88° S., and camped in 88° 9' S. A great surprise awaited us in the tent that evening. I expected to find, as on the previous evening, that the boiling-point had fallen somewhat; in other words, that it would show a continued rise of the ground, but to our astonishment this was not so. The water boiled at exactly the same temperature as on the preceding day. I tried it several times, to convince myself that there was nothing wrong, each time with the same result. There was great rejoicing among us all when I was able to announce that we had arrived on the top of the plateau.

December 7 began like the 6th, with absolutely thick weather, but, as they say, you never know what the day is like before sunset. Possibly I might have chosen a better expression than this last – one more in agreement with the natural conditions – but I will let it stand. Though for several weeks now the sun had not set, my readers will not be so critical as to reproach me with inaccuracy. With a light wind from the north-east, we now went southward at a good speed over the perfectly level plain, with excellent going. The uphill work had taken it out of our dogs, though not to any serious extent. They had turned greedy – there is no denying that – and the half kilo of pemmican they got each day was not enough to fill their stomachs. Early and late they were looking for something – no matter what – to devour. To begin with they contented themselves with such loose objects as ski-bindings, whips, boots, and the like; but as we came to know their proclivities, we took such care of everything that they found no extra meals lying about. But that was not the end of the matter. They then went for the fixed lashings of the sledges, and – if we had allowed it – would very quickly have resolved the various sledges into their component parts. But we found a way of stopping that: every evening, on halting, the sledges were buried in the snow, so as to hide all the lashings. That was successful; curiously enough, they never tried to force the "snow rampart." I may mention as a curious thing that these ravenous animals, that devoured everything they came across, even to the ebonite points of our ski-sticks, never made any attempt to break into the provision cases. They lay there and went about among the sledges with their noses just on a level with the split cases, seeing and scenting the pemmican, without once making a sign of taking any. But if one raised a lid, they were not long in showing themselves. Then they all came in a great hurry and flocked about the sledges in the hope of getting a little extra bit. I am at a loss to explain this behaviour; that bashfulness was not at the root of it, I am tolerably certain.

During the forenoon the thick, grey curtain of cloud began to grow thinner on the horizon, and for the first time for three days we could see a few miles about us. The feeling was something like that one has on waking from a good nap, rubbing one's eyes and looking around. We had become so accustomed to the grey twilight that this positively dazzled us. Meanwhile, the upper layer of air seemed obstinately to remain the same and to be doing its best to prevent the sun from showing itself.

We badly wanted to get a meridian altitude, so that we could determine our latitude. Since 86° 47' S. we had had no observation, and it was not easy to say when we should get one. Hitherto, the weather conditions on the high ground had not been particularly favourable. Although the prospects were not very promising, we halted at 11 a.m. and made ready to catch the sun if it should be kind enough to look out. Hassel and Wisting used one sextant and artificial horizon, Hanssen and I the other set.

I don't know that I have ever stood and absolutely pulled at the sun to get it out as I did that time. If we got an observation here which agreed with our reckoning, then it would be possible, if the worst came to the worst, to go to the Pole on dead reckoning; but if we got none now, it was a question whether our claim to the Pole would be admitted on the dead reckoning we should be able to produce. Whether my pulling helped or not, it is certain that the sun appeared. It was not very brilliant to begin with, but, practised as we now were in availing ourselves of even the poorest chances, it was good enough. Down it came, was checked by all, and the altitude written down. The curtain of cloud was rent more and more, and before we had finished our work – that is to say, caught the sun at its highest, and convinced ourselves that it was descending again – it was shining in all its glory. We had put away our instruments and were sitting on the sledges, engaged in the calculations. I can safely say that we were excited. What would the result be, after marching blindly for so long and over such impossible ground, as we had been doing? We added and subtracted, and at last there was the result. We looked at each other in sheer incredulity: the result was as astonishing as the most consummate conjuring trick – 88° 16' S., precisely to a minute the same as our reckoning, 88° 16' S. If we were forced to go to the Pole on dead reckoning, then surely the most exacting would admit our right to do so. We put away our observation books, ate one or two biscuits, and went at it again.

We had a great piece of work before us that day nothing less than carrying our flag farther south than the foot of man had trod. We had our silk flag ready; it was made fast to two ski-sticks and laid on Hanssen's sledge. I had given him orders that as soon as we had covered the distance to 88°S., which was Shackleton's farthest south, the flag was to be hoisted on his sledge. It was my turn as forerunner, and I pushed on. There was no longer any difficulty in holding one's course; I had the grandest cloud-formations to steer by, and everything now went like a machine. First came the forerunner for the time being, then Hanssen, then Wisting, and finally Bjaaland. The forerunner who was not on duty went where he liked; as a rule he accompanied one or other of the sledges.

I had long ago fallen into a reverie – far removed from the scene in which I was moving; what I thought about I do not remember now, but I was so preoccupied that I had entirely forgotten my surroundings. Then suddenly I was roused from my dreaming by a jubilant shout, followed by ringing cheers. I turned round quickly to discover the reason of this unwonted occurrence, and stood speechless and overcome.

I find it impossible to express the feelings that possessed me at this moment. All the sledges had stopped, and from the foremost of them the Norwegian flag was flying. It shook itself out, waved and flapped so that the silk rustled; it looked wonderfully well in the pure, clear air and the shining white surroundings. 88° 23' was past; we were farther south than any human being had been. No other moment of the whole trip affected me like this. The tears forced their way to my eyes; by no effort of will could I keep them back. It was the flag yonder that conquered me and my will. Luckily I was some way in advance of the others, so that I had time to pull myself together and master my feelings before reaching my comrades. We all shook hands, with mutual congratulations; we had won our way far by holding together, and we would go farther yet – to the end.

We did not pass that spot without according our highest tribute of admiration to the man, who – together with his gallant companions – had planted his country's flag so infinitely nearer to the goal than any of his precursors. Sir Ernest Shackleton's name will always be written in the annals of Antarctic exploration in letters of fire. Pluck and grit can work wonders, and I know of no better example of this than what that man has accomplished.

The cameras of course had to come out, and we got an excellent photograph of the scene which none of us will ever forget. We went on a couple of miles more, to 88° 25', and then camped. The weather had improved, and kept on improving all the time. It was now almost perfectly calm, radiantly clear, and, under the circumstances, quite summer-like: -0.4° F. Inside the tent it was quite sultry. This was more than we had expected. After much consideration and discussion we had come to the conclusion that we ought to lay down a depot – the last one – at this spot. The advantages of lightening our sledges were so great that we should have to risk it. Nor would there be any great risk attached to it, after all, since we should adopt a system of marks that would lead even a blind man back to the place. We had determined to mark it not only at right angles to our course – that is, from east to west – but by snow beacons at every two geographical miles to the south.

We stayed here on the following day to arrange this depot. Hanssen's dogs were real marvels, all of them; nothing seemed to have any effect on them. They had grown rather thinner, of course, but they were still as strong as ever. It was therefore decided not to lighten Hanssen's sledge, but only the two others; both Wisting's and Bjaaland's teams had suffered, especially the latter's. The reduction in weight that was effected was considerable – nearly 110 pounds on each of the two sledges; there was thus about 220 pounds in the depot. The snow here was ill-adapted for building, but we put up quite a respectable monument all the same. It was dogs' pemmican and biscuits that were left behind; we carried with us on the sledges provisions for about a month. If, therefore, contrary to expectation, we should be so unlucky as to miss this depot, we should nevertheless be fairly sure of reaching our depot in 86° 21' before supplies ran short. The cross-marking of the depot was done with sixty splinters of black packing-case on each side, with 100 paces between each. Every other one had a shred of black cloth on the top. The splinters on the east side were all marked, so that on seeing them we should know instantly that we were to the east of the depot. Those on the west had no marks.

The warmth of the past few days seemed to have matured our frost-sores, and we presented an awful appearance. It was

Wisting, Hanssen, and I who had suffered the worst damage in the last south-east blizzard; the left side of our faces was one mass of sore, bathed in matter and serum. We looked like the worst type of tramps and ruffians, and would probably not have been recognized by our nearest relations. These sores were a great trouble to us during the latter part of the journey. The slightest gust of wind produced a sensation as if one's face were being cut backwards and forwards with a blunt knife. They lasted a long time, too; I can remember Hanssen removing the last scab when we were coming into Hobart – three months later. We were very lucky in the weather during this depot work; the sun came out all at once, and we had an excellent opportunity of taking some good azimuth observations, the last of any use that we got on the journey.

December 9 arrived with the same fine weather and sunshine. True, we felt our frost-sores rather sharply that day, with -18.4° F. and a little breeze dead against us, but that could not be helped. We at once began to put up beacons – a work which was continued with great regularity right up to the Pole. These beacons were not so big as those we had built down on the Barrier; we could see that they would be quite large enough with a height of about 3 feet, as it was, very easy to see the slightest irregularity on this perfectly flat surface. While thus engaged we had an opportunity of becoming thoroughly acquainted with the nature of the snow. Often – very often indeed – on this part of the plateau, to the south of 88° 25', we had difficulty in getting snow good enough – that is, solid enough for cutting blocks. The snow up here seemed to have fallen very quietly, in light breezes or calms. We could thrust the tent-pole, which was

441

6 feet long, right down without meeting resistance, which showed that there was no hard layer of snow. The surface was also perfectly level; there was not a sign of sastrugi in any direction.

Every step we now took in advance brought us rapidly nearer the goal; we could feel fairly certain of reaching it on the afternoon of the 14th. It was very natural that our conversation should be chiefly concerned with the time of arrival. None of us would admit that he was nervous, but I am inclined to think that we all had a little touch of that malady. What should we see when we got there? A vast, endless plain, that no eye had yet seen and no foot yet trodden; or ... No, it was an impossibility; with the speed at which we had travelled, we must reach the goal first, there could be no doubt about that. And yet – and yet – Wherever there is the smallest loophole, doubt creeps in and gnaws and gnaws and never leaves a poor wretch in peace. "What on earth is Uroa scenting?" It was Bjaaland who made this remark, on one of these last days, when I was going by the side of his sledge and talking to him. "And the strange thing is that he's scenting to the south. It can never be ..." Mylius, Ring, and Suggen, showed the same interest in the southerly direction; it was quite extraordinary to see how they raised their heads, with every sign of curiosity, put their noses in the air, and sniffed due south. One would really have thought there was something remarkable to be found there.

From 88° 25' S. the barometer and hypsometer indicated slowly but surely that the plateau was beginning to descend towards the other side. This was a pleasant surprise to us; we had thus not only found the very summit of the plateau, but also the slope down on the far side. This would have a very important bearing for obtaining an idea of the construction of the whole plateau. On December 9 observations and dead reckoning agreed within a mile. The same result again on the 10th: observation 2 kilometres behind reckoning. The weather and going remained about the same as on the preceding days: light southeasterly breeze, temperature -18.4° F. The snow surface was loose, but ski and sledges glided over it well. On the 11th, the same weather conditions. Temperature -13° F. Observation and reckoning again agreed exactly. Our latitude was 89° 15' S. On the 12th we reached 89° 30', reckoning 1 kilometre behind observation. Going and surface as good as ever. Weather splendid – calm with sunshine. The noon observation on the 13th gave 89° 37' S. Reckoning 89° 38.5' S. We halted in the afternoon, after going eight geographical miles, and camped in 89° 45', according to reckoning.

The weather during the forenoon had been just as fine as before; in the afternoon we had some snow-showers from the south-east. It was like the eve of some great festival that night in the tent. One could feel that a great event was at hand. Our flag was taken out again and lashed to the same two ski-sticks as before. Then it was rolled up and laid aside, to be ready when the time came. I was awake several times during the night, and had the same feeling that I can remember as a little boy on the night before Christmas Eve – an intense expectation of what was going to happen. Otherwise I think we slept just as well that night as any other.

On the morning of December 14 the weather was of the finest, just as if it had been made for arriving at the Pole. I am not quite sure, but I believe we despatched our breakfast rather more quickly than usual and were out of the tent sooner, though I must admit that we always accomplished this with all reasonable haste. We went in the usual order – the forerunner, Hanssen, Wisting, Bjaaland, and the reserve forerunner. By noon we had reached 89° 53' by dead reckoning, and made ready to take the rest in one stage. At 10 a.m. a light breeze had sprung up from the south-east, and it had clouded over, so that we got no noon altitude; but the clouds were not thick, and from time to time we had a glimpse of the sun through them. The going on that day was rather different from what it had been; sometimes the skis went over it well, but at others it was pretty bad. We advanced that day in the same mechanical way as before; not much was said, but eyes were used all the more. Hanssen's neck grew twice as long as before in his endeavour to see a few inches farther. I had asked him before we started to spy out ahead for all he was worth, and he did so with a vengeance. But, however keenly he stared, he could not descry anything but the endless flat plain ahead of us. The dogs had dropped their scenting, and appeared to have lost their interest in the regions about the earth's axis.

At three in the afternoon a simultaneous "Halt!" rang out from the drivers. They had carefully examined their sledge-meters, and they all showed the full distance – our Pole by reckoning. The goal was reached, the journey ended. I cannot say – though I know it would sound much more effective – that the object of my life was attained. That would be romancing rather too bare-facedly. I had better be honest and admit straight out that I have never known any man to be placed in such a diametrically opposite position to the goal of his desires as I was at that moment. The regions around the North Pole – well, yes, the North Pole itself – had attracted me from childhood, and here I was at the South Pole. Can anything more topsy-turvy be imagined?

We reckoned now that we were at the Pole. Of course, every one of us knew that we were not standing on the absolute spot; it would be an impossibility with the time and the instruments at our disposal to ascertain that exact spot. But we were so near it that the few miles which possibly separated us from it could not be of the slightest importance. It was our intention to make a circle round this camp, with a radius of twelve and a half miles (20 kilometres), and to be satisfied with that. After we had halted we collected and congratulated each other. We had good grounds for mutual respect in what had been achieved, and I think that was just the feeling that was expressed in the firm and powerful grasps of the fist that were exchanged. After this we proceeded to the greatest and most solemn act of the whole journey – the planting of our flag. Pride and affection shone in the five pairs of eyes that gazed upon the flag, as it unfurled itself with a sharp crack, and waved over the Pole. I had determined that the act of planting it – the historic event – should be equally divided among us all. It was not for one man to do this; it was for all who had staked their lives in the struggle, and held together through thick and thin. This was the only way in which I could show my gratitude to my comrades in this desolate spot. I could see that they understood and accepted it in the spirit in which it was offered. Five weather-beaten, frost-bitten fists they were that grasped the pole, raised the waving flag in the air, and planted it as the first at the geographical South Pole. "Thus we plant thee, beloved flag, at the South Pole, and give to the plain on which it lies the name of King Haakon VII's Plateau." That moment will certainly be remembered by all of us who stood there.

One gets out of the way of protracted ceremonies in those regions – the shorter they are the better. Everyday life began again at once. When we had got the tent up, Hanssen set about slaughtering Helge, and it was hard for him to have to part from his best friend. Helge had been an uncommonly useful and good-natured dog; without making any fuss he had pulled from morning to night, and had been a shining example to the team. But during the last week he had quite fallen away, and on our arrival at the Pole there was only a shadow of the old Helge left. He was only a drag on the others, and did absolutely no work. One blow on the skull, and Helge had ceased to live. "What is death to one is food to another," is a saying that can scarcely find a better application than these dog meals. Helge was portioned out on the spot, and within a couple of hours there was nothing left of him but his teeth and the tuft at the end of his tail. This was the second of our eighteen dogs that we had lost. The Major, one of Wisting's fine dogs, left us in 88° 25' S., and never returned. He was fearfully worn out, and must have gone away to die. We now had sixteen dogs left, and these we intended to divide into two equal teams, leaving Bjaaland's sledge behind.

Of course, there was a festivity in the tent that evening – not that champagne corks were popping and wine flowing – no, we contented ourselves with a little piece of seal meat each, and it tasted well and did us good. There was no other sign of festival indoors. Outside we heard the flag flapping in the breeze. Conversation was lively in the tent that evening, and we talked of many things. Perhaps, too, our thoughts sent messages home of what we had done.

Everything we had with us had now to be marked with the words "South Pole" and the date, to serve afterwards as souvenirs. Wisting proved to be a first-class engraver, and many were the articles he had to mark. Tobacco – in the form of smoke – had hitherto never made its appearance in the tent. From time to time I had seen one or two of the others take a quid, but now these things were to be altered. I had brought with me an old briar pipe, which bore inscriptions from many places in the Arctic regions, and now I wanted it marked "South Pole." When I produced my pipe and was about to mark it, I received an unexpected gift Wisting offered me tobacco for the rest of the journey. He had some cakes of plug in his kit-bag, which he would prefer to see me smoke. Can anyone grasp what such an offer meant at such a spot, made to a man who, to tell the truth, is very fond of a smoke after meals? There are not many who can understand it fully. I accepted the offer, jumping with joy, and on the way home I had a pipe of fresh, fine-cut plug every evening. Ah! that Wisting, he spoiled me entirely. Not only did he give me tobacco, but every evening – and I must confess I yielded to the temptation after a while, and had a morning smoke as well – he undertook the disagreeable work of cutting the plug and filling my pipe in all kinds of weather.

But we did not let our talk make us forget other things. As we had got no noon altitude, we should have to try and take

447

one at midnight. The weather had brightened again, and it looked as if midnight would be a good time for the observation. We therefore crept into our bags to get a little nap in the intervening hours. In good time – soon after 11 p.m. – we were out again, and ready to catch the sun; the weather was of the best, and the opportunity excellent. We four navigators all had a share in it, as usual, and stood watching the course of the sun. This was a labour of patience, as the difference of altitude was now very slight. The result at which we finally arrived was of great interest, as it clearly shows how unreliable and valueless a single observation like this is in these regions. At 12.30 a.m. we put our instruments away, well satisfied with our work, and quite convinced that it was the midnight altitude that we had observed. The calculations which were carried out immediately afterwards gave us 89° 56' S. We were all well pleased with this result.

The arrangement now was that we should encircle this camp with a radius of about twelve and a half miles. By encircling I do not, of course, mean that we should go round in a circle with this radius; that would have taken us days, and was not to be thought of. The encircling was accomplished in this way: Three men went out in three different directions, two at right angles to the course we had been steering, and one in continuation of that course. To carry out this work I had chosen Wisting, Hassel, and Bjaaland. Having concluded our observations, we put the kettle on to give ourselves a drop of chocolate; the pleasure of standing out there in rather light attire had not exactly put warmth into our bodies. As we were engaged in swallowing the scalding drink, Bjaaland suddenly observed: "I'd like to tackle this encircling straight away. We shall have lots of time to sleep when we get back." Hassel and Wisting were quite of the same opinion, and it was agreed that they should start the work immediately. Here we have yet another example of the good spirit that prevailed in our little community. We had only lately come in from our day's work – a march of about eighteen and a half miles – and now they were asking to be allowed to go on another twenty-five miles. It seemed as if these fellows could never be tired. We therefore turned this meal into a little breakfast – that is to say, each man ate what he wanted of his bread ration, and then they began to get ready for the work. First, three small bags of light windproof stuff were made, and in each of these was placed a paper, giving the position of our camp. In addition, each of them carried a large square flag of the same dark brown material, which could be easily seen at a distance. As flag-poles we elected to use our spare sledge-runners, which were both long – 12 feet – and strong, and which we were going to take off here in any case, to lighten the sledges as much as possible for the return journey.

Thus equipped, and with thirty biscuits as an extra ration, the three men started off in the directions laid down. Their march was by no means free from danger, and does great honour to those who undertook it, not merely without raising the smallest objection, but with the greatest keenness. Let us consider for a moment the risk they ran. Our tent on the boundless plain, without marks of any kind, may very well be compared with a needle in a haystack. From this the three men were to steer out for a distance of twelve and a half miles. Compasses would have been good things to take on such a walk, but our sledge-compasses were too heavy and unsuitable for carrying. They therefore had to go without. They had the sun to go by, certainly, when they started, but who could say how long it would last? The weather was then fine enough, but it was impossible to guarantee that no sudden change would take place. If by bad luck the sun should be hidden, then their own tracks might help them. But to trust to tracks in these regions is a dangerous thing. Before you know where you are the whole plain may be one mass of driving snow, obliterating all tracks as soon as they are made. With the rapid changes of weather we had so often experienced, such a thing was not impossible. That these three risked their lives that morning, when they left the tent at 2.30, there can be no doubt at all, and they all three knew it very well. But if anyone thinks that on this account they took a solemn farewell of us who stayed behind, he is much mistaken. Not a bit; they all vanished in their different directions amid laughter and chaff.

The first thing we did – Hanssen and I – was to set about arranging a lot of trifling matters; there was something to be done here, something there, and above all we had to be ready for the series of observations we were to carry out together, so as to get as accurate a determination of our position as possible. The first observation told us at once how necessary this was. For it turned out that this, instead of giving us a greater altitude than the midnight observation, gave us a smaller one, and it was then clear that we had gone out of the meridian we thought we were following. Now the first thing to be done was to get our north and south line and latitude determined, so that we could find our position once more. Luckily for us, the weather looked as if it would hold. We measured the sun's altitude at every hour from 6 a.m. to 7 p.m., and from these observations found, with some degree of certainty, our latitude and the direction of the meridian.

By nine in the morning we began to expect the return of our comrades; according to our calculation they should then have covered the distance – twenty-five miles. It was not till ten o'-clock that Hanssen made out the first black dot on the horizon, and not long after the second and third appeared. We both gave a sigh of relief as they came on; almost simultaneously the three arrived at the tent. We told them the result of our observations up to that time; it looked as if our camp was in about 89° 54' 30" S., and that with our encircling we had therefore included the actual Pole. With this result we might very well have been content, but as the weather was so good and gave the impression that it would continue so, and our store of provisions proved on examination to be very ample, we decided to go on for the remaining ten kilometres (five and a half geographical miles), and get our position determined as near to the Pole as possible. Meanwhile the three wanderers turned in – not so much because they were tired, as because it was the right thing to do – and Hanssen and I continued the series of observations.

In the afternoon we again went very carefully through our provision supply before discussing the future. The result was that we had food enough for ourselves and the dogs for eighteen days. The surviving sixteen dogs were divided into two teams of eight each, and the contents of Bjaaland's sledge were shared between Hanssen's and Wisting's. The abandoned sledge was set upright in the snow, and proved to be a splendid mark.

The sledge-meter was screwed to the sledge, and we left it there; our other two were quite sufficient for the return journey; they had all shown themselves very accurate. A couple of empty provision cases were also left behind. I wrote in pencil on a piece of case the information that our tent – "Polheim" – would be found five and a half geographical miles north-west quarter west by compass from the sledge. Having put all these things in order the same day, we turned in, very well satisfied.

Early next morning, December 16, we were on our feet again. Bjaaland, who had now left the company of the drivers and been received with jubilation into that of the forerunners, was immediately entrusted with the honourable task of leading the expedition forward to the Pole itself. I assigned this duty, which we all regarded as a distinction, to him as a mark of gratitude to the gallant Telemarkers for their pre-eminent work in the advancement of ski spot. The leader that day had to keep as straight as a line, and if possible to follow the direction of our meridian. A little way after Bjaaland came Hassel, then Hanssen, then Wisting, and I followed a good way behind. I could thus check the direction of the march very accurately, and see that no great deviation was made. Bjaaland on this occasion showed himself a matchless forerunner; he went perfectly straight the whole time. Not once did he incline to one side or the other, and when we arrived at the end of the distance, we could still clearly see the sledge we had set up and take its bearing. This showed it to be absolutely in the right direction.

It was 11 a.m. when we reached our destination. While some of us were putting up the tent, others began to get everything ready for the coming observations. A solid snow pedestal was put up, on which the artificial horizon was to be placed, and a smaller one to rest the sextant on when it was not in use. At 11.30 a.m. the first observation was taken. We divided ourselves into two parties – Hanssen and I in one, Hassel and Wisting in the other. While one party slept, the other took the observations, and the watches were of six hours each. The weather was altogether grand, though the sky was not perfectly bright the whole time. A very light, fine, vaporous curtain would spread across the sky from time to time, and then quickly disappear again. This film of cloud was not thick enough to hide the sun, which we could see the whole time, but the atmosphere seemed to be disturbed. The effect of this was that the sun appeared not to change its altitude for several hours, until it suddenly made a jump.

Observations were now taken every hour through the whole twenty-four. It was very strange to turn in at 6 p.m., and then on turning out again at midnight to find the sun apparently still at the same altitude, and then once more at 6 a.m. to see it still no higher. The altitude had changed, of course, but so slightly that it was imperceptible with the naked eye. To us it appeared as though the sun made the circuit of the heavens at exactly the same altitude. The times of day that I have given here are calculated according to the meridian of Framheim; we continued to reckon our time from this. The observations soon told us that we were not on the absolute Pole, but as close to it as we could hope to get with our instruments. The observations, which have been submitted to Mr. Anton Alexander, will be published, and the result given later in this book.

On December 17 at noon we had completed our observations, and it is certain that we had done all that could be done. In order if possible to come a few inches nearer to the actual Pole, Hanssen and Bjaaland went out four geographical miles (seven kilometres) in the direction of the newly found meridian.

Bjaaland astonished me at dinner that day. Speeches had not hitherto been a feature of this journey, but now Bjaaland evidently thought the time had come, and surprised us all with a really fine oration. My amazement reached its culmination when, at the conclusion of his speech, he produced a cigar-case full of cigars and offered it round. A cigar at the Pole! What do you say to that? But it did not end there. When the cigars had gone round, there were still four left. I was quite touched when he handed the case and cigars to me with the words: "Keep this to remind you of the Pole." I have taken good care of the case, and shall preserve it as one of the many happy signs of my comrades' devotion on this journey. The cigars I shared out afterwards, on Christmas Eve, and they gave us a visible mark of that occasion.

When this festival dinner at the Pole was ended, we began our preparations for departure. First we set up the little tent we had brought with us in case we should be compelled to divide into two parties. It had been made by our able sailmaker, Ronne, and was of very thin windproof gabardine. Its drab colour made it easily visible against the white surface. Another pole was lashed to the tent-pole, making its total height about 13 feet. On the top of this a little Norwegian flag was lashed fast, and underneath it a pennant, on which "*Fram*" was painted. The tent was well secured with guy-ropes on all sides. Inside the tent, in a little bag, I left a letter, addressed to H.M. the King, giving information of what we had accomplished. The way home was a long one, and so many things might happen to make it impossible for us to give an account of our expedition. Besides this letter, I wrote a short epistle to Captain Scott, who, I assumed, would be the first to find the tent. Other things we left there were a sextant with a glass horizon, a hypsometer case, three reindeer-skin foot-bags, some kamiks and mits.

When everything had been laid inside, we went into the tent, one by one, to write our names on a tablet we had fastened to the tent-pole. On this occasion we received the congratulations of our companions on the successful result, for the following messages were written on a couple of strips of leather, sewed to the tent

"Good luck," and "Welcome to 90°." These good wishes, which we suddenly discovered, put us in very good spirits. They were signed by Beck and Rönne. They had good faith in us. When we had finished this we came out, and the tent-door was securely laced together, so that there was no danger of the wind getting a hold on that side.

And so good-bye to Polheim. It was a solemn moment when we bared our heads and bade farewell to our home and our flag. And then the travelling tent was taken down and the sledges packed. Now the homeward journey was to begin – homeward, step by step, mile after mile, until the whole distance was accomplished. We drove at once into our old tracks and followed them. Many were the times we turned to send a last look to Polheim. The vaporous, white air set in again, and it was not long before the last of Polheim, our little flag, disappeared from view.

CHAPTER 13

THE RETURN TO FRAMHEIM

The going was splendid and all were in good spirits, so we went along at a great pace. One would almost have thought the dogs knew they were homeward bound. A mild, summer-like wind, with a temperature of -22° F., was our last greeting from the Pole.

When we came to our last camp, where the sledge was left, we stopped and took a few things with us. From this point we came into the line of beacons. Our tracks had already become very indistinct, but, thanks to his excellent sight, Bjaaland kept in them quite well. The beacons, however, served their purpose so satisfactorily that the tracks were almost superfluous. Although these beacons were not more than about 3 feet high, they were extremely conspicuous on the level surface. When the sun was on them, they shone like electric lighthouses; and when the sun was on the other side, they looked so dark in the shadow that one would have taken them for black rocks. We intended in future to travel at night; the advantages of this were many and great. In the first place, we should have the sun behind us, which meant a good deal to our eyes. Going against the sun on a snow surface like this tells fearfully on the eyes, even if one has good snow-goggles; but with the sun at one's back it is only play. Another great advantage – which we did not reap till later – was that it gave us the warmest part of the twenty-four hours in the tent, during which time we had an opportunity of drying wet clothes, and so on. This last advantage was, however, a doubtful one, as we shall see in due course.

It was a great comfort to turn our backs to the south. The wind, which had nearly always been in this quarter, had often been very painful to our cracked faces; now we should always have it at our backs, and it would help us on our way, besides giving our faces time to heal. Another thing we were longing for was to come down to the Barrier again, so that we could breathe freely. Up here we were seldom able to draw a good long breath; if we only had to say "Yes," we had to do it in two instalments. The asthmatic condition in which we found ourselves during our six weeks' stay on the plateau was anything but pleasant. We had fixed fifteen geographical miles (seventeen and three-eighths statute miles) as a suitable day's march on the home-ward journey. We had, of course, many advantages now as compared with the southward journey, which would have enabled us to do longer marches than this; but we were afraid of over-working the dogs, and possibly using them up before we had gone very far, if we attempted too great a distance daily. It soon proved, however, that we had underestimated our dogs' powers; it only took us five hours to cover the appointed distance, and our rest was therefore a long one.

On December 19 we killed the first dog on the homeward trip. This was Lasse, my own favourite dog. He had worn himself out completely, and was no longer worth anything. He was divided into fifteen portions, as nearly equal as possible, and given to his companions. They had now learnt to set great store by fresh meat, and it is certain that the extra feeds, like this one, that took place from time to time on the way home, had no small share in the remarkably successful result. They seemed to benefit by these meals of fresh meat for several days afterwards, and worked much more easily.

December 20 began with bitter weather, a breeze from the south-east, grey and thick. We lost the trail, and for some time had to go by compass. But as usual it suddenly cleared, and once more the plain lay before us, light and warm. Yes, too warm it was. We had to take off everything – nearly – and still the sweat poured off us. It was not for long that we were uncertain of the way: our excellent beacons did us brilliant service, and one after another they came up on the horizon, flashed and shone, and drew us on to our all-important depot in 88° 25′ S. We were now going slightly uphill, but so slightly that it was unnoticeable. The hypsometer and barometer, however, were not to be deceived, and both fell in precisely the same degree as they had risen before. Even if we had not exactly noticed the rise, the feeling of it was present. It may perhaps be called imagination, but I certainly thought I could notice the rise by my breathing.

Our appetite had increased alarmingly during the last few days. It appeared that we ski-runners evinced a far greater voracity than the drivers. There were days – only a few days, be it said – when I believe any of us three – Bjaaland, Hassel, and myself – would have swallowed pebbles without winking. The drivers never showed such signs of starvation. It has occurred to me that this may possibly have been due to their being able

459

to lean on the sledges as they went along, and thus have a rest and support which we had to do without. It seems little enough simply to rest one's hand on a sledge on the march, but in the long run, day after day, it may perhaps make itself felt. Fortunately we were so well supplied that when this sensation of hunger came over us, we could increase our daily rations. On leaving the Pole we added to our pemmican ration, with the result that our wild-beast appetites soon gave way and shrank to an ordinary good, everyday twist. Our daily programme on entering upon the return journey was so arranged that we began to get breakfast ready at 6 p.m., and by 8 p.m. we were usually quite ready to start the day's march. An hour or so after midnight the fifteen geographical miles were accomplished, and we could once more put up our tent, cook our food, and seek our rest. But this rest soon became so insufferably long. And then there was the fearful heat – considering the circumstances – which often made us get out of our sleeping-bags and lie with nothing over us. These rests of twelve, fourteen, sometimes as much as sixteen hours, were what most tried our patience during the early part of the return journey. We could see so well that all this rest was unnecessary, but still we kept it up as long as we were on the high ground. Our conversation at this time used to turn very often on the best way of filling up these long, unnecessary waits.

That day – December 20 – Per – good, faithful, conscientious Per – broke down utterly and had to be taken on the sledge the last part of the way. On arrival at the camping-ground he had his reward. A little blow of the back of the axe was enough for him; without making a sound the worn-out animal collapsed.

In him Wisting lost one of his best dogs. He was a curious animal – always went about quietly and peaceably, and never took part in the others' battles; from his looks and behaviour one would have judged him, quite mistakenly, to be a queer sort of beast who was good for nothing. But when he was in harness he showed what he could do. Without needing any shouts or cuts of the whip, he put himself into it from morning to night, and was priceless as a draught dog. But, like others of the same character, he could not keep it going any longer; he collapsed, was killed and eaten.

Christmas Eve was rapidly approaching. For us it could not be particularly festive, but we should have to try to make as much of it as circumstances would permit. We ought, therefore, to reach our depot that evening, so as to keep Christmas with a dish of porridge. The night before Christmas Eve we slaughtered Svartflekken. There was no mourning on this occasion Svartflekken was one of Hassel's dogs, and had always been a reprobate. I find the following in my diary, written the same evening: "Slaughtered Svartflekken this evening. He would not do any more, although there was not much wrong with his looks. Bad character. If a man, he would have ended in penal servitude." He was comparatively fat, and was consumed with evident satisfaction.

Christmas Eve came; the weather was rather changeable – now overcast, now clear – when we set out at 8 p.m. the night before. We had not far to go before reaching our depot. At 12 midnight we arrived there in the most glorious weather, calm and warm. Now we had the whole of Christmas Eve before us, and could enjoy it at our ease. Our depot was at once taken down and divided between the two sledges. All crumbs of biscuit were carefully collected by Wisting, the cook for the day, and put into a bag. This was taken into the tent and vigorously beaten and kneaded; the result was pulverized biscuit. With this product and a sausage of dried milk, Wisting succeeded in making a capital dish of Christmas porridge. I doubt whether anyone at home enjoyed his Christmas dinner so much as we did that morning in the tent. One of Bjaaland's cigars to follow brought a festival spirit over the whole camp.

Another thing we had to rejoice about that day was that we had again reached the summit of the plateau, and after two or three more days' march would begin to go downhill, finally reaching the Barrier and our old haunts. Our daily march had hitherto been interrupted by one or two halts; we stopped to rest both the dogs and ourselves. On Christmas Eve we instituted a new order of things, and did the whole distance – fifteen geographical miles – without a stop. We liked this arrangement best, after all, and it seemed as if the dogs did the same. As a rule it was hard to begin the march again after the rest; one got rather stiff lazy, too, perhaps – and had to become supple again.

On the 26th we passed 88° S., going well. The surface appeared to have been exposed to powerful sunshine since we left it, as it had become quite polished. Going over these polished levels was like crossing smooth ice, but with the important difference that here the dogs had a good foothold. This time we sighted high land even in 88°, and it had great surprises in store for us. It was clear that this was the same mighty range running to the south-east as we had seen before, but this time it stretched considerably farther to the south. The weather was radiantly clear, and we could see by the land that the range of vision was very great. Summit after summit the range extended to the south-east, until it gradually disappeared; but to judge from the atmosphere, it was continued beyond our range of vision in the same direction. That this chain traverses the Antarctic continent I therefore consider beyond a doubt. Here we had a very good example of how deceptive the atmosphere is in these regions. On a day that appeared perfectly clear we had lost sight of the mountains in 87°, and now we saw them as far as the eye could reach in 88°. That we were astonished is a mild expression. We looked and looked, entirely unable to recognize our position; little did we guess that the huge mountain-mass that stood up so high and clear on the horizon was Mount Thorvald Nilsen. How utterly different it had looked in the misty air when we said good-bye to it. It is amusing to read my diary of this time and see how persistently we took the bearings of land every day, and thought it was new. We did not recognize that vast mountain until Mount Helmer Hanssen began to stick up out of the plain.

On December 28 we left the summit of the plateau, and began the descent. Although the incline was not perceptible to the naked eye, its effect could easily be seen in the dogs. Wisting now used a sail on his sledge, and was thus able to keep up with Hanssen. If anyone had seen the procession that came marching over the plateau at that time, he would hardly have thought we had been out for seventy days at a stretch, for we came at a swinging pace. We always had the wind at our backs, with sunshine and warmth the whole time. There was never a thought of using the whip now; the dogs were bursting with health, and tugged at their harness to get away. It was a hard time for our worthy forerunner; he often had to spurt as much as he could to keep clear of Hanssen's dogs. Wisting in full sail, with his dogs howling for joy, came close behind. Hassel had his work cut out to follow, and, indeed, I had the same. The surface was absolutely polished, and for long stretches at a time we could push ourselves along with our sticks. The dogs were completely changed since we had left the Pole; strange as it may sound, it is nevertheless true that they were putting on flesh day by day, and getting quite fat. I believe it must have been feeding them on fresh meat and pemmican together that did this. We were again able to increase our ration of pemmican from December 28; the daily ration was 1 pound (450 grams) per man, and we could not manage more – at least, I think not.

On December 29 we went downhill more and more, and it was indeed tough work being a ski-runner. The drivers stood so jauntily by the side of their sledges, letting themselves be carried over the plain at a phenomenal pace. The surface consisted of sastrugi, alternating with smooth stretches like ice. Heaven help me, how we ski-runners had to struggle to keep up! It was all very well for Bjaaland; he had flown faster on even worse ground. But for Hassel and me it was different. I saw Hassel put out, now an arm; now a leg, and make the most desperate efforts to keep on his feet. Fortunately I could not see myself; if I had been able to, I am sure I should have been in fits of laughter. Early that day Mount Helmer Hanssen appeared. The ground now went in great undulations – a thing we had not noticed in the mist when we were going south. So high were these undulations that they suddenly hid the view from us. The first

464

we saw of Mount Hanssen was from the top of one of these big waves; it then looked like the top of a pressure hummock that was just sticking up above the surface. At first we did not understand at all what it was; it was not till the next day that we really grasped it, when the pointed blocks of ice covering the top of the mountain came into view. As I have said, it was only then that we made sure of being on the right course; all the rest of the land that we saw was so entirely strange to us. We recognized absolutely nothing.

On the 30th we passed 87° S., and were thus rapidly nearing the Devil's Ballroom and Glacier. The next day was brilliantly fine-temperature -2.2° F. – with a good breeze right aft. To our great joy, we got sight of the land around the Butcher's Shop. It was still a long way off, of course, but was miraged up in the warm, sunny air. We were extraordinarily lucky on our homeward trip; we escaped the Devil's Ballroom altogether.

On January 1 we ought, according to our reckoning, to reach the Devil's Glacier, and this held good. We could see it at a great distance; huge hummocks and ice-waves towered into the sky. But what astonished us was that between these disturbances and on the far side of them, we seemed to see an even, unbroken plain, entirely unaffected by the broken surface. Mounts Hassel, Wisting, and Bjaaland, lay as we had left them; they were easy to recognize when we came a little nearer to them. Now Mount Helmer Hanssen again towered high into the air; it flashed and sparkled like diamonds as it lay bathed in the rays of the morning sun. We assumed that we had come nearer to this range than when we were going south, and that this was the reason of our finding the ground so changed. When we were going south, it certainly looked impassable between us and the mountains; but who could tell? Perhaps in the middle of all the broken ground that we then saw there was a good even stretch, and that we had now been lucky enough to stumble upon it. But it was once more the atmosphere that deceived us, as we found out on the following day, for instead of being nearer the range we had come farther out from it, and this was the reason of our only getting a little strip of this undesirable glacier.

We had our camp that evening in the middle of a big, filled-up crevasse. We were a trifle anxious as to what kind of surface we should find farther on; that these few hummocks and old crevasses were all the glacier had to offer us this time, was more than we dared to hope. But the 2nd came, and brought – thank God! – no disappointment. With incredible luck we had slipped past all those ugly and dangerous places, and now, before we knew where we were, we found ourselves safe and sound on the plain below the glacier. The weather was not first-rate when we started at seven in the evening. It was fairly thick, and we could only just distinguish the top of Mount Bjaaland. This was bad, as we were now in the neighbourhood of our depot, and would have liked clear weather to find out where it lay; but instead of clearing, as we hoped, it grew thicker and thicker, and when we had gone about six and three-quarter miles, it was so bad that we thought it best to stop and wait for a while. We had all the time been going on the erroneous assumption that we had come too far to the east-that is, too near the mountains – and under the circumstances – in the short gleams that had come from time to time – we had not been able to recognize the ground below the glacier. According to our idea, we were on the east of the depot. The bearings, which had been taken in thick air, and were now to guide us in this heavy mist, gave no result whatever. There was no depot to be seen.

We had just swallowed the grateful warm pemmican when the sun suddenly showed itself. I don't think the camp was ever broken and the sledges packed in such a short time. From the moment we jumped out of our bags till the sledges were ready, it only took us fifteen minutes, which is incredibly quick. "What on earth is that shining over there through the fog?" The question came from one of the lads. The mist had divided, and was rolling away on both sides; in the western bank something big and white peeped through – along ridge running north and south. Hurrah! it's Helland Hansen. Can't possibly be anything else. Our only landmark on the west. We all shouted with joy on meeting this old acquaintance. But in the direction of the depot the fog hung thick. We held a brief consultation, and agreed to let it go, to steer for the Butcher's and put on the pace. We had food enough, anyhow. No sooner said than done, and we started off. It rapidly cleared, and then, on our way towards Helland Hansen, we found out that we had come, not too far to the east, but too far to the west. But to turn round and begin to search for our depot was not to our liking. Below Mount Helland Hansen we came up on a fairly high ridge. We had now gone our fixed distance, and so halted.

Behind us, in the brightest, clearest weather, lay the glacier, as we had seen it for the first time on our way to the south: break after break, crevasse after crevasse. But in among all this nastiness there ran a white, unbroken line, the very path we had stood and looked at a few weeks back. And directly below that white stripe we knew, as sure as anything could be, that our depot lay. We stood there expressing our annoyance rather forcibly at the depot having escaped us so easily, and talking of how jolly it would have been to have picked up all our depots from the plain we had strewed them over. Dead tired as I felt that evening, I had not the least desire to go back the fifteen miles that separated us from it. "If anybody would like to make the trip, he shall have many thanks." They all wanted to make it – all as one man. There was no lack of volunteers in that company. I chose Hanssen and Bjaaland. They took nearly everything off the sledge, and went away with it empty.

It was then five in the morning. At three in the afternoon they came back to the tent, Bjaaland running in front, Hanssen driving the sedge. That was a notable feat, both for men and dogs. Hanssen, Bjaaland, and that team had covered about fifty miles that day, at an average rate of three to three and a half miles an hour. They had found the depot without much search. Their greatest difficulty had been in the undulating surface; for long stretches at a time they were in the hollows between the waves, which shut in their view entirely. Ridge succeeded ridge, endlessly. We had taken care that everything was ready for their return – above all great quantities of water. Water, water was the first thing, and generally the last, that was in request. When their thirst was a little quenched, great interest was shown in the pemmican. While these two were being well looked after, the depot they had brought in was divided between the two sledges, and in a short time all was ready for our departure. Meanwhile, the weather had been getting finer and finer, and before us lay the mountains, sharp and clear. We thought we recognized Fridtjof Nansen and Don Pedro Christophersen, and took good bearings of them in case the fog should return. With most of us the ideas of day and night began to get rather mixed. "Six o'clock," someone would answer, when asked the time. "Yes, in the morning," remarks the other. "No; what are you talking about?" answers the first one again; "it's evening, of course." The date was hopeless; it was a good thing if we remembered the year. Only when writing in our diaries and observation books did we come across such things as dates; while at work we had not the remotest idea of them.

Splendid weather it was when we turned out on the morning of January 3. We had now agreed to go as it suited us, and take no notice of day or night; for some time past we had all been sick of the long hours of rest, and wanted to break them up at any price. As I have said, the weather could not have been finer brilliantly clear and a dead calm. The temperature of -2.2° F. felt altogether like summer in this bright, still air. Before we began our march all unnecessary clothes were taken off and put on the sledges. It almost looked as if everything would be considered superfluous, and the costume in which we finally started would no doubt have been regarded as somewhat unseemly in our latitudes. We smiled and congratulated ourselves that at present no ladies had reached the Antarctic regions, or they might have objected to our extremely comfortable and serviceable costume. The high land now stood out still more sharply. It was very interesting to see in these conditions the country we had gone through on, the southward trip in the thickest blizzard. We had then been going along the foot of this immense mountain chain without a suspicion of how near we were to it, or how colossal it was. The ground was fortunately quite undisturbed in this part. I say fortunately, as Heaven knows what would have happened to us if we had been obliged to cross a crevassed surface in such weather as we then had. Perhaps we should have managed it – perhaps not.

The journey before us was a stiff one, as the Butcher's lay 2,680 feet higher than the place where we were. We had been expecting to stumble upon one of our beacons before long, but this did not happen until we had gone twelve and a half miles. Then one of them suddenly came in sight, and was greeted with joy. We knew well enough that we were on the right track, but an old acquaintance like this was very welcome all the same. The sun had evidently been at work up here while we were in the south, as some of the beacons were quite bent over, and great icicles told us clearly enough how powerful the sunshine had been. After a march of about twenty-five miles we halted at the beacon we had built right under the hill, where we had been forced to stop by thick weather on November 25.

January 4 was one of the days to which we looked forward with anxiety, as we were then due at our depot at the Butcher's, and had to find it. This depot, which consisted of the finest, fresh dogs' flesh, was of immense importance to us. Not only had our animals got into the way of preferring this food to pemmican, but, what was of still greater importance, it had an extremely good effect on the dogs' state of health. No doubt our pemmican was good enough – indeed, it could not have been better – but a variation of diet is a great consideration, and seems, according to my experience, to mean even more to the dogs than to the men on a long journey like this. On former occasions I have seen dogs refuse pemmican, presumably because they were tired of it, having no variety; the result was that the dogs grew thin and weak, although we had food enough. The pemmican I am referring to on that occasion was made for human use, so that their distaste cannot have been due to the quality.

It was 1.15 a.m. when we set out. We had not had a long sleep, but it was very important to avail ourselves of this fine, clear weather while it lasted; we knew by experience that up here in the neighbourhood of the Butcher's the weather was not to be depended upon. From the outward journey we knew that the distance from the beacon where our camp was to the depot at the Butcher's was thirteen and a half miles. We had not put up more than two beacons on this stretch, but the ground was of such a nature that we thought we could not go wrong. That it was not so easy to find the way, in spite of the beacons, we were soon to discover. In the fine, clear weather, and with Hanssen's sharp eyes, we picked up both our beacons. Meanwhile we were astonished at the appearance of the mountains. As I have already mentioned, we thought the weather was perfectly clear when we reached the Butcher's for the first time, on November 20. I then took a bearing from the tent of the way we had come up on to the plateau between the mountains, and carefully recorded it. After passing our last beacon, when we were beginning to approach the Butcher's – as we reckoned – we were greatly surprised at the aspect of our surroundings. Last time – on November 20 – we had seen mountains on the west and north, but a long way off: Now the whole of that part of the horizon seemed to be filled with colossal mountain masses, which were right over us. What in the world was the meaning of this? Was it witchcraft? I am sure I began to think so for a moment. I would readily have taken my most solemn oath that I had never seen that landscape before in my life. We had now gone the full distance, and according to the beacons we had passed, we ought to be on the spot. This was very strange; in the direction in which I had taken the bearing of our ascent, we now only saw the side of a perfectly unknown mountain, sticking up from the plain. There could be absolutely no way down in that precipitous wall. Only on the north-west did the ground give the impression of allowing a descent; there a natural depression seemed to be formed, running down towards the Barrier, which we could see far, far away.

We halted and discussed the situation. "Hullo!" Hanssen suddenly exclaimed, "somebody has been here before." – "Yes," broke in Wisting; "I'm hanged if that isn't my broken ski that I stuck up by the depot." So it was Wisting's broken ski that brought us out of this unpleasant situation. It was a good thing he put it there – very thoughtful, in any case. I now examined the place with the glasses, and by the side of a snow mound, which proved to be our depot, but might easily have escaped our notice, we could see the ski sticking up out of the snow. We cheerfully set our course for the spot, but did not reach it until we had gone three miles.

There was rejoicing in our little band when we arrived and saw that what we had considered the most important point of our homeward journey had been reached. It was not so much for the sake of the food it contained that we considered it so necessary to find this spot, as for discovering the way down to the Barrier again. And now that we stood there, we recognized this necessity more than ever. For although we now knew, from our bearings, exactly where the descent lay, we could see nothing of it at all. The plateau there seemed to go right up to the mountain, without any opening towards the lower ground beyond; and yet the compass told us that such an opening must exist, and would take us down. The mountain, on which we had thus walked all day on the outward journey, without knowing anything of it, was Mount Fridtjof Nansen. Yes, the difference in the light made a surprising alteration in the appearance of things.

The first thing we did on reaching the depot was to take out the dogs' carcasses that lay there and cut them into big lumps, that were divided among the dogs. They looked rather surprised; they had not been accustomed to such rations. We threw three carcasses on to the sledges, so as to have a little extra food for them on the way down. The Butcher's was not a very friendly spot this time, either. True, it was not the same awful weather as on our first visit, but it was blowing a fresh breeze with a temperature of -9.4° F., which, after the heat of the last few days, seemed to go to one's marrow, and did not invite us to stay longer than was absolutely necessary. Therefore, as soon as we had finished feeding the dogs and putting our sledges in order, we set out.

Although the ground had not given us the impression of sloping, we soon found out that it did so when we got under way. It was not only downhill, but the pace became so great that we had to stop and put brakes under the sledges. As we advanced, the apparently unbroken wall opened more and more, and showed us at last our old familiar ascent. There lay Mount Ole Engelstad, snowclad and cold, as we saw it the first time. As we rounded it we came on to the severe, steep slope, where, on the way south, I had so much admired the work done by my companions and the dogs that day. But now I had an even better opportunity of seeing how steep this ascent really had been. Many were the brakes we had to put on before we could reduce the speed to a moderate pace, but even so we came down rapidly, and soon the first part of the descent lay behind us. So as not to be exposed to possible gusts from the plain, we went round Mount Engelstad and camped under the lee of it, well content with the day's work. The snow lay here as on our first visit, deep and loose, and it was difficult to find anything like a good place for the tent. We could soon feel that we had descended a couple of thousand feet and come down among the mountains. It was still, absolutely still, and the sun broiled us as on a day of high summer at home. I thought, too, that I could notice a difference in my breathing; it seemed to work much more easily and pleasantly – perhaps it was only imagination.

At one o'clock on the following morning we were out again. The sight that met our eyes that morning, when we came out of the tent, was one of those that will always live in our memories. The tent stood in the narrow gap between Fridtjof Nansen and Ole Engelstad. The sun, which now stood in the south, was completely hidden by the latter mountain, and our camp was thus in the deepest shadow; but right against us on the other side the Nansen mountain raised its splendid ice-clad summit high towards heaven, gleaming and sparkling in the rays of the midnight sun. The shining white passed gradually, very gradually, into pale blue, then deeper and deeper blue, until the shadow swallowed it up. But down below, right on the Heiberg Glacier, its ice-covered side was exposed – dark and solemn the mountain mass stood out. Mount Engelstad lay in shadow, but on its summit rested a beautiful light little cirrus cloud, red with an edge of gold. Down over its side the blocks of ice lay scattered pell-mell. And farther down on the east rose Don Pedro Christophersen, partly in shadow, partly gleaming in the sun – a marvellously beautiful sight. And all was so still; one almost feared to disturb the incomparable splendour of the scene.

We now knew the ground well enough to be able to go straight ahead without any detours. The huge avalanches were more frequent than on the outward journey. One mass of snow after another plunged down; Don Pedro was getting rid of his winter coat. The going was precisely the same – loose, fairly deep snow. We went quite easily over it, however, and it was all downhill. On the ridge where the descent to the glacier began we halted to make our preparations. Brakes were put under the sledges, and our two ski-sticks were fastened together to make one strong one; we should have to be able to stop instantly if surprised by a crevasse as we were going. We ski-runners went in front. The going was ideal here on the steep slope, just enough loose snow to give one good steering on ski. We went whizzing down, and it was not many minutes before we were on the Heiberg Glacier. For the drivers it was not quite such plain sailing: they followed our tracks, but had to be extremely careful on the steep fall.

We camped that evening on the selfsame spot where we had had our tent on November 18, at about 3,100 feet above the sea.

From here one could see the course of the Axel Heiberg Glacier right down to its junction with the Barrier. It looked fine and even, and we decided to follow it instead of climbing over the mountain, as we had done on the way south. Perhaps the distance would be somewhat longer, but probably we should make a considerable saving of time. We had now agreed upon a new arrangement of our time; the long spells of rest were becoming almost unbearable. Another very important side of the question was that, by a reasonable arrangement, we should be able to save a lot of time, and reach home several days sooner than we had reckoned. After a great deal of talk on one side and on the other, we agreed to arrange matters thus: we were to do our fifteen geographical miles, or twenty-eight kilometres, and then have a sleep of six hours, turn out again and do fifteen miles more, and so on. In this way we should accomplish a very good average distance on our day's march. We kept to this arrangement for the rest of the journey, and thus saved a good many days.

Our progress down the Heiberg Glacier did not encounter any obstructions; only at the transition from the glacier to the Barrier were there a few crevasses that had to be circumvented. At 7 a.m. on January 6 we halted at the angle of land that forms the entrance to the Heiberg Glacier, and thence extends northward. We had not yet recognized any of the land we lay under, but that was quite natural, as we now saw it from the opposite side. We knew, though, that we were not far away from our main depot in 85° 5' S. On the afternoon of the same day we were off again.

From a little ridge we crossed immediately after starting, Bjaaland thought he could see the depot down on the Barrier, and it was not very long before we came in sight of Mount Betty and our way up. And now we could make sure with the glasses that it really was our depot that we saw – the same that Bjaaland thought he had seen before. We therefore set our course straight for it, and in a few minutes we were once more on the Barrier – January 6, 11 p.m. – after a stay of fifty-one days on land. It was on November 17 that we had begun the ascent.

We reached the depot, and found everything in order. The heat here must have been very powerful; our lofty, solid depot was melted by the sun into a rather low mound of snow. The pemmican rations that had been exposed to the direct action of the sun's rays had assumed the strangest forms, and, of course, they had become rancid. We got the sledges ready at once, taking all the provisions out of the depot and loading them. We left behind some of the old clothes we had been wearing all the way from here to the Pole and back. When we had completed all this repacking and had everything ready, two of us went over to Mount Betty, and collected as many different specimens of rock as we could lay our hands on. At the same time we built a great cairn, and left there a can of 17 litres of paraffin, two packets of matches – containing twenty boxes – and an account of our expedition. Possibly someone may find a use for these things in the future.

We had to kill Frithjof, one of Bjaaland's dogs, at this camp. He had latterly been showing marked signs of shortness of breath, and finally this became so painful to the animal that we decided to put an end to him. Thus brave Frithjof ended his career. On cutting him open it appeared that his lungs were quite shrivelled up; nevertheless, the remains disappeared pretty quickly into his companions' stomachs. What they had lost in quantity did not apparently affect their quality. Nigger, one of Hassel's dogs, had been destroyed on the way down from the plateau. We thus reached this point again with twelve dogs, as we had reckoned on doing, and left it with eleven. I see in my diary the following remark: "The dogs look just as well as when we left Framheim." On leaving the place a few hours later we had provisions for thirty-five days on the sledges. Besides this, of course, we had a depot at every degree of latitude up to 80°.

It looked as though we had found our depot at the right moment, for when we came out to continue our journey the whole Barrier was in a blizzard. A gale was blowing from the south, with a sky completely clouded over; falling snow and drift united in a delightful dance, and made it difficult to see. The lucky thing was that now we had the wind with us, and thus escaped getting it all in our eyes, as, we had been accustomed to. The big crevasse, which, as we knew, lay right across the line of our route, made us go very carefully. To avoid any risk, Bjaaland and Hassel, who went in advance, fastened an alpine rope between them. The snow was very deep and loose, and the going very heavy. Fortunately, we were warned in time of our approach to the expected cracks by the appearance of some bare ice ridges. These told us clearly enough that disturbances had taken place here, and that even greater ones might be expected, probably near at hand. At that moment the thick curtain of cloud was torn asunder, and the sun pierced the whirling mass of snow. Instantly Hanssen shouted: "Stop, Bjaaland!" He was just on the edge of the yawning crevasse. Bjaaland himself has splendid sight, but his excellent snow-goggles – his own patent – entirely prevented his seeing. Well, Bjaaland would not have been in any serious danger if he had fallen into the crevasse, as he was roped to Hassel, but it would have been confoundedly unpleasant all the same.

As I have said before, I assume that these great disturbances here mark the boundary between the Barrier and the land. This time, curiously enough, they seemed also to form a boundary between good and bad weather, for on the far side of them – to the north – the Barrier lay bathed in sunshine. On the south the blizzard raged worse than ever. Mount Betty was the last to send us its farewell. South Victoria Land had gone into hiding, and did not show itself again. As soon as we came into the sunshine, we ran upon one of our beacons; our course lay straight towards it. That was not bad steering in the dark. At 9 p.m. we reached the depot in 85° S. Now we could begin to be liberal with the dogs' food, too; they had double pemmican rations, besides as many oatmeal biscuits as they would eat. We had such masses of biscuits now that we could positively throw them about. Of course, we might have left a large part of these provisions behind; but there was a great satisfaction in being so well supplied with food, and the dogs did not seem to mind the little extra weight in the least. As long as things went so capitally as they were going – that is, with men and dogs exactly keeping pace with one another – we could ask for nothing better. But the weather that had cheered us was not of long duration. "Same beastly weather," my diary says of the next stage. The wind had shifted to the north-west, with overcast, thick weather, and very troublesome drifting snow. In spite of these unfavourable conditions, we passed beacon after beacon, and at the end of our march had picked up all the beacons we had erected on this distance of seventeen miles and three-eighths. But, as before, we owed this to Hanssen's good eyes.

On our way southward we had taken a good deal of seal meat and had divided it among the depots we built on the Barrier in such a way that we were now able to eat fresh meat every day. This had not been done without an object; if we should be visited with scurvy, this fresh meat would be invaluable. As we were – sound and healthy as we had never been before – the seal-beef was a pleasant distraction in our menu, nothing more. The temperature had risen greatly since we came down on to the Barrier, and kept steady at about + 14° F. We were so warm in our sleeping-bags that we had to turn them with the hair out. That was better; we breathed more freely and felt happier. "Just like going into an ice-cellar," somebody remarked. The same feeling as when on a really warm summer day one comes out of the hot sun into cool shade.

January 9. – "Same beastly weather; snow, snow, snow, nothing but snow. Is there no end to it? Thick too, so that we have not been able to see ten yards ahead. Temperature + 17.6° F. Thawing everywhere on the sledges. Everything getting wet. Have not found a single beacon in this blind man's weather. The snow was very deep to begin with and the going exceedingly heavy, but in spite of this the dogs managed their sledges very well." That evening the weather improved, fortunately, and became comparatively clear by the time we resumed our journey at 10 p.m. Not long after we sighted one of our beacons. It lay to the west, about 200 yards away. We were thus not far out of our course; we turned aside and went up to it, as it was interesting to see whether our reckoning was in order. The beacon was somewhat damaged by sunshine and storms, but we found the paper left in it, which told us that this beacon was erected on November 14, in 84° 26' S. It also told us what course to steer by compass to reach the next beacon, which lay five kilometres from this one.

As we were leaving this old friend and setting our course as it advised, to our unspeakable astonishment two great birds – skua gulls – suddenly came flying straight towards us. They circled round us once or twice and then settled on the beacon. Can anyone who reads these lines form an idea of the effect this had upon us? It is hardly likely. They brought us a message from the living world into this realm of death – a message of all that was dear to us. I think the same thoughts filled us all. They did not allow themselves a long rest, these first messengers from another world; they sat still a while, no doubt wondering who we were, then rose aloft and flew on to the south. Mysterious creatures! they were now exactly half-way between Framheim and the Pole, and yet they were going farther inland. Were they going over to the other side?

Our march ended this time at one of our beacons, in 84° 15'. It felt so good and safe to lie beside one of these; it always gave us a sure starting-point for the following stage. We were up at 4 a.m. and left the place a few hours later, with the result that the day's march brought us thirty-four miles nearer Framheim. With our present arrangement, we had these long-day marches every other day. Our dogs need no better testimonial than this – one day seventeen miles, the next day thirty-four, and fresh all the way home. The two birds, agreeably as their first appearance had affected me, led my thoughts after a while in another direction, which was anything but agreeable. It occurred to me that these two might only be representatives of a larger collection of these voracious birds, and that the remainder might now be occupied in consuming all the fresh meat we had so laboriously transported with us and spread all over the plain in our depots. It is incredible what a flock of these birds of prey can get rid of; it would not matter if the meat were frozen as hard as iron, they would have managed it, even if it had been a good deal harder than iron. Of the seals' carcasses we had lying in 80°, I saw in my thoughts nothing but the bones. Of the various dogs we had killed on our way south and laid on the tops of beacons I did not see even so much as that. Well, it was possible that my thoughts had begun to assume too dark a hue; perhaps the reality would be brighter.

Weather and going began by degrees to right themselves; it looked as if things would improve in proportion to our distance from land. Finally, both became perfect; the sun shone from a cloudless sky, and the sledges ran on the fine, even surface with all the ease and speed that could be desired. Bjaaland, who had occupied the position of forerunner all the way from the Pole, performed his duties admirably; but the old saying that nobody is perfect applied even to him. None of us – no matter who it may be – can keep in a straight line, when he has no marks to follow. All the more difficult is this when, as so often happened with us, one has to go blindly. Most of us, I suppose, would swerve now to one side, now to the other, and possibly end, after all this groping, by keeping pretty well to the line. Not so with Bjaaland; he was a right-hand man. I can see him now;

Hanssen has given him the direction by compass, and Bjaaland turns round, points his skis in the line indicated and sets of with decision. His movements clearly show that he has made up his mind, cost what it may, to keep in the right direction. He sends his ski firmly along, so that the snow spurts from them, and looks straight before him. But the result is the same; if Hanssen had let Bjaaland go on without any correction, in the course of an hour or so the latter would probably have described a beautiful circle and brought himself back to the spot from which he had started. Perhaps. after all, this was not a fault to complain of, since we always knew with absolute certainty that, when we had got out of the line of beacons, we were to the right of it and had to search for the beacons to the west. This conclusion proved very useful to us more than once, and we gradually became so familiar with Bjaaland's right-handed tendencies that we actually counted on them.

On January 13, according to our reckoning, we ought to reach the depot in 83° S. This was the last of our depots that was not marked at right angles to the route, and therefore the last critical point. The day was not altogether suited for finding the needle in the haystack. It was calm with a thick fog, so thick that we could only see a few yards in front of us. We did not see a single beacon on the whole march. At 4 p.m. we had completed the distance, according to the sledge-meters, and reckoned that we ought to be in 83° S., by the depot; but there was nothing to be seen. We decided, therefore, to set our tent and wait till it cleared. While we were at work with this, there was a rift in the thick mass of fog, and there, not many yards away – to the west, of course – lay our depot. We quickly took the tent down again, packed it on the sledge, and drove up to our food mound, which proved to be quite in order. There was no sign of the birds having paid it a visit. But what was that? Fresh, well-marked dog-tracks in the newly-fallen snow. We soon saw that they must be the tracks of the runaways that we had lost here on the way south. Judging by appearances, they must have lain under the lee of the depot for a considerable time; two deep hollows in the snow told us that plainly. And evidently they must have had enough food, but where on earth had they got it from? The depot was absolutely untouched, in spite of the fact that the lumps of pemmican lay exposed to the light of day and were very easy to get at; besides which, the snow on the depot was not so hard as to prevent the dogs pulling it down and eating up all the food. Meanwhile the dogs had left the place again, as shown by the fresh trail, which pointed to the north. We examined the tracks very closely, and agreed that they were not more than two days old. They went northward, and we followed them from time to time on our next stage. At the beacon in 82° 45', where we halted, we saw them still going to the north. In 82° 24' the trail began to be much confused, and ended by pointing due west. That was the last we saw of the tracks; but we had not done with these dogs, or rather with their deeds. We stopped at the beacon in 82° 20'. Else, who had been laid on the top of it, had fallen down and lay by the side; the sun had thawed away the lower part of the beacon. So the roving dogs had not been here; so much was certain, for otherwise we should not have found Else as we did. We camped at the end of that stage by the beacon in 82° 15', and shared out Else's body. Although she had been lying in the strong sunshine, the flesh was quite good, when we had scraped away a little mouldiness. It smelt rather old, perhaps, but our dogs were not fastidious when it was a question of meat.

On January 16 we arrived at the depot in 82° S. We could see from a long way off that the order in which we had left it no longer prevailed. When we came up to it, we saw at once what had happened. The innumerable dog-tracks that had trampled the snow quite hard round the depot declared plainly enough that the runaways had spent a good deal of time here. Several of the cases belonging to the depot had fallen down, presumably from the same cause as Else, and the rascals had succeeded in breaking into one of them. Of the biscuits and pemmican which it had contained, nothing, of course, was left; but that made no difference to us now, as we had food in abundance. The two dogs' carcasses that we had placed on the top of the depot – Uranus and Jaala – were gone, not even the teeth were to be seen. Yet they had left the teeth of Lucy, whom they had eaten in 82° 3'. Jaala's eight puppies were still lying on the top of a case; curiously enough, they had not fallen down. In addition to all the rest, the beasts had devoured some ski-bindings and things of that sort. It was no loss to us, as it happened; but who could tell which way these creatures had gone? If they had succeeded in finding the depot in 80° S., they would probably by this time have finished our supply of seal meat there. Of course it would be regrettable if this had happened, although it would entail no danger either to ourselves or our animals. If we got as far as 80°, we should come through all right. For the time being, we had to console ourselves with the fact that we could see no continuation of the trail northward.

We permitted ourselves a little feast here in 82°. The "chocolate pudding" that Wisting served as dessert is still fresh in my memory; we all agreed that it came nearer perfection than anything it had hitherto fallen to our lot to taste. I may disclose the receipt: biscuit-crumbs, dried milk and chocolate are put into a kettle of boiling water. What happens afterwards, I don't know; for further information apply to Wisting. Between 82° and 81° we came into our old marks of the second depot journey; on that trip we had marked this distance with splinters of packing-case at every geographical mile. That was in March, 1911, and now we were following these splinters in the second half of January, 1912. Apparently they stood exactly as they had been put in. This marking stopped in 81° 33' S., with two pieces of case on a snow pedestal. The pedestal was still intact and good.

I shall let my diary describe what we saw on January 18: "Unusually fine weather to-day. Light south-south-west breeze, which in the course of our march cleared the whole sky. In 81° 20' we came abreast of our old big pressure ridges. We now saw far more of them than ever before. They extended as far as the eye could see, running north-east to south-west, in ridges and peaks. Great was our surprise when, a short time after, we made out high, bare land in the same direction, and not long after that two lofty, white summits to the south-east, probably in about 82° S. It could be seen by the look of the sky that the land extended from north-east to south-west. This must be the same land that we saw lose itself in the horizon in about 84°S., when we stood at a height of about 4,000 feet and looked out over the Barrier, during our ascent. We now have sufficient indications to enable us without hesitation to draw this land as continuous – Carmen Land. The surface against the land is violently disturbed – crevasses and pressure ridges, waves and valleys, in all directions. We shall no doubt feel the effect of it to-morrow." Although what we have seen apparently justifies us in concluding that Carmen Land extends from 86° S. to this position – about 81° 30' S. – and possibly farther to the north-east, I have not ventured to lay it down thus on the map. I have contented myself with giving the name of Carmen Land to the land between 86° and 84°, and have called the rest "Appearance of Land." It will be a profitable task for an explorer to investigate this district more closely.

As we had expected, on our next stage we were made to feel the effect of the disturbances. Three times we had now gone over this stretch of the Barrier without having really clear weather. This time we had it, and were able to see what it actually looked like. The irregularities began in 81° 12' S., and did not extend very far from north to south-possibly about five kilometres (three and a quarter miles). How far they extended from east to west it is difficult to say, but at any rate as far as the eye could reach. Immense pieces of the surface had fallen away and opened up the most horrible yawning gulfs, big enough to swallow many caravans of the size of ours. From these open holes, ugly wide cracks ran out in all directions; besides which, mounds and haycocks were everywhere to be seen. Perhaps the most remarkable thing of all was that we had passed over here unharmed. We went across as light-footedly as possible, and at top speed. Hanssen went halfway into a crevasse, but luckily got out of it again without difficulty.

The depot in 81° S. was in perfect order; no dog-tracks to be seen there. Our hopes that the depot in 80° S. would be intact rose considerably. In 80° 45' S. lay the first dog we had killed – Bone. He was particularly fat, and was immensely appreciated. The dogs no longer cared very much for pemmican. On January 21 we passed our last beacon, which stood in 80° 23' S. Glad as we were to leave it behind, I cannot deny that it was with a certain feeling of melancholy that we saw it vanish. We had grown so fond of our beacons, and whenever we met them we greeted them as old friends. Many and great were the services these silent watchers did us on our long and lonely way.

On the same day we reached our big depot in 80° S., and now we considered that we were back. We could see at once that others had been at the depot since we had left it, and we found a message from Lieutenant Prestrud, the leader of the eastern party, saying that he, with Stubberud and Johansen, had passed here on November 12, with two sledges, sixteen dogs, and supplies for thirty days. Everything thus appeared to be in the best of order. Immediately on arriving at the depot we let the dogs loose, and they made a dash for the heap of seal's flesh, which had been attacked neither by birds nor dogs in our absence. It was not so much for the sake of eating that our dogs made their way to the meat mound, as for the sake of fighting. Now they really had something to fight about. They went round the seals' carcasses a few times, looked askance at the food and at each other, and then flung themselves into the wildest scrimmage. When this had been duly brought to a conclusion, they went away and lay round their sledges. The depot in 80° S. is still large, well supplied and well marked, so it is not impossible that it may be found useful later.

The journey from 80° S. to Framheim has been so often described that there is nothing new to say about it. On January 25, at 4 a.m., we reached our good little house again, with two sledges and eleven dogs; men and animals all hale and hearty. We stood and waited for each other outside the door in the early morning; our appearance must be made all together. It was so still and quiet – they must be all asleep. We came in. Stubberud started up in his bunk and glared at us; no doubt he took us for ghosts. One after another they woke up – not grasping what was happening. Then there was a hearty welcome home on all sides "Where's the *Fram*?" was of course our first question Our joy was great when we heard all was well. "And what about the Pole? Have you been there?" – "Yes, of course; otherwise you would hardly have seen us again." Then the coffee kettle was put on, and the perfume of "hot cakes" rose as in old days. We agreed that it was good outside, but still better at home. Ninety-nine days the trip had taken. Distance about 1,860 miles.

The *Franz* had come in to the Barrier on January 8, after a three months' voyage from Buenos Aires; all were well on board. Meanwhile, bad weather had forced her to put out again. On the following day the lookout man reported that the *Fram* was approaching. There was life in the camp; on with furs and out with the dogs. They should see that our dogs were not worn out yet. We heard the engine panting and grunting, saw the crow's-nest appear over the edge of the Barrier, and at last she glided in, sure and steady. It was with a joyful heart I went on board and greeted all these gallant men, who had brought the *Franz* to her destination through so many fatigues and perils, and had accomplished so much excellent work on the way. They all looked pleased and happy, but nobody asked about the Pole. At last it slipped out of Gjertsen: "Have you been there?" Joy is a poor name for the feeling that beamed in my comrades' faces; it was something more.

I shut myself up in the chart-house with Captain Nilsen, who gave me my mail and all the news. Three names stood high above the rest, when I was able to understand all that had happened – the names of the three who gave me their support when it was most needed. I shall always remember them in respectful gratitude –

H. M. THE KING,
PROFESSOR FRIDTJOF NANSEN,
DON PEDRO CHRISTOPHERSEN.

CHAPTER 14

NORTHWARD

After two days of bustle in getting on board the things we were to take with us, we managed to be ready for sea on the afternoon of January 30. There could scarcely have been anything at that moment that rejoiced us more than just that fact, that we were able at so early a date to set our course northward and thus take the first step on the way to that world which, as we knew, would soon begin to expect news from us, or of us. And yet, I wonder whether there was not a little feeling of melancholy in the midst of all our joy? It can hardly be doubted that such was really the case, although to many this may seem a flat contradiction. But it is not altogether so easy to part from a place that has been one's home for any length of time, even though this home lie in the 79th degree of latitude, more or less buried in snow and ice. We human beings are far too dependent on habit to be able to tear ourselves abruptly from the surroundings with which we have been obliged to be familiar for many months. That outsiders would perhaps pray all the powers of goodness to preserve them from such surroundings, does not counteract the full validity of this rule. To an overwhelming majority of our fellow-men Framheim will certainly appear as one of those spots on our planet where they would least of all wish to find themselves – a God-forsaken, out-of-the-way hole that could offer nothing but the very climax of desolation, discomfort, and boredom. To us nine, who stood on the gangway ready to leave this place, things appeared somewhat differently. That strong little house, that now lay entirely hidden beneath the snow behind Mount Nelson, had for a whole year been our home, and a thoroughly good and comfortable home it was, where after so many a hard day's work we had found all the rest and quiet we wanted. Through the whole Antarctic winter – and it is a winter – those four walls had protected us so well that many a poor wretch in milder latitudes would have envied us with all his heart, if he could have seen us. In conditions so hard that every form of life flies headlong from them, we had lived on at Framheim undisturbed and untroubled, and lived, be it said, not as animals, but as civilized human beings, who had always within their reach most of the good things that are found in a well-ordered home. Darkness and cold reigned outside, and the blizzards no doubt did their best to blot out most traces of our activity, but these enemies never came within the door of our excellent dwelling; there we shared quarters with light and warmth and comfort. What wonder was it that this spot exercised a strong attraction upon each of us at the moment when we were to turn our backs upon it for good? Outside the great world beckoned to us, that is true; and it might have much to offer us that we had had to forego for a long time; but in what awaited us there was certainly a great deal that we would gladly have put off for as long as possible. When everyday life came with its cares and worries, it might well happen that we should look back with regret to our peaceful and untroubled existence at Framheim.

However, this feeling of melancholy was hardly so strong that we could not all get over it comparatively quickly. Judging by the faces, at any rate, one would have thought that joy was the most predominant mood. And why not? It was no use dwelling on the past, however attractive it might seem just then, and as to the future, we had every right to expect the best of it. Who cared to think of coming troubles? No one. Therefore the *Fram* was dressed with flags from stem to stern, and therefore faces beamed at each other as we said good-bye to our home on the Barrier. We could leave it with the consciousness that the object of our year's stay had been attained, and, after all, this consciousness was of considerably more weight than the thought that we had been so happy there. One thing that in the course of our two years' association on this expedition contributed enormously to making time pass easily and keeping each of us in full vigour was the entire absence of what I may call "dead periods." As soon as one problem was solved, another instantly appeared. No sooner was one goal reached, than the next one beckoned from afar. In this way we always had our hands full, and when that is the case, as everyone knows, time flies quickly. One often hears it asked, How is it possible to make the time pass on such a trip? My good friends, I would answer, if anything caused us worry, it was the thought of how we should find time enough for all we had to do. Perhaps to many this assertion will bear the stamp of improbability; it is, nevertheless, absolutely true. Those who have read this narrative through will, in any case, have received the impression that unemployment was an evil that was utterly unknown in our little community.

At the stage where we now found ourselves, with the main object of our enterprise achieved, there might have been reason to expect a certain degree of relaxation of interest. This, however, was not the case. The fact was that what we had done would have no real value until it was brought to the knowledge of mankind, and this communication had to be made with as little loss of time as possible. If anyone was interested in being first in the market it was certainly ourselves. The probability was, no doubt, that we were out in good time; but, in spite of all, it was only a probability. On the other hand, it was absolutely certain that we had a voyage of 2,400 nautical miles to Hobart, which had been selected as our first port of call; and it was almost equally certain that this voyage would be both slow and troublesome. A year before our trip through Ross Sea had turned out almost like a pleasure cruise, but that was in the middle of summer. Now we were in February, and autumn was at hand. As regards the belt of drift-ice, Captain Nilsen thought that would cause us no delay in future. He had discovered a patent and infallible way of getting through! This sounded like a rather bold assertion, but, as will be seen later, he was as good as his word. Our worst troubles would be up in the westerlies, where we should this time be exposed to the unpleasant possibility of having to beat. The difference in longitude between the Bay of Whales and Hobart is nearly fifty degrees. If we could have sailed off this difference in longitude in the latitudes where we then were, and where a degree of longitude is only about thirteen nautical miles, it would all have been done in a twinkling; but the mighty mountain ranges of North Victoria Land were a decisive obstacle. We should first have to follow a northerly course until we had rounded the Antarctic Continent's northern outpost, Cape Adare, and the Balleny Islands to the north of it. Not till then would the way be open for us to work to the west; but then we should be in a region where in all probability the wind would be dead against us, and as to tacking with the *Fram* – no, thank you! Every single man on board knew enough of the conditions to be well aware of what awaited us, and it is equally certain that the thoughts of all were centred upon how we might conquer our coming difficulties in the best and quickest way. It was the one great, common object that still bound, and would continue to bind, us all together in our joint efforts.

Among the items of news that we had just received from the outer world was the message that the Australian Antarctic Expedition under Dr. Douglas Mawson would be glad to take over some of our dogs, if we had any to spare. The base of this expedition was Hobart, and as far as that went, this suited us very well. It chanced that we were able to do our esteemed colleague this small service. On leaving the Barrier we could show a pack of thirty-nine dogs, many of which had grown up during our year's stay there; about half had survived the whole trip from Norway, and eleven had been at the South Pole. It had been our intention only to keep a suitable number as the progenitors of a new pack for the approaching voyage in the Arctic Ocean, but Dr. Mawson's request caused us to take all the thirty-nine on board. Of these dogs, if nothing unforeseen happened, we should be able to make over twenty-one to him. When the last load was brought down, there was nothing to do but to pull the dogs over the side, and then we were ready. It was quite curious to see how several of the old veterans seemed at home again on the *Fram's* deck. Wisting's brave dog, the old Colonel, with his two adjutants, Suggen and Arne, at once took possession of the places where they had stood for so many a long day on the voyage south – on the starboard side of the mainmast; the two twins, Mylius and Ring, Helmer Hanssen's special favourites, began their games away in the corner of the fore-deck to port, as though nothing had happened. To look at those two merry rascals no one would have thought they had trotted at the head of the whole caravan both to and from the Pole. One solitary dog could be seen stalking about, lonely and reserved, in a continual uneasy search. This was the boss of Bjaaland's team. He was unaffected by any advances; no one could take the place of his fallen comrade and friend, Frithjof, who had long ago found a grave in the stomachs of his companions many hundreds of miles across the Barrier.

No sooner was the last dog helped on board, and the two ice-anchors released, than the engine-room telegraph rang, and the engine was at once set going to keep us from any closer contact with the ice-foot in the Bay of Whales. Our farewell to this snug harbour took almost the form of a leap from one world to another; the fog hung over us as thick as gruel, concealing all the surrounding outlines behind its clammy curtain, as we stood out. After a lapse of three or four hours, it lifted quite suddenly, but astern of us the bank of fog still stood like a wall; behind it the panorama, which we knew would have looked wonderful in clear weather, and which we should so gladly have let our eyes rest upon as long as we could, was entirely concealed.

The same course we had steered when coming in a year before could safely be taken in the opposite direction now we were going out. The outlines of the bay had remained absolutely unchanged during the year that had elapsed. Even the most projecting point of the wall on the west side of the bay, Cape Man's Head, stood serenely in its old place, and it looked as if it was in no particular hurry to remove itself. It will probably stay where it is for many a long day yet, for if any movement of the ice mass is taking place at the inner end of the bay, it is in any case very slight. Only in one respect did the condition of things differ somewhat this year from the preceding. Whereas in 1911 the greater part of the bay was free of sea-ice as early as January 14, in 1912 there was no opening until about fourteen days later. The ice-sheet had stubbornly held on until the fresh northeasterly breeze, that appeared on the very day the southern party returned, had rapidly provided a channel of open water. The breaking up of the ice could not possibly have taken place at a more convenient moment; the breeze in question saved us a great deal, both of time and trouble, as the way to the place where the *Fram* lay before the ice broke up was about five times as long as the distance we now had to go. This difference of fourteen days in the time of the disappearance of the ice in two summers showed us how lucky we had been to choose that particular year – 1911 – for our landing here. The work which we carried out in three weeks in 1911, thanks to the early breaking up of the ice, would certainly have taken us double the time in 1912, and would have caused us far more difficulty and trouble.

The thick fog that, as I have said, lay over the Bay of Whales when we left it, prevented us also from seeing what our friends the Japanese were doing. The *Kainan Maru* had put to sea in company with the *Fram* during the gale of January 27, and since that time we had seen nothing of them. Those members of the expedition who had been left behind in a tent on the edge of the Barrier to the north of Framheim had also been very retiring of late. On the day we left the place, one of our own party had an interview with two of the foreigners. Prestrud had gone to fetch the flag that had been set up on Cape Man's Head as a signal to the *Fram* that all had returned. By the side of the flag a tent had been put up, which was intended as a shelter for a lookout man, in case the *Fram* had been delayed. When Prestrud came up, he was no doubt rather surprised to find himself face to face with two sons of Nippon, who were engaged in inspecting our tent and its contents, which, however, only consisted of a sleeping-bag and a Primus. The Japanese had opened the conversation with enthusiastic phrases about "nice day" and "plenty ice"; when our man had expressed his absolute agreement on these indisputable facts, he tried to get information on matters of more special interest. The two strangers told him that for the moment they were the only inhabitants of the tent out on the edge of the Barrier. Two of their companions had gone on a tour into the Barrier to make meteorological observations, and were to be away about a week. The *Kainan Maru* had gone on another cruise in the direction of King Edward Land. As far as they knew, it was intended that the ship should be back before February 10, and that all the members of the expedition should then go on board and sail to the north. Prestrud had invited his two new acquaintances to visit us at Framheim, the sooner the better; they delayed their coming too long, however, for us to be able to wait for them. If they have since been at Framheim, they will at any rate be able to bear witness that we did our best to make things comfortable for any successors.

When the fog lifted, we found ourselves surrounded by open sea, practically free from ice, on all sides. A blue-black sea, with a heavy, dark sky above it, is not usually reckoned among the sights that delight the eye. To our organs of vision it was a real relief to come into surroundings where dark colours predominated. For months we had been staring at a dazzling sea of white, where artificial means had constantly to be employed to protect the eyes against the excessive flood of light. As a rule, it was even necessary to limit the exposure of the pupils to a minimum, and to draw the eyelids together. Now we could once more look on the world with open eyes, literally "without winking "; even such a commonplace thing as this is an experience in one's life. Ross Sea showed itself again on its most favourable side. A cat's paw of south-westerly wind enabled us to use the sails, so that after a lapse of two days we were already about two hundred miles from the Barrier. Modest as this distance may be in itself, when seen on the chart it looked quite imposing in our eyes. It must be remembered that, with the means of transport we had employed on land, it cost us many a hard day's march to cover a distance of two hundred geographical miles.

Nilsen had marked on the chart the limits of the belt of drift-ice during the three passages the *Fram* had already made. The supposition that an available opening is always to be found in the neighbourhood of the 150th meridian appears to be confirmed. The slight changes in the position of the channel were only caused, according to Nilsen's experiences, by variations in the direction of the wind. He had found that it always answered his purpose to turn and try to windward, if the pack showed signs of being close. This mode of procedure naturally had the effect of making the course somewhat crooked, but to make up for this it had always resulted in his finding open water. On this trip we reached the edge of the pack-ice belt three days after leaving the Barrier. The position of the belt proved to be very nearly the same as on previous passages. After we had held our course for some hours, however, the ice became so thick that it looked badly for our further progress. Now was the time to try Nilsen's method: the wind, which, by the way, was quite light, came about due west, and accordingly the helm was put to starboard and the bow turned to the west. For a good while we even steered true south, but it proved that this fairly long turn had not been made in vain; after we had worked our way to windward for a few hours, we found openings in numbers. If we had held our course as we began, it is not at all impossible that we should have been delayed for a long time, with a free passage a few miles away.

After having accomplished this first long turn, we escaped having to make any more in future. The ice continued slack, and on February 6 the rapidly increasing swell told us that we had done with the Antarctic drift-ice for good. I doubt if we saw a single seal during our passage through the ice-belt this time; and if we had seen any, we should scarcely have allowed the time for shooting them. There was plenty of good food both for men and dogs this time, without our having recourse to seal-beef. For the dogs we had brought all our remaining store of the excellent dogs' pemmican, and that was not a little. Besides this, we had a good lot of dried fish. They had fish and pemmican on alternate days. On this diet the animals kept in such splendid condition that, when on arrival at Hobart they had shed most of their rough winter coats, they looked as if they had been in clover for a year.

For the nine of us who had just joined the ship, our comrades on board had brought all the way from Buenos Aires several fat pigs, that were now living in luxury in their pen on the after-deck; in addition to these, three fine sheep's carcasses hung in the workroom. It need scarcely be said that we were fully capable of appreciating these unexpected luxuries. Seal-beef, no doubt, had done excellent service, but this did not prevent roast mutton and pork being a welcome change, especially as they came as a complete surprise. I hardly think one of us had counted on the possibility of getting fresh meat before we were back again in civilization.

On her arrival at the Bay of Whales there were eleven men on board the *Fram,* all included. Instead of Kutschin and Nödtvedt, who had gone home from Buenos Aires while the ship was there in the autumn of 1911, three new men were engaged – namely, Halvorsen, Olsen and Steller; the two first-named were from Bergen; Steller was a German, who had lived for several years in Norway, and talked Norwegian like a native.

All three were remarkably efficient and friendly men; it was a pleasure to have any dealings with them. I venture to think that they, too, found themselves at home in our company; they were really only engaged until the *Fram* called at the first port, but they stayed on board all the way to Buenos Aires, and will certainly go with us farther still.

When the shore party came on board, Lieutenant Prestrud took up his old position as first officer; the others began duty at once. All told, we were now twenty men on board, and after the *Fram* had sailed for a year rather short-handed, she could now be said to have a full crew again. On this voyage we had no special work outside the usual sea routine, and so long as the weather was fair, we had thus a comparatively quiet life on board. But the hours of watch on deck passed quickly enough, I expect; there was material in plenty for many a long chat now. If we, who came from land, showed a high degree of curiosity about what had been going on in the world, the sea-party were at least as eager to have full information of every detail of our year-long stay on the Barrier. One must almost have experienced something similar oneself to be able to form an idea of the hail of questions that is showered upon one on such an occasion. What we land-lubbers had to relate has been given in outline in the preceding chapters. Of the news we heard from outside, perhaps nothing interested us so much as the story of how the change in the plan of the expedition had been received at home and abroad.

It must have been at least a week before there was any noticeable ebb in the flood of questions and answers. That week went by quickly; perhaps more quickly than we really cared for, since it proved that the *Fram* was not really able to keep pace with time.

The weather remained quite well behaved, but not exactly in the way we wished. We had reckoned that the south-easterly and easterly winds, so frequent around Framheim, would also show themselves out in Ross Sea, but they entirely forgot to do so. We had little wind, and when there was any, it was, as a rule, a slant from the north, always enough to delay our honest old ship. It was impossible to take any observations for the first eight days, the sky was continuously overcast. If one occasionally asked the skipper about her position, he usually replied that the only thing that could be said for certain was that we were in Ross Sea. On February 7, however, according to a fairly good noon observation, we were well to the north of Cape Adare, and therefore beyond the limits of the Antarctic Continent. On the way northward we passed Cape Adare at a distance hardly greater than could have been covered with a good day's sailing; but our desire of making this detour had to give way to the chief consideration – northward, northward as quickly as possible.

There is usually plenty of wind in the neighbourhood of bold promontories, and Cape Adare is no exception in this respect; it is well known as a centre of bad weather. Nor did we slip by without getting a taste of this; but it could not have been more welcome, as it happened that the wind was going the same way as ourselves. Two days of fresh south-east wind took us comparatively quickly past the Balleny Islands, and on February 9 we could congratulate ourselves on being well out of the south frigid zone. It was with joy that we had crossed the Antarctic Circle over a year ago, going south; perhaps we rejoiced no less at crossing it this time in the opposite direction.

In the bustle of getting away from our winter-quarters there had been no time for any celebration of the fortunate reunion of the land and sea parties. As this occasion for festivity had been let slip, we had to look out for another, and we agreed that the day of our passage from the frigid to the temperate zone afforded a very good excuse. The pre-arranged part of the programme was extremely simple: an extra cup of coffee, duly accompanied by punch and cigars, and some music on the gramophone. Our worthy gramophone could not offer anything that had the interest of novelty to us nine who had wintered at Framheim: we knew the whole repertoire pretty well by heart; but the well-known melodies awakened memories of many a pleasant Saturday evening around the toddy table in our cosy winter home down at the head of the Bay of Whales – memories which we need not be ashamed of recalling. On board the *Fram* gramophone music had not been heard since Christmas Eve, 1910, and the members of the sea party were glad enough to encore more than one number.

Outside the limits of the programme we were treated to an extra number by a singer, who imitated the gramophone in utilizing a big megaphone, to make up for the deficiencies of his voice – according to his own statement. He hid behind the curtain of Captain Nilsen's cabin, and through the megaphone came a ditty intended to describe life on the Barrier from its humorous side. It was completely successful, and we again had a laugh that did us good. Performances of this kind, of course, only have a value to those who have taken part in or are acquainted with the events to which they refer. In case any outsider may be interested in seeing what our entertainment was like, a few of the verses are given here.

It must be remarked that the author composed his production in the supposition that we should be able to meet by Christmas, and he therefore proposed that for the moment we should imagine ourselves to be celebrating that festival. We made no difficulty about acceding to his request:

Well, here we are assembled to jollity once more, Some from off the ocean and the rest from off the shore. A year has passed since last we met and all are safe and sound, Then let us banish all our cares and join our hands all round. Christmas, happy Christmas! let us pass the flowing bowl, Fill your glasses all, and let's make "Sails" a wee bit full. For all I'll say is this – that it's in his country's cause; If he staggers just a little, it is in his country's cause.

Now you sailor boys shall hear about the time we have gone through: The winter – well, it wasn't long, we had so much to do. There was digging snow, and sleeping – you can bet we're good at that – And eating, too – no wonder that we're all a little fat. We had hot cakes for our breakfast and "hermetik" each day, Mutton pies, ragouts and curries, for that is Lindström's way. But all I'll say is this – that 'twas in our country's cause, If we stuffed ourselves with dainties, it was in our country's cause.

September came and off we went – that trip was pretty tough; Our compasses all went on strike, they thought it cold enough. The brandy in the Captain's flask froze to a lump of ice; We all agreed, both men and dogs, such weather wasn't nice. So back we went to Framheim to thaw our heels and toes; It could not be quite healthy when our feet and fingers froze. But all I say is this – that 'twas in our country's cause, And we did not mind a frost-bite when 'twas in our country's cause.

The sun came up and warmed us then a little day by day; Five men went out again and toiled along the southern way. This time they conquered snow and ice, and all the world may hear That Norway's flag flies at the Pole. Now, boys, a ringing cheer For him who led

them forward through the mountains and the plain, Up to the goal
they aimed at, and safely back again. But all I'll say is this – that
'twas in his country's cause; If he went through and won the Pole,
'twas in his country's cause.

It could soon be noticed, in one way and another, that we
had reached latitudes where existence took a very different aspect from what we had been accustomed to south of the 66th
parallel. One welcome change was the rise in temperature; the
mercury now climbed well above freezing-point, and those individuals on board who were still more or less clad in skins,
shed the last remnants of their Polar garb for a lighter and more
convenient costume. Those who waited longest before making
the change were the ones who belonged to the shore party. The
numerous people who imagine that a long stay in the Polar regions makes a man less susceptible of cold than other mortals
are completely mistaken. The direct opposite is more likely to
be the case. A man who stays some time in a place where the
everyday temperature is down in the fifties below zero, or more
than that, will not trouble himself greatly about the cold, so
long as he has good and serviceable skin clothing. Let the same
man, rigged out in civilized clothes, be suddenly put down in
the streets of Christiania on a winter day, with thirty or thirty-
five degrees of frost, and the poor fellow's teeth will chatter till
they fall out of his mouth. The fact is, that on a Polar trip one
defends oneself effectively against the cold; when one comes
back, and has to go about with the protection afforded by an
overcoat, a stiff collar, and a hard hat – well, then one feels it.

A less welcome consequence of the difference in latitude was
the darkening of the nights. It may be admitted that continual

daylight would be unpleasant in the long run ashore, but aboard ship an everlasting day would certainly be preferred, if such a thing could be had. Even if we might now consider that we had done with the principal mass of Antarctic ice, we still had to reckon with its disagreeable outposts – the icebergs. It has already been remarked that a practised look-out man can see the blink of one of the larger bergs a long way off in the dark, but when it is a question of one of the smaller masses of ice, of which only an inconsiderable part rises above the surface, there is no such brightness, and therefore no warning. A little lump like this is just as dangerous as a big berg; you run the same risks in a possible collision of knocking a hole in the bows or carrying away the rigging. In these transitional regions, where the temperature of the water is always very low, the thermometer is a very doubtful guide.

The waters in which we were sailing are not yet so well known as to exclude the possibility of meeting with land. Captain Colbeck, who commanded one of the relief ships sent south during Scott's first expedition, came quite unexpectedly upon a little island to the east of Cape Adare; this island was afterwards named after Captain Scott. When Captain Colbeck made his discovery, he was about on the course that has usually been taken by ships whose destination was within the limits of Ross Sea. There is still a possibility that in going out of one's course, voluntarily or involuntarily, one may find more groups of islands in that part.

On the current charts of the South Pacific there are marked several archipelagoes and islands, the position of which is not a little doubtful. One of these – Emerald Island – is charted as lying almost directly in the course we had to follow to reach Hobart. Captain Davis, who took Shackleton's ship, the *Nimrod*, home to England in 1909, sailed, however, right over the point where Emerald Island should be found according to the chart without seeing anything of it. If it exists at all, it is, at any rate, incorrectly charted. In order to avoid its vicinity, and still more in order to get as far as possible to the west before we came into the westerly belt proper, we pressed on as much as we could for one hard week, or perhaps nearer two; but a continual northwest wind seemed for a long time to leave us only two disagreeable possibilities, either of drifting to the eastward, or of finding ourselves down in the drift-ice to the north of Wilkes Land.

Those weeks were a very severe trial of patience to the many on board who were burning with eagerness to get ashore with our news, and perhaps to hear some in return. When the first three weeks of February were past, we were not much more than half-way; with anything like favourable conditions we ought to have arrived by that time. The optimists always consoled us by saying that sooner or later there would be a change for the better, and at last it came. A good spell of favourable wind took us at a bound well to the windward both of the doubtful Emerald Island and of the authentic Macquarie group to the north of it. It may be mentioned in passing, that at the time we went by, the most southerly wireless telegraphy station in the world was located on one of the Macquarie Islands. The installation belonged to Dr. Mawson's Antarctic expedition. Dr. Mawson also took with him apparatus for installing a station on the Antarctic Continent itself, but, so far as is known, no connection was accomplished the first year.

During this fortunate run we had come so far to the west that our course to Hobart was rapidly approaching true north. On the other hand, we should have liked to be able to take advantage of the prevailing winds, – the westerlies. These vary little from one year to another, and we found them much the same as we had been accustomed to before: frequent, stiff breezes from the north-west, which generally held for about twelve hours, and then veered to west or south-west. So long as the north-wester was blowing, there was nothing to do but to lie to with shortened sail; when the change of wind came, we made a few hours' progress in the right direction. In this way we crept step by step northward to our destination. It was slow enough, no doubt; but every day the line of our course on the chart grew a little longer, and towards the end of February the distance between us and the southern point of Tasmania had shrunk to very modest dimensions.

With the constant heavy westerly swell, the *Fram*, light as she now was, surpassed herself in rolling, and that is indeed saying a great deal. This rolling brought us a little damage to the rigging, the gaff of the mainsail breaking; however, that affair did not stop us long. The broken spar was quickly replaced by a spare gaff. Our hopes of arriving before the end of February came to naught, and a quarter of March went by before our voyage was at an end.

On the afternoon of March 4, we had our first glimpse of land; but, as the weather was by no means clear and we had not been able to determine our longitude with certainty for two days, we were uncertain which point of Tasmania we had before us. To explain the situation, a short description of the coast-line is necessary. The southern angle of Tasmania runs out in three promontories; off the easternmost of these, and only divided from it by a very narrow channel, lies a steep and apparently inaccessible island, called Tasman Island. It is, however, accessible, for on the top of it – 900 feet above the sea – stands a lighthouse. The middle promontory is called Tasman Head, and between this and the eastern one we have Storm Bay, which forms the approach to Hobart; there, then, lay our course. The question was, which of the three heads we had sighted. This was difficult, or rather impossible, to decide, so indistinct was the outline of the land in the misty air; it was also entirely unknown to us, as not one of us had ever before been in this corner of the world. When darkness came on, a heavy rain set in, and without being able to see anything at all, we lay there feeling our way all night. With the appearance of daylight a fresh southwest wind came and swept away most of the rain, so that we could again make out the land. We decided that what we saw was the middle promontory, Tasman Head, and gaily set our course into Storm Bay – as we thought. With the rapidly strengthening breeze we went spinningly, and the possibility of reaching Hobart in a few hours began to appear as a dead certainty. With this comfortable feeling we had just sat down to the breakfast table in the fore-saloon, when the door was pulled open with what seemed unnecessary violence, and the face of the officer of the watch appeared in the doorway. "We're on the wrong side of the head," was the sinister message, and the face disappeared. Good-bye to our pleasant plans, good-bye to our breakfast! All hands went on deck at once, and it was seen only too well that the melancholy information was correct. We had made a mistake in the thick rain. The wind, that had now increased to a stiff breeze, had chased the rain-clouds from the tops of the hills, and on the point we had taken for Tasman Head, we now saw the lighthouse. It was therefore Tasman Island, and instead of being in Storm Bay, we were out in the open Pacific, far to leeward of the infamous headland.

There was nothing to be done but to beat and attempt to work our way back to windward, although we knew it would be practically labour in vain. The breeze increased to a gale, and instead of making any headway we had every prospect of drifting well to leeward; that was the usual result of trying to beat with the *Fram*. Rather annoyed though we were, we set to work to do what could be done, and with every square foot of canvas set the *Fram* pitched on her way close-hauled. To begin with, it looked as if we held our own more or less, but as the distance from land increased and the wind got more force, our bearings soon showed us that we were going the way the hen kicks. About midday we went about and stood in towards land again; immediately after came a violent squall which tore the outer jib to ribbons; with that we were also obliged to take in the mainsail, otherwise it would pretty soon have been caught aback, and there would have been further damage to the rigging. With the remaining sails any further attempt was useless; there was nothing left but to get as close under the lee of the land as we could and try with the help of the engine to hold our own till the weather moderated. How it blew that afternoon! One gust after another came dancing down the slopes of the hills, and tore at the rigging till the whole vessel shook. The feeling on board was, as might be expected, somewhat sultry, and found an outlet in various expressions the reverse of gentle. Wind, weather, fate, and life in general were inveighed against, but this availed little. The peninsula that separated us from Storm Bay still lay there firm and immovable, and the gale went on as if it was in no hurry to let us get round. The whole day went by, and the greater part of the night, without any change taking place. Not till the morning of the 6th did our prospects begin to improve. The wind became lighter and went more to the south; that was, of course, the way we had to go, but by hugging the shore, where we had perfectly smooth water, we succeeded in working our way down to Tasman Island before darkness fell. The night brought a calm, and that gave us our chance. The engine worked furiously, and a slight favourable current contributed to set us on our way. By dawn on the 7th we were far up Storm Bay and could at last consider ourselves masters of the situation.

It was a sunny day, and our faces shone in rivalry with the sun; all trace of the last two days' annoyances had vanished. And soon the *Fram*, too, began to shine. The white paint on deck had a thorough overhauling with soap and water in strong solution. The Ripolin was again as fresh as when new. When this had been seen to, the outward appearance of the men also began to undergo a striking change. The Iceland jackets and "blanket costumes" from Horten gave way to "shore clothes" of the most varied cut, hauled out after a two years' rest; razors and scissors had made a rich harvest, and sailmaker Rönne's fashionable Burberry caps figured on most heads. Even Lindström, who up to date had held the position among the land party of being its heaviest, fattest, and blackest member, showed unmistakable signs of having been in close contact with water.

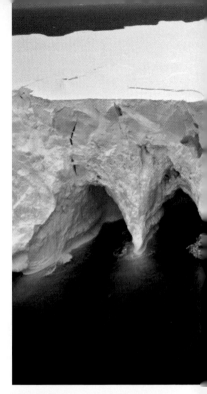

I *A helicopter lands on a snow-covered island near the Antarctic Peninsula.*
(© Bill Curtsinger)

II bottom *On Signy Island, a scientist is surveying near an arch-shaped iceberg.*
(© Rick Price/Corbis)

II-III *An iceberg extends its frozen "roots" into the sea like sharp claws.*
(© Winfred Wisniewski/Corbis)

III bottom *The inventive shape of the walls of this ice formation, off Signy Island, is due to the action of wind and weather.*
(© Rick Price/Corbis)

III

IV-V *Things have changed since Amundsen's era, and
today those who venture to the frozen expanses of
Antarctica use high-tech equipment and clothing.*
(© Paul A. Souders/Corbis)

V top *Sheets of ice float on the calm surface
of the Antarctic Sea.*
(© Tui De Roy/Hedgehog House)

V bottom *An iceberg rises like a rocky wall over the
Antarctic Sea, appearing here as a vast, frozen expanse.*
(© Kerry Lorimer/Hedgehog House)

VI-VII *Adélie penguins open their wings as they get ready to dive into the sea
near Ross Island, where they breed.*

VII top *A penguin dives from an iceberg, creating a spectacular kaleidoscope of spray,
water and ice, and the contrasting colors of its coat.*
(All photographs © Tim Davis/Corbis)

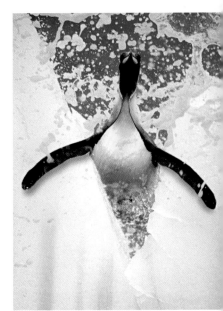

VII bottom and VIII *After extended dives, Weddell seals rise from the sea depths to the frozen surface, using cracks and blowholes to breathe.*
(VII © Colin Monteath/ Hegdehog House; VIII © Bill Curtsinger)

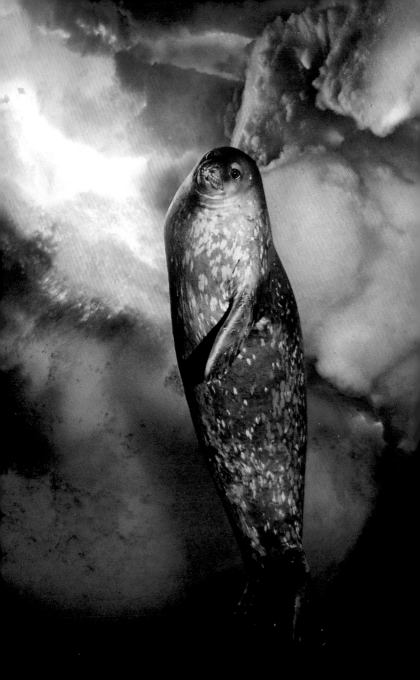

Meanwhile we were nearing a pilot station, and a bustling little motor launch swung alongside. "Want a pilot, captain?" One positively started at the sound of the first new human voice. Communication with the outer world was again established. The pilot – a brisk, good-humoured old man – looked about him in surprise when he came up on to our deck. "I should never have imagined things were so clean and bright on board a Polar ship," he said; "nor should I have thought from the look of you that you had come from Antarctica. You look as if you had had nothing but a good time." We could assure him of that, but as to the rest, it was not our intention just yet to allow ourselves to be pumped, and the old man could see that. He had no objection to our pumping him, though he had no very great store of news to give us. He had heard nothing of the *Terra Nova*; on the other hand, he was able to tell us that Dr. Mawson's ship, the *Aurora*, commanded by Captain Davis, might be expected at Hobart any day. They had been looking out for the *Fram* since the beginning of February, and had given us up long ago. That was a surprise, anyhow.

Our guest evidently had no desire to make the acquaintance of our cuisine; at any rate, he very energetically declined our invitation to breakfast. Presumably he was afraid of being treated to dog's flesh or similar original dishes. On the other hand, he showed great appreciation of our Norwegian tobacco. He had his handbag pretty nearly full when he left us.

Hobart Town lies on the bank of the Derwent River, which runs into Storm Bay. The surroundings are beautiful, and the soil evidently extremely fertile; but woods and fields were almost burnt up on our arrival; a prolonged drought had prevailed, and made an end of all green things. To our eyes it was, however, an unmixed delight to look upon meadows and woods, even if their colours were not absolutely fresh. We were not very difficult to please on that score.

The harbour of Hobart is an almost ideal one, large and remarkably well protected. As we approached the town, the usual procession of harbour-master, doctor, and Custom-house officers came aboard. The doctor soon saw that there was no work for his department, and the Custom-house officers were easily convinced that we had no contraband goods. The anchor was dropped, and we were free to land. I took my cablegrams, and accompanied the harbour-master ashore.

CHAPTER 15

THE EASTERN SLEDGE JOURNEY
by Lieutenant K. Prestrud

On October 20, 1911, the southern party started on their long journey. The departure took place without much ceremony, and with the smallest possible expenditure of words. A hearty grasp of the hand serves the purpose quite as well on such occasions. I accompanied them to the place we called the starting-point, on the south side of the bay. After a final "Good luck" to our Chief and comrades – as sincere a wish as I have ever bestowed upon anyone – I cinematographed the caravan, and very soon after it was out of sight. Those fellows went southward at a great pace, Helmer Hanssen's quick-footed team leading as usual.

There I stood, utterly alone, and I cannot deny that I was a prey to somewhat mixed feelings. When should we see those five again, who had just disappeared from view on the boundless plain, and in what conditions? What sort of a report would they bring of the result? There was plenty of room for guesses here, and abundant opportunity for weighing every possibility, good and bad; but there was very little to be gained by indulging in speculations of that sort. The immediate facts first claimed attention. One fact, amongst others, was that Framheim was a good three miles away; another was that the cinematograph apparatus weighed a good many pounds; and a third that Lindström would be mightily put out if I arrived too late for dinner. Our chef insisted on a high standard of punctuality in the matter of meal-times. Homeward, then, at the best speed possible. The speed, however, was not particularly good, and I began to prepare for the consequences of a long delay. On the other side of the bay I could just make out a little black speck, that seemed to be in motion towards me. I thought at first it was a seal, but, fortunately, it turned out to be Jörgen Stubberud with six dogs and a sledge. This was quite encouraging: in the first place, I should get rid of my unmanageable burden, and in the second I might expect to get on faster. Stubberud's team consisted, however, of four intractable puppies, besides Puss and another courser of similar breed; the result was that our pace was a modest one and our course anything but straight, so that we arrived at Framheim two hours after the time appointed for dinner. Those who know anything of Master Lindström and his disposition will easily be able from this explanation to form an idea of his state of mind at the moment when we entered the door. Yes, he was undoubtedly angry, but we were at least equally hungry; and if anything can soften the heart of a Norwegian caterer, it is a ravenous appetite in those he has to feed, provided, of course, that he have enough to offer them, and Lindström's supplies were practically unlimited.

I remember that dinner well: at the same table where eight of us had sat for so many months, there were now only three left – Johansen, Stubberud, and I. We had more room, it is true, but that gain was a poor satisfaction. We missed those who had gone very badly, and our thoughts were always following them.

The first thing we discussed on this occasion was how many miles they might be expected to do that day: nor was this the last dispute we had on the same theme. During the weeks and months that followed, it was constantly to the fore, and gave plenty of material for conversation when we had exhausted our own concerns. As regards these latter, my instructions were:

1. To go to King Edward VII. Land, and there carry out what exploration time and circumstances might permit.

2. To survey and map the Bay of Whales and its immediate surroundings.

3. As far as possible to keep the station at Framheim in order, in case we might have to spend another winter there.

As regards time, my orders were to be back at Framheim before we could reasonably expect the arrival of the *Fram*. This was, and would necessarily remain, somewhat uncertain. No doubt we all had a great idea of the *Fram*'s capacity for keeping time, and Lieutenant Nilsen had announced his intention of being back by Christmas or the New Year; but nevertheless a year is a long time, and there are many miles in a trip round the world. If we assumed that no mishap had occurred to the *Fram* and that she had left Buenos Aires at the time fixed in the plan – October 1, 1911 – she would in all probability be able to arrive at the Bay of Whales about the middle of January, 1912. On the basis of this calculation we decided, if possible, to get the sledge journey to King Edward Land done before Christmas, while the surveying work around the bay would have to be postponed to the first half of January, 1912. I thought, however, seeing the advantages of working while the bay was still frozen over, that it would pay to devote a few days – immediately following the departure of the southern party – to the preparatory work of measuring. But this did not pay at all. We had reckoned without the weather, and in consequence were well taken in. When one thinks over it afterwards, it seems reasonable enough that the final victory of mild weather over the remains of the Antarctic winter cannot be accomplished without serious disturbances of the atmospheric conditions. The expulsion of one evil has to be effected by the help of another; and the weather was bad with a vengeance. During the two weeks that followed October 20 there were only three or four days that offered any chance of working with the theodolite and plane-table. We managed to get a base-line measured, 1,000 metres long, and to lay out the greater part of the east side of the bay, as well as the most prominent points round the camp; but one had positively to snatch one's opportunities by stealth, and every excursion ended regularly in bringing the instruments home well covered with snow.

If the bad weather thus put hindrances in the way of the work we were anxious to do, it made up for it by providing us with a lot of extra work which we could very well have done without. There was incessant shovelling of snow to keep any sort of passage open to the four dog-tents that were left standing, as well as to our own underground dwelling, over which the snow covering had been growing constantly higher. The fairly high wall that we had originally built on the east side of the entrance door was now entirely buried in the snow-drift. It had given us good protection; now the drift had unimpeded access, and the opening, like the descent into a cellar, that led down to the door, was filled up in the course of a few hours when the wind was in the right quarter. Lindström shook his head when we sometimes asked him how he would get on by himself if the weather continued in this way. "So long as there's nothing but snow in the way, I'll manage to get out," said he. One day he came and told us that he could no longer get at the coal, and on further investigation it looked rather difficult. The roof of the place where the coal was stored had yielded to the pressure of the mass of snow, and the whole edifice had collapsed. There was nothing to be done but to set to work at once, and after a great deal of hard labour we got the remainder of the precious fuel moved into the long snow tunnel that led from the house to the coal-store. With that our "black diamonds" were in safety for the time being. This job made us about as black as the "diamonds." When we came in the cook, as it happened, had just been doing a big wash on his own account – a comparatively rare event – and there was surprise on both sides. The cook was as much taken aback at seeing us so black as we were at seeing him so clean.

All the snow-shovelling that resulted from the continued bad weather, in conjunction with the necessary preparations for the sledge journey, gave us plenty of occupation, but I will venture to say that none of us would care to go through those days again. We were delayed in our real work, and delay, which is unpleasant enough in any circumstances, was all the more unwelcome down here, where time is so precious. As we only had two sledges on which to transport supplies for three men and sixteen dogs, besides all our outfit, and as on our trip we should have no depots to fall back on, the duration of the journey could not be extended much beyond six weeks. In order to be back again by Christmas, we had, therefore, to leave before the middle of November. It would do no harm, however, to be off before this, and as soon as November arrived we took the first opportunity of disappearing.

On account of getting on the right course, we preferred that the start should take place in clear weather. The fact was that we were obliged to go round by the depot in 80° S. As King Edward Land lies to the east, or rather north-east, of Framheim, this was a considerable detour; it had to be made, because in September we had left at this depot all the packed sledging provisions, a good deal of our personal equipment, and, finally, some of the necessary instruments.

On the way to the depot, about thirty geographical miles south of Framheim, we had the nasty crevassed surface that had been met with for the first time on the third depot journey in the autumn of 1911 – in the month of April. At that time we came upon it altogether unawares, and it was somewhat remarkable that we escaped from it with the loss of two dogs. This broken surface lay in a depression about a mile to the west of the route originally marked out; but, however it may have been, it seems ever since that time to have exercised an irresistible attraction. On our first attempt to go south, in September, 1911, we came right into the middle of it, in spite of the fact that it was then perfectly clear. I afterwards heard that in spite of all their efforts, the southern party, on their last trip, landed in this dangerous region, and that one man had a very narrow escape of falling in with sledge and dogs. I had no wish to expose myself to the risk of such accidents – at any rate, while we were on familiar ground. That would have been a bad beginning to my first independent piece of work as a Polar explorer. A day or two of fine weather to begin with would enable us to follow the line originally marked out, and thus keep safe ground under our feet until the ugly place was passed.

In the opening days of November the weather conditions began to improve somewhat; in any case, there was not the continual driving snow. Lindström asked us before we left to bring up a sufficient quantity of seals, to save him that work as long as possible. The supply we had had during the winter was almost exhausted; there was only a certain amount of blubber left. We thought it only fair to accede to his wish, as it is an awkward business to transport those heavy beasts alone, especially when one has only a pack of unbroken puppies to drive. We afterwards heard that Lindström had some amusing experiences with them during the time he was left alone.

Leaving the transport out of the question, this seal-hunting is a very tame sport. An old Arctic hand or an Eskimo would certainly be astounded to see the placid calm with which the Antarctic seal allows itself to be shot and cut up. To them Antarctica would landed in this dangerous region, and that one man had a very narrow escape of falling in with sledge and dogs. I had no wish to expose myself to the risk of such accidents – at any rate, while we were on familiar ground. That would have been a bad beginning to my first independent piece of work as a Polar explorer. A day or two of fine weather to begin with would enable us to follow the line originally marked out, and thus keep safe ground under our feet until the ugly place was passed.

In the opening days of November the weather conditions began to improve somewhat; in any case, there was not the continual driving snow. Lindström asked us before we left to bring up a sufficient quantity of seals, to save him that work as long as possible. The supply we had had during the winter was almost exhausted; there was only a certain amount of blubber left. We thought it only fair to accede to his wish, as it is an awkward business to transport those heavy beasts alone, especially when one has only a pack of unbroken puppies to drive. We afterwards heard that Lindström had some amusing experiences with them during the time he was left alone.

Leaving the transport out of the question, this seal-hunting is a very tame sport. An old Arctic hand or an Eskimo would certainly be astounded to see the placid calm with which the Antarctic seal allows itself to be shot and cut up. To them Antarctica would but it seldom removes itself many yards at a time, for the motions of the seal are just as clumsy and slow on land as they are active and swift in the water. When it has crawled with great pains to a little distance, there is no sign that the interruption has made any lasting impression on it. It looks more as if it took it all as an unpleasant dream or nightmare, which it would be best to sleep off as soon as possible. If one shoots a single seal, this may happen without those lying round so much as raising their heads. Indeed, we could open and cut up a seal right before the noses of its companions without this making the slightest impression on them.

About the beginning of November the seals began to have their young. So far as we could make out, the females kept out of the water for several days without taking any food, until the young one was big enough to be able to go to sea; otherwise, it did not seem that the mothers cared very much for their little ones. Some, it is true, made a sort of attempt to protect their offspring if they were disturbed, but the majority simply left their young ones in the lurch.

As far as we were concerned, we left the females and their young as much as possible in peace. We killed two or three new-born seals to get the skins for our collection. It was another matter with the dogs. With them seal-hunting was far too favourite a sport for the opportunity to be neglected. Against a full-grown seal, however, they could do nothing; its body offered no particularly vulnerable spots, and the thick, tight-fitting skin was too much even for dogs' teeth. The utmost the rascals could accomplish was to annoy and torment the object of their attack. It was quite another matter when the young ones began to arrive. Among this small game the enterprising hunters could easily satisfy their inborn craving for murder, for the scoundrels only killed for the sake of killing; they were not at all hungry, as they had as much food as they liked. Of course, we did all we could to put a stop to this state of things, and so long as there were several of us at the hut, we saw that the whole pack was tied up; but when Lindström was left by himself, he could not manage to hold them fast. His tents were altogether snowed under in the weather that prevailed on the seaboard in December. There were not many dogs left in his charge, but I am afraid those few wrought great havoc among the young seals out on the ice of the bay. The poor mothers could hardly have done anything against a lot of dogs, even if they had been more courageous. Their enemies were too active. For them it was the work of a moment to snatch the young one from the side of its mother, and then they were able to take the poor thing's life undisturbed.

Unfortunately, there were no sea-leopards in the neighbourhood of Framheim. These, which are far quicker in their movements than the Weddell seal, and are, moreover, furnished with a formidable set of teeth, would certainly have made the four-footed seal-hunters more careful in their behaviour.

After we had brought up to the house enough seals' carcasses to keep the ten or twelve dogs that would be left supplied for a good while, and had cut up a sufficient quantity for our own use on the way to 80° S., we took the first opportunity of getting away. Before I pass on to give an account of our trip, I wish to say a few words about my companions – Johansen and Stubberud. It goes without saying that it gave me, as a beginner, a great feeling of security to have with me such a man as Johansen, who possessed many years' experience of all that pertains to sledging expeditions; and as regards Stubberud, I could not have wished for a better travelling companion than him either – a first-rate fellow, steady and efficient in word and deed. As it turned out, we were not to encounter very many difficulties, but one never escapes scot-free on a sledge journey in these regions. I owe my comrades thanks for the way in which they both did their best to smooth our path.

Johansen and Stubberud drove their dog-teams; I myself acted as "forerunner." The drivers had seven dogs apiece. We took so many, because we were not quite sure of what the animals we had were fit for. As was right and proper, the southern party had picked out the best. Among those at our disposal there were several that had previously shown signs of being rather quickly tired. True, this happened under very severe conditions. As it turned out, our dogs exceeded all our expectations in the easier conditions of work that prevailed during the summer. On the first part of the way – as far as the depot in 80° S. – the loads were quite modest. Besides the tent, the sleeping-bags, our personal outfit, and instruments, we only had provisions for eight days-seals' flesh for the dogs, and tinned food for ourselves. Our real supplies were to be taken from the depot, where there was enough of everything.

On November 8 we left Framheim, where in future Lindström was to reside as monarch of all he surveyed. The weather was as fine as could be wished. I was out with the cinematograph apparatus, in order if possible to immortalize the start. To complete the series of pictures, Lindström was to take the forerunner, who was now, be it said, a good way behind those he was supposed to be leading. With all possible emphasis I enjoined Lindström only to give the crank five or six turns, and then started off to catch up the drivers. When I had nearly reached the provision store I pulled up, struck by a sudden apprehension. Yes, I was right on looking back I discovered that incorrigible person still hard at work with the crank, as though he were going to be paid a pound for every yard of film showing the back view of the forerunner. By making threatening gestures with a ski-pole I stopped the too persistent cinematograph, and then went on to join Stubberud, who was only a few yards ahead. Johansen had disappeared like a meteor. The last I saw of him was the soles of his boots, as he quite unexpectedly made an elegant backward somersault off the sledge when it was passing over a little unevenness by the provision store. The dogs, of course, made off at full speed, and Johansen after them like the wind. We all met again safe and sound at the ascent to the Barrier. Here a proper order of march was formed, and we proceeded southward.

The Barrier greeted us with a fresh south wind, that now and then made an attempt to freeze the tip of one's nose; it did not succeed in this, but it delayed us a little. It does not take a great deal of wind on this level plain to diminish the rate of one's progress. But the sun shone too gaily that day to allow a trifle of wind to interfere very much with our enjoyment of life. The surface was so firm that there was hardly a sign of drift-snow. As it was perfectly clear, the mark-flags could be followed the whole time, thus assuring us that, at any rate, the first day's march would be accomplished without any deviation from the right track.

At five o'clock we camped, and when we had fed the dogs and come into the tent we could feel how much easier and pleasanter everything was at this season than on the former journeys in autumn and spring. We could move freely in a con-venient costume; if we wished, there was nothing to prevent our performing all the work of the camp with bare hands and still preserving our finger-tips unharmed. As I had no dog-team to look after, I undertook the duty of attending to our own needs; that is to say, I acted as cook. This occupation also was consid-erably easier now than it had been when the temperature was below -60° F. At that time it took half an hour to turn the snow in the cooker into water; now it was done in ten minutes, and the cook ran no risk whatever of getting his fingers frozen in the process.

Ever since we landed on the Barrier in January, 1911, we had been expecting to hear a violent cannonade as the result of the movement of the mass of ice. We had now lived a whole winter at Framheim without having observed, as far as I know, the slightest sign of a sound. This was one of many indications that the ice round our winter-quarters was not in motion at all.

No one, I believe, had noticed anything of the expected noise on the sledge journeys either, but at the place where we camped on the night of November 8 we did hear it. There was a report about once in two minutes, not exactly loud, but still, there it was. It sounded just as if there was a whole battery of small guns in action down in the depths below us. A few hundred yards to the west of the camp there were a number of small hummocks, which might indicate the presence of crevasses, but otherwise the surface looked safe enough. The small guns kept up a lively crackle all through the night, and combined with a good deal of uproar among the dogs to shorten our sleep. But the first night of a sledge journey is almost always a bad one. Stubberud declared that he could not close his eyes on account of "that filthy row." He probably expected the ice to open and swallow him up every time he heard it. The surface, however, held securely, and we turned out to the finest day one could wish to see. It did not require any very great strength of mind to get out of one's sleeping-bag now. The stockings that had been hung up in the evening could be put on again as dry as a bone; the sun had seen to that. Our ski boots were as soft as ever; there was not a sign of frost on them. It is quite curious to see the behaviour of the dogs when the first head appears through the tent-door in the morning. They greet their lord and master with the most unmistakable signs of joy, although, of course, they must know that his arrival will be followed by many hours of toil, with, perhaps, a few doses of the whip thrown in; but from the moment he begins to handle the sledge, the dogs look as if they had no desire in the world but to get into the harness as soon as possible and start away. On days like this their troubles would be few; with the light load and good going we had no difficulty in covering nineteen geographical miles in eight hours. Johansen's team was on my heels the whole time, and Stubberud's animals followed faithfully behind. From time to time we saw sledge-tracks quite plainly; we also kept the mark-flags in sight all day. In the temperatures we now had to deal with our costume was comparatively light – certainly much lighter than most people imagine; for there is a kind of summer even in Antarctica, although the daily readings of the thermometer at this season would perhaps rather remind our friends at home of what they are accustomed to regard as winter.

In undertaking a sledge journey down there in autumn or spring, the most extraordinary precautions have to be taken to protect oneself against the cold. Skin clothing is then the only thing that is of any use; but at this time of year, when the sun is above the horizon for the whole twenty-four hours, one can go for a long time without being more heavily clad than a lumberman working in the woods. During the march our clothing was usually the following: two sets of woollen underclothes, of which that nearest the skin was quite thin. Outside the shirt we wore either an ordinary waistcoat or a comparatively light knitted woollen jersey. Outside all came our excellent Burberry clothes – trousers and jacket. When it was calm, with full sun-shine, the Burberry jacket was too warm; we could then go all day in our shirt-sleeves. To be provided for emergencies, we all had our thinnest reindeer-skin clothes with us; but, so far as I know, these were never used, except as pillows or mattresses.

The subject of sleeping-bags has no doubt been thoroughly threshed out on every Polar expedition. I do not know how many times we discussed this question, nor can I remember the number of more or less successful patents that were the fruit of these discussions. In any case, one thing is certain, that the ad-herents of one-man bags were in an overwhelming majority, and no doubt rightly. As regards two-man bags, it cannot be denied that they enable their occupants to keep warm longer; but it is always difficult to find room for two big men in one sack, and if the sack is to be used for sleeping in, and one of the big men takes to snoring into the other's ear, the situation may become quite unendurable. In the temperatures we had on the summer journeys there was no difficulty in keeping warm enough with the one-man bags, and they were used by all of us.

On the first southern journey, in September, Johansen and I used a double bag between us; in the intense cold that prevailed at that time we managed to get through the night without freez-ing; but if the weather is so cold that one cannot keep warmth in one's body in good, roomy one-man bags, then it is altogeth-er unfit for sledging journeys.

November 10. – Immediately after the start this morning we tried how we could get on without a forerunner. As long as we were in the line of flags this answered very well; the dogs gal-loped from one flag to another, while I was able to adopt the easy method of hanging on to Stubberud's sledge. About midday we were abreast of the depression already mentioned, where, on the third depot journey last autumn, we ran into a regular net of crevasses. This time we were aware of the danger, and kept to the left; but at the last moment the leading team ran out to the wrong side, and we cut across the eastern part of the dangerous zone. Fortunately it was taken at full gallop. It is quite possible that I inwardly wished we were all a few pounds lighter, as our little caravan raced across those thin snow bridges, through which could be seen the blue colour of the ugly gulfs below. But after the lapse of a few long minutes we could congratulate ourselves on getting over with our full numbers.

Not for anything would I have gone that mile without ski on my feet; it would practically have meant falling in and going out. It is, perhaps, saying a good deal to claim that with ski on, one is absolutely secured against the danger these crevasses present; if misfortunes are abroad, anything may happen. But it would require a very considerable amount of bad luck for man and ski to fall through.

November 11. – In weather like this, going on the march is like going to a dance: tent, sleeping-bags, and clothes keep soft and dry as a bone. The thermometer is about -4° F. A fellow-man suddenly put down in our midst from civilized surroundings would possibly shake his head at so many degrees of frost, but it must be remembered that we have long ago abandoned the ordinary ideas of civilized people as to what is endurable in the way of temperature. We are enthusiastic about the spring-like weather, especially when we remember what it was like down here two months ago, when the thermometer showed - 76° F., and the rime hung an inch thick inside the tent, ready to drop on everything and everybody at the slightest movement. Now there is no rime to be seen; the sun clears it away. For now there is a sun; not the feeble imitation of one that stuck its red face above the northern horizon in August, but our good old acquaintance of lower latitudes, with his wealth of light and warmth.

After two hours' march we came in sight, at ten o'clock in the morning, of the two snow-huts that were built on the last trip. We made straight for them, thinking we might possibly find some trace of the southern party. So we did, though in a very different way from what we expected. We were, perhaps, about a mile off when we all three suddenly halted and stared at the huts. "There are men," said Stubberud. At any rate there was something black that moved, and after confused thoughts of Japanese, Englishmen, and the like had flashed through our minds, we at last got out the glasses. It was not men, but a dog. Well, the presence of a live dog here, seventy-five miles up the Barrier, was in itself a remarkable thing. It must, of course, be one of the southern party's dogs, but how the runaway had kept himself alive all that time was for the present a mystery. On coming to closer quarters we soon found that it was one of Hassel's dogs, Peary by name. He was a little shy to begin with, but when he heard his name he quickly understood that we were friends come on a visit, and no longer hesitated to approach us. He was fat and round, and evidently pleased to see us again. The hermit had lived on the lamentable remains of poor Sara, whom we had been obliged to kill here in September. Sara's lean and frozen body did not seem particularly adapted for making anyone fat, and yet our newly-found friend Peary looked as if he had been feasting for weeks. Possibly he had begun by devouring Neptune, another of his companions, who had also given the southern party the slip on the way to the depot in 80° S. However this may be, Peary's rest cure came to an abrupt conclusion. Stubberud took him and put him in his team.

We had thought of reaching the depot before the close of the day, and this we could easily have done if the good going had continued; but during the afternoon the surface became so loose that the dogs sank in up to their chests, and when – at about six in the evening – the sledge-meter showed twenty-one geographical miles, the animals were so done up that it was no use going on.

At eleven o'clock the next morning – Sunday, November 12 – we reached the depot. Captain Amundsen had promised to leave a brief report when the southern party left here, and the first thing we did on arrival was, of course, to search for the document in the place agreed upon. There were not many words on the little slip of paper, but they gave us the welcome intelligence: "All well so far."

We had expected that the southern party's dogs would have finished the greater part, if not the whole, of the seal meat that was laid down here in April; but fortunately this was not the case. There was a great quantity left, so that we could give our own dogs a hearty feed with easy consciences. They had it, too, and it was no trifling amount that they got through. The four days' trot from Framheim had been enough to produce an unusual appetite. There was a puppy in Johansen's team that was exposed for the first time in his life to the fatigues of a sledge journey. This was a plucky little chap that went by the name of Lillegut. The sudden change from short commons to abundance was too much for his small stomach, and the poor puppy lay shrieking in the snow most of the afternoon.

We also looked after ourselves that day, and had a good meal of fresh seal meat; after that we supplied ourselves from the large stores that lay here with the necessary provisions for a sledge journey of five weeks: three cases of dogs' pemmican, one case of men's pemmican, containing ninety rations, 20 pounds of dried milk, 55 pounds of oatmeal biscuits, and three tins of malted milk, besides instruments, Alpine rope, and clothing. The necessary quantity of chocolate had been brought with us from *Fram* heim, as there was none of this to spare out in the field. Our stock of paraffin was 6 1/2 gallons, divided between two tanks, one on each sledge. Our cooking outfit was exactly the same as that used by the southern party.

The instruments we carried were a theodolite, a hypsometer, two aneroids, one of which was no larger than an ordinary watch, two thermometers, one chronometer watch, one ordinary watch, and one photographic camera (Kodak 3 x 3 inches), adapted for using either plates or films. We had three spools of film, and one dozen plates.

Our medical outfit was exceedingly simple. It consisted of nothing but a box of laxative pills, three small rolls of gauze bandage, and a small pair of scissors, which also did duty for beard-cutting. Both pills and gauze were untouched when we returned; it may therefore be safely said that our state of health during the journey was excellent.

While the drivers were packing and lashing their loads, which now weighed nearly 600 pounds, I wrote a report to the Chief, and took an azimuth observation to determine the direction of our course. According to our instructions we should really have taken a north-easterly course from here; but as our dogs seemed to be capable of more and better work than we had expected, and as there was believed to be a possibility that bare land was to be found due east of the spot where we were, it was decided to make an attempt in that direction.

Our old enemy the fog had made its appearance in the course of the night, and now hung, grey and disgusting, under the sky, when we broke camp at the depot on the morning of November 13. However, it was not so bad as to prevent our following the flags that marked the depot on the east.

My duty as forerunner was immediately found to be considerably lighter than before. With the greatly increased weight behind them the dogs had all they could do to follow, if I went at an ordinary walking pace. At 11 a.m. we passed the easternmost flag, at five geographical miles from the depot, and then we found ourselves on untrodden ground. A light southerly breeze appeared very opportunely and swept away the fog; the sun again shed its light over the Barrier, which lay before us, shining and level, as we had been accustomed to see it. There was, however, one difference: with every mile we covered there was the possibility of seeing something new. The going was excellent, although the surface was rather looser than one could have wished. The skis flew over it finely, of course, while dogs' feet and sledge-runners sank in. I hope I shall never have to go here without skis; that would be a terrible punishment; but with skis on one's feet and in such weather it was pure enjoyment.

Meanwhile the new sights we expected were slow in coming. We marched for four days due east without seeing a sign of change in the ground; there was the same undulating surface that we knew so well from previous expeditions. The readings of the hypsometer gave practically the same result day after day; the ascent we were looking for failed to appear.

Stubberud, who for the first day or two after leaving the depot had been constantly stretching himself on tiptoe and looking out for mountain-tops, finally gave it as his heartfelt conviction that this King Edward Land we were hunting for was only a confounded "Flyaway Land," which had nothing to do with reality. We others were not yet quite prepared to share this view; for my own part, in any case, I was loth to give up the theory that assumed a southward continuation of King Edward Land along the 158th meridian; this theory had acquired a certain force during the winter, and was mainly supported by the fact that on the second depot journey we had seen, between the 81st and 82nd parallels, some big pressure-ridges, which suggested the presence of bare land in a south-easterly direction.

On November 16 we found ourselves at the 158th meridian, but on every side the eye encountered the level, uninterrupted snow surface and nothing else. Should we go on? It was tempting enough, as the probability was that sooner or later we should come upon something; but there was a point in our instructions that had to be followed, and it said: Go to the point where land is marked on the chart. This point was now about 120 geographical miles to the north of us. Therefore, instead of going on to the east in uncertainty, we decided to turn to the left and go north. The position of the spot where we altered our course was determined, and it was marked by a snow beacon 7 feet high, on the top of which was placed a tin box containing a brief report.

On that part of the way which we now had before us there was little prospect of meeting with surprises; nor did any fall to our lot. In day's marches that varied from seventeen to twenty geographical miles, we went forward over practically level ground. The nature of the surface was at first ideal; but as we came farther north and thus nearer to the sea, our progress was impeded by a great number of big snow-waves (sastrugi), which had probably been formed during the long period of bad weather that preceded our departure from Framheim. We did not escape damage on this bad surface. Stubberud broke the forward part of the spare ski he had lashed under his sledge, and Johansen's sledge also suffered from the continual bumping against the hard sastrugi. Luckily he had been foreseeing enough to bring a little hickory bar, which came in very handy as a splint for the broken part.

As we were now following the direction of the meridian, or in other words, as our course was now true north, the daily observations of latitude gave a direct check on the readings of the sledge-meter. As a rule they agreed to the nearest minute. Whilst I was taking the noon altitude my companions had the choice of standing by the side of their sledges and eating their lunch, or setting the tent and taking shelter. They generally chose the latter alternative, making up for it by going an hour longer in the afternoon. Besides the astronomical observations, the barometric pressure, temperature, force and direction of the wind, and amount of cloud were noted three times daily; every evening a hypsometer reading was taken.

If I were to undertake the description of a long series of days like those that passed while we were travelling on the flat Barrier, I am afraid the narrative would be strikingly reminiscent of the celebrated song of a hundred and twenty verses, all with the same rhyme. One day was very much like another. One would think that this monotony would make the time long, but the direct opposite was the case. I have never known time fly so rapidly as on these sledge journeys, and seldom have I seen men more happy and contented with their existence than we three, when after a successful day's march we could set about taking our simple meal, with a pipe of cut plug to follow. The bill of fare was identically the same every day, perhaps a fault in the eyes of many; variety of diet is supposed to be the thing. Hang variety, say I; appetite is what matters. To a man who is really hungry it is a very subordinate matter what he shall eat; the main thing is to have something to satisfy his hunger.

After going north for seven days, we found that according to observations and sledge-meter we ought to be in the neighbourhood of the sea. This was correct. My diary for November 23 reads:

"To-day we were to see something besides sky and snow. An hour after breaking camp this morning two snowy petrels came sailing over us; a little while later a couple of skua gulls. We welcomed them as the first living creatures we had seen since leaving winter-quarters. The constantly increasing 'water-sky' to the north had long ago warned us that we were approaching the sea; the presence of the birds told us it was not far off. The skua gulls settled very near us, and the dogs, no doubt taking them for baby seals, were of course ready to break the line of march, and go off hunting, but their keenness soon passed when they discovered that the game had wings.

"The edge of the Barrier was difficult to see, and, profiting by previous experience of how easy it is to go down when the light is bad, we felt our way forward step by step. At four o'clock we thought we could see the precipice. A halt was made at a safe distance, and I went in advance to look over. To my surprise I found that there was open water right in to the wall of ice. We had expected the sea-ice to extend a good way out still, seeing it was so early in summer; but there lay the sea, almost free of ice as far as the horizon. Black and threatening it was to look at, but still a beneficent contrast to the everlasting snow surface on which we had now tramped for 300 geographical miles.

The perpendicular drop of 100 feet that forms the boundary between the dead Barrier and the sea, with its varied swarm of life, is truly an abrupt and imposing transition. The panorama from the top of the ice-wall is always grand, and it can be beautiful as well. On a sunny day, or still more on a moonlit night, it has a fairylike beauty. To-day a heavy, black sky hung above a still blacker sea, and the ice-wall, which shines in the light with a dazzling white purity, looked more like an old white-washed wall than anything else. There was not a breath of wind; the sound of the surf at the bottom of the precipice now and then reached my ears – this was the only thing that broke the vast silence. One's own dear self becomes so miserably small in these mighty surroundings; it was a sheer relief to get back to the company of my comrades."

As things now were, with open water up to the Barrier itself, our prospect of getting seals here at the edge of the ice seemed a poor one. Next morning, however, we found, a few miles farther east, a bay about four miles long, and almost entirely enclosed. It was still frozen over, and seals were lying on the ice by the dozen. Here was food enough to give both ourselves and the dogs an extra feed and to replenish our supplies. We camped and went off to examine the ground more closely. There were plenty of crevasses, but a practicable descent was found, and in a very short time three full-grown seals and a fat young one were despatched. We hauled half a carcass up to the camp with the Alpine rope. As we were hard at work dragging our spoil up the steep slope, we heard Stubberud sing out, "Below, there!" – and away he went like a stone in a well. He had gone through the snow-bridge on which we were standing, but a lucky projection stopped our friend from going very far down, besides which he had taken a firm round turn with the rope round his wrist. It was, therefore, a comparatively easy matter to get him up on the surface again. This little intermezzo would probably have been avoided if we had not been without our ski, but the slope was so steep and smooth that we could not use them. After a few more hauls we had the seal up by the tent, where a large quantity of it disappeared in a surprisingly short time down the throats of fifteen hungry dogs.

The ice of the bay was furrowed by numerous leads, and while the hunters were busy cutting up the seals, I tried to get a sounding, but the thirty fathoms of Alpine rope I had were not enough; no bottom was reached. After having something to eat we went down again, in order if possible to find out the depth.

This time we were better supplied with sounding tackle two reels of thread, a marlinspike, and our geological hammer.

First the marlinspike was sent down with the thread as a line. An inquisitive lout of a seal did all it could to bite through the thread, but whether this was too strong or its teeth too poor, we managed after a lot of trouble to coax the marlinspike up again, and the interfering rascal, who had to come up to the surface now and then to take breath, got the spike of a ski-pole in his thick hide. This unexpected treatment was evidently not at all to his liking, and after acknowledging it by a roar of disgust, he vanished into the depths. Now we got on better. The marlinspike sank and sank until it had drawn with it 130 fathoms of thread. A very small piece of seaweed clung to the thread as we hauled it in again; on the spike there was nothing to be seen. As its weight was rather light for so great a depth – a possible setting of current might have carried it a little to one side – we decided to try once more with the hammer, which was considerably heavier, in order to check the result. The hammer, on the other hand, was so heavy, that with the delicate thread as a line the probability of successfully carrying out the experiment seemed small, but we had to risk it. The improvised sinker was well smeared with blubber, and this time it sank so rapidly to the bottom as to leave no doubt of the correctness of the sounding – 130 fathoms again. By using extreme care we succeeded in getting the hammer up again in safety, but no specimen of the bottom was clinging to it.

On the way back to camp we dragged with us the carcass of the young seal. It was past three when we got into our sleeping-bags that night, and, in consequence, we slept a good deal later than usual the next morning. The forenoon was spent by Johansen and Stubberud in hauling up another seal from the bay and packing as much flesh on the sledges as possible. As fresh meat is a commodity that takes up a great deal of space in proportion to its weight, the quantity we were able to take with us was not large. The chief advantage we had gained was that a considerable supply could be stored on the spot, and it might be useful to fall back upon in case of delay or other mishaps.

I took the observation for longitude and latitude, found the height by hypsometer, and took some photographs. After laying down the depot and erecting beacons, we broke camp at 3 p.m. South of the head of the bay there were a number of elevations and pressure masses, exactly like the formations to be found about Framheim. To the east a prominent ridge appeared, and with the glass it could be seen to extend inland in a south-easterly direction. According to our observations this must be the same that Captain Scott has marked with land-shading on his chart.

We made a wide detour outside the worst pressure-ridges, and then set our course east-north-east towards the ridge just mentioned. It was a pretty steep rise, which was not at all a good thing for the dogs. They had overeaten themselves shockingly, and most of the seal's flesh came up again. So that their feast should not be altogether wasted, we stopped as soon as we had come far enough up the ridge to be able to regard the surface as comparatively safe; for in the depression round the bay it was somewhat doubtful.

On the following morning – Sunday, November 26 – there was a gale from the north-east with sky and Barrier lost in driving snow. That put an end to our plans of a long Sunday march. In the midst of our disappointment I had a sudden bright idea. It was Queen Maud's birthday! If we could not go on, we could at least celebrate the day in a modest fashion. In one of the provision cases there was still a solitary Stavanger tin, containing salt beef and peas. It was opened at once, and its contents provided a banquet that tasted better to us than the most carefully chosen menu had ever done. In this connection I cannot help thinking of the joy it would bring to many a household in this world if its master were possessed of an appetite like ours. The wife would then have no need to dread the consequences, however serious the shortcomings of the cuisine might be. But to return to the feast. Her Majesty's health was drunk in a very small, but, at the same time, very good tot of aquavit, served in enamelled iron mugs. Carrying alcohol was, of course, against regulations, strictly speaking; but, as everyone knows, prohibition is not an easy thing to put into practice. Even in Antarctica this proved to be the case. Lindström had a habit of sending a little surprise packet with each sledging party that went out, and on our departure he had handed us one of these, with the injunction that the packet was only to be opened on some festive occasion; we chose as such Her Majesty's birthday. On examination the packet was found to contain a little flask of spirits, in which we at once agreed to drink the Queen's health.

The 27th brought the same nasty weather, and the 28th was not much better, though not bad enough to stop us. After a deal of hard work in hauling our buried belongings out of the snow, we got away and continued our course to the north-eastward. It was not exactly an agreeable morning: a brisk wind with driving snow right in one's face. After trudging against this for a couple of hours I heard Stubberud call "Halt!" – half his team were hanging by the traces in a crevasse. I had gone across without noticing anything; no doubt owing to the snow in my face. One would think the dogs would be suspicious of a place like this; but they are not – they plunge on till the snow-bridge breaks under them. Luckily the harness held, so that it was the affair of a moment to pull the poor beasts up again. Even a dog might well be expected to be a trifle shaken after hanging head downwards over such a fearful chasm; but apparently they took it very calmly, and were quite prepared to do the same thing over again.

For my own part I looked out more carefully after this, and although there were a good many ugly fissures on the remaining part of the ascent, we crossed them all without further incident.

Unpleasant as these crevasses are, they do not involve any direct danger, so long as the weather is clear and the light favourable. One can then judge by the appearance of the surface whether there is danger ahead; and if crevasses are seen in time, there is always a suitable crossing to be found. The case is somewhat different in fog, drift, or when the light is such that the small inequalities marking the course of the crevasse do not show up. This last is often the case in cloudy weather, when even a fairly prominent rise will not be noticed on the absolutely white surface until one falls over it. In such conditions it is safest to feel one's way forward with the ski-pole; though this mode of proceeding is more troublesome than effective.

In the course of the 28th the ascent came to an end, and with it the crevasses. The wind fell quite light, and the blinding drift was succeeded by clear sunshine. We had now come sufficiently high up to have a view of the sea far to the north-west. During the high wind a quantity of ice had been driven southward, so that for a great distance there was no open water to be seen, but a number of huge icebergs. From the distance of the sea horizon we guessed our height to be about 1,000 feet, and in the evening the hypsometer showed the guess to be very nearly right.

November 29. – Weather and going all that could be wished on breaking camp this morning; before us we had a level plateau, which appeared to be quite free from unpleasant obstructions. When we halted for the noon observation the sledge-meter showed ten geographical miles, and before evening we had brought the day's distance up to twenty. The latitude was then 77° 32'. The distance to the Barrier edge on the north was, at a guess, about twenty geographical miles. We were now a good way along the peninsula, the northern point of which Captain Scott named Cape Colbeck, and at the same time a good way to the east of the meridian in which he put land-shading on his chart. Our height above the sea, which was now about 1,000 feet, was evidence enough that we had firm land under us, but it was still sheathed in ice. In that respect the landscape offered no change from what we had learnt to know by the name of "Barrier." It cannot be denied that at this juncture I began to entertain a certain doubt of the existence of bare land in this quarter.

This doubt was not diminished when we had done another good day's march to the eastward on November 30. According to our observations we were then just below the point where the Alexandra Mountains should begin, but there was no sign of mountain ranges; the surface was a little rougher, perhaps. However, it was still too soon to abandon the hope. It would be unreasonable to expect any great degree of accuracy of the chart we had to go by; its scale was far too large for that. It was, moreover, more than probable that our own determination of longitude was open to doubt.

Assuming the approximate accuracy of the chart, by holding on to the north-east we ought soon to come down to the seaboard, and with this object in view we continued our march. On December 1, in the middle of the day, we saw that everything agreed. From the top of an eminence the sea was visible due north, and on the east two domed summits were outlined, apparently high enough to be worthy of the name of mountains. They were covered with snow, but on the north side of them there was an abrupt precipice, in which many black patches showed up sharply against the white background. It was still too soon to form an idea as to whether they were bare rock or not; they might possibly be fissures in the mass of ice. The appearance of the summits agreed exactly with Captain Scott's description of what he saw from the deck of the Discovery in 1902. He assumed that the black patches were rocks emerging from the snow-slopes. As will be seen later, our respected precursor was right.

In order to examine the nature of the seaboard, we began by steering down towards it; but in the meantime the weather underwent an unfavourable change. The sky clouded over and the light became as vile as it could be. The point we were anxious to clear up was whether there was any Barrier wall here, or whether the land and sea-ice gradually passed into each other in an easy slope. As the light was, there might well have been a drop of 100 feet without our seeing anything of it. Securely roped together we made our way down, until our progress was stopped by a huge pressure-ridge, which, as far as could be made out, formed the boundary between land and sea-ice. It was, however, impossible in the circumstances to get any clear view of the surroundings, and after trudging back to the sledges, which had been left up on the slope, we turned to the east to make a closer examination of the summits already mentioned. I went in front, as usual, in the cheerful belief that we had a fairly level stretch before us, but I was far out in my calculation. My ski began to slip along at a terrific speed, and it was advisable to put on the brake. This was easily done as far as I was concerned, but with the dogs it was a different matter. Nothing could stop them when they felt that the sledge was running by its own weight; they went in a wild gallop down the slope, the end of which could not at present be seen. I suppose it will sound like a tall story, but it is a fact, nevertheless, that to our eyes the surface appeared to be horizontal all the time. Snow, horizon and sky all ran together in a white chaos, in which all lines of demarcation were obliterated.

Fortunately nothing came of our expectation that the scamper would have a frightful ending in some insidious abyss. It was stopped quite naturally by an opposing slope, which appeared to be as steep as the one we had just slid down. If the pace had been rather too rapid before, there was now no ground of complaint on that score. Step by step we crawled up to the top of the ridge; but the ground was carefully surveyed before we proceeded farther.

In the course of the afternoon we groped our way forward over a whole series of ridges and intervening depressions. Although nothing could be seen, it was obvious enough that our surroundings were now of an entirely different character from anything we had previously been accustomed to. The two mountain summits had disappeared in the fleecy mist, but the increasing unevenness of the ground showed that we were approaching them. Meanwhile I considered it inadvisable to come to close quarters with them so long as we were unable to use our eyes, and, remembering what happens when the blind leads the blind, we camped. For the first time during the trip I had a touch of snow-blindness that afternoon. This troublesome and rightly dreaded complaint was a thing that we had hitherto succeeded in keeping off by a judicious use of our excellent snow-goggles. Among my duties as forerunner was that of maintaining the direction, and this, at times, involved a very severe strain on the eyes. In thick weather it is only too easy to yield to the temptation of throwing off the protective goggles, with the idea that one can see better without them. Although I knew perfectly well what the consequence would be, I had that afternoon broken the commandment of prudence. The trifling smart I felt in my eyes was cured by keeping the goggles on for a couple of hours after we were in the tent. Like all other ills, snow-blindness may easily be dispelled by taking it in time.

Next morning the sun's disc could just be made out through a veil of thin stratus clouds, and then the light was more or less normal again. As soon as we could see what our surroundings were, it was clear enough that we had done right in stopping the game of blind man's buff we had been playing on the previous day. It might otherwise have had an unpleasant ending. Right across our line of route and about 500 yards from our camp the surface was so broken up that it was more like a sieve than anything else. In the background the masses of snow were piled in huge drifts down a steep slope on the north-west side of the two mountains. It was impossible to take the sledges any farther on the way we had hitherto been following, but in the course of the day we worked round by a long detour to the foot of the most westerly of the mountains. We were then about 1,000 feet above the sea; to the north of us we had the abrupt descent already mentioned, to the south it was quite flat. Our view to the east was shut in by the two mountains, and our first idea was to ascend to the tops of them, but the powers of the weather again opposed us with their full force. A stiff south-east wind set in and increased in the course of half an hour to a regular blizzard. Little as it suited our wishes, there was nothing to be done but to creep back into the tent. For a whole month now we had seen scarcely anything but fair weather, and the advance of summer had given us hopes that it would hold; but just when it suited us least of all came a dismal change.

The light Antarctic summer night ran its course, while the gusts of wind tugged and tore at the thin sides of our tent; no snowfall accompanied the south-easterly wind, but the loose snow of the surface was whirled up into a drift that stood like an impenetrable wall round the tent. After midnight it moderated a little, and by four o'clock there was comparatively fair weather. We were on our feet at once, put together camera, glasses, aneroids, axe, Alpine rope, with some lumps of pemmican to eat on the way, and then went off for a morning walk with the nearer of the two hills as our goal. All three of us went, leaving the dogs in charge of the camp. They were not so fresh now that they would not gladly accept all the rest that was offered them. We had no need to fear any invasion of strangers; the land we had come to appeared to be absolutely devoid of living creatures of any kind.

The hill was farther off and higher than it appeared at first; the aneroid showed a rise of 700 feet when we reached the top. As our camp lay at a height of 1,000 feet, this gave us 1,700 feet as the height of this hill above the sea. The side we went up was covered by névé, which, to judge from the depth of the cracks, must have been immense. As we approached the summit and our view over the surrounding ground became wider, the belief that we should see so much as a crag of this King Edward Land grew weaker and weaker. There was nothing but white on every side, not a single consolatory little black patch, however carefully we looked. And to think that we had been dreaming of great mountain masses in the style of McMurdo Sound, with sunny slopes, penguins by the thousand, seals and all the rest! All these visions were slowly but surely sunk in an endless sea of snow, and when at last we stood on the highest point, we certainly thought there could be no chance of a revival of our hopes.

But the unexpected happened after all. On the precipitous northern side of the adjacent hill our eyes fell upon bare rock – the first glimpse we had had of positive land during the year we had been in Antarctica. Our next thought was of how to get to it and take specimens, and with this object we at once began to scale the neighbouring hill, which was a trifle higher than the one we had first ascended. The precipice was, however, per-pendicular, with a huge snow cornice over-hanging it. Lowering a man on the rope would be rather too hazardous a proceeding; besides which, a length of thirty yards would not go very far. If we were to get at the rock, it would have to be from below. In the meantime we availed ourselves of the opportunity offered by the clear weather to make a closer examination of our sur-roundings. From the isolated summit, 1,700 feet high, on which we stood, the view was fairly extensive. Down to the sea on the north the distance was about five geographical miles. The surface descended in terraces towards the edge of the wa-ter, where there was quite a low Barrier wall. As might be ex-pected, this stretch of the ice-field was broken by innumerable crevasses, rendering any passage across it impossible.

On the east extended a well-marked mountain-ridge, about twenty geographical miles in length, and somewhat lower than the summit on which we stood. This was the Alexandra Moun-tains. It could not be called an imposing range, and it was snow-clad from one end to the other. Only on the most easter-ly spur was the rock just visible.

On the south and south-west nothing was to be seen but the usual undulating Barrier surface. Biscoe Bay, as Captain Scott has named it, was for the moment a gathering-place for numer-ous icebergs; one or two of these seemed to be aground. The in-most corner of the bay was covered with sea-ice. On its eastern side the Barrier edge could be seen to continue northward, as marked in Captain Scott's chart; but no indication of bare land was visible in that quarter.

Having built a snow beacon, 6 feet high, on the summit, we

put on our skis again and went down the eastern slope of the hill at a whizzing pace. On this side there was an approach to the level on the north of the precipice, and we availed ourselves of it. Seen from below the mountain crest looked quite grand, with a perpendicular drop of about 1,000 feet. The cliff was covered with ice up to a height of about 100 feet, and this circumstance threatened to be a serious obstacle to our obtaining specimens of the rocks. But in one place a nunatak about 250 feet high stood out in front of the precipice, and the ascent of this offered no great difficulty.

A wall of rock of very ordinary appearance is not usually reckoned among things capable of attracting the attention of the human eye to any marked extent; nevertheless, we three stood and gazed at it, as though we had something of extraordinary beauty and interest before us. The explanation is very simple, if we remember the old saying about the charm of variety. A sailor, who for months has seen nothing but sea and sky, will lose himself in contemplation of a little islet, be it never so barren and desolate. To us, who for nearly a year had been staring our eyes out in a dazzling white infinity of snow and ice, it was indeed an experience to see once more a bit of the earth's crust. That this fragment was as poor and bare as it could be was not taken into consideration at the moment.

The mere sight of the naked rock was, however, only an anticipatory pleasure. A more substantial one was the feeling of again being able to move on ground that afforded a sure and trustworthy foothold. It is possible that we behaved rather like children on first reaching bare land. One of us, in any case, found immense enjoyment in rolling one big block after another down the steep slopes of the nunatak. At any rate, the sport had the interest of novelty.

This little peak was built up of very heterogenous materials. As the practical result of our visit, we brought away a fairly abundant collection of specimens of all the rocks to be found there. Not being a specialist, I cannot undertake any classification of the specimens. It will be the task of geologists to deal with them, and to obtain if possible some information as to the structure of the country. I will only mention that some of the stones were so heavy that they must certainly have contained metallic ore of one kind or another. On returning to camp that evening, we tried them with the compass-needle, and it showed very marked attraction in the case of one or two of the specimens. These must, therefore, contain iron-ore.

This spur, which had been severely handled by ice-pressure and the ravages of time, offered a poor chance of finding what we coveted most – namely, fossils – and the most diligent search proved unsuccessful in this respect. From finds that have been made in other parts of Antarctica it is known that in former geological periods – the Jurassic epoch – even this desolate continent possessed a rich and luxurious vegetation. The leader of the Swedish expedition to Graham Land, Dr. Nordenskjöld, and his companion, Gunnar Andersson, were the first to make this exceedingly interesting and important discovery.

While it did not fall to our lot to furnish any proof of the existence of an earlier flora in King Edward Land, we found living plants of the most primitive form. Even on that tiny islet in the ocean of snow the rock was in many places covered with thick moss. How did that moss come there? Its occurrence might, perhaps, be quoted in support of the hypothesis of the genesis of organic life from, dead matter. This disputed question must here be left open, but it may be mentioned in the same connection that we found the remains of birds' nests in many places among the rocks. Possibly the occupants of these nests may have been instrumental in the conveyance of the moss.

Otherwise, the signs of bird life were very few. One or two solitary snowy petrels circled round the summit while we were there; that was all.

It was highly important to obtain some successful photographs from this spot, and I was setting about the necessary preparations, when one of my companions made a remark about the changed appearance of the sky. Busy with other things, I had entirely neglected to keep an eye on the weather, an omission for which, as will be seen, we might have had to pay dearly. Fortunately, another had been more watchful than I, and the warning came in time. A glance was enough to convince me of the imminent approach of a snow-storm; the fiery red sky and the heavy ring round the sun spoke a language that was only too clear. We had a good hour's march to the tent, and the possibility of being surprised by the storm before we arrived was practically equivalent to never arriving at all.

We very soon put our things together, and came down the nunatak even more quickly. On the steep slopes leading up to the plateau on which the tent stood the pace was a good deal slower, though we made every possible effort to hurry. There was no need to trouble about the course; we had only to follow the trail of our own ski – so long as it was visible. But the drift was beginning to blot it out, and if it once did that, any attempt at finding the tent would be hopeless. For a long and anxious quarter of an hour it looked as if we should be too late, until at last the tent came in sight, and we were saved. We had escaped the blizzard so far; a few minutes later it burst in all its fury, and the whirling snow was so thick that it would have been impossible to see the tent at a distance of ten paces, but by then we were all safe and sound inside. Ravenously hungry after the twelve hours that had passed since our last proper meal, we cooked an extra large portion of pemmican and the same of chocolate, and with this sumptuous repast we celebrated the event of the day – the discovery of land. From what we had seen in the course of the day it might be regarded as certain that we should be disappointed in our hopes of finding any great and interesting field for our labours in this quarter; King Edward Land was still far too well hidden under eternal snow and ice to give us that. But even the establishment of this, to us, somewhat unwelcome fact marked an increase of positive human knowledge of the territory that bears the name of King Edward VII.; and with the geological specimens that we had collected, we were in possession of a tangible proof of the actual existence of solid ground in a region which otherwise bore the greatest resemblance to what we called "Barrier" elsewhere, or in any case to the Barrier as it appears in the neighbourhood of our winterquarters at Framheim.

Monday, December 4. – The gale kept on at full force all night, and increased rather than moderated as the day advanced. As usual, the storm was accompanied by a very marked rise of temperature. At the noon observation to-day the reading was + 26.6° F. This is the highest temperature we have had so

554

far on this trip, and a good deal higher than we care about. When the mercury comes so near freezing-point as this, the floor of the tent is always damp.

To-day, for once in a way, we have falling snow, and enough of it. It is snowing incessantly – big, hard flakes, almost like hail. When the cooker was filled to provide water for dinner, the half-melted mass looked like sago. The heavy flakes of snow make a noise against the tent that reminds one of the safety-valve of a large boiler blowing off: Inside the tent it is difficult to hear oneself speak; when we have anything to say to each other we have to shout.

These days of involuntary idleness on a sledge journey may safely be reckoned among the experiences it is difficult to go through without a good deal of mental suffering. I say nothing of the purely physical discomfort of having to pass the day in a sleeping-bag. That may be endured; in any case, so long as the bag is fairly dry. It is a far worse matter to reconcile oneself to the loss of the many solid hours that might otherwise have been put to a useful purpose, and to the irritating consciousness that every bit of food that is consumed is so much wasted of the limited store. At this spot of all others we should have been so glad to spend the time in exploring round about, or still more in going farther. But if we are to go on, we must be certain of having a chance of getting seals at a reasonable distance from here. With our remaining supply of dogs' food we cannot go on for more than three days.

What we have left will be just enough for the return journey, even if we should not find the depot of seals' flesh left on the way. There remained the resource of killing dogs, if it was a question of getting as far to the east as possible, but for many reasons I shrank from availing myself of that expedient. We could form no idea of what would happen to the southern party's animals. The probability was that they would have none left on their return. Supposing their return were delayed so long as to involve spending another winter on the Barrier, the transport of supplies from the ship could hardly be carried out in the necessary time with the ten untrained puppies that were left with Lindström. We had picked out the useful ones, and I thought that, should the necessity arise, they could be used with greater advantage for this work than we should derive from slaughtering them here, and thereby somewhat prolonging the distance covered; the more so as, to judge from all appearance, there was a poor prospect of our finding anything of interest within a reasonable time.

Tuesday, December 5. – It looks as if our patience is to be given a really hard trial this time. Outside the same state of things continues, and the barometer is going down. A mass of snow has fallen in the last twenty-four hours. The drift on the windward side of the tent is constantly growing; if it keeps on a little longer it will be as high as the top of the tent. The sledges are completely snowed under, and so are the dogs; we had to haul them out one by one in the middle of the day. Most of them are now loose, as there is nothing exposed to the attacks of their teeth. It is now blowing a regular gale; the direction of the wind is about true east. Occasionally squalls of hurricane-like violence occur. Fortunately the big snow-drift keeps us comfortable, and we are under the lee of a hill, otherwise it would look badly for our tent. Hitherto it has held well, but it is beginning to be rather damp inside. The temperature remains very high (+ 27.2° F. at noon to-day), and the mass of snow pressing against the tent causes the formation of rime.

In order to while away the time to some extent under depressing circumstances like these, I put into my diary on leaving Framheim a few loose leaves of a Russian grammar; Johansen solaced himself with a serial cut out of the Aftenpost; as far as I remember, the title of it was "The Red Rose and the White." Unfortunately the story of the Two Roses was very soon finished; but Johansen had a good remedy for that: he simply began it over again. My reading had the advantage of being incomparably stiffer. Russian verbs are uncommonly difficult of digestion, and not to be swallowed in a hurry. For lack of mental nutriment, Stubberud with great resignation consoled himself with a pipe, but his enjoyment must have been somewhat diminished by the thought that his stock of tobacco was shrinking at an alarming rate. Every time he filled his pipe, I could see him cast longing looks in the direction of my pouch, which was still comparatively full. I could not help promising a fraternal sharing in case he should run short; and after that our friend puffed on with an easy mind.

Although I look at it at least every half-hour, the barometer will not go up. At 8 p.m. it was down to 27.30. If this means anything, it can only be that we shall have the pleasure of being imprisoned here another day. Some poor consolation is to be had in the thought of how lucky we were to reach the tent at the last moment the day before yesterday. A storm as lasting as this one would in all probability have been too much for us if we had not got in.

Wednesday, December 6. – the third day of idleness has at last crept away after its predecessors. We have done with it. It has not brought any marked variation. The weather has been just as violent, until now – 8 p.m. – the wind shows a slight tendency to moderate. It is, surely, time it did; three days and nights should be enough for it. The heavy snowfall continues. Big, wet flakes come dancing down through the opening in the drift in which the peak of the tent still manages to show itself. In the course of three days we have had more snowfall here than we had at Framheim in ten whole months. It will be interesting to compare our meteorological log with Lindström's; probably he has had his share of the storm, and in that case it will have given him some exercise in snow-shovelling.

The moisture is beginning to be rather troublesome now; most of our wardrobe is wet through, and the sleeping-bags will soon meet with the same fate. The snow-drift outside is now so high that it shuts out most of the daylight; we are in twilight. To-morrow we shall be obliged to dig out the tent, whatever the weather is like, otherwise we shall be buried entirely, and run the additional risk of having the tent split by the weight of snow. I am afraid it will be a day's work to dig out the tent and the two sledges; we have only one little shovel to do it with.

A slight rise of both barometer and thermometer tells us that at last we are on the eve of the change we have been longing for. Stubberud is certain of fair weather to-morrow, he says. I am by no means so sure, and offer to bet pretty heavily that there will be no change. Two inches of Norwegian plug tobacco is the stake, and with a heartfelt desire that Jörgen may win I await the morrow.

Thursday, December 7. – Early this morning I owned to having lost my bet, as the weather, so far as I could tell, was no longer of the same tempestuous character; but Stubberud thought the contrary. "It seems to me just as bad," said he. He was right enough, as a matter of fact, but this did not prevent my persuading him to accept payment. Meanwhile we were obliged to make an attempt to dig out the tent, regardless of the weather; the situation was no longer endurable. We waited all the forenoon in the hope of an improvement; but as none came, we set to work at twelve o'clock. Our implements showed some originality and diversity: a little spade, a biscuit-tin, and a cooker. The drift did its best to undo our work as fast as we dug, but we managed to hold our own against it. Digging out the tent-pegs gave most trouble. After six hours' hard work we got the tent set up a few yards to windward of its first position; the place where it had stood was now a well about seven feet deep. Unfortunately there was no chance of immortalizing this scene of excavation. It would have been amusing enough to have it on the plate; but drifting snow is a serious obstacle to an amateur photographer – besides which, my camera was on Stubberud's sledge, buried at least four feet down.

In the course of our digging we had had the misfortune to make two or three serious rents in the thin canvas of the tent, and the drift was not long in finding a way through these when the tent was up again. To conclude my day's work I had, therefore, a longish tailor's job, while the other two men were digging out a good feed for the dogs, who had been on half-rations for the last two days. That night we went rather short of sleep. Vulcan, the oldest dog in Johansen's team, was chiefly to blame for this. In his old age Vulcan was afflicted with a bad digestion, for even Eskimo dogs may be liable to this infirmity, hardy as they generally are. The protracted blizzard had given the old fellow a relapse, and he proclaimed this distressing fact by incessant howling. This kind of music was not calculated to lull us to sleep, and it was three or four in the morning before we could snatch a nap. During a pause I was just dropping off, when the sun showed faintly through the tent. This unwonted sight at once banished all further thoughts of sleep; the Primus was lighted, a cup of chocolate swallowed, and out we went. Stubberud and Johansen set to work at the hard task of digging out the sledges; they had to go down four feet to get hold of them. I dragged our wet clothes, sleeping-bags, and so forth out of the tent, and hung them all up to dry. In the course of the morning observations were taken for determining the geographical longitude and latitude, as well as a few photographs, which will give some idea of what our camp looked like after the blizzard. Having made good the damage and put everything fairly in order, we hurried away to our peaks, to secure some photographs while the light was favourable. This time we were able to achieve our object: "Scott's Nunataks," as they were afterwards named – after Captain Scott, who first saw them – were now for the first time recorded by the camera. Before we left the summit the Norwegian flag was planted there, a snow beacon erected, and a report of our visit deposited in it. The weather would not keep clear; before we were back at the camp there was a thick fog, and once more we had to thank the tracks of our ski for showing us the way. During the time we had been involuntarily detained at this spot, our store of provisions had decreased alarmingly; there was only a bare week's supply left, and in less than a week we should hardly be able to make home; probably it would take more than a week, but in that case we had the depot at our Bay of Seals to fall back upon. In the immediate neighbourhood of our present position we could not reckon on being able to replenish our supply in the continued unfavourable state of the weather. We therefore made up our minds on the morning of December 9 to break off the journey and turn our faces homeward. For three days more we had to struggle with high wind and thick snow, but as things now were, we had no choice but to keep going, and by the evening of the 11th we had dragged ourselves fifty geographical miles to the west. The weather cleared during the night, and at last, on December 12, we had a day of real sunshine. All our discomforts were forgotten; everything went easily again. In the course of nine hours we covered twenty-six geographical miles that day, without any great strain on either dogs or men.

At our midday rest we found ourselves abreast of the bay, where, on the outward journey, we had laid down our depot of seals' flesh. I had intended to turn aside to the depot and replenish our supply of meat as a precaution, but Johansen suggested leaving out this detour and going straight on. We might thereby run the risk of having to go on short rations; but Johansen thought it a greater risk to cross the treacherous ground about the bay, and, after some deliberation, I saw he was right. It was better to go on while we were about it.

From this time on we met with no difficulty, and rapidly drew near to our destination in regular daily marches of twenty geographical miles. After men and dogs had received their daily ration on the evening of the 15th, our sledge cases were practically empty; but, according to our last position, we should not have more than twenty geographical miles more to Framheim.

Saturday, December 16. – We broke camp at the usual time, in overcast but perfectly clear weather, and began what was to be our last day's march on this trip. A dark water-sky hung over the Barrier on the west and north-west, showing that there was open sea off the mouth of the Bay of Whales. We went on till 10.30, our course being true west, when we made out far to the north-west an ice-cape that was taken to be the extreme point on the western side of the bay. Immediately after we were on the edge of the Barrier, the direction of which was here south-west and north-east. We altered our course and followed the edge at a proper distance until we saw a familiar iceberg that had broken off to the north of Framheim, but had been stopped by the sea-ice from drifting out. With this excellent mark in view the rest of the way was plain sailing. The sledge-meter showed 19.5 geographical miles, when in the afternoon we came in sight of our winter home. Quiet and peaceful it lay there, if possible more deeply covered in snow than when we had left it. At first we could see no sign of life, but soon the glasses discovered a lonely wanderer on his way from the house to the "meteorological institute." So Lindström was still alive and performing his duties.

When we left, our friend had expressed his satisfaction at "getting us out of the way"; but I have a suspicion that he was quite as pleased to see us back again. I am not quite certain, though, that he did see us for the moment, as he was about as snow-blind as a man can be. Lindström was the last person we should have suspected of that malady. On our asking him how it came about, he seemed at first unwilling to give any explanation; but by degrees it came out that the misfortune had happened a couple of days before, when he had gone out after seals. His team, composed of nothing but puppies, had run away and pulled up at a big hummock out by the western cape, ten miles from the station. But Lindström, who is a determined man, would not give up before he had caught the runaways; and this was too much for his eyes, as he had no goggles with him. "When I got home I couldn't see what the time was," he said; "but it must have been somewhere about six in the morning." When we had made him put on plenty of red eye-ointment and supplied him with a proper pair of goggles, he was soon cured.

Framheim had had the same protracted storms with heavy snowfall. On several mornings the master of the house had had to dig his way out through the snow-wall outside the door; but during the last three fine days he had managed to clear a passage, not only to the door, but to the window as well. Daylight came down into the room through a well nine feet deep. This had been a tremendous piece of work; but, as already hinted, nothing can stop Lindström when he makes up his mind. His stock of seals' flesh was down to a minimum; the little there was vanished on the appearance of our ravenous dogs. We ourselves were in no such straits; sweets were the only things in special demand.

We stayed at home one day. After bringing up two loads of seals' flesh, filling our empty provision cases, carrying out a number of small repairs, and checking our watches, we were again on the road on Monday the 18th. We were not very loth to leave the house; indoor existence had become rather uncomfortable on account of constant dripping from the ceiling. In the course of the winter a quantity of ice had formed in the loft. As the kitchen fire was always going after our return, the temperature became high enough to melt the ice, and the water streamed down. Lindström was annoyed and undertook to put a stop to it. He disappeared into the loft, and sent down a hail of ice, bottle-straw, broken cases, and other treasures through the trap-door.

We fled before the storm and drove away. This time we had to carry out our instructions as to the exploration of the long eastern arm of the Bay of Whales. During the autumn several Sunday excursions had been made along this remarkable formation; but although some of these ski-runs had extended as far as twelve miles in one direction, there was no sign of the hummocks coming to an end. These great disturbances of the ice-mass must have a cause, and the only conceivable one was that the subjacent land had brought about this disruption of the surface. For immediately to the south there was undoubtedly land, as there the surface rose somewhat rapidly to a height of 1,000 feet; but it was covered with snow. There was a possibility that the rock might project among the evidences of heavy pressure at the foot of this slope; and with this possibility in view we made a five days' trip, following the great fissure, or "bay," as we generally called it, right up to its head, twenty-three geographical miles to the east of our winter-quarters.

Although we came across no bare rock, and in that respect the journey was a disappointment, it was nevertheless very interesting to observe the effects of the mighty forces that had here been at work, the disruption of the solid ice-sheath by the still more solid rock.

The day before Christmas Eve we were back at Framheim. Lindström had made good use of his time in our absence. The ice had disappeared from the loft, and therewith the rain from the ceiling. New linoleum had been laid down over half the floor, and marks of the paint-brush were visible on the ceiling. These efforts had possibly been made with an eye to the approaching festival, but in other respects we abstained from any attempt at keeping Christmas. It did not agree with the time of year; constant blazing sunshine all through the twenty-four hours could not be reconciled with a northerner's idea of Christmas. And for that reason we had kept the festival six months before. Christmas Eve fell on a Sunday, and it passed just like any ordinary Sunday. Perhaps the only difference was that we used a razor that day instead of the usual beard-clipper. On Christmas Day we took a holiday, and Lindström prepared a banquet of skua gulls. Despise this dish as one may, it tasted undeniably of – bird.

The numerous snow-houses were now in a sad way. Under the weight of the constantly increasing mass, the roofs of most of the rooms were pressed so far in that there was just enough space to crawl on hands and knees. In the Crystal Palace and the Clothing Store we kept all our skin clothing, besides a good deal of outfit, which it was intended to take on board the *Fram* when she and the southern party arrived. If the sinking continued, it would be a long business digging these things out again, and in order to have everything ready we made up our minds to devote a few days to this work at once. We hauled the snow up from these two rooms through a well twelve feet deep by means of tackles. It was a long job, but when we had finished this part of the labyrinth was as good as ever. We had no time to deal with the vapour-bath or the carpenter's shop just then. There still remained the survey of the south-western corner of the Bay of Whales and its surroundings. On an eight days' sledge journey, starting at the New Year, we ranged about this district, where we were surprised to find the solid Barrier divided into small islands, separated by comparatively broad sounds. These isolated masses of ice could not possibly be afloat, although the depth in one or two places, where we had a chance of making soundings, proved to be as much as 200 fathoms. The only rational explanation we could think of was that there must be a group of low-lying islands here, or in any case shoals. These "ice islands," if one may call them so, had a height of 90 feet and sloped evenly down to the water on the greater part of their circumference. One of the sounds, that penetrated into the Barrier a short distance inside the western cape of the bay, continued southward and gradually narrowed to a mere fissure. We followed this until it lost itself, thirty geographical miles within the Barrier.

The last day of this trip – Thursday, January 11 – will always be fixed in our memory; it was destined to bring us experiences of the kind that are never forgotten. Our start in the morning was made at exactly the same time and in exactly the same way as so many times before. We felt pretty certain of reaching Framheim in the course of the day, but that prospect was for the moment of minor importance. In the existing state of the weather our tent offered us as comfortable quarters as our snowed-up winter home. What made us look forward to our return with some excitement was the possibility of seeing the *Fram* again, and this thought was no doubt in the minds of all of us that January morning, though we did not say much about it.

After two hours' march we caught sight of West Cape, at the entrance to the bay, in our line of route, and a little later we saw a black strip of sea far out on the horizon. As usual, a number of bergs of all sizes were floating on this strip, in every variety of shade from white to dark grey, as the light fell on them. One particular lump appeared to us so dark that it could hardly be made of ice; but we had been taken in too many times to make any remark about it.

As the dogs now had a mark to go by, Johansen was driving in front without my help; I went by the side of Stubberud's sledge. The man at my side kept staring out to sea, without uttering a word. On my asking him what in the world he was looking at, he replied "I could almost swear it was a ship, but of course it's only a wretched iceberg." We were just agreed upon this, when suddenly Johansen stopped short and began a hurried search for his long glass. "Are you going to look at the *Fram*?" I asked ironically. "Yes, I am," he said; and while he turned the telescope upon the doubtful object far out in Ross Sea, we two stood waiting for a few endless seconds. "It's the *Fram* sure enough, as large as life!" was the welcome announcement that broke our suspense. I glanced at Stubberud and saw his face expanding into its most amiable smile. Though I had not much doubt of the correctness of Johansen's statement, I borrowed his glass, and a fraction of a second was enough to convince me. That ship was easily recognized; she was our own old *Fram* safely back again.

We had still fourteen long miles to Framheim and an obstinate wind right in our faces, but that part of the way was covered in a remarkably short time. On arriving at home at two in the afternoon we had some expectation of finding a crowd of people in front of the house; but there was not a living soul to be seen. Even Lindström remained concealed, though as a rule he was always about when anyone arrived. Thinking that perhaps our friend had had a relapse of snow-blindness, I went in to announce our return. Lindström was standing before his range in the best of health when I entered the kitchen. "The *Fram's* come!" he shouted, before I had shut the door. "Tell me something I don't know," said I, "and be so kind as to give me a cup of water with a little syrup in it if you can." I thought somehow that the cook had a sly grin on his face when he brought what I asked for, but with the thirst I had after the stiff march, I gave a great part of my attention to the drink. I had consumed the best part of a quart, when Lindström went off to his bunk and asked if I could guess what he had hidden there. There was no time to guess anything before the blankets were thrown on to the floor, and after them bounded a bearded ruffian clad in a jersey and a pair of overalls of indeterminable age and colour. "Hullo!" said the ruffian, and the voice was that of Lieutenant Gjertsen. Lindström was shaking with laughter while I stood open-mouthed before this apparition; I had been given a good surprise. We agreed to treat Johansen and Stubberud in the same way, and as soon as they were heard outside, Gjertsen hid himself again among the blankets. But Stubberud had smelt a rat in some way or other. "There are more than two in this room," he said, as soon as he came in. It was no surprise to him to find a man from the *Fram* in Lindström's bunk.

When we heard that the visitor had been under our roof for a whole day, we assumed that in the course of that time he had heard all about our own concerns from Lindström. We were therefore not inclined to talk about ourselves; we wanted news from without, and Gjertsen was more than ready to give us them. The *Fram* had arrived two days before, all well. After lying at the ice edge for a day and a night, keeping a constant lookout for the "natives," Gjertsen had grown so curious to know how things were at Framheim that he had asked Captain Nilsen for "shore leave." The careful skipper had hesitated a while before giving permission; it was a long way up to the house, and the sea-ice was scored with lanes, some of them fairly wide. Finally Gjertsen had his way, and he left the ship, taking a signal flag with him. He found it rather difficult to recognize his surroundings, to begin with; one ice cape was very like another, and ugly ideas of calvings suggested themselves, until at last he caught sight of Cape Man's Head, and then he knew that the foundations of Framheim had not given way. Cheered by this knowledge, he made his way towards Mount Nelson, but on arriving at the top of this ridge, from which there was a view over Framheim, the eager explorer felt his heart sink. Where our new house had made such a brave show a year before on the surface of the Barrier, there was now no house at all to be seen. All that met the eyes of the visitor was a sombre pile of ruins. But his anxiety quickly vanished when a man emerged from the confusion. The man was Lindström, and the supposed ruin was the most ingenious of all winter-quarters. Lindström was ignorant of the *Fram*'s arrival, and the face he showed on seeing Gjertsen must have been worth some money to look at.

When our first curiosity was satisfied, our thoughts turned to our comrades on board the *Fram*. We snatched some food, and then went down to the sea-ice, making our way across the little bay due north of the house. Our well-trained team were not long in getting there, but we had some trouble with them in crossing the cracks in the ice, as some of the dogs, especially the puppies, had a terror of water.

The *Fram* was cruising some way out, but when we came near enough for them to see us, they made all haste to come in to the ice-foot. Yes, there lay our good little ship, as trim as when we had last seen her; the long voyage round the world had left no mark on her strong hull. Along the bulwarks appeared a row of smiling faces, which we were able to recognize in spite of the big beards that half concealed many of them. While clean-shaven chins had been the fashion at Framheim, almost every man on board appeared with a flowing beard. As we came over the gangway questions began to hail upon us. I had to ask for a moment's grace to give the captain and crew a hearty shake of the hand, and then I collected them all about me and gave a short account of the most important events of the past year. When this was done, Captain Nilsen pulled me into the chart-house, where we had a talk that lasted till about four the next morning – to both of us certainly one of the most interesting we have ever had. On Nilsen's asking about the prospects of the southern party, I ventured to assure him that in all probability we should have our Chief and his companions back in a few days with the Pole in their pockets.

Our letters from home brought nothing but good news. What interested us most in the newspapers was, of course, the account of how the expedition's change of route had been received.

At 8 a.m. we left the *Fram* and returned home. For the next few days we were occupied with the work of surveying and charting, which went comparatively quickly in the favourable weather. When we returned after our day's work on the afternoon of the 17th, we found Lieutenant Gjertsen back at the hut. He asked us if we could guess the news, and as we had no answer ready, he told us that the ship of the Japanese expedition had arrived. We hurriedly got out the cinematograph apparatus and the camera, and went off as fast as the dogs could go, since Gjertsen thought this visit would not be of long duration.

When we caught sight of the *Fram* she had her flag up, and just beyond the nearest cape lay the *Kainan Maru*, with the ensign of the Rising Sun at the peak. Banzai! We had come in time. Although it was rather late in the evening, Nilsen and I decided to pay her a visit, and if possible to see the leader of the expedition. We were received at the gangway by a young, smiling fellow, who beamed still more when I produced the only Japanese word I knew: Oheio – Good-day. There the conversation came to a full stop, but soon a number of the inquisitive sons of Nippon came up, and some of them understood a little English. We did not get very far, however. We found out that the *Kainan Maru* had been on a cruise in the direction of King Edward VII. Land; but we could not ascertain whether any landing had been attempted or not.

As the leader of the expedition and the captain of the ship had turned in, we did not want to disturb them by prolonging our visit; but we did not escape before the genial first officer had offered us a glass of wine and a cigar in the chart-house. With an invitation to come again next day, and permission to take some photographs, we returned to the *Fram*; but nothing came of the projected second visit to our Japanese friends. Both ships put out to sea in a gale that sprang up during the night, and before we had another opportunity of going on board the *Kainan Maru* the southern party had returned.

The days immediately preceding the departure of the expedition for the north fell about the middle of the short Antarctic summer, just at the time when the comparatively rich animal life of the Bay of Whales shows itself at its best.

The name of the Bay of Whales is due to Shackleton, and is appropriate enough; for from the time of the break-up of the sea-ice this huge inlet in the Barrier forms a favourite playground for whales, of which we often saw schools of as many as fifty disporting themselves for hours together. We had no means of disturbing their peaceful sport, although the sight of all these monsters, each worth a small fortune, was well calculated to make our fingers itch. It was the whaling demon that possessed us.

For one who has no special knowledge of the industry it is difficult to form an adequate opinion as to whether this part of Antarctica is capable of ever becoming a field for whaling enterprise. In any case, it will probably be a long time before such a thing happens. In the first place, the distance to the nearest inhabited country is very great – over 2,000 geographical miles – and in the second, there is a serious obstruction on this route in the shape of the belt of pack-ice, which, narrow and loose as it may be at times, will always necessitate the employment of timber-built vessels for the work of transport.

The conditions prevailing in the Bay of Whales must presumably offer a decisive obstacle to the establishment of a permanent station. Our winter house was snowed under in the course of two months, and to us this was only a source of satisfaction, as our quarters became all the warmer on this account; but whether a whaling station would find a similar fate equally convenient is rather doubtful. Lastly, it must be said that, although in the bay itself huge schools of whales were of frequent occurrence, we did not receive the impression that there was any very great number of them out in Ross Sea. The species most commonly seen was the Finner; after that the Blue Whale.

As regards seals, they appeared in great quantities along the edge of the Barrier so long as the sea-ice still lay there; after the break-up of the ice the Bay of Whales was a favourite resort of theirs all through the summer. This was due to its offering them an easy access to the dry surface, where they could abandon themselves to their favourite occupation of basking in the sunshine.

During our whole stay we must have killed some two hundred and fifty of them, by far the greater number of which were shot in the autumn immediately after our arrival. This little inroad had no appreciable effect. The numerous survivors, who had been eye-witnesses of their companions' sudden death, did not seem to have the slightest idea that the Bay of Whales had become for the time being a somewhat unsafe place of residence.

The name crab-eater may possibly evoke ideas of some ferocious creature; in that case it is misleading. The animal that bears it is, without question, the most amicable of the three species. It is of about the same size as our native seal, brisk and active in its movements, and is constantly exercising itself in high jumps from the water on to the ice-foot. Even on the ice it can work its way along so fast that it is all a man can do to keep up. Its skin is extraordinarily beautiful – grey, with a sheen of silver and small dark spots.

One is often asked whether seal's flesh does not taste of train oil. It seems to be a common assumption that it does so. This, however, is a mistake; the oil and the taste of it are only present in the layer of blubber, an inch thick, which covers the seal's body like a protective armour. The flesh itself contains no fat; on the other hand, it is extremely rich in blood and its taste in consequence reminds one of black-puddings. The flesh of the Weddell seal is very dark in colour; in the frying-pan it turns quite black. The flesh of the crab-eater is of about the same colour as beef, and to us, at any rate, its taste was equally good. We therefore always tried to get crab-eater when providing food for ourselves.

We found the penguins as amusing as the seals were useful. So much has been written recently about these remarkable creatures, and they have been photographed and cinematographed so many times, that everyone is acquainted with them. Nevertheless, anyone who sees a living penguin for the first time will always be attracted and interested, both by the dignified Emperor penguin, with his three feet of stature, and by the bustling little Adelie.

Not only in their upright walk, but also in their manners and antics, these birds remind one strikingly of human beings. It has been remarked that an Emperor is the very image of "an old gentleman in evening dress," and the resemblance is indeed very noticeable. It becomes still more so when the Emperor – as is always his habit – approaches the stranger with a series of ceremonious bows; such is their good breeding!

When this ceremony is over, the penguin will usually come quite close; he is entirely unsuspecting and is not frightened even if one goes slowly towards him. On the other hand, if one approaches rapidly or touches him, he is afraid and immediately takes to flight. It sometimes happens, though, that he shows fight, and then it is wiser to keep out of range of his flippers; for in these he has a very powerful weapon, which might easily break a man's arm. If you wish to attack him, it is better to do so from behind; both flippers must be seized firmly at the same time and bent backwards along his back; then the fight is over.

The little Adelie is always comic. On meeting a flock of these little busybodies the most ill-humoured observer is forced to burst into laughter. During the first weeks of our stay in the Bay of Whales, while we were still unloading stores, it was always a welcome distraction to see a flock of Adélie penguins, to the number of a dozen or so, suddenly jump out of the water, as though at a word of command, and then sit still for some moments, stiff with astonishment at the extraordinary things they saw. When they had recovered from the first surprise, they generally dived into the sea again, but their intense curiosity soon drove them back to look at us more closely.

In contradistinction to their calm and self-controlled relative, the Emperor penguin, these active little creatures have an extremely fiery temperament, which makes them fly into a passion at the slightest interference with their affairs; and this, of course, only makes them still more amusing.

The penguins are birds of passage; they spend the winter on the various small groups of islands that are scattered about the southern ocean. On the arrival of spring they betake themselves to Antarctica, where they have their regular rookeries in places where there is bare ground. They have a pronounced taste for roaming, and as soon as the chicks are grown they set out, young and old together, on their travels. It was only as tourists that the penguins visited Framheim and its environs; for there was, of course, no bare land in our neighbourhood that might offer them a place of residence. For this reason we really saw comparatively little of them; an Emperor was a very rare visitor; but the few occasions on which we met these peculiar "bird people" of Antarctica will remain among the most delightful memories of our stay in the Bay of Whales.

CHAPTER 16

THE VOYAGE OF THE *FRAM*
by First-Lieutenant Thorvald Nilsen

From Norway to the Barrier

After the *Fram* had undergone extensive repairs in Horten Dockyard, and had loaded provisions and equipment in Christiania, we left the latter port on June 7, 1910. According to the plan we were first to make an oceanographical cruise of about two months in the North Atlantic, and then to return to Norway, where the *Fram* was to be docked and the remaining outfit and dogs taken on board.

This oceanographical cruise was in many respects successful. In the first place, we gained familiarity with the vessel, and got everything shipshape for the long voyage to come; but the best of all was, that we acquired valuable experience of our auxiliary engine. This is a 180 h.p. Diesel motor, constructed for solar oil, of which we were taking about 90,000 litres (about 19,800 gallons). In this connection it may be mentioned that we consumed about 500 litres (about 110 gallons) a day, and that the *Fram's* radius of action was thus about six months. For the first day or two the engine went well enough, but after that it went slower and slower, and finally stopped of its own accord. After this it was known as the "Whooping Cough." This happened several times in the course of the trip; the piston-rods had constantly to be taken out and cleared of a thick black deposit. As possibly our whole South Polar Expedition would depend on the motor doing its work properly, the result of this was that the projected cruise was cut short, and after a lapse of three weeks our course was set for Bergen, where we changed the oil for refined paraffin, and at the same time had the motor thoroughly overhauled. Since then there has never been anything wrong with the engine.

From Bergen we went to Christiansand, where the *Fram* was docked, and, as already mentioned, the remaining outfit, with the dogs and dog-food, was taken on board. The number of living creatures on board when we left Norway was nineteen men, ninety-seven dogs, four pigs, six carrier pigeons, and one canary.

At last we were ready to leave Christiansand on Thursday, August 9, 1910, and at nine o'clock that evening the anchor was got up and the motor started. After the busy time we had had, no doubt we were all glad to get off. As our departure had not been made public, only the pilot and a few acquaintances accompanied us a little way out. It was glorious weather, and everyone stayed on deck till far into the light night, watching the land slowly disappear. All the ninety-seven dogs were chained round the deck, on which we also had coal, oil, timber and other things, so that there was not much room to move about.

The rest of the vessel was absolutely full. To take an example, in the fore-saloon we had placed forty-three sledging cases, which were filled with books, Christmas presents, underclothing, and the like. In addition to these, one hundred complete sets of dog-harness, all our ski, ski-poles, snow-shoes, etc. Smaller articles were stowed in the cabins, and every man had something. When I complained, as happened pretty often, that I could not imagine where this or that was to be put, the Chief of the expedition used generally to say: "Oh, that's all right; you can just put it in your cabin!" Thus it was with every imaginable thing – from barrels of paraffin and new-born pups to writing materials and charts.

As the story of this voyage has already been told, it may be rapidly passed over here. After much delay through headwinds in the Channel, we picked up the north-east trade in about the latitude of Gibraltar, and arrived at Madeira on September 6. At 9 p.m. on September 9 we weighed anchor for the last time, and left Madeira. As soon as we were clear of the land we got the north-east trade again, and it held more or less fresh till about lat. 11° N.

After our departure from Madeira I took over the morning watch, from 4 to 8 a.m.; Prestrud and Gjertsen divided the remainder of the twenty-four hours. In order if possible to get a little more way on the ship, a studding-sail and a skysail were rigged up with two awnings; it did not increase our speed very much, but no doubt it helped a little.

The highest temperature we observed was 84° F. In the trade winds we constantly saw flying-fish, but as far as I know not one was ever found on deck; those that came on board were of course instantly snapped up by the dogs.

In about lat. 11° N. we lost the north-east trade, and thus came into the "belt of calms," a belt that extends on each side of the Equator, between the north-east and south-east trades.

Here, as a rule, one encounters violent rain-squalls; to sailing ships in general and ourselves in particular this heavy rain is welcome, as water-tanks can be filled up. Only on one day were we lucky enough to have rain, but as it was accompanied by a strong squall of wind, we did not catch all the water we wanted. All hands were on deck carrying water, some in oil-skins, some in Adam's costume; the Chief in a white tropical suit, and, as far as I remember, clogs. As the latter were rather slippery, and the *Fram* suddenly gave an unexpected lurch, he was carried off his legs, and left sitting on the deck, while his bucket of water poured all over him. But "it was all in his country's cause," so he did not mind. We caught about 3 tons of water, and then had our tanks full, or about 30 tons, when the shower passed off; later in the voyage we filled a bucket now and again, but it never amounted to much, and if we had not been as careful as we were, our water-supply would hardly have lasted out.

On October 4 we crossed the Equator. The south-east trade was not so fresh as we had expected, and the engine had to be kept going the whole time. At the beginning of November we came down into the west wind belt, or the "Roaring Forties," as they are called, and from that time we ran down our easting at a great rate. We were very lucky there, and had strong fair winds for nearly seven weeks at a stretch. In the heavy sea we found out what it was to sail in the *Fram*; she rolls incessantly, and there is never a moment's rest. The dogs were thrown backwards and forwards over the deck, and when one of them rolled into another, it was taken as a personal insult, and a fight followed at once. But for all that the *Fram* is a first-rate sea boat, and hardly ever ships any water. If this had been otherwise, the dogs would have been far worse off than they were.

The weather in the "Foggy Fifties " varied between gales, calms, fogs, snowstorms, and other delights. As a rule, the engine was now kept constantly ready, in case of our being so unlucky as to come too near an iceberg. Fortunately, however, we did not meet any of these until early on the morning of January 1, 1911, when we saw some typical Antarctic bergs; that is to say, entirely tabular. Our latitude was then a little over 60° S., and we were not far off the pack. On the 1st and 2nd we sailed southward without seeing anything but scattered bergs and a constantly increasing number of lumps of ice, which showed us we were getting near. By 10 p.m. on the 2nd we came into slack drift-ice; the weather was foggy, and we therefore kept going as near as might be on the course to the Bay of Whales, which was destined to be our base.

A good many seals were lying on the ice-floes, and as we went forward we shot some. As soon as the first seal was brought on board, all our dogs had their first meat meal since Madeira; they were given as much as they wanted, and ate as much as they could. We, too, had our share of the seal, and from this time forward we had fresh seal-steak for breakfast at least every day; it tasted excellent to us, who for nearly half a year had been living on nothing but tinned meat. With the steak whortleberries were always served, which of course helped to make it appreciated. The biggest seal we got in the pack-ice was about 12 feet long, and weighed nearly half a ton. A few penguins were also shot, mostly Adélie penguins; these are extraordinarily amusing, and as inquisitive as an animal can be. When any of them saw us, they at once came nearer to get a better view of the unbidden guests. If they became too impertinent, we did not hesitate to take them, for their flesh, especially the liver, was excellent. The albatrosses, which had followed us through the whole of the west wind belt, had now departed, and in their place came the beautiful snowy petrels and Antarctic petrels.

We had more or less fog all through the pack-ice. Only on the night of the 5th did we have sun and fine weather, when we saw the midnight sun for the first time. A more beautiful morning it would be difficult to imagine: radiantly clear, with thick ice everywhere, as far as the eye could see; the lanes of water between the floes gleamed in the sun, and the ice-crystals glittered like thousands of diamonds. It was a pure delight to go on deck and drink in the fresh air; one felt altogether a new man. I believe everyone on board found this passage through the pack the most interesting part of the whole voyage, and, of course, it all had the charm of novelty. Those who had not been in the ice before, myself among them, and who were hunting for the first time, ran about after seals and penguins, and amused themselves like children.

At 10 p.m. on the 6th we were already out of the ice after a passage of exactly four days; we had been extremely lucky, and the *Fram* went very easily through the ice.

After coming out of the pack, our course was continued through the open Ross Sea to the Bay of Whales, which from the previous description was to be found in about long. 164° W. On the afternoon of the 11th we had strong ice-blink ahead, by which is meant the luminous stripe that is seen above a considerable accumulation of ice; the nearest thing one can compare it to is the glare that is always seen over a great city on approaching it at night. We knew at once that this was the glare of the mighty Ross Barrier, named after Sir James Clark Ross, who first saw it in 1841. The Barrier is a wall of ice, several hundred miles long, and about 100 feet high, which forms the southern boundary of Ross Sea. We were, of course, very intent upon seeing what it looked like, but to me it did not appear so imposing as I had imagined it. Possibly this was because I had become familiar with it, in a way, from the many descriptions of it. From these descriptions we had expected to find a comparatively narrow opening into Balloon Bight, as shown in the photographs we had before us; but as we went along the Barrier, on the 12th, we could find no opening. In long. 164° W., on the other hand, there was a great break in the wall, forming a cape (West Cape); from here to the other side of the Barrier was about eight geographical miles, and southward, as far as we could see, lay loose bay ice. We held on to the east outside this drift-ice and along the eastern Barrier till past midnight, but as Balloon Bight was not to be found, we returned to the above-mentioned break or cape, where we lay during the whole forenoon of the 13th, as the ice was too thick to allow us to make any progress. After midday, however, the ice loosened, and began to drift out; at the same time we went in, and having gone as far as possible, the *Fram* was moored to the fast ice-foot on the western side of the great bay we had entered. It proved that Balloon Bight and another bight had merged to form a great bay, exactly as described by Sir Ernest Shackleton, and named by him the Bay of Whales.

After mooring here, the Chief and one or two others went on a reconnoitring tour; but it began to snow pretty thickly, and, as far as I am aware, nothing was accomplished beyond seeing that the Barrier at the southernmost end of the bay sloped evenly down to the sea-ice; but between the latter and the slope there was open water, so that they could not go any farther. We lay all night drifting in the ice, which was constantly breaking up, and during this time several seals and penguins were shot. Towards morning on the 14th it became quite clear, and we had a splendid view of the surroundings. Right over on the eastern side of the bay it looked as if there was more open water; we therefore went along the fast ice-foot and moored off the eastern Barrier at about three in the afternoon. The cape in the Barrier, under which we lay, was given the name of "Man's Head," on account of its resemblance to a human profile. All the time we were going along the ice we were shooting seals, so that on arrival at our final moorings we already had a good supply of meat.

For my part I was rather unlucky on one of these hunts: Four seals were lying on the ice-foot, and I jumped down with rifle and five cartridges; to take any cartridges in reserve did not occur to me, as, of course, I regarded myself as a mighty hunter, and thought that one shot per seal was quite enough. The three first died without a groan; but the fourth took the alarm, and made off as fast as it could. I fired my fourth cartridge, but it did not hit as it ought to have done, and the seal was in full flight, leaving a streak of blood behind it. I was not anxious to let a wounded seal go, and as I had only one cartridge left, and the seal had its tail turned towards me, I wanted to come to close quarters to make sure of it. I therefore ran as hard as I could, but the seal was quicker, and it determined the range. After running half-way to the South Pole, I summoned my remaining strength and fired the last shot. Whether the bullet went above or below, I have no idea. All I know is, that on arriving on board I was met by scornful smiles and had to stand a good deal of chaff.

As already mentioned, we left Norway on August 9, 1910, and arrived at our final moorings on January 14, 1911, in the course of which time we had only called at Madeira. The Barrier is 16,000 geographical miles from Norway, a distance which we took five months to cover. From Madeira we had had 127 days in open sea, and therewith the first part of the voyage was brought to an end.

Off the Barrier

As soon as we had moored, the Chief, Prestrud, Johansen and I went up on to the Barrier on a tour of reconnaissance. The ascent from the sea-ice to the Barrier was fine, a perfectly even slope. When no more than a mile from the ship, we found a good site for the first dog-camp, and another mile to the south it was decided that the house was to stand, on the slope of a hill, where it would be least exposed to the strong south-easterly gales which might be expected from previous descriptions. Up on the Barrier all was absolutely still, and there was not a sign of life; indeed, what should anything live on? This delightful ski-run was extended a little farther to the south, and after a couple of hours we returned on board. Here in the meantime the slaughtering of seals had been going on, and there were plenty to be had, as several hundreds of them lay about on the ice.

After the rather long sea voyage, and the cramped quarters on board, I must say it was a pleasure to have firm ground under one's feet and to be able to move about a little. The dogs evidently thought the same; when they came down on to the ice, they rolled in the snow and ran about, wild with delight. During our whole stay a great part of the time was spent in ski-runs and seal-hunts, and an agreeable change it was.

Sunday the 15th was spent in setting up tents at the first dog-camp and at Framheim, as the winter station was named. A team of dogs was used, and, as they were unused to being driven, it is not surprising that some lay down, others fought, a few wanted to go on board, but hardly any of them appreciated the seriousness of the situation or understood that their good time had come to an end. On Monday all the dogs were landed, and on the following day the supplies began to be put ashore.

The landing of the cases was done in this way: the sea-party brought up on deck as many cases as the drivers could take in one journey; as the sledges came down to the vessel, the cases were sent down on to the ice on skids, so that it all went very rapidly. We would not put the cases out on the ice before the sledges came back, as, in case the ice should break up, we should be obliged to heave them all on board again, or we might even lose them. At night no one was ever allowed to stay on the ice.

Before we reached the ice, we had counted on having 50 per cent. of idle days – that is, from previous descriptions we had reckoned on having such bad weather half the time that the *Fram* would be obliged to leave her moorings. In this respect we were far luckier than we expected, and only had to put out twice. The first time was on the night of January 25, when we had a stiff breeze from the north with some sea, so that the vessel was bumping rather hard against the ice. Drifting floes came down upon us, and so as not to be caught by any iceberg that might suddenly come sailing in from the point of the Barrier we called Man's Head, we took our moorings on board and went. When the shore party next morning came down as usual at a swinging pace, they saw to their astonishment that the *Fram* was gone. In the course of the day the weather became fine, and we tried to go back about noon; but the bay was so full of drift-ice that we could not come in to the fast ice-foot. About nine in the evening we saw from the crow's nest that the ice was loosening; we made the attempt, and by midnight we were again moored.

But the day was not wasted by the shore party, for on the day before Kristensen, L. Hansen and I had been out on skis and had shot forty seals, which were taken up to the station while we were away.

Only once or twice more did we have to leave our berth, until on February 7, when almost all the ice had left the bay, we were able to moor alongside the low, fast Barrier, where we lay in peace until we went for good.

There was a great deal of animal life about us. A number of whales came close in to the vessel, where they stayed still to look at the uninvited guests. On the ice seals came right up to the ship, as did large and small flocks of penguins, to have a look at us. These latter were altogether extraordinarily inquisitive creatures. Two Emperor penguins often came to our last moorings to watch us laying out an ice-anchor or hauling on a hawser, while they put their heads on one side and jabbered, and they were given the names of "the Harbour-master and his Missis." A great number of birds, skua gulls, snowy petrels and Antarctic petrels, flew round the ship and gave us many a good "roast ptarmigan."

On the morning of February 4, about 1 a.m., the watchman, Beck, came and called me with the news that a vessel was coming in. I guessed at once, of course, that it was the *Terra Nova*; but I must confess that I did not feel inclined to turn out and look at her. We hoisted the colours, however.

As soon as she was moored, Beck told me, some of her party went ashore, presumably to look for the house. They did not find it, though, and at 3 a.m. Beck came below again, and said that now they were coming on board. So then I turned out and received them. They were Lieutenant Campbell, the leader of Captain Scott's second shore party, and Lieutenant Pennell, the commander of the *Terra Nova*. They naturally asked a number of questions, and evidently had some difficulty in believing that it was actually the *Fram* that was lying here. We had at first been taken for a whaler. They offered to take our mail to New Zealand; but we had no mail ready, and had to decline the offer with thanks. Later in the day a number of the *Terra Nova*'s officers went to breakfast at Framheim, and the Chief, Prestrud and I lunched with them. At about two in the afternoon the *Terra Nova* sailed again.

On Friday, February 16, a number of the shore party started

on the first trip to lay down depots. We cleared up, filled our water-tanks with snow, and made the ship ready for sea. We had finished this by the evening of the 14th.

From the Bay of Whales to Buenos Aires

The sea party consisted of the following ten men Thorvald Nilsen, L. Hansen, H. Kristensen and J. Nödtvedt; H. F. Gjertsen, A. Beck, M. Rönne, A. Kutschin and O. K. Sundbeck. The first four formed one watch, from eight to two, and the last five the other, from two to eight. Last, but not least, comes K. Olsen, cook.

Having made ready for sea, we let go our moorings on the Ice Barrier at 9 a.m. on February 15, 1911. Hassel, Wisting, Bjaaland, and Stubberud came down to see us off. As in the course of the last few days the ice had broken up right to the end of the bay, we went as far south as possible to take a sounding; the shallowest we got was 155 3/4 fathoms (285 metres). The bay ended in a ridge of ice on the east, which was continued in a northerly direction, so that at the spot where we were stopped by the Barrier, we reached the most southerly point that a vessel can attain, so long as the Barrier remains as it is now. Highest latitude 78° 41' S. When the *Terra Nova* was here, her latitude and ours was 78° 38' S.

The last two days before our departure had been calm, and a thick, dense sludge lay over the whole bay; so dense was it that the *Fram* lost her way altogether, and we had to keep going ahead and astern until we came out into a channel. Seals by the hundred were lying on the floes, but as we had a quantity of seal's flesh, we left them in peace for a change.

Before the Chief began the laying out of depots, I received from him the following orders:

"To First-lieutenant Thorvald Nilsen.

With the departure of the *Fram* from the Ice Barrier, you will take over the command on board. In accordance with the plan we have mutually agreed upon:

"1. You will sail direct to Buenos Aires, where the necessary repairs will be executed, provisions taken on board, and the crew completed. When this has been done,

"2. You will sail from Buenos Aires to carry out oceano-graphical observations in the South Atlantic Ocean. It would be desirable if you could investigate the conditions between South America and Africa in two sections. These investigations must, however, be dependent on the prevailing conditions, and on the time at your disposal. When the time arrives you will return to Buenos Aires, where the final preparations will be made for

"3. Your departure for the Ice Barrier to take off the shore party. The sooner you can make your way in to the Barrier in 1912, the better. I mention no time, as everything depends on circumstances, and I leave it to you to act according to your judgment.

"In all else that concerns the interests of the Expedition, I leave you entire freedom of action.

"If on your return to the Barrier you should find that I am prevented by illness or death from taking over the leadership of the Expedition, I place this in your hands, and beg you most earnestly to endeavour to carry out the original plan of the Expedition – the exploration of the North Polar basin.

"With thanks for the time we have spent together, and in the hope that when we meet again we shall have reached our respective goals,

"I am,

"Yours sincerely,

"Roald Amundsen."

When Sir James Ross was in these waters for the first time, in 1842, he marked "Appearance of land" in long. 160° W., and lat. about 78° S. Afterwards, in 1902, Captain Scott named this land "King Edward VII. Land." One of the *Terra Nova*'s objects was to explore this land; but when we met the ship on February 4, they told us on board that on account of the ice conditions they had not been able to land. As no one had ever been ashore there, I thought it might be interesting to go and see what it looked like. Consequently our course was laid northeastward along the Barrier. During the night a thick sea-fog came on, and it was only now and then that we could see the Barrier over our heads. All of a sudden we were close upon a lofty iceberg, so that we had to put the helm hard over to go clear. The *Fram* steers splendidly, however, when she is in proper trim, and turns as if on a pivot; besides which, it was calm.

As the day advanced, the weather cleared more and more, and by noon it was perfectly clear. The sight that then met us was the lofty Barrier to starboard, and elsewhere all round about some fifty icebergs, great and small. The Barrier rose from about 100 feet at its edge to something like 1,200 feet.

We followed the Barrier for some distance, but in the neighbourhood of Cape Colbeck we met the drift-ice, and as I had no wish to come between this and the Barrier, we stood out in a north-westerly direction. There is, besides, the disadvantage about a propeller like ours, that it is apt to wear out the brasses, so that these have to be renewed from time to time. It was imperative that this should be done before we came into the pack-ice, and the sooner the better. When, therefore, we had gone along the Barrier for about a day and a half without seeing any bare land, we set our course north-west in open water, and after we had come some way out we got a slant of easterly wind, so that the sails could be set. We saw the snow-covered land and the glare above it all night. The date had not yet been changed, but as this had to be done, it was changed on February 15.

At noon on the 16th the propeller was lifted, and by the evening of the 17th the job was done – a record in spite of the temperature. Capital fellows to work, our engineers. On the night of the 15th we saw the midnight sun unfortunately for the last time. The same night something dark was sighted on the port bow; in that light it looked very like an islet. The sounding apparatus was got ready, and we who were on watch of course saw ourselves in our minds as great discoverers. I was already wondering what would be the most appropriate name to give it, but, alas! the "discovery" became clearer and the name – well, it was a rather prosaic one: "Dead Whale Islet"; for it turned out to be a huge inflated whale, that was drifting, covered with birds.

We went rather slowly north-westward under sail alone. On the morning of the 17th we saw ice-blink on the starboard bow, and about noon we were close to the pack itself; it was here quite thick, and raised by pressure, so that an attempt to get through it was out of the question. We were, therefore, obliged to follow the ice to the west. Due aft we saw in the sky the same glare as above the great Ice Barrier, which may possibly show that the Barrier turns towards the north and north-west; besides which, the masses of pressure-ice that collect here must go to show that it encounters an obstruction, probably the Barrier. When we went out in 1912 the ice lay in exactly the same place and in the same way.

Our course was still to the west along the pack-ice, and it was not till the 20th that we could turn her nose northward again. For a change we now had a stiff breeze from the south-east, with thick snow, so we got on very well. On the whole, the *Fram* goes much more easily through the water now than on the way south. Her bottom has probably been cleaned by the cold water and all the scraping against the ice; besides which, we have no more than a third of the load with which we left Norway.

On the night of the 20th we had to light the binnacle-lamps again, and now the days grew rapidly shorter. It may possibly be a good thing to have dark nights on land, but at sea it ought always to be light, especially in these waters, which are more or less unknown, and full of drifting icebergs.

At 4 p.m. on the 22nd we entered the drift-ice in lat. 70.5° S., long. 177.5° E. The ice was much higher and uglier than when we were going south, but as there was nothing but ice as far as we could see both east and west, and it was fairly loose, we had to make the attempt where there seemed to be the best chance of getting through.

The seals, which to the south of the ice had been following

us in decreasing numbers, had now disappeared almost entirely, and curiously enough we saw very few seals in the pack. Luckily, however, Lieutenant Gjertsen's watch got three seals, and for a week we were able to enjoy seal-beef, popularly known as "crocodile beef," three times a day. Seal-beef and fresh whortleberries – delicioso!

We went comparatively well through the ice, though at night – from eleven to one – we had to slacken speed, as it was impossible to steer clear on account of the darkness, and towards morning we had a heavy fall of snow, so that nothing could be seen, and the engine had to be stopped. When it cleared, at about 9 a.m., we had come into a dam, out of which we luckily managed to turn fairly easily, coming out into a bay. This was formed by over a hundred icebergs, many of which lay in contact with each other and had packed the ice close together. On the west was the outlet, which we steered for, and by 10 p.m. on February 23 we were already out of the ice and in open water. Our latitude was then 69° S., longitude 175.5° E.

It is very curious to find such calm weather in Ross Sea; in the two months we have been here we have hardly had a strong breeze. Thus, when I was relieved at 2 a.m. on the 25th, I wrote in my diary ... It is calm, not a ripple on the water. The three men forming the watch walk up and down the deck. Now and then one hears the penguins' cry, kva, kva, but except these there is no other sound than the tuff, tuff of the motor, 220 times a minute. Ah, that motor! it goes unweariedly. It has now gone for 1,000 hours without being cleaned, while on our Atlantic cruise last year it stopped dead after going for eighty hours ....Right over us we have the Southern Cross, all round glow the splendid southern lights, and in the darkness can be seen the gleaming outline of an iceberg ..."

On the 26th we crossed the Antarctic Circle, and the same day the temperature both of air and water rose above 32° F.

It was with sorrow in our hearts that we ate our last piece of "crocodile beef," but I hoped we should get a good many albatrosses, which we saw as soon as we came out of the ice. They were mostly the sooty albatross, that tireless bird that generally circles alone about the ship and is so difficult to catch, as he seldom tries to bite at the pork that is used as bait. When I saw these birds for the first time, as a deck boy, I was told they were called parsons, because they were the souls of ungodly clergymen, who had to wait down here till doomsday without rest.

More or less in our course to Cape Horn there are supposed to be two groups of islands, the Nimrod group in about long. 158° W., and Dougherty Island in about long. 120° W. They are both marked "D" (Doubtful) on the English charts. Lieutenant Shackleton's vessel, the *Nimrod*, Captain Davis, searched for both, but found neither; Dougherty Island, however, is said to have been twice sighted. The *Fram's* course was therefore laid for the Nimrod group. For a time things went very well, but then we had a week of northerly winds – that is, head winds – and when at last we had a fair wind again, we were so far to the south-east of them that there was no sense in sailing back to the north-west to look for doubtful islands; it would certainly have taken us weeks. Consequently, our course was laid for Dougherty Island. We had westerly winds for about two weeks, and were only two or three days' sail from the island in question, when suddenly we had a gale from the north-east, which lasted for three days, and ended in a hurricane from the same quarter. When this was over, we had come according to dead reckoning about eighty nautical miles to the south-east of the island; the heavy swell, which lasted for days, made it out of the question to attempt to go against it with the motor. We hardly had a glimpse of sun or stars, and weeks passed without our being able to get an observation, so that for that matter we might easily be a degree or two out in our reckoning. For the present, therefore, we must continue to regard these islands as doubtful.

Moral: Don't go on voyages of discovery, my friend; you're no good at it!

As soon as we were out of Ross Sea and had entered the South Pacific Ocean, the old circus started again – in other words, the *Fram* began her everlasting rolling from one side to the other. When this was at its worst, and cups and plates were dancing the fandango in the galley, its occupant's only wish was, "Oh, to be in Buenos Aires!" For that matter, it is not a very easy job to be cook in such circumstances, but ours was always in a good humour, singing and whistling all day long. How well the *Fram* understands the art of rolling is shown by the following little episode.

One afternoon a couple of us were sitting drinking coffee on a tool-box that stood outside the galley. As ill-luck would have it, during one of the lurches the lashing came loose, and the box shot along the deck. Suddenly it was checked by an obstacle, and one of those who were sitting on it flew into the air, through the galley door, and dashed past the cook with a splendid tiger's leap, until he landed face downwards at the other end of the galley, still clinging like grim death to his cup, as though he wanted something to hold on to. The face he presented after this successful feat of aviation was extremely comical, and those who saw it had a hearty fit of laughter.

As has already been said, we went very well for a time after reaching the Pacific, a fair wind for fourteen days together, and I began to hope that we were once more in what are called the "westerlies." However, nothing is perfect in this world, and we found that out here, as we had icebergs every day, and were constantly bothered by snow-squalls or fog; the former were, of course, to be preferred, as it was at any rate clear between the squalls; but fog is the worst thing of all. It sometimes happened that all hands were on deck the whole night to work the ship at a moment's notice, and there were never less than two men on the lookout forward. The engine, too, was always ready to be started instantly. A little example will show how ready the crew were at any time.

One Sunday afternoon, when Hansen, Kristensen and I were on watch, the wind began to draw ahead, so that we had to beat. It was blowing quite freshly, but I did not want to call the watch below, as they might need all the sleep they could get, and Hansen and I were to put the ship about. Kristensen was steering, but gave us a hand when he could leave the wheel. As the ship luffed up into the wind and the sails began to flap pretty violently, the whole of the watch below suddenly came rushing on deck in nothing but their unmentionables and started to haul. Chance willed it that at the same moment an iceberg came out of the fog, right in front of our bows. It was not many minutes, either, before we were on the other tack, and the watch below did not linger long on deck. With so few clothes on it was no pleasure to be out in that cold, foggy air. They slept so lightly, then, that it took no more noise than that to wake them. When I afterwards asked one of them – I think it was Beck – what made them think of coming up, he replied that they thought we were going to run into an iceberg and were trying to get out of the way.

It has happened at night that I have seen the ice-blink as far off as eight miles, and then there is nothing to fear; but sometimes in the middle of the day we have sailed close to icebergs that have only been seen a few minutes before we were right on them. As the voyage was long, we sailed as fast as we could, as a rule; but on two or three nights we had to reduce our way to a minimum, as we could not see much farther than the end of the bowsprit.

After two or three weeks' sailing the icebergs began gradually to decrease, and I hoped we should soon come to the end of them; but on Sunday, March 5, when it was fairly clear, we saw about midday a whole lot of big bergs ahead. One of the watch below, who had just come on deck, exclaimed: "What the devil is this beastly mess you fellows have got into?" He might well ask, for in the course of that afternoon we passed no less than about a hundred bergs. They were big tabular bergs, all of the same height, about 100 feet, or about as high as the crow's-nest of the *Fram*. The bergs were not the least worn, but looked as if they had calved quite recently. As I said, it was clear enough, we even got an observation that day (lat. 61° S., long. 150° W.), and as we had a west wind, we twisted quite elegantly past one iceberg after another. The sea, which during the morning had been high enough for the spray to dash over the tops of the bergs, gradually went down, and in the evening, when we were well to leeward of them all, it was as smooth as if we had been in harbour. In the course of the night we passed a good many more bergs, and the next day we only saw about twenty.

In the various descriptions of voyages in these waters, opinions are divided as to the temperature of the water falling in the neighbourhood of icebergs. That it falls steadily as one approaches the pack-ice is certain enough, but whether it falls for one or a few scattered icebergs, no doubt depends on circumstances.

One night at 12 o'clock we had a temperature in the water of 34.1° F., at 4 a.m. 33.8° F., and at 8 a.m. 33.6° F.; at 6 a.m. we passed an iceberg. At 12 noon the temperature had risen to 33.9° F. In this case one might say that the temperature gave warning, but, as a rule, in high latitudes it has been constant both before and after passing an iceberg.

On Christmas Eve, 1911, when on our second trip southward we saw the first real iceberg, the temperature of the water fell in four hours from 35.6° F. to 32.7° F., which was the temperature when the bergs were passed, after which it rose rather rapidly to 35° F.

In the west wind belt I believe one can tell with some degree of certainty when one is approaching ice. In the middle of November, 1911, between Prince Edward Island and the Crozet Islands (about lat. 47° S.) the temperature fell. Towards morning I remarked to someone: "The temperature of the water is falling as if we were getting near the ice." On the forenoon of the same day we sailed past a very small berg; the temperature again rose to the normal, and we met no more ice until Christmas Eve.

On Saturday, March 4, the day before we met that large collection of bergs, the temperature fell pretty rapidly from 33.9° F. to 32.5° F. We had not then seen ice for nearly twenty-four hours. At the same time the colour of the water became unusually green, and it is possible that we had come into a cold current. The temperature remained as low as this till Sunday morning, when at 8 a. m. it rose to 32.7° F.; at 12 noon, close to a berg, to 32.9° F., and a mile to lee of it, to 33° F. It continued to rise, and at 4 p.m., when the bergs were thickest, it was 33.4° F.; at 8 p.m. 33.6° F., and at midnight 33.8° F. If there had been a fog, we should certainly have thought we were leaving the ice instead of approaching it; it is very curious, too, that the temperature of the water should not be more constant in the presence of such a great quantity of ice; but, as I have said, it may have been a current.

In the course of the week following March 5 the bergs became rarer, but the same kind of weather prevailed. Our speed was irreproachable, and in one day's work (from noon to noon) we covered a distance of 200 nautical miles, or an average of about 82 knots an hour, which was the best day's work the *Fram* had done up to that time. The wind; which had been westerly and north-westerly, went by degrees to the north, and ended in a hurricane from the north-east on Sunday, March 12. I shall quote here what I wrote about this in my diary on the 13th:

"Well, now we have experienced the first hurricane on the *Fram* . On Saturday afternoon, the 11th, the wind went to the north-east, as an ordinary breeze with rain. The barometer had been steady between 29.29 inches (744 millimetres) and 29.33 inches (745 millimetres). During the afternoon it began to fall, and at 8 p.m. it was 29.25 inches (743 millimetres) without the wind having freshened at all. The outer jib was taken in, however. By midnight the barometer had fallen to 29.0 inches (737 millimetres), while the wind had increased to a stiff breeze. We took in the foresail, mainsail, and inner jib, and had now only the topsail and a storm-trysail left. The wind gradually increased to a gale. At 4 a.m. on Sunday the barometer had fallen again to 28.66 inches (728 millimetres), and at 6 a.m. the topsail was made fast.

The wind increased and the seas ran higher, but we did not ship much water. At 8 a.m. the barometer was 28.30 inches (719 millimetres), and at 9 a.m. 28.26 inches (718 millimetres), when at last it stopped going down and remained steady till about noon, during which time a furious hurricane was blowing. The clouds were brown, the colour of chocolate; I cannot remember ever having seen such an ugly sky. Little by little the wind went to the north, and we sailed large under two storm-trysails. Finally, we had the seas on our beam, and now the *Fram* showed herself in all her glory as the best sea-boat in the world. It was extraordinary to watch how she behaved. Enormous seas came surging high to windward, and we, who were standing on the bridge, turned our backs to receive them, with some such remark as: 'Ugh, that's a nasty one coming.' But the sea never came. A few yards from the ship it looked over the bulwarks and got ready to hurl itself upon her. But at the last moment the *Fram* gave a wriggle of her body and was instantly at the top of the wave, which slipped under the vessel. Can anyone be surprised if one gets fond of such a ship? Then she went down with the speed of lightning from the top of the wave into the trough, a fall of fourteen or fifteen yards. When we sank like this, it gave one the same feeling as dropping from the twelfth to the ground-floor in an American express elevator, 'as if everything inside you was coming up.' It was so quick that we seemed to be lifted off the deck. We went up and down like this all the afternoon and evening, till during the night the wind gradually dropped and it became calm. That the storm would not be of long duration might almost be assumed from its suddenness, and the English rule – Long foretold, long last; Short notice, soon past' – may thus be said to have held good.

"When there is a strong wind on her beam, the *Fram* does not roll so much as usual, except for an occasional leeward lurch; nor was any excessive quantity of water shipped in this boisterous sea. The watch went below as usual when they were relieved, and, as somebody very truly remarked, all hands might quite well have turned in, if we had not had to keep a lookout for ice. And fortune willed it that the day of the hurricane was the first since we had left the Barrier that we did not see ice – whether this was because the spray was so high that it hid our view, or because there really was none. Be that as it may, the main thing was that we saw no ice.

During the night we had a glimpse of the full moon, which gave the man at the wheel occasion to call out 'Hurrah!' – and with good reason, as we had been waiting a long time for the moon to help us in looking out for ice.

"In weather like this one notices nothing out of the ordinary below deck. Here hardly anything is heard of the wind, and in the after-saloon, which is below the water-line, it is perfectly comfortable. The cook, who resides below, therefore reckons 'ugly weather' according to the motion of the vessel, and not according to storms, fog, or rain. On deck we do not mind much how it blows, so long as it is only clear, and the wind is not against us. How little one hears below deck may be understood from the fact that yesterday morning, while it was blowing a hurricane, the cook went about as usual, whistling his two verses of 'The Whistling Bowery Boy.' While he was in the middle of the first, I came by and told him that it was blowing a hurricane if he cared to see what it looked like. 'Oh, yes,' he said, 'I could guess it was blowing, for the galley fire has never drawn so well; the bits of coal are flying up the chimney'; and then he whistled through the second verse. All the same, he could not resist going up to see. It was not long before he came down again, with a 'My word, it is blowing, and waves up to the sky!' No; it was warmer and more cosy below among his pots and pans.

"For dinner, which was eaten as usual amid cheerful conversation, we had green-pea soup, roast sirloin, with a glass of aquavit, and caramel pudding; so it may be seen that the cook was not behindhand in opening tins, even in a hurricane. After dinner we enjoyed our usual Sunday cigar, while the canary, which has become Kristensen's pet, and hangs in his cabin, sang at the top of its voice."

On March 14 we saw the last iceberg; during the whole trip we had seen and passed between 500 and 600 bergs.

The wind held steady from the north-east for a week and a half, and I was beginning to think we should be stuck down here to play the *Flying Dutchman*. There was every possible sign of a west wind, but it did not come. On the night of the 17th it cleared; light cirrus clouds covered the sky, and there was a ring about the moon. This, together with the heavy swell and the pronounced fall of the barometer, showed that something might be expected. And, sure enough, on Sunday, March 19, we were in a cyclone. By manoeuvring according to the rules for avoiding a cyclone in the southern hemisphere, we at any rate went well clear of one semicircle. About 4 p.m. on Sunday afternoon the barometer was down to 27.56 inches (700 millimetres), the lowest barometer reading I have ever heard of. From noon to 4 p.m. there was a calm, with heavy sea. Immediately after a gale sprang up from the north-west, and in the course of a couple of days it slowly moderated to a breeze from the same quarter.

Sunday, March 5, a hundred icebergs; Sunday March 12, a hurricane; and Sunday, March 19, a cyclone: truly three pleasant "days of rest." The curves given on the next page, which show the course of barometric pressure for a week, from Monday to Monday, are interesting. By way of comparison a third curve is given from the north-east trade, where there is an almost constant breeze and fine weather.

On this trip the fore-saloon was converted into a sail-loft, where Rönne and Hansen carried on their work, each in his watch. The after-saloon was used as a common mess-room, as it is warmer, and the motion is far less felt than forward.

From the middle of March it looked as if the equinoctial gales were over, for we had quite fine weather all the way to Buenos Aires. Cape Horn was passed on March 31 in the most delightful weather – a light westerly breeze, not a cloud in the sky, and only a very slight swell from the west. Who would have guessed that such splendid weather was to be found in these parts? – and that in March, the most stormy month of the year.

Lieutenant Gjertsen and Kutschin collected plankton all the time; the latter smiled all over his face whenever he chanced to get one or two "tadpoles" in his tow-net.

From the Falkland Islands onward the *Fram* was washed and painted, so that we might not present too "Polar" an appearance on arrival at Buenos Aires.

It may be mentioned as a curious fact that the snow with which we filled our water-tanks on the Barrier did not melt till we were in the River La Plata, which shows what an even temperature is maintained in the *Fram's* hold.

About midday on Easter Sunday we were at the mouth of the River La Plata, without seeing land, however. During the night the weather became perfect, a breeze from the south, moonlight and starry, and we went up the river by soundings and observations of the stars until at 1 a.m. on Monday, when we had the Recalada light-ship right ahead. We had not seen any light since we left Madeira on September 9. At 2.30 the same morning we got a pilot aboard, and at seven in the evening we anchored in the roads of Buenos Aires.

We had then been nearly once round the world, and for over seven months the anchor had not been out. We had reckoned on a two months' voyage from the ice, and it had taken us sixty-two days.

The Oceanographical Cruise

According to the programme, the *Fram* was to go on an oceanographical cruise in the South Atlantic, and my orders were that this was to be arranged to suit the existing circumstances. I had reckoned on a cruise of about three months. We should have to leave Buenos Aires at the beginning of October to be down in the ice at the right time (about the New Year).

As we were too short-handed to work the ship, take soundings, etc., the following four seamen were engaged: H. Halvorsen, A. Olsen, F. Steller, and J. Andersen. At last we were more or less ready, and the *Fram* sailed from Buenos Aires on June 8, 1911, the anniversary of our leaving Horten on our first hydrographic cruise in the North Atlantic. I suppose there was no one on board on June 8, 1910, who dreamed that a year later we should go on a similar cruise in the South.

We had a pilot on board as far as Montevideo, where we arrived on the afternoon of the 9th; but on account of an increasing wind (pampero) we had to lie at anchor here for a day and a half, as the pilot could not be taken off. On Saturday afternoon, the 10th, he was fetched off by a big tug-boat, on board of which was the Secretary of the Norwegian Consulate. This gentleman asked us if we could not come into the harbour, as "people would like to see the ship." I promised to come in on the way back, "if we had time."

On Sunday morning, the 11th, we weighed anchor, and went out in the most lovely weather that can be imagined. Gradually the land disappeared, and in the course of the evening we lost the lights; we were once more out in the Atlantic, and immediately everything resumed its old course.

In order to save our supply of preserved provisions as much as possible, we took with us a quantity of live poultry, and no fewer than twenty live sheep, which were quartered in the "farmyard" on the port side of the vessel's fore-deck. Sheep and hens were all together, and there was always a most beautiful scent of hay, so that we had not only sea air, but "country air." In spite of all this delightful air, three or four of the crew were down with influenza, and had to keep their berths for some days.

I reckoned on being back at Buenos Aires by the beginning of September, and on getting, if possible, one station a day. The distance, according to a rough calculation, was about 8,000 nautical miles, and I laid down the following plan: To go about east by north with the prevailing northerly and north-westerly winds to the coast of Africa, and there get hold of the south-east trade. If we could not reach Africa before that date, then to turn on July 22 and lay our course with the south-east trade for St. Helena, which we could reach before August 1; from there again with the same wind to South Trinidad (August 11 or 12); on again with easterly and north-easterly winds on a south-westerly course until about August 22, when the observations were to be concluded, and we should try to make Buenos Aires in the shortest time.

That was the plan that we attempted. On account of the fresh water from the River La Plata, we did not begin at once to take samples of water, and with a head-wind, north-east, we lay close-hauled for some days. We also had a pretty stiff breeze, which was another reason for delaying the soundings until the 17th.

For taking samples of water a winch is used, with a sound-ing-line of, let us say, 5,000 metres (2,734 fathoms), on which are hung one or more tubes for catching water; we used three at once to save time. Now, supposing water and temperatures are to be taken at depths of 300, 400, and 500 metres (164, 218, and 273 fathoms), Apparatus III. (see diagram) is first hung on, about 20 metres (10 fathoms) from the end of the line, where a small weight (a) hangs; then it is lowered until the indicator-wheel, over which the line passes, shows 100 metres (54 fathoms); Apparatus II. is then put on, and it is lowered again for another 100 metres, when Apparatus I. is put on and the line paid out for 300 metres (164 fathoms) – that is, until the indicator-wheel shows 500 metres (273 fathoms). The upper Apparatus (I.) is then at 300 metres (164 fathoms), No. II. at 400 metres (218 fathoms), and No. III. at 500 metres (273 fathoms). Under Apparatus I. and II. is hung a slipping sinker (about 8 centimetres, or 3 1/4 inches, long, and 3 centimetres, or 1 1/4 inches, in diameter). To the water-samplers are attached thermometers (b) in tubes arranged for the purpose.

The water-samplers themselves consist of a brass cylinder (c), about 38 centimetres (15 inches) long and 4 centimetres (1 1/2 inches) in diameter (about half a litre of water), set in a *Fram* e (d). At about the middle of the cylinder are pivots, which rest in bearings on the *Fram* e, so that the cylinder can be swung 180 degrees (straight up and down).

The cylinder, while being lowered in an inverted position, is open at both ends, so that the water can pass through. But at its upper and lower ends are valves, working on hinges and provided with packing. When the apparatus is released, the cylinder swings round, and these valves then automatically close the ends of the cylinder. The water that is thus caught in the cylinder at the required depth remains in it while it is being heaved up, and is collected in bottles. When the apparatus is released, the column of mercury in the thermometer is broken, and the temperature of the water is read at the same depth as the water is taken from.

The release takes place in the following manner: when all the cylinders have been lowered to the required depths, they are left hanging for a few minutes, so that the thermometers may be set at the right temperature before the column of mercury is broken. Then a slipping sinker is sent down the line. When this sinker strikes the first apparatus, a spring is pressed, a hook (e) which has held the cylinder slips loose, and the cylinder turns completely over (Apparatus I.). As it does this, the valves, as already mentioned, close the ends of the cylinder, which is fixed in its new position by a hook in the bottom of the frame. At the same instant the slipping sinker that hangs under Apparatus I. is released, and continues the journey to Apparatus II., where the same thing happens. It is then repeated with Apparatus III. When they are all ready, they are heaved in.

By holding one's finger on the line one can feel, at all events in fairly calm weather, when the sinkers strike against the cylinders; but I used to look at my watch, as it takes about half a minute for the sinker to go down 100 metres. The necessary data are entered in a book.

On the morning of the 17th, then, the sails were clewed up, and the *Fram* began to roll even worse than with the sails set. We first tried taking soundings with a sinker of 66 pounds, and a tube for taking specimens of the sea-bed. At 2,000 metres (1,093 fathoms) or more the line (piano wire) broke, so that sinker, tube, and over 2,000 metres of line continued their way unhindered to the bottom. I had thought of taking samples of water at 4,000, 3,000, and 2,000 metres (2,187, 1,639, 1,093 fathoms), and so on, and water-cylinders were put on from 0 to 2,000 metres. This, however, took six hours. Next day, on account of the heavy sea, only a few samples from 0 to 100 metres (54 fathoms) were taken. On the third day we made another attempt to get the bottom. This time we got specimens of the sea-bed from about 4,500 metres (about 2,500 fathoms); but the heaving in and taking of water samples and temperatures occupied eight hours, from 7 a.m. till 3 p.m., or a third part of the twenty-four hours.

In this way we should want at least nine months on the route that had been laid down; but as, unfortunately, this time was not at our disposal, we at once gave up taking specimens of the bottom and samples of water at greater depths than 1,000 metres (546 fathoms).

For the remainder of the trip we took temperatures and samples of water at the following depths: 0, 5, 10, 25, 50, 75, 100, 150, 200, 250, 300, 400, 500, 750, and 1,000 metres (0, 2 3/4, 5 1/2, 13 1/2, 27, 41, 54, 81, 108, 135, 164, 218, 273, 410, and 546 fathoms), in all, fifteen samples from each station, and from this time forward we went on regularly with one station every day. Finally, we managed to heave up two water-cylinders on the same line by hand without great difficulty. At first this was done with the motor and sounding-machine, but this took too long, and we afterwards used nothing but a light hand-winch. Before very long we were so practised that the whole business only took two hours.

These two hours were those we liked best of the twenty-four. All kinds of funny stories were told, especially about experiences in Buenos Aires, and every day there was something new. Here is a little yarn.

One of the members of the expedition had been knocked down by a motor-car in one of the busiest streets; the car stopped and of course a crowd collected at once. Our friend lay there, wondering whether he ought not to be dead, or at least to have broken a leg, so as to get compensation. While he lay thus, being prodded and examined by the public, he suddenly remembered that he had half a dollar in his pocket. With all that money it didn't matter so much about the compensation; up jumped our friend like an india-rubber ball, and in a second he had vanished in the crowd, who stood open-mouthed, gazing after the "dead" man.

Our speed on this cruise was regulated as nearly as possible so that there might be about 100 nautical miles between each station, and I must say we were uncommonly lucky in the weather. We made two fairly parallel sections with comparatively regular intervals between the stations; as regular, in any case, as one can hope to get with a vessel like the *Fram,* which really has too little both of sail area and engine power. The number of stations was 60 in all and 891 samples of water were taken. Of plankton specimens 190 were sent home. The further examination of these specimens in Norway will show whether the material collected is of any value, and whether the cruise has yielded satisfactory results.

As regards the weather on the trip, it was uniformly good the whole time; we had a good deal of wind now and then, with seas and rolling, but for the most part there was a fresh breeze. In the south-east trade we sailed for four weeks at a stretch without using the engine, which then had a thorough over-hauling. At the same time we had a good opportunity of smartening up the ship, which she needed badly. All the iron was freed from rust, and the whole vessel painted both below and above deck. The decks themselves were smeared with a mixture of oil, tar and turpentine, after being scoured. All the rigging was examined. At the anchorage at Buenos Aires nearly the whole ship was painted again, masts and yards, the outside of the vessel and everything inboard, both deck-houses, the boats and the various winches, pumps, etc. In the engine-room everything was either shining bright or freshly painted, every-thing hung in its place and such order and cleanliness reigned that it was a pleasure to go down there. The result of all this renovating and smartening up was that, when we fetched up by the quay at Buenos Aires, the *Fram* looked brighter than I suppose she has ever done since she was new. During the trip the holds were also cleaned up, and all the provisions re-stowed and an inventory made of them.

A whole suit of sails was completely worn out on this voyage; but what can one expect when the ship is being worked every single day, with clewing up, making fast and setting of sails both in calms and winds? This work every day reminded me of the corvette *Ellida*, when the order was "all hands aloft." As a rule, though, it was only clewing up the sails that had to be done, as we always had to take soundings on the weather side, so that the sounding-line should not foul the bottom of the vessel and smash the apparatus. And we did not lose more than one ther-mometer in about nine hundred soundings.

On account of all this wear and tear of sails Rönne was occupied the whole time, both at sea and in Buenos Aires, in making and patching sails, as there was not much more than the leeches left of those that had been used, and on the approaching trip (to the Ice Barrier) we should have to have absolutely first-class things in the "Roaring Forties."

June 30, 1911, is a red-letter day in the *Fram's* history, as on that day we intersected our course from Norway to the Barrier, and the *Franz* thus completed her first circumnavigation of the globe. Bravo, *Fram!* It was well done, especially after the bad character you have been given as a sailer and a sea-boat. In honour of the occasion we had a better dinner than usual, and the *Franz* was congratulated by all present on having done her work well.

On the evening of July 29 St. Helena was passed. It was the first time I had seen this historic island. It was very strange to think that "the greatest spirit of a hundred centuries," as some author has called Napoleon, should have ending his restless life on this lonely island of the South Atlantic.

On August 12, when daylight came, we sighted the little Martin Vaz Islands ahead, and a little later South Trinidad (in 1910 this island was passed on October 16). We checked our chronometers, which, however, proved to be correct. From noon till 2 p.m., while we were lying still and taking our daily hydrographic observations, a sailing ship appeared to the north of us, lying close-hauled to the south. She bore down on us and ran up her flag, and we exchanged the usual greetings; she was a Norwegian barque bound for Australia. Otherwise we did not see more than four or five ships on the whole voyage, and those were pretty far off.

Never since leaving Madeira (September, 1910) had we been troubled with animals or insects of any kind whatever; but when we were in Buenos Aires for the first time, at least half a million flies came aboard to look at the vessel. I hoped they would go ashore when the *Fram* sailed; but no, they followed us, until by degrees they passed peacefully away on fly-paper.

Well, flies are one thing, but we had something else that was worse – namely, rats – our horror and dread, and for the future our deadly enemies. The first signs of them I found in my bunk and on the table in the fore-saloon; they were certainly not particular. What I said on that occasion had better not be printed, though no expression could be strong enough to give vent to one's annoyance at such a discovery. We set traps, but what was the use of that, when the cargo consisted exclusively of provisions?

One morning, as Rönne was sitting at work making sails, he observed a "shadow" flying past his feet, and, according to his account, into the fore-saloon. The cook came roaring: "There's a rat in the fore-saloon!" Then there was a lively scene; the door was shut, and all hands started hunting. All the cabins were emptied and rummaged, the piano, too; everything was turned upside down, but the rat had vanished into thin air.

About a fortnight later I noticed a corpse-like smell in Hassel's cabin, which was empty. On closer sniffing and examination it turned out to be the dead rat, a big black one, unfortunately a male rat. The poor brute, that had starved to death, had tried to keep itself alive by devouring a couple of novels that lay in a locked drawer. How the rat got into that drawer beats me.

On cleaning out the provision hold nests were found with

several rats in them: six were killed, but at least as many escaped, so now no doubt we have a whole colony. A reward was promised of ten cigars for each rat; traps were tried again, but all this did very little good. When we were in Buenos Aires for the second time we got a cat on board; it certainly kept the rats down, but it was shot on the Barrier. At Hobart we provided a few traps, which caught a good many; but we shall hardly get rid of them altogether until we have landed most of the provisions, and smoked them out. We have also had a lot of moth; at present they have done nothing beyond eating a couple of holes in my best trousers.

During the whole of this cruise we had a fishing-line hanging out, but it hung for a whole month without there being a sign of a fish, in spite of the most delicate little white rag that was attached to the hook. One morning the keenest of our fishermen came up as usual and felt the line. Yes, by Jove! at last there was one, and a big one, too, as he could hardly haul in the line by himself. There was a shout for assistance. "Hi, you beggar! come and lend a hand; there's a big fish!" Help came in a second, and they both hauled for all they were worth. "Ah! he's a fine, glistening fish; it'll be grand to get fresh fish for dinner!" At last the fish appeared over the rail; but, alas! it was seen to have no head. It was an ordinary stockfish, about three-quarters of a yard long, that some joker had hung on the line during the night. That we all had a hearty laugh goes without saying, the fishermen included, as they took it all in good part.

As a fishing-boat the *Fram* is on the whole not very successful. The only fish we caught, besides the above-mentioned stockfish, was a real live fish; but, unfortunately, it fell off the hook as it was being hauled in. According to the account of eye-witnesses, this fish was ... six feet long and one broad. Now we don't fish any more.

On August 19 the hydrographic observations were brought to an end, and a course was laid for Buenos Aires, where we anchored in the roads at midnight on September 1.

At Buenos Aires

To arrive at Buenos Aires in the early part of 1911 was not an unmixed pleasure, especially when one had no money. The *Fram* Expedition was apparently not very popular at that time, and our cash balance amounted to about forty pesos (about (L)3 10s.), but that would not go very far; our supply of provisions had shrunk to almost nothing, and we had not enough to be able to leave the port. I had been told that a sum had been placed to the credit of the *Fram* for our stay in Buenos Aires, but I neither saw nor heard anything of it while we were there, and it was no doubt somewhat imaginary.

If we were to be at all able to go down and take off the shore party money must be found. We had come to the end of sail-cloth and ropes, we had too little food and a minimum of oil; all this would have to be provided. At the worst the oceanographical cruise could be cut out, and we could lie still at Buenos Aires; then, as our comrades could not very well be left to perish on the ice, enough would have to be sent us from Norway to enable us to go down there; but that would finish the whole expedition, as in such a case the *Fram* had orders to go back to Norway.

As usual, however, the *Fram's* luck helped her again. A few days before we left Norway our distinguished compatriot in Buenos Aires, Don Pedro Christophersen, had cabled that he would supply us with what provisions we might require, if, after leaving Madeira, we would call at Buenos Aires. Of course, he did not know at that time that the voyage would be extended to include the South Pole, and that the *Fram* on arrival at Buenos Aires would be almost empty instead of having a full cargo, but that did not prevent his helping us. I immediately called on him and his brother, the Norwegian Minister; fortunately, they were both very enthusiastic about our Chief's change of plan.

When, on a subsequent occasion, I expressed my astonishment at not hearing from home, I was told that the funds of the Expedition were exhausted, and Mr. Christophersen promised me, on hearing what straits we were in, to pay all our expenses in Buenos Aires, and to supply us with provisions and fuel. That brought us out of our difficulties at a bound, and we had no more need to take thought for the morrow. Everyone on board received a sum of money for his personal expenses from the Norwegian colony of the River Plate, and we were invited to their dinner on Independence Day, May 17.

Our second stay at Buenos Aires was very pleasant; everyone was amiability itself, and festivities were even got up for us. We took on board provisions that had been sent out from Norway by Mr. Christophersen's orders, about 50,000 litres (11,000 gallons) of petroleum, ship's stores, and so on; enough for a year. But this was not all. Just before we sailed Mr. Christophersen said he would send a relief expedition, if the *Fram* did not return to Australia by a certain date; but, as everyone knows, this was happily unnecessary.

During the three weeks we were lying at the quay in Buenos Aires we were occupied in getting everything on board, and making the vessel ready for sea. We had finished this by the afternoon of Wednesday, October 4, and next morning the Pram was ready to continue her second circumnavigation of the globe. In Buenos Aires we lay at the same quay as the *Deutschland*, the German Antarctic Expedition's ship. A. Kutschin and the second engineer, J. Nödtvedt, went home, and seaman J. Andersen was discharged.

From Buenos Aires to the Ross Barrier

On the trip from Buenos Aires to the Barrier the watches were divided as follows: From eight to two: T. Nilsen, L. Hansen, H. Halvorsen, and A. Olsen. From two to eight: H. Gjertsen, A. Beck, M. Rönne, and F. Steller. In the engine-room: K. Sundbeck and H. Kristensen. Lastly, K. Olsen, cook. In all eleven men.

It is said that "well begun is half done," and it almost seems as if a bad beginning were likely to have a similar continuation. When we left the northern basin on the morning of October 5, there was a head wind, and it was not till twenty-four hours later that we could drop the pilot at the Recalada lightship. After a time it fell calm, and we made small progress down the River La Plata, until, on the night of the 6th, we were clear of the land, and the lights disappeared on the horizon.

Properly speaking, we ought to have been in the west wind

belt as soon as we came out, and the drift of the clouds and movement of the barograph were examined at least twenty-four times a day, but it still remained calm. At last, after the lapse of several days, we had a little fresh south-westerly wind with hail showers, and then, of course, I thought we had made a beginning; but unfortunately it only lasted a night, so that our joy was short-lived.

We took with us from Buenos Aires fifteen live sheep and fifteen live little pigs, for which two houses were built on the after-deck; as, however, one of the pigs was found dead on the morning after the south-westerly breeze just mentioned, I assumed that this was on account of the cold, and another house was at once built for them between decks (in the work-room), where it was very warm. They were down here the whole time; but as their house was cleaned out twice a day and dry straw put on the floor, they did not cause us much inconvenience; besides which, their house was raised more than half a foot above the deck itself, so that the space below could always be kept clean. The pigs thrived so well down here that we could almost see them growing; on arrival at the Barrier we had no fewer than nine alive.

The sheep had a weather-tight house with a tarpaulin over the roof, and they grew fatter and fatter; we had every opportunity of noticing this, as we killed one of them regularly every Saturday until we came into the pack-ice and got seal-meat. We had four sheep left on reaching the Barrier.

We did wretchedly in October – calms and east winds, nothing but east winds; as regards distance it was the worst month we had had since leaving Norway, notwithstanding that the

Fram had been in dry dock, had a clean bottom and a light cargo. When close-hauled with any head sea, we scarcely move; a stiff fair wind is what is wanted if we are to get on. Somebody said we got on so badly because we had thirteen pigs on board; another said it was because we caught so many birds, and I had caught no less than fourteen albatrosses and four Cape pigeons. Altogether there is quite enough of what I will call superstition at sea. One particular bird brings fine weather, another storms; it is very important to notice which way the whale swims or the dolphin leaps; the success of seal-hunting depends on whether the first seal is seen ahead or astern, and so on. Enough of that.

October went out and November came in with a fresh breeze from the south-south-west, so that we did nine and a half knots. This promised well for November, but the promise was scarcely fulfilled. We had northerly wind or southerly wind continually, generally a little to the east of north or south, and I believe I am not saying too much when I state that in the "west wind belt" with an easterly course we lay close-hauled on one tack or the other for about two-thirds of the way. For only three days out of three months did we have a real west wind, a wind which, with south-westerly and north-westerly winds, I had reckoned on having for 75 per cent of the trip from Buenos Aires to about the longitude of Tasmania.

In my enthusiasm over the west wind in question, I went so far as to write in my diary at 2 a.m. on November 11: "There is a gale from the west, and we are making nine knots with foresail and topsail. The sea is pretty high and breaking on both sides of the vessel, so that everything about us is a mass of spray. In spite of this, not a drop of water comes on deck, and it is so dry that the watch are going about in clogs. For my part I am wearing felt slippers, which will not stand wet. Sea-boots and oilskins hang ready in the chart-house, in case it should rain. On a watch like to-night, when the moon is kind enough to shine, everyone on deck is in the best of humours, whistling, chattering, and singing. Somebody comes up with the remark that 'She took that sea finely,' or 'Now she's flying properly.' 'Fine' is almost too feeble an expression; one ought to say 'lightly and elegantly' when speaking of the *Fram* ... What more can one wish?" etc.

But whatever time Adam may have spent in Paradise, we were not there more than three days, and then the same wretched state of things began again. What I wrote when there was a head wind or calm, I should be sorry to reproduce. Woe to him who then came and said it was fine weather.

It was lucky for us that the *Fram* sails so much more easily now than in 1910, otherwise we should have taken six months to reach the Barrier. When we had wind, we used it to the utmost; but we did not do this without the loss of one or two things; the new jib-sheet broke a couple of times, and one night we carried away the outer bobstay of the jib-boom. The foresail and topsail were neither made fast nor reefed during the whole trip.

The last time the jib-sheet broke there was a strong breeze from the south-west with a heavy sea; all sail was set with the exception of the spanker, as the ship would not steer with that. There was an extra preventer on the double jib-sheet, but in spite of that the sheets broke and the jib was split with a fearful crack. Within a minute the mainsail and gaff-topsail were hauled down, so that the ship might fall off, and the jib hauled down. This was instantly unbent and a new one bent. The man at the helm, of course, got the blame for this, and the first thing he said to me was "I couldn't help it, she was twisting on the top of a wave." We were then making ten knots, and more than that we shall not do.

The *Fram* rolled well that day. A little earlier in the afternoon, at two o'clock, when the watch had gone below to dinner and were just eating the sweet, which on that occasion consisted of preserved pears, we felt that there was an unusually big lurch coming. Although, of course, we had fiddles on the table, the plates, with meat, potatoes, etc., jumped over the fiddles, which they didn't care a button for, into Beck's cabin. I caught one of the pears in its flight, but the plate with the rest of them went on its way. Of course there was a great shout of laughter, which stopped dead as we heard a violent noise on deck, over our heads; I guessed at once it was an empty water-tank that had broken loose, and with my mouth full of pear I yelled "Tank!" and flew on deck with the whole watch below at my heels. A sea had come in over the after-deck, and had lifted the tank up from its lashings. All hands threw themselves upon the tank, and held on to it till the water had poured off the deck, when it was again fixed in its place. When this was done, my watch went below again and lit their pipes as if nothing had happened.

On November 13 we passed the northernmost of the Prince Edward Islands, and on the 18th close to Penguin Island, the most south-westerly of the Crozets. In the neighbourhood of the latter we saw a great quantity of birds, a number of seals and penguins, and even a little iceberg. I went close to the land to check the chronometers, which an observation and bearings of the islands showed to be correct.

Our course was then laid for Kerguelen Island, but we went too far north to see it, as for two weeks the wind was south-easterly and southerly, and the leeway we made when sailing close-hauled took us every day a little to the north of east. When we were in the same waters in 1910, there was gale after gale; then we did not put in at Kerguelen on account of the force of the wind; this time we could not approach the island because of the wind's direction. In no respect can the second trip be compared with the first; I should never have dreamed that there could be so much difference in the "Roaring Forties" in two different years at the same season. In the "Foggy Fifties" the weather was calm and fine, and we had no fog until lat. 58° S.

As regards the distance sailed, November, 1911, is the best month the *Fram* has had.

In December, which began with a speed of one and a half knots, calm, swell against us, and the engine at full speed, we had a fair wind for three days, all the rest calms and head winds; the first part of the month from the north-east and east, so that we came much too far south; even in long. 150 E. we were in lat. 60° S. In Christmas week we had calms and light winds from the south-east, so that we managed to steal eastward to long. 170° E. and lat. 65° S., where, on the edge of the pack-ice, we had a stiff breeze from the north-north-east, that is, straight on to the ice.

Between Buenos Aires and the pack-ice we caught, as I have said, a good many birds, mostly albatrosses, and about thirty skins were prepared by L. Hansen. The largest albatross we got measured twelve feet between the tips of its wings, and the smallest bird was of a land species, not much bigger than a humming-bird.

Talking of albatrosses, it is both amusing and interesting to watch their elegant flight in a high wind. Without a movement of the wings they sail, now with, now against, the wind; at one instant they touch the surface of the water with the points of their wings, at the next they go straight into the air like an arrow. An interesting and instructive study for an aviator.

In a wind, when there is generally a number of them hovering about the vessel, they will dash down after anything that is thrown overboard; but of course it is useless to try to catch them when the ship has so much way. This must be done the next day, when the wind is lighter.

The birds are caught with an iron triangle, which ought to be enclosed in wood, so that it will float on the water. At the apex, which is very acute, the iron is filed as sharp as a knife, and pork is hung on each of the sides. When this is thrown in the wake of the ship, the bird settles on the water to feed. The upper part of its beak is hooked like that of a bird of prey, and as the albatross opens its beak and bites at the pork, you give a jerk, so that the triangle catches the upper part of the beak by two small notches, and the bird is left hanging. If the line should break, the whole thing simply falls off and the bird is unharmed. In hauling in, therefore, you have to be very careful to hold the line quite tight, even if the bird flies towards you, otherwise it will easily fall off: A bird may be pulled half-way in several times, and will immediately take the bait again.

On the night of December 11 an unusually beautiful aurora was seen; it lasted over an hour, and moved in a direction from west to east. On the 14th all the white paint was washed; the temperature was 43° F., and we were in shirt-sleeves.

For a whole week before Christmas the cook was busy baking Christmas cakes. I am bound to say he is industrious; and the day before Christmas Eve one of the little pigs, named Tulla, was killed. The swineherd, A. Olsen, whose special favourite this pig was, had to keep away during the operation, that we might not witness his emotion.

Early on the morning of Christmas Eve we saw the three first icebergs; there was an absolute calm all day, with misty air.

To keep Christmas the engine was stopped at 5 p.m., and then all hands came to dinner. Unfortunately we had no gramophone to sing to us, as in 1910; as a substitute the "orchestra" played "Glade Jul, hellige Jul," when all were seated. The orchestra was composed of Beck on the violin, Sundbeck on the mandolin, and the undersigned on the flute. I puffed out my cheeks as much as I could, and that is not saying a little, so that the others might see how proficient I was. I hardly think it was much of a musical treat; but the public was neither critical nor ceremonious, and the prevalent costume was jerseys. The dinner consisted of soup, roast pork, with fresh potatoes and whortleberries, ten-years-old aquavit and Norwegian bock beer, followed by wine-jelly and "kransekake," with – champagne. The toasts of their Majesties the King and Queen, Don Pedro Christophersen, Captain Amundsen, and the *Fram* were drunk.

I had decorated the saloon in a small way with artificial flowers, embroideries, and flags, to give a little colour. Dinner was followed by cigars and the distribution of Christmas presents. L. Hansen played the accordion, and Lieutenant Gjertsen and Rönne danced "folk dances"; the latter was, as usual, so amusing that he kept us in fits of laughter. At ten o'clock it was all over, the engine was started again, one watch went to bed and the other on deck; Olsen cleaned out the pigsty, as usual at this time of night. That finished Christmas for this year.

As has been said before, Sir James Ross was down here in the 1840's. Two years in succession he sailed from the Pacific into Ross Sea with two ships that had no auxiliary steam-power. I assumed, therefore, that if he could get through so easily, there must be some place between South Victoria Land and the Barrier (or land) on the other side, where there was little or no ice. Following this assumption, I intended to go down to the western pack-ice (that lying off South Victoria Land) and steer along it till we were in Ross Sea, or, at all events, until we found a place where we could easily get through. It is quite possible that Ross was very lucky in the time at which he encountered the ice, and that he only sailed in clear weather. We had no time to spare, however, but had to make use of whatever wind there was, even if we could not see very far.

As early as December 28, at 5 p.m., in lat. 65° S. and long. 171.5° E., it was reported that we were off the pack. I was a good deal surprised, as recent expeditions had not met the pack until 66.5° S., or about one hundred nautical miles farther south, nor had there been any sign of our being so near the ice. The wind for the last few days had been south-easterly, but for the moment it was calm; we therefore held on to the east along the edge of the pack, with the ice to starboard. About midnight the wind freshened from the north, and we lay close-hauled along the edge of the ice till midday on the 29th, when the direction of the ice became more southerly. The northerly wind, which gradually increased to a stiff breeze, was good enough for getting us on, but it must inevitably bring fog and snow in its train. These came, sure enough, as thick as a wall, and for a couple of days we sailed perfectly blindly.

Outside the pack-ice proper lie long streams of floes and loose scattered lumps, which become more frequent as one nears the pack. For two days we sailed simply by the lumps of ice; the more of them we saw, the more easterly was our course, until they began to decrease, when we steered more to the south. In this way we went in forty-eight hours from lat. 65° S. and long. 174° E. to lat. 69° S. and long. 178° E., a distance of about two hundred and fifty nautical miles, without entering the pack. Once we very nearly went into the trap, but fortunately got out again. The wind was so fresh that we did as much as eight and a half knots; when sailing at such a rate through a loose stream of ice, we sometimes ran upon a floe, which went under the ship's bottom, and came up alongside the other way up.

During the afternoon of the 31st the streams of ice became closer and closer, and then I made the mistake of continuing to sail to the eastward; instead of this, I ought to have stood off, and steered due south or to the west of south, with this ice on ourport side. The farther we advanced, the more certain I was that we had come into the eastern pack-ice. It must be remembered, however, that owing to fog and thick snow we had seen nothing for over two days. Observations there were none, of course; our speed had varied between two and eight and a half knots, and we had steered all manner of courses. That our dead reckoning was not very correct in such circumstances goes without saying, and an observation on January 2 showed us that we were somewhat farther to the east than we had reckoned. On the evening of December 31 the fog lifted for a while, and we saw nothing but ice all round. Our course was then set due south. We had come right down in lat. 69.5° S., and I hoped soon to be clear altogether; in 1910 we got out of the ice in 70°S., and were then in the same longitude as now.

Now, indeed, our progress began to be slow, and the old year went out in a far from pleasant fashion. The fog was so thick that I may safely say we did not see more than fifty yards from the ship, whereas we ought to have had the midnight sun; ice and snow-sludge were so thick that at times we lay still. The wind had, unfortunately, fallen off, but we still had a little breeze from the north, so that both sails and engine could be used. We went simply at haphazard; now and then we were lucky enough to come into great open channels and even lakes, but then the ice closed again absolutely tight. It could hardly be called real ice, however, but was rather a snow-sludge, about two feet thick, and as tough as dough; it looked as if it had all just been broken off a single thick mass. The floes lay close together, and we could see how one floe fitted into the other. The ice remained more or less close until we were right down in lat. 73°S. and long. 179° W.; the last part of it was old drift-ice.

From here to the Bay of Whales we saw a few scattered streams of floes and some icebergs. A few seals were shot in the ice, so that we had fresh meat enough, and could save the sheep and pigs until the shore party came on board. I was sure they would appreciate fresh roast pork.

The chart of Ross Sea has been drawn chiefly as a guide to future expeditions. It may be taken as certain that the best place to go through the ice is between long. 176° E. and 180°, and that the best time is about the beginning of February. Take, for instance, our southward route in 1911 – 1912: as has been said, the ice was met with as early as in 65° S., and we were not clear of it till about 73° S.; between 68° S. and 69° S. the line is interrupted, and it was there that I ought to have steered to the south.

Now follow the course from the Bay of Whales in 1912. Only in about 75° S. was ice seen (almost as in 1911), and we followed it. After that time we saw absolutely no more ice, as the chart shows; therefore in the course of about a month and a half all the ice that we met when going south had drifted out. The stippled line shows how I assume the ice to have lain; the heavy broken line shows what our course ought to have been.

The midnight sun was not seen till the night of January 7, 1912, to the south of lat. 77° S.; it was already 9.5° above the horizon. On the night of January 8 we arrived off the Barrier in extremely bitter weather. South-westerly and southerly winds had held for a few days, with fair weather; but that night there was thick snow, and the wind gradually fell calm, after which a fresh breeze sprang up from the south-east, with biting snow, and at the same time a lot of drift-ice. The engine went very slowly, and the ship kept head to wind. About midnight the weather cleared a little, and a dark line, which proved to be the Barrier, came in sight. The engine went ahead at full speed, and the sails were set, so that we might get under the lee of the perpendicular wall. By degrees the ice-blink above the Barrier became lighter and lighter, and before very long we were so close under it that we only just had room to go about. The Barrier here runs east and west, and with a south-easterly wind we went along it to the east. The watch that had gone below at eight o'clock, when we were still in open sea, came up again at two to find us close to the long-desired wall of ice.

Some hours passed in the same way, but then, of course, the wind became easterly – dead ahead – so that we had tack after tack till 6 p.m. the same day, when we were at the western point of the Bay of Whales.

The ice lay right out to West Cape, and we sailed across the mouth of the bay and up under the lee of the eastern Barrier, in order, if possible, to find slack ice or open water; but no, the fast ice came just as far on that side. It turned out that we could not get farther south than 78°30' – that is, eleven nautical miles farther north than the previous year, and no less than fifteen nautical miles from Framheim, taking into consideration the turn in the bay.

We were thus back at the same place we had left on February 14, 1911, and had since been round the world. The distance covered on this voyage of circumnavigation was 25,000 nautical miles, of which 8,000 belong to the oceanographical cruise in the South Atlantic.

We did not lie under the lee of the eastern Barrier for more than four hours; the wind, which had so often been against us, was true to its principles to the last. Of course it went to the north and blew right up the bay; the drift-ice from Ross Sea came in, and at midnight (January 9 – 10) we stood out again.

I had thought of sending a man up to Framheim to report that we had arrived, but the state of the weather did not allow it. Besides, I had only one pair of private skis on board and should therefore only have been able to send one man. It would have been better if several had gone together. During the forenoon of the 10th it gradually cleared, the wind fell light and we stood inshore again. As at the same time the barometer was rising steadily, Lieutenant Gjertsen went ashore on skis about one o'clock.

Later in the afternoon a dog came running out across the sea-ice, and I thought it had come down on Lieutenant Gjertsen's track; but I was afterwards told it was one of the half-wild dogs that ran about on the ice and did not show themselves up at the hut.

Meanwhile the wind freshened again; we had to put out for another twenty-four hours and lay first one way and then the other with shortened sail; then there was fine weather again and we came in. At 4 p.m. on the 11th Lieutenant Gjertsen returned with Lieutenant Prestrud, Johansen and Stubberud. Of course we were very glad to see one another again and all sorts of questions were asked on both sides. The Chief and the southern party were not yet back. They stayed on board till the 12th, got their letters and a big pile of newspapers and went ashore again; we followed them with the glasses as far as possible, so as to take them on board again if they could not get across the cracks in the ice.

During the days that followed we lay moored to the ice or went out, according to the weather.

At 7 p.m. on the 16th we were somewhat surprised to see a vessel bearing down. For my part, I guessed her to be the *Aurora*, Dr. Mawson's ship. She came very slowly, but at last what should we see but the Japanese flag! I had no idea that expedition was out again. The ship came right in, went past us twice and moored alongside the loose ice. Immediately afterwards ten men armed with picks and shovels went up the Barrier, while the rest rushed wildly about after penguins, and their shots were heard all night. Next morning the commander of the *Kainan Maru*, whose name was Homura, came on board. The same day a tent was set up on the edge of the Barrier, and cases, sledges, and so on, were put out on the ice. *Kainan Maru* means, I have been told, "the ship that opens the South."

Prestrud and I went on board her later in the day, to see what she was like, but we met neither the leader of the expedition nor the captain of the ship. Prestrud had the cinematograph apparatus with him, and a lot of photographs were also taken.

The leader of the Japanese expedition has written somewhere or other that the reason of Shackleton's losing all his ponies was that the ponies were not kept in tents at night, but had to lie outside. He thought the ponies ought to be in the tents and the men outside. From this one would think they were great lovers of animals, but I must confess that was not the impression I received. They had put penguins into little boxes to take them alive to Japan! Round about the deck lay dead and half-dead skua gulls in heaps. On the ice close to the vessel was a seal ripped open, with part of its entrails on the ice; but the seal was still alive. Neither Prestrud nor I had any sort of weapon that we could kill the seal with, so we asked the Japanese to do it, but

632

they only grinned and laughed. A little way off two of them were coming across the ice with a seal in front of them; they drove it on with two long poles, with which they pricked it when it would not go. If it fell into a crack, they dug it up again as you would see men quarrying stone at home; it had not enough life in it to be able to escape its tormentors. All this was accompanied by laughter and jokes. On arrival at the ship the animal was nearly dead, and it was left there till it expired.

On the 19th we had a fresh south-westerly wind and a lot of ice went out. The Japanese were occupied most of the night in going round among the floes and picking up men, dogs, cases, and so on, as they had put a good deal on to the ice in the course of the day. As the ice came out, so the *Fram* went in, right up to fat. 78°35' S., while the *Kainan Maru* drifted farther and farther out, till at last she disappeared. Nor did we see the vessel again, but a couple of men with a tent stayed on the Barrier as long as we were in the bay.

On the night of the 24th there was a stiff breeze from the west, and we drifted so far out in the thick snow that it was only on the afternoon of the 27th that we could make our way in again through a mass of ice. In the course of these two days so much ice had broken up that we came right in to fat. 78°39' S., or almost to Framheim, and that was very lucky. As we stood in over the Bay of Whales, we caught sight of a big Norwegian naval ensign flying on the Barrier at Cape Man's Head, and I then knew that the southern party had arrived. We went therefore as far south as possible and blew our powerful siren; nor was it very long before eight men came tearing down. There was great enthusiasm. The first man on board was the Chief; I was so certain he had reached the goal that I never asked him. Not till an hour later, when we had discussed all kinds of other things, did I enquire "Well, of course you have been at the South Pole?"

We lay there for a couple of days; on account of the short distance from Framheim, provisions, outfit, etc., were brought on board. If such great masses of ice had not drifted out in the last few days, it would probably have taken us a week or two to get the same quantity on board.

At 9.30 p.m. on January 30, 1912, in a thick fog, we took our moorings on board and waved a last farewell to the mighty Barrier.

From the Barrier to Buenos Aires, Via Hobart

The first day after our departure from the Barrier everything we had taken on board was stowed away, so that one would not have thought our numbers were doubled, or that we had taken several hundred cases and a lot of outfit on board. The change was only noticed on deck, where thirty-nine powerful dogs made an uproar all day long, and in the fore-saloon, which was entirely changed. This saloon, after being deserted for a year, was now full of men, and it was a pleasure to be there; especially as everyone had something to tell – the Chief of his trip, Prestrud of his, and Gjertsen and I of the *Fram*'s.

However, there was not very much time for yarning. The Chief at once began writing cablegrams and lectures, which Prestrud and I translated into English, and the Chief then copied again on a typewriter. In addition to this I was occupied the whole time in drawing charts, so that on arrival at Hobart everything was ready; the time passed quickly, though the voyage was fearfully long.

As regards the pack-ice we were extremely lucky. It lay in exactly the same spot where we had met with it in 1911 – that is, in about lat. 75° S. We went along the edge of it for a very short time, and then it was done with. To the north of 75° we saw nothing but a few small icebergs. We made terribly slow progress to the northward, how slow may perhaps be understood if I quote my diary for February 27:

"This trip is slower than anything we have had before; now and then we manage an average rate of two knots an hour in a day's run. In the last four days we have covered a distance that before would have been too little for a single day. We have been at it now for nearly a month, and are still only between lat. 52° and 53° S. Gales from the north are almost the order of the day," etc. However, it is an ill wind that blows nobody any good, and the time was well employed with all we had to do. After a five weeks' struggle we at last reached Hobart and anchored in the splendid harbour on March 7.

Our fresh provisions from Buenos Aires just lasted out; the last of the fresh potatoes were finished a couple of days before our arrival, and the last pig was killed when we had been at Hobart two days.

The *Fram* remained here for thirteen days, which were chiefly spent in repairing the propeller and cleaning the engine; in addition to this the topsail-yard, which was nearly broken in the middle, was spliced, as we had no opportunity of getting a new one. The first week was quiet on board, as, owing to the circumstances, there was no communication with the shore; but after that the ship was full of visitors, so that we were not very sorry to get away again.

Twenty-one of our dogs were presented to Dr. Mawson, the leader of the Australian expedition, and only those dogs that had been to the South Pole and a few puppies, eighteen in all, were left on board. While we lay in Hobart, Dr. Mawson's ship, the *Aurora*, came in. I went aboard her one day, and have thus been on board the vessels of all the present Antarctic expeditions. On the *Terra Nova*, the British ship, on February 4, 1911, in the Bay of Whales; on the *Deutschland*, the German, in September and October, 1911, in Buenos Aires; on the *Kainan Maru*, the Japanese, on January 17, 1912, in the Bay of Whales; and finally on the *Aurora* in Hobart. Not forgetting the *Fram,* which, of course, I think best of all.

On March 20 the *Fram* weighed anchor and left Tasmania. We made very poor progress to begin with, as we had calms for nearly three weeks, in spite of its being the month of March in the west wind belt of the South Pacific. On the morning of Easter Sunday, April 7, the wind first freshened from the northwest and blew day after day, a stiff breeze and a gale alternately, so that we went splendidly all the way to the Falkland Islands, in spite of the fact that the topsail was reefed for nearly five weeks on account of the fragile state of the yard. I believe most of us wanted to get on fast; the trip was now over for the present, and those who had families at home naturally wanted to be with them as soon as they could; perhaps that was why we went so well.

On April 1 Mrs. Snuppesen gave birth to eight pups; four of

these were killed, while the rest, two of each sex, were allowed to live.

On Maundy Thursday, April 4, we were in long. 180° and changed the date, so that we had two Maundy Thursdays in one week; this gave us a good many holidays running, and I cannot say the effect is altogether cheerful; it was a good thing when Easter Tuesday came round as an ordinary week-day.

On May 6 we passed Cape Horn in very fair weather; it is true we, had a snow-squall of hurricane violence, but it did not last much more than half an hour. For a few days the temperature was a little below freezing-point, but it rose rapidly as soon as we were out in the Atlantic. From Hobart to Cape Horn we saw no ice. After passing the Falkland Islands we had a head wind, so that the last part of the trip was nothing to boast of.

On the night of May 21 we passed Montevideo, where the Chief had arrived a few hours before. From here up the River La Plata we went so slowly on account of head wind that we did not anchor in the roads of Buenos Aires till the afternoon of the 23rd, almost exactly at the same time as the Chief landed at Buenos Aires. When I went ashore next morning and met Mr. P. Christophersen, he was in great good-humour. "This is just like a fairy tale," he said; and it could not be denied that it was an amusing coincidence. The Chief, of course, was equally pleased.

On the 25th, the Argentine National Fête, the *Fram* was moored at the same quay that we had left on October 5, 1911. At our departure there were exactly seven people on board to say good-bye, but, as far as I could see, there were more than this when we arrived; and I was able to make out, from newspapers and other sources, that in the course of a couple of months the third *Fram* Expedition had grown considerably in popularity.

In conclusion I will give one or two data. Since the *Fram* left Christiania on June 7, 1910, we have been two and a half times round the globe; the distance covered is about 54,400 nautical miles; the lowest reading of the barometer during this time was 27.56 inches (700 millimetres) in March, 1911, in the South Pacific, and the highest 30.82 inches (783 millimetres) in October, 1911, in the South Atlantic.

On June 7, 1912, the second anniversary of our leaving Christiania, all the members of the Expedition, except the Chief and myself, left for Norway, and the first half of the Expedition was thus brought to a fortunate conclusion.